D0777262

LORD BULLOCK of Leafield, head of the discussion group, was the Founding Master of St. Catherine's College, Oxford, and former Vice-Chancellor of Oxford University. SHAUN JOHNSON, the editor of the volume, is a political writer on the *Johannesburg Weekly Mail*. He was a Rhodes Scholar at Oxford.

SOUTH AFRICA: NO TURNING BACK

South Africa: No Turning Back

Edited by
Shaun Johnson

Foreword by Lord Bullock

Indiana University Press
Bloomington and Indianapolis

Manufactured in Great Britain.

Library of Congress Cataloging-in-Publication Data
South Africa : no turning back.
Includes index.
1. South Africa—Politics and government—1978–
2. Apartheid—South Africa. I. Johnson, Shaun.
DT779.952.S655 1989 968.06'3 88–22988
ISBN 0–253–35395–5

1 2 3 4 5 93 92 91 90 89

Contents

Notes on the Contributors and Members of the Study Group

Lord Bullock, FBA Founding Master of St Catherine's College, Oxford. Vice-Chancellor of Oxford University (1969–73). Historian, and former Chairman, Research Committee, Royal Institute of International Affairs.

Howard Barrell South African journalist living in Zimbabwe. He has specialised in the affairs of the outlawed South African liberation movements since 1981. He works through a news feature agency, Agenda Press, which has offices in Harare and Johannesburg.

John Brewer Lecturer in Sociology at Queen's University, Belfast. Author of *After Soweto* (1987). He is the editor of a collection of essays examining South Africa's prospects of survival entitled *Can South Africa Survive? Five Minutes to Midnight* (London: Macmillan). He is also the author of *Police, Public Order and the State* (London: Macmillan), and his work in this volume on the South African police is being extended into a book.

Christopher Coker Lecturer in International Relations at the London School of Economics. His most recent publications include *The United States and South Africa: Constructive engagement and its critics* (1986), and *South Africa's Security Dilemmas*, Washington Paper No.126, 1987.

Shaun Johnson Political writer and journalistic training officer for the Johannesburg *Weekly Mail*. Educated at Rhodes University, South Africa and the University of Oxford, where he was a Rhodes Scholar. Has wide experience in the South African media, and has long been involved in the 'alternative' press, writing the feasibility study for the *New Nation* in 1982. A former president of the South African Students' Press Union, he now also contributes occasional features to the London *Times* and various journals.

Ian Linden General Secretary of the Catholic Institute for International Relations, London. He has a doctorate in developmental biology and in African studies. He has taught in African universities and has written a number of monographs on the social and political role of Christianity in Africa.

Merle Lipton Author of *Capitalism and Apartheid* (1985), and of *Sanctions Against South Africa* (1988). She has held teaching or research posts at Yale University, the School of Advanced International Studies in Washington DC, the Wilson Center in Washington DC, the Royal Institute of International Affairs, London and Sussex University.

Shula Marks Director of the Institute of Commonwealth Studies and Professor of Commonwealth History in the University of London. She has written extensively on South African history from the Iron Age to the present and is currently interested in the history of health and health care in South Africa.

James Mayall Reader in International Relations at the London School of Economics. He has written widely on African and Third World international relations and on international theory. He is currently completing a book on the impact of nationalism on international order.

Kumi Naidoo Political Science Honours graduate, University of Durban-Westville, now reading for a M.Litt. in politics at Oxford University. He is a former office bearer in student, youth and community organisations in South Africa.

Sam Nolutshungu Lecturer in Government at the University of Manchester. He has taught at the University of Ibadan (Nigeria) and York (Toronto), and was recently Visiting Professor of Government at Dartmouth College in the USA. His publications include *South Africa in Africa: a study of ideology and foreign policy* (1975) and *Changing South Africa: political considerations* (1982), as well as numerous papers on various aspects of African politics and international relations.

Peter Slinn Senior lecturer in law at the School of Oriental and African Studies, London, specialising in international and constitutional law. He is joint general editor of Law Reports of the

Commonwealth and has published a number of articles on Commonwealth Constitutional subjects.

Jack Spence Professor and Head of the Department of Politics at the University of Leicester. He has published a number of books and articles on Southern Africa, and was Bradlow Fellow at the South African Institute of International Affairs in 1985/6. He contributed a chapter on southern Africa to *Small is Dangerous* (1986).

Stanley Trapido Oxford University Lecturer in the Government of New States at Queen Elizabeth House, Oxford, and Murray Senior Research Fellow in African Studies at Lincoln College. Former co-editor of the *Journal of Southern African Studies.* Recent publications include *The Politics of Race, Class and Nationalism in Twentieth Century South Africa* (1977), edited with Shula Marks, and *Putting the Plough to the Ground: Accumulation and Dispossession in Rural South Africa, 1850-1930* (1986), edited with William Beinart and Peter Delius.

Stanley Uys Former political editor, Johannesburg *Sunday Times*, and South African correspondent of *The Guardian* and *The Observer.* He is a regular contributor to the BBC. He has recently been London editor of South African morning newspapers. Presently co-editor of *Front File*, newsletter on southern Africa. Lecturer.

Phillip van Niekerk Began his career in journalism in 1980 on the *Diamond Fields Advertiser* in Kimberley, then worked for the East London *Daily Dispatch*, the *Cape Times* and the *Rand Daily Mail.* A specialist in labour and political reporting, he is now a freelance journalist for international and local newspapers, including the *Boston Globe*, *Volkskrant* and the *Weekly Mail.*

Anne Yates Educated at Witwatersrand and Oxford Universities, she was lecturer, 1949–60, at Witwatersrand University and organised the South African Committee for Higher Education from its beginning in 1959 until 1971. From 1971 she has lived in Oxford. She was adviser to overseas students at Oxford 1973–85 and has been director of the Southern African Advanced Education Project since 1986.

Foreword

This book is about a country which has captured the imagination of the world. The struggle in South Africa is seen by many as the last great battle against legislated racism. But of course it is much more complex than that: history, and more particularly the history of decolonisation in Africa, offers no comfortable parallels for the situation in South Africa.

In an attempt to do justice to this complexity, and to provide an accessible analysis of the forces at play in contemporary South Africa, this book follows a thematic course. Each contributor has made a study of a specific area of South African society; described it, and speculated about its possible influence on the future of that benighted country.

In some chapters, description outweighs analysis; in others the reverse is true. Both approaches sit happily together, given the fact that some of the areas upon which we focus are well documented in academic and journalistic writing, while others are gravely under-researched.

Thanks to a formula developed by the David Davies Memorial Institute, the book is more than a collection of essays. Each chapter is the product of the individual researches of the different authors, but all have been submitted for discussion and criticism by the members of the Study Group in a series of meetings between January 1986 and September 1987.

The members of this Group, which included most of the authors as well as other southern African specialists, share the broad basic agreement that fundamental change in South Africa is inevitable and long overdue. Beyond that, many of them hold sharply differing views and come from a variety of professional backgrounds, and this led to rigorous debate on ways in which the situation might and should develop. As a result of these discussions, all the chapters were altered and adapted – to greater or lesser degrees. Now that the arguments are over, however, the individual chapters remain the sole responsibility of the authors, and not of the Study Group or Institute. I believe that the book has benefited greatly from the exchanges, but the reader will not be surprised to find that there are still important areas of disagreement.

The extraordinary fluidity of the South African situation was demonstrated over the time that the Group sat. Meeting first during the last days of a selective State of Emergency, the Group's deliberations have spanned the lifting of that Emergency; the climax of 'insurrectionary' politics in the townships; and the reimposition of 'law and order' through the most comprehensive clampdown in South African history.

To the question 'How will it all end?', we offer no prescriptive answer. What we do claim for the book is an attention to detail and a highlighting of key factors which are not readily available elsewhere. In our focus on the forces of resistance in South Africa, for example, we give substantial consideration to the various components which make up that resistance, rather than providing a mere overview of 'black politics' as is often the case.

My own role in the Study Group requires brief comment. While all contributors and members were invited to serve because of their expertise in one or other area of South African politics, I was asked to be chairman for precisely the opposite reason. I came to the Group with no specialist knowledge of South Africa, and no 'track record' on the question. This, it was felt, would facilitate fruitful debate among participants with very different points of view. I am grateful to the members of the Group for their willingness to make such an arrangement work and for the friendly spirit in which they accepted my interventions from the Chair.

I could not have played this role without the help which I received throughout from Shaun Johnson whose contribution has been central to the success of the enterprise. He was in South Africa for the whole of 1986 researching his chapter on the role of youth in the resistance and he made a follow-up visit in April 1987. As a result, his chapter contains remarkable first-hand material never published before. He won the confidence of the members of the Group and did a great deal to hold it together, and finally he has been responsible for completing the editing of the finished version to an exacting timetable.

Books on South Africa are legion. The topic excites such fascination – and passion – that there are likely to be hundreds more before the crisis is resolved, or at least fundamentally altered in nature. This does not lead us to apologise for adding to that already weighty body of literature; indeed, we believe ours to be a small but distinctive contribution to the debate.

And should we, or our readers, feel disappointment at our inability to map out a 'solution', it is as well to recall Gladstone's words. When speaking in the House of Commons more than a century ago, he said: 'South Africa is destined to become the one great unsolved, perhaps unsolveable, problem of our colonial system.' At the very least, we hope that this book will add to a better understanding of the problem.

ALAN BULLOCK

Editor's Introduction

Because the chapters which go to make up *South Africa: No Turning Back* were so widely discussed by the Study Group before publication, the task of the editor was not a particularly onerous one. It was made still easier – and more pleasurable – by the energetic and expert support of Sheila Harden, the Director; and Mary Unwin and Esme Allen, the staff of the David Davies Memorial Institute of International Studies. Mary, in particular, shouldered much of the editorial burden with incisiveness and humour.

It is important for readers to note that the length of individual chapters in no way reflects the importance attached to them. It was our intention that while contributions should as far as possible conform to a 'style' running through the book, authors should be allowed to retain their own approaches intact. Hence, some felt it necessary to supply a great deal of empirical evidence while others concentrated on analysis.

Similarly, the order in which chapters appear does not imply a 'ranking'. Editorial prerogative was used to group the pieces. They could well have been differently arranged. The book opens with an historical overview, followed by, broadly speaking, an assessment of the state of resistance; the position of the state; and the influence of other key groups and phenomena.

One or two stylistic decisions require explanation. Where it is essential for clarity, the terms African, Indian, coloured and white are used to distinguish between the South African state's racial categories. We have not used inverted commas to indicate our reluctance to accept the state's terms uncritically, as such usage is stylistically cumbersome. This introduction should therefore be read as inserting invisible inverted commas throughout the text. Where the term 'black' is used, it refers to all people not classified as 'white'. These distinctions, although seemingly trivial, have tremendous political resonance within South Africa.

Any book about South African politics is unavoidably peppered with acronyms. The List of Abbreviations is provided as an aid to the reader in making sense of them.

Both as editor of this book and as participant in the Study Group, I have been privileged to work with an extraordinary group of people. My sincere thanks to those listed on pp. vii–ix will, I hope, be taken as read. However, several others were of inestimable help. Above all,

David and Bridget Astor offered succour, encouragement, wisdom, and a friendship I cannot place a value upon.

Sir Philip Adams was tireless in his efforts on behalf of the project, and in his enthusiasm for it. The chairman, Lord Bullock, gave freely of his incomparable vision and sense of history which served to offset my inexperience. He was also a source of kindness and encouragement far beyond his 'duties' as chairman. Anthony Sampson played a valuable part in some of the meetings of the Study Group and was also of great help to me personally. Tim Farmiloe, editorial director of Macmillan, embraced the book quickly and wholeheartedly. Kumi Naidoo, who acted as editorial assistant as well as contributor in the frenetic final stages of the preparation of this book, brought fresh energy and a delightful direct approach to the project. Finally, my thanks go to Jo Hanlon, who participated in our early meetings.

South Africa: No Turning Back, like any book about a country undergoing its greatest ever crisis, cannot hope to please all its readers. For many of us, our feelings about South Africa's future run so deep that we find it difficult to countenance positions opposing our own. The strength of this volume, I hope, is its variety. There should be something for everybody who hopes to live to see the day that true democracy comes to South Africa.

SHAUN JOHNSON

POSTSCRIPT

It should come as no surprise that the situation we attempt to describe and analyse has changed in the period between the book's completion in Autumn 1987 and final publication. Equally, given the country with which we are dealing, it is not surprising that some of these shifts have been marked. We have decided not to allow authors to update their contributions – their analysis stands as a reflection of a particular period – but it is worth recording some major developments.

Perhaps the most noteworthy was the effective banning, in February 1988, of the most significant organisations of internal resistance. The United Democratic Front, the Azanian People's Organisation and 16 other groups have been precluded, in terms of Emergency regulations, from engaging in political programmes. In addition, the Congress of South African Trade Unions (COSATU) has been prohibited from political, as opposed to purely labour, activity. This has necessitated the fashioning of new strategies among extra-parliamentary groups, the results of which will not be clear for some time.

The national State of Emergency has been redeclared for a third time, and its provisions have been made more stringent – notably as regards the scope left for the media to record events in South Africa. The government has revived and expanded upon the notion of a form of national advisory council which proposes to include Africans. Cross-border raids have continued, and there has been an increase in the number of assassination attempts on exiled leaders, as well as in the incidence of bomb blasts in South Africa's urban areas. The townships remain tense, but relatively quiet.

List of Abbreviations

AAC	Alexandra Action Committee
ANC	African National Congress
ASB	Afrikaanse Studentebond (Afrikaans National Students' Association)
AWB	Afrikaner Weerstandsbeweging (Afrikaner Resistance Movement)
AYCO	Alexandra Youth Congress
AZACTU	Azanian Confederation of Trade Unions
AZANYU	Azanian National Youth Unity
AZAPO	Azanian Peoples' Organisation
AZASM	Azanian Students Movement
AZASO	Azanian Students Organisation
AZAYO	Azanian Youth Organisation
BC	Black Consciousness
BCMA	Black Consciousness Movement of Azania
BICSA	British Industry Committee on South Africa
BPC	Black Peoples' Convention
BOSS	Bureau of State Security
CAL	Cape Action League
CASA	Catholic Students Association
CAYCO	Cape Youth Congress
CCAWUSA	Commercial Catering and Allied Workers Union of South Africa
CMEA	Council for Mutual Economic Assistance (COMECON)
COSAS	Congress of South African Students
COD	Congress of Democrats
COSATU	Congress of South African Trade Unions
COSAW	Congress of South African Writers
CP	Conservative Party
CTMWA	Cape Town Municipal Workers Association
CUSA	Council of Unions of South Africa
CWIU	Chemical Workers Industrial Union
DET	Department of Education and Training
DFA	Department of Foreign Affairs
DMI	Department of Military Intelligence
ECC	End Conscription Campaign

EEC	European Economic Community
EPG	(Commonwealth) Eminent Persons Group
FAK	Federasie van Afrikaanse Kultuurvereenigings
FCWU	Food and Canning Workers Union
FEDSAW	Federation of South African Women
FLS	Front Line States
FOSATU	Federation of South African Trade Unions
FRELIMO	Frente de Libertacao de Mozambique (Front for the Liberation of Mozambique)
GWU	General Workers Union
HNP	Herstigte Nasionale Party ('Purified' National Party)
IDAF	International Defence and Aid Fund
IDASA	Institute for a Democratic Alternative for South Africa
IYB	Inkatha Youth Brigade
JMC	Joint Management Committees
JSE	Johannesburg Stock Exchange
MAWU	Metal and Allied Workers Union
MICWU	Motor Industry Combined Workers Union
MK	Umkhonto We Sizwe (Spear of the Nation)
MNR	Mozambique National Resistance (also known as RENAMO)
MPLA	Movimento Popular de Libertacao de Angola (Popular Movement for the Liberation of Angola)
MWU	Mineworkers Union
NAM	Non-Aligned Movement
NAAWU	National Automobile and Allied Workers Union
NACTU	National Council of Trade Unions
NECC	National Education Crisis Committee
NF	National Forum
NGK	Nederduitse Gereformeerde Kerk (Dutch Reformed Church)
NIC	Natal Indian Congress
NIS	National Intelligence Service
NOW	Natal Organisation of Women
NP	National Party
NSMS	National Security Management System
NUM	National Union of Mineworkers
NUMSA	National Union of Metalworkers of South Africa
NUSAS	National Union of South African Students
NUTW	National Union of Textile Workers

OAU	Organisation of African Unity
PAC	Pan Africanist Congress
PFP	Progressive Federal Party
PWAWU	Paper Wood and Allied Workers Union
SAAWU	South African Allied Workers Union
SABC	South African Broadcasting Corporation
SACC	South African Council of Churches
SACOL	South African Confederation of Labour
SACP	South African Communist Party
SACPO	South African Coloured Peoples' Organisation
SACTU	South African Congress of Trade Unions
SACWU	South African Chemical Workers Union
SADCC	Southern African Development Co-ordination Conference
SADF	South African Defence Force
SANSCO	South African National Students Congress
SAP	South African Police
SASM	South African Students' Movement
SASO	South African Students' Organisation
SATS	South African Transport Services
SAYCO	South African Youth Congress
SCA	Soweto Civic Association
SFAWU	Sweet Food and Allied Workers Union
SOSCO	Soweto Students Congress
SOYA	Students of Young Azania
SOYCO	Soweto Youth Congress
SPCC	Soweto Parents Crisis Committee
SSC	State Security Council
SSRC	Soweto Students Representative Council
STYCO	Southern Transvaal Youth Congress
TAWU	Transport and Allied Workers Union
TGWU	Transport and General Workers Union
TIC	Transvaal Indian Congress
TUCSA	Trade Union Council of South Africa
UBC	Urban Bantu Council
UDF	United Democratic Front
UMSA	Unity Movement of South Africa
UNITA	Uniao Nacional para a Independencia Total de Angola (National Union for the Total Independence of Angola)
UNITRA	University of Transkei

UNO	United Nations Organisation
UWUSA	United Workers' Union of South Africa
ZANU	Zimbabwe African National Union
ZAPU	Zimbabwe African Peoples' Union

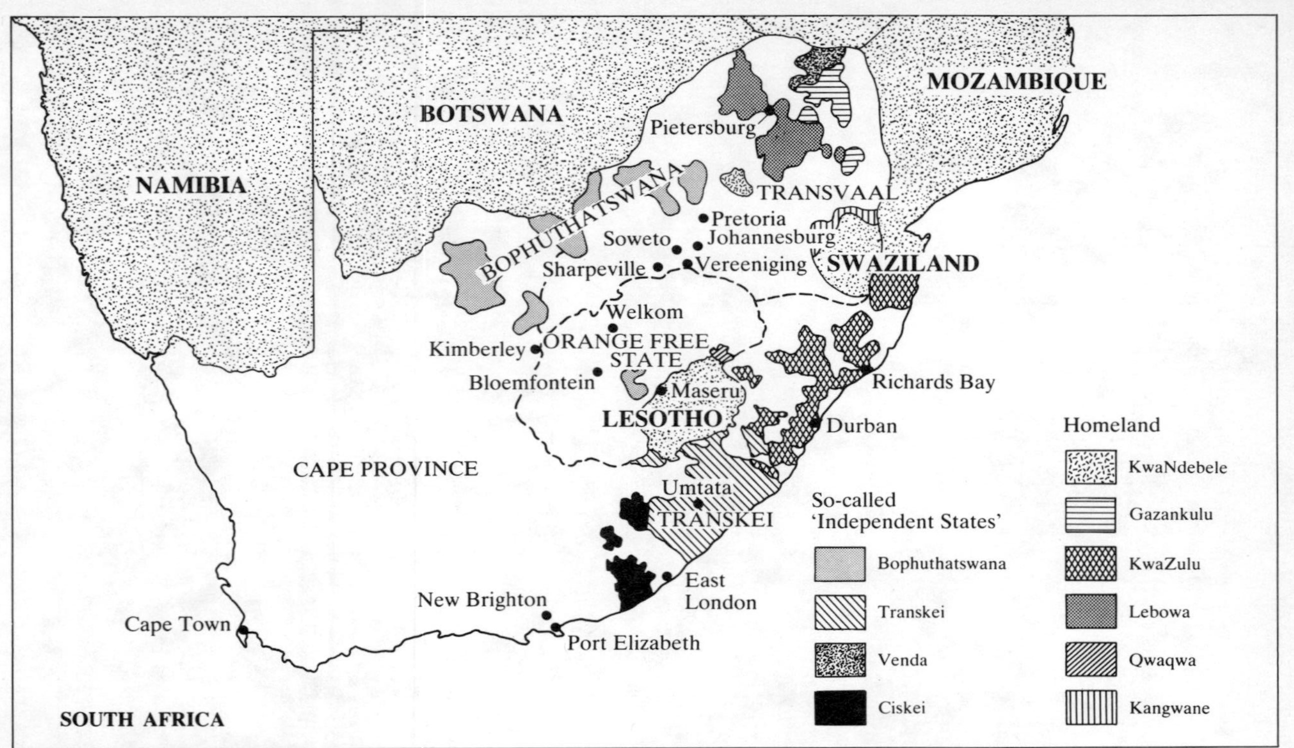

Source: Martin Murray, *South Africa: Time of Agony, Time of Destiny* (London: Verso, 1987).

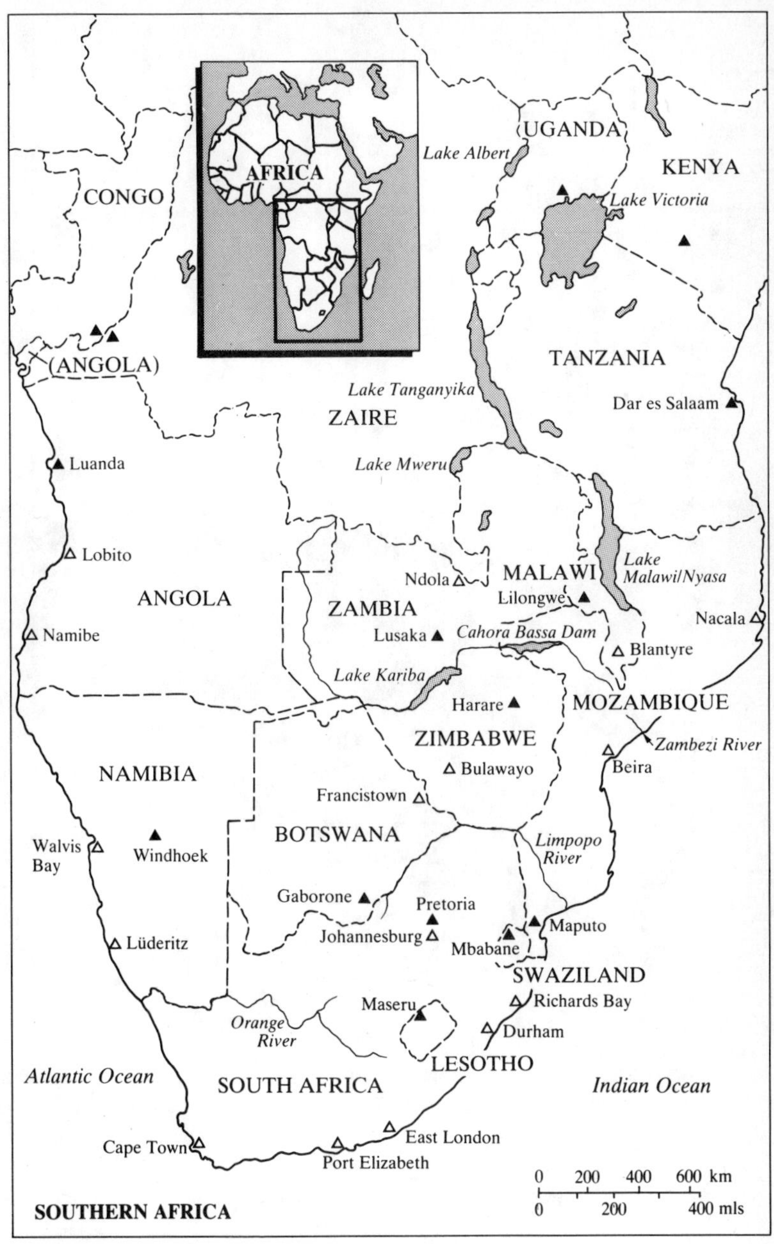

Source: Joseph Hanlon, *Apartheid's Second Front* (Harmondsworth: Penguin, 1986).

1 South Africa since 1976: An Historical Perspective

Shula Marks and Stanley Trapido

From the mid-1970s to the mid-1980s, events in South Africa were subjected to a bewildering diversity of interpretations. Observers of state actions were divided between those who asserted that peaceful reform was possible and those who were equally adamant that no change had taken place. Commentators on the insurrection among South Africa's urban blacks were equally divided between those who portrayed it as a display of mindless violence and those who viewed it as an indication that the revolution was around the corner.

None of these characteristics, however, did justice to the complexities of the current situation. Since then, the state has ruled almost continuously with Emergency powers, and some 30 000 activists have, at some point, been detained. A white general election has been held which has seemed to strengthen the right-wing opponents of reform, and both community and trade union activities have been subjected to severe restriction. Even the proponents of reform would now concede that the process has stalled, although some would claim that the delay is purely temporary.

In the analysis which follows we hope to set recent developments in their historical and differentiated local contexts. We also hope to analyse both the essential continuities with the past which constrain the present and the critical transformations which have taken place over the past ten years as the state has responded to structural changes and increasing black militancy.

The term apartheid has come to be used synonymously with white domination in South Africa. In fact, twentieth-century South Africa has seen two main forms of white domination: segregation and apartheid. These are different forms of state which have emerged to ensure the continuation of white domination in different politico-economic circumstances. Initially, confronted by economic change and black political demands, there appear to have been attempts to restructure the state in order to ensure the continuation of a new form of white domination to replace apartheid. As these attempts simply seemed to fuel black anger, the advocates of direct coercion have asserted their control over state policy.

Over the past decade, multiple challenges resulting from economic change and black resistance led to the jettisoning of aspects of orthodox apartheid. Perhaps the most significant of the reforms were the recognition accorded African trade unions, the ostensible abolition of the 'pass laws', which drastically control black urbanisation, attempts at the co-option of a black middle- and skilled working class through the granting of limited urban and welfare rights (health and education), and of Indians and coloureds through constitutional change. There has even been some recognition of the failure of the bantustans and talk of regional councils as an alternative.

There were serious limitations to all these reforms, and many were relegated to the back shelf during the States of Emergency, still in force; nevertheless, it would be wrong simply to dismiss the reforms as spurious. Although they were not designed to hand over power, no reform ever is. Even the 1832 and 1867 franchise acts in Britain and the establishment of compulsory education in 1872 which underpin the modern British parliamentary system were intended to contain protest against this system rather than to surrender to it. No ruling group willingly and knowingly hands over power. Yet all reform has unanticipated and unintended consequences. The paradox of the situation in South Africa today is that while the government has made some changes in the nature of apartheid which would have been inconceivable in the 1960s, what blacks are demanding is the end of white domination. The situation is reminiscent of the occasion in 1899 before the outbreak of the South African War when President Paul Kruger, under pressure from mine magnates and imperial authorities to 'reform' the South African Republic, complained bitterly that what they wanted was not reform, but his country.[1]

I

The origins of the contemporary South African state are to be sought in the first decade of the twentieth century in the aftermath of the South African War. In response to the changes wrought in a previously agrarian economy by the mineral discoveries in the last third of the nineteenth century, a new state, the Union of South Africa, was formed with powers greatly exceeding those of its predecessors. While neither white racism nor capitalism were new to South Africa in the late nineteenth century, the scale of industrialisation and the consequent class formation and state intervention marked a decisive transformation.

Since the 1890s, gold has been central to the South African economy and still remains the single most important earner of foreign exchange; no government in South Africa has been able to ignore its imperatives. Historically, the gold price could not be increased in response to rising costs; nor was there a mass consumer market. In South Africa, the average grade of ore is low, and producers had little control over costs other than labour. White labour, because of its scarcity and political power, was able to maintain a relatively high wage structure; black labour, in the quantities needed and at the low wages offered, had to be forcibly conquered and then excluded from any significant political and trade union rights. Almost from the start, the South African mining industry was based on a migrant labour system, which originated in the resistance of blacks to proletarianisation but which soon proved invaluable to the mine owners. Workers left their families behind in those rural areas which had been retained by Africans after the wars of expropriation. (These areas came to be known as 'reserves'.) The mining industry defined all Africans as single male 'target' workers and wages were appallingly low. Thus, the costs of supporting the workers' families and of the workers themselves in childhood, sickness and old age were subsidised by agricultural production in the reserves. At the same time the possibility of unionisation and political opposition was diminished. Workers were housed in compounds which increased the capacity of management to cut costs and to control desertion and workers' organisation.

The conquest and control of the workforce lent a specific racial form to the nature of the social and economic order, even before the twentieth century. After the South African War, however, when the British controlled the whole of South Africa, the segregationist state was born. The British High Commissioner, Lord Milner, reshaped and rationalised the institutions of 'Native administration', in order to cope with the demands of the mining industry for vast supplies of cheap labour and the reaction which this provoked from the surviving authorities in once powerful African politics. By 1910, when the separate colonies were brought together in the Union of South Africa, and power handed over to white settlers, a specific form of racial capitalism had been entrenched.[2]

However significant the mining industry in forging the 'new' South Africa, the Union which was formed in 1910 was still characterised by enormous regional diversities, which continue to shape South African politics to the present. Even in the Transvaal, the rural community – still at that time the major political constituency of the ruling party – continued to exact a tribute from the state. The demands of white farmers for labour, state subsidies and protection had to be balanced against the needs of the mining industry. The resulting compromise has been dubbed 'the alliance of maize and gold'. With the development of secondary industry from the mid-1930s, further compromises had to be made between conflicting white interest groups.

At a wider regional level, recently conquered African kingdoms existed side by side with the colonies of settlement. At the time called 'reserves', they were later to form the basis of South Africa's bantustan or 'homelands' policy. The Cape Colony, with a proletariat descended from the indigenous population, East Indian slaves and European settlers, now known as coloureds, had a history of incorporating blacks into its political structure through a non-racial property and income-based franchise which distinguished it from the rest of South Africa. The Cape incorporationist strategy and the endeavours of Christian missionaries preaching the brotherhood of man were sufficiently successful to inspire Africans all over South Africa to believe in the evolution of a multiracial democracy. Alongside this liberal tradition ran a deep strand of nationalism among Africans in the Eastern Cape (as elsewhere), who vividly remembered the defeat and subordination of their communities.[3]

In Natal, white settlers, predominantly of British origin, dominated the indigenous Zulu-speaking Africans and a considerable Indian population, initially brought there as indentured labourers to work in the sugar plantations. Like the Coloureds in the Cape, Indians in Natal have occupied an intermediary role between white settlers and the majority African population: a position which imperial administrators and white politicians have attempted to manipulate since at least the beginning of this century. Flanked by the powerful military kingdom of the Zulu which was only conquered in 1879 and incorporated into Natal nearly twenty years later, Natal settlers were always heavily outnumbered by blacks and aware of the tenuousness of their control. White insecurities and the continuities in the Zulu political tradition, real and invented, have coloured the politics of Natal to the present.

It was Natal which provided many of the precedents for South Africa's twentieth-century segregationist policies: the allocation of reserved lands for African tribal occupation, the codification of an arbitrarily defined 'customary' law, administration through acceptable 'traditional' authorities, the exemption of Christian Africans from customary law, and the attempt to prevent large-scale African urbanisation through the institution of a system of labour registration.

In the years before the Second World War, segregation was systematised by a series of Union governments regardless of party political persuasion. The ideologues of segregation were increasingly conscious of the dangers of a class-conscious and organised proletariat. As George Heaton Nicholls, the United Party's most important spokesman on segregation, put it: 'Bantu communalism is the answer to Bantu Communism'. Essential to the segregationist state was the exclusion of blacks from the central political institutions of the South African state; the refinement of the migrant labour system, based on the unequal division of the land between blacks and whites; a nexus of laws controlling African movement, residence and trade union organisation; and the recognition and 'refurbishing' of chiefly authorities in the rural areas.[4]

The increasing impoverishment of the African 'reserves' and the growth of manufacturing industry in the late 1930s and 1940s, led to a massive influx of rural blacks to the urban areas, and a call from some members of the governing United Party for a more stable workforce. For a time, during the Second World War and immediately after it, liberal voices within the state and in industry advocating improved conditions for Africans in the urban areas and a recognition of their right to be there were able to make themselves heard. Humanitarians called for improved wages, decent housing and education, and a national health service to remedy the squalid conditions in towns. The serious social dislocations and ill-health resulting from the migrant labour system were increasingly recognised. Although their views were never uncontested, for a brief spell it seemed possible that the segregationist state would be reformed and welfare measures introduced for blacks. The moves were cautious; recommendations that the already existing African trade unions be recognised, for example, were quashed by the opposition of the Chamber of Mines, and African strikes remained illegal. Although minimal social security was offered to blacks, and school feeding schemes implemented, there was certainly no extension of African political rights.[5]

The need for state action was spurred by increasing African nationalist demands and black working-class organisation. By the 1940s, the black nationalist organisation, the African National Congress (ANC), which had been founded by the educated Christian middle class as early as 1912, was beginning to change its character as it incorporated a new urban working-class constituency. This was signalled in 1944 by the formation of the Congress's Youth League and its response to the Atlantic Charter. For this radicalised organisation the attempts of the state to defuse discontent through welfare, rather than through the extension of political rights, were wholly inadequate.[6]

Far from responding to African demands, the victory of the Afrikaner nationalists in the white election of 1948 reversed even the modest welfare measures introduced by the Smuts government. Although there were substantial continuities in the National Party's programme with the segregationist policies of previous Union governments, a new group of men came into power determined to redress powerfully felt inequalities between English- and Afrikaans-speaking whites.

A comparatively recent phenomenon, Afrikaner nationalism – like African nationalism – had its roots in the late nineteenth century, largely in reaction to British imperialism and the dislocations of South Africa's mining and agrarian transformations. The South African War from 1899–1902 acted as a forcing house. The high death rate of Afrikaner women and children in what were known as concentration camps and the loss of Republican independence intensified nationalist sentiment, while the British scorched earth policy accelerated the process of Afrikaner impoverishment. By the late 1920s, under the continued impact of land loss and drought, one in five Afrikaners were classified as 'poor white'. Unskilled and barely literate, they competed in town with skilled and highly paid English-speaking workers on the one hand, and with low-paid Africans who still had some access to rural productive resources on the other.

Afrikaner clerics, teachers, lawyers and journalists who found themselves disadvantaged in the new social order under Union provided the leadership for an Afrikaner nationalism that took different forms in the first half of this century. By the 1930s, in the aftermath of the Depression, this intelligentsia sought to mobilise the Afrikaner underclasses in a variety of economic, cultural and political institutions in their bid to capture state power. Informing these institutions was an ideology of Christian nationalism, constructed out of late nineteenth-century neo-Calvinist and populist beliefs which portrayed Afrikaners as the 'chosen people' and opposed both British imperialism and international communism. Language, culture and nation were endangered by an alien capitalism and an equally alien communism. It was not capitalism *per se* that was the enemy, but the control of the capitalist system by non-Afrikaners. Only through control over government could they take hold of what was rightfully theirs.[7]

II

Using the slogan 'apartheid' and essentially capitalising on post-war dissatisfaction with the Smuts government, the Afrikaner nationalists won a narrow electoral victory in 1948. Contrary to conventional wisdom, however, they did not immediately proceed to implement a monolithic apartheid blueprint. Although the 1948 election was fought under this banner, the word meant different and at times contradictory things to the different groups of Afrikaners who were brought together in a nationalist alliance. Whereas Afrikaner farmers were most concerned about the consequences of African urbanisation for their labour supply, and Afrikaner workers feared black competition on the shop floor, Afrikaner commercial and financial interests and the embryonic class of manufacturers wanted government control over those Africans already in town. A degree of ideological respectability was given to this alliance by the Afrikaner intelligentsia's espousal of ideas of 'separate development'. Contingency operated every bit as forcefully as ideology and interest in crystalising new policies. The first political priority of the National Party after 1948 was to ensure its parliamentary majority. Given the narrowness of that majority, it carried out a virtual parliamentary coup by manipulating electoral boundaries, incorporating South West African seats and eliminating the coloured vote – thus making it impossible for any other party to regain office through the ballot box. It was only in the later 1950s under Prime Minister Verwoerd that apartheid as a coherent set of policies acquired a greater practical influence.[8]

During the 1950s Afrikaner nationalists used their control over the state to increase their share in an expanding economy. Industrial expansion and National Party policies ensured a transformation in the position of the Afrikaner middle and working class. Although the establishment of public corporations pre-dated National Party rule, between 1946 and 1973 public sector investment rose ten times, and has risen even more dramatically since then. To the dismay of latter-day free marketeers, the South African economy was increasingly state controlled and state-owned.[9] This vast expansion of public corporations and state initiated enterprises greatly assisted Afrikaner economic advancement, while the special relationship since 1948 of the Afrikaner businessman to political control was of great importance in fostering Afrikaner advance in the private sector. The preferential allocation of state contracts, and interlocking directorates between the state corporations and Afrikaner private capital ensured the emergence by the late 1970s of a new class of Afrikaner entrepreneurs who could compete successfully with their English-speaking peers, who shared many of the same economic interests and who sat on many of the same boards of directors. By 1978 it was estimated that 30 per cent of the gold mines were under Afrikaner control, 40 per cent of the platinum, 35 per cent of the coal, 50 per cent of the asbestos and 40 per cent of the chrome.[10]

At the same time, the years between 1950 and 1970 saw a remarkable shift in the position of Afrikaner workers. Whereas in 1951 there was still a substantial white working class – with 38 per cent of white male workers employed in factories, building sites, transport and mines, and thousands more in low-level white collar work – by 1970, 38 per cent of whites were in professional/technical and managerial administrative jobs. The production/building/transport category was down to 26 per cent. Thirty-seven per cent had white collar jobs, while 60 per cent of white school-leavers qualified for university entrance.[11]

For all these groups, control over the African labour supply was of the essence. They were intent on stemming the flow of Africans to the towns, and controlling those who could not be removed. Through the 1950s the National Party tightened the nexus of laws which governed the daily lives of Africans. The penalties for contravention of the pass laws were stepped up and labour bureaux were created in the rural areas to direct labour to the mines, factories and farms. The job colour bar, which reserved certain work for whites only, was extended. Although employers were always able to bypass both the influx control regulations and the job colour bar (in the first case through special permission to recruit migrant labour, in the second by manipulating job descriptions), the effect was to keep African wages low and African workers powerless. Although Africans were allowed to form trade unions, these were not recognised in wage negotiations, and to strike was a criminal offence. Given the low level of skill of most African workers, any sign of assertiveness was met with instant dismissal and potential deportation back to the rural reserves, the 13 per cent of the land set aside for African occupation under the Land Acts of 1913 and 1936.

The reserves, now renamed Bantu homelands by the government and derided by their critics as 'bantustans', had long served as labour pools for the white controlled economy. They now became a cornerstone of state policy. In 1956 a government appointed Commission under Professor F. R. Tomlinson argued that an expenditure of about £104 million was needed over the next ten years to make the reserves economically viable. These proposals were initially rejected by the state and very little additional money was made available. As their material base declined, however, it became increasingly important to refurbish chiefly instruments of control while the state also attempted to deflect African urban politics into these impoverished areas by establishing in them forms of severely circumscribed local self-government.

Aware of the role of the African Christian urban based intelligentsia in nationalist movements, and in the face of a mounting tide of black opposition, the government attempted to establish an alternative rural collaborating class of chiefs and headmen. At the same time, Christian mission education with its universal ideals of a common society came under attack. The Bantu Education Act of 1953 had two goals. It aimed to provide the minimal education demanded by employers – basic literacy and some knowledge of English or Afrikaans – and to bring under state control the mission schools which up to this time had provided virtually all African education.

In the early 1950s the National Party appears to have been almost as preoccupied with the position of the minority coloured population (predominantly in the Cape province) and Indians (mainly in Natal) as with the majority African populace. Numbering one and half million coloureds and almost half a million Asians in the 1950s and some two and a half million and 800 000 respectively in the mid-1980s, the coloureds and Indians constituted a particular challenge to the racial ideologues of the National Party.

For much of the twentieth century, Afrikaner nationalists (and whites more widely) have had an ambivalent attitude toward the coloureds, who are claimed by some in the Cape to be 'brown Afrikaners'. In the first decade of the century, the British High Commissioner in South Africa, Lord Selborne, warned of the dangers of driving the 'respectable Coloured' into the arms of the 'native'. In the 1920s, too, General Hertzog, concerned at evidence of an increasing political alliance between coloureds and Africans, made overtures to incorporate the coloured population. Nothing came of this, however. The coloureds were to receive renewed attention after the Afrikaner nationalist victory of 1948.

In the early 1950s a cluster of laws were passed which attempted to confine South Africa's population groups within newly defined ethnic boundaries. The Population Registration, Group Areas, Immorality and Mixed Marriage Acts all had very specific connotations for coloureds and Indians, isolating them from each other and from Africans and whites. Substantial energy was expended in trying to remove coloureds from the common voters' roll. The motivation was partly ideological but mainly political, since the Nationalist majority in parliament was still slender. It was widely believed that the coloured vote went almost entirely to the opposition United Party. At the same time, however, other sections of the National Party sought to create a new 'coloured' identity, and to win their loyalty through the Coloured Labour Preference Policy which secured jobs for coloureds in the Western Cape at the expense of Africans.[12]

If attitudes to coloureds were marked by ambivalence, until comparatively recently there was no such ambivalence in relation to the Indian population who were affected by the same nexus of laws. The majority of Indians were Hindu from South India first brought to South Africa in the second half of the nineteenth century as indentured labourers for the sugar plantations and coal mines of Natal. This migration was paralleled by a smaller number of largely Gujerati Muslim merchants and traders, who initially attempted to achieve political acceptance at the expense of poorer Indians. Their identity as a community was forged in the face of bitter discrimination and the constantly reiterated demand from white politicians that they be repatriated to India.

In the 1930s and 1940s Afrikaner nationalist economic mobilisation focused on 'unfair' competition from Indian traders, while in Natal the expansion of Indian property holding and competition from skilled Indian workers were also fiercely resented. In the 1940s the state was also concerned by evidence of the radicalisation of the Indian working class and an incipient unity between Indian and African trade unionists. In the event, however, as the 1949 anti-Indian riots tragically revealed, the relationship between major elements in the African and Indian populations was characterised more by hostility than co-operation. In 1946 the Smuts government attempted to placate white opinion through the passage of legislation which was designed to confine Indian property holding to its existing limits. As a *quid pro quo*, the United Party offered the Indians two seats in Parliament which were, however, rejected. Passive resistance to the Smuts legislation marked the radicalisation of Indian politics. This, together with the lessons learnt from the 1949 anti-Indian riots, resulted in an alliance between the Indian and African National Congresses. The 1946 legislation, coupled with National Party legislation affecting Indians, led to the increasingly articulate criticism of South Africa's policies from the government of India at the United Nations. Discrimination against Indians in South

Africa became both an international and a Commonwealth issue.[13]

For the Commonwealth, the South African question came to the fore most prominently in 1961 when the Afrikaner nationalists were able to achieve their goal of declaring South Africa a Republic. Internally, the significance of this move lay in its removal of alternative symbols of authority. The overriding hegemony of the British Crown had seemed to legitimate what was seen as a British ideology of pragmatic liberalism which ultimately threatened white rule. Its removal opened the way for the incorporation of English-speaking South Africans into the apartheid design. Throughout the 1950s, English-speaking South Africans opposed government policies, more because they were hostile to Afrikaner nationalism than because they were in fundamental disagreement with the general thrust of apartheid doctrines, although there was always a handful of liberal whites (organised in the Liberal Party from 1953) who attacked the state's racial policies. Paradoxically, the act declaring South Africa a Republic, which was intended to strengthen internal Afrikaner legitimacy among whites, paved the way for the ousting of South Africa from the Commonwealth in March 1961 and for the further erosion of South Africa's international standing.

By this time South Africa's international image had been further damaged by the police shootings in March 1961 on a crowd of anti-pass law protesters at Sharpeville in the Transvaal. This came at the end of a decade of rising African nationalist and trade union protest, led by the African National Congress. Frequently taking advantage of local and regionally differentiated grassroots dissatisfaction, the ANC provided the framework for resistance, and launched itself in this period as the most legitimate vehicle for the expression of African grievances. From being a small elitist organisation it achieved a mass following, although paid-up membership remained low and it always suffered from a lack of funds and personnel. Throughout the 1950s, the African National Congress mounted a series of campaigns against apartheid legislation, in alliance with the South African Indian Congress, the South African Coloured Peoples' Organisation (SACPO), the white Congress of Democrats (COD) and, after 1956, the associated trade union federation, the South African Congress of Trade Unions (SACTU). In addition, by the late 1950s some of the whites in the Liberal Party had become increasingly involved in radical opposition to the government.[14]

The state's response was to harass and repress opposition. As early as 1950, the Nationalists passed the Suppression of Communism Act, giving themselves wide powers to ban any individual or organisation accused of furthering the aims of communism. The definition of communism was all-embracing, and its interpretation left to the discretion of the Minister of Justice. Paradoxically, the Suppression of Communism Act led to far closer collaboration between the radical left and the African nationalists than in the past.

In the early 1950s the banning of trade unionists under the Suppression of Communism Act contributed to the decline in working-class organisation at a time when the economic gains made by black workers during the war years were being eroded. Nevertheless, by 1955, multiracial unions had regrouped in SACTU, which provided a focus within the Congress Alliance for working-class demands in a broader political context, and working-class and nationalist militancy mounted. The role of ex-Communist Party members within the Congress alliance was considerable and led to dissatisfaction among some members of the ANC who both resisted their radical 'foreign' ideology and resented what they saw as continued white domination. In 1959, the 'Africanist' group as they were known broke away to form the Pan Africanist Congress (PAC). Although the PAC never challenged the national authority of the ANC in the Western Cape and in some of the towns of the Eastern Cape, they expressed widespread popular anti-white sentiment. It was the PAC which called the pass-burning demonstrations that led to the shootings at Sharpeville, and which was followed shortly after by the banning of both the ANC and the PAC. Forced underground and frustrated at their inability to effect any change through peaceful protest, the leaders of these organisations decided to change their strategy of non-violence. This was followed by a short-lived campaign of sabotage by the ANC's newly formed Umkhonto we Sizwe, the military wing, PAC's Poqo, and a small band of individuals drawn in the main from the Liberal Party. These tactics were rapidly defeated by the state.

III

The suppression of political organisations and the banning, exile and imprisonment of nationalist, radical and trade union leaders in the early 1960s led to a decade of apparent political quiescence. This surface stability encouraged overseas investment in the South African economy which contributed to the Republic's high rate of growth: an average of 6 per cent per annum from 1963 to 1971. Nevertheless, throughout the 1960s the vast majority of Africans continued to earn wages well below the minimum effective level and more than half remained below the poverty datum line – a very stringent measurement indeed.[15]

As a result of its political control and the high rate of economic growth, the state was now able to engage in social engineering on an unprecedented scale. Through the 1960s large numbers of Africans were removed to the bantustans from white owned farms, towns and so-called 'black spots' (i.e. black owned land in areas designated as white by the state). In some cases people were uprooted two or even three times and literally dumped in the barren *veld*, with no access to clean water or decent shelter. The physical toll was appalling and the psychological consequences virtually unrecorded and probably immeasurable. The 'success' of this social engineering can be seen from the figures: according to one economist, while 39 per cent of Africans were living in the bantustans in 1960, by 1980 the figure had reached 53 per cent. To take one by no means isolated example: the tiny bantustan of Qwaqwa in the Orange Free State saw its population explode from approximately 20 000 in 1970 to about half a million by the mid-1980s.[16] Although there had been a slight relative decline in urban numbers, the major change came in the white rural areas, where the black population decreased from 31 per cent in 1960 to 21 per cent in 1980.[17]

Much of this is to be attributed to the increased capitalisation of white agriculture since the war. Thus, whereas in 1948 wages constituted 68 per cent of farming costs, labour costs had gone down to 29 per cent by the early 1970s. At the same time, the value of capital goods on white farms had gone up from R135 million in 1947 to R763 million by 1971. Although the number of white farms decreased in this period from 117 000 in 1950 to 77,500 by 1975, the actual land under cultivation increased by more than 4 million morgen.[18] To the usual dislocations of expropriation and mechanisation, however, were added state induced removals which destroyed families, communities and survival networks on a vast scale.

The limited rights which Africans had had in urban areas under section ten of the 1945 Urban Areas (Amendment) Act were whittled away, as all new workers had to register with labour bureaux in the rural areas before being engaged, and were only granted migrant status. Government planners believed that the answer to South Africa's problems lay in the decentralisation of industry and its re-siting on the borders of the rural reserves. The congestion of the existing industrial areas would be relieved; new opportunities would be opened up for Afrikaner entrepreneurs, where wage and safety conditions in factories would be relaxed; and the mounting tide of African urban militancy would be defused. Although decentralisation hardly got off the ground, increasing attempts were made to channel all African social, political and economic aspirations to the impoverished rural reserves.

Using the language of decolonisation, a variety of new constitutional devices were implemented to grant the bantustans increased local self-government, although they remained totally dependent on South Africa economically and for their internal and external security. The new collaborating bureaucracy was further bolstered and given a vested interest in the bantustans, and increasingly African welfare rights were displaced to the rural areas, in order to given them some kind of material reality. Some attempt was also made to introduce development schemes but they failed dismally to provide employment on the scale needed. It was during the 1960s that the state ethnographers began to reconstruct and manipulate African ethnic identity, making use of elements of older and often abandoned traditions, in an attempt to break the hold of pan-South African nationalism. It was only in 1976, however, that the Transkei, the most geographically coherent and ethnically homogeneous of the bantustans, achieved 'independence', followed by Bophutatswana, Venda and the Ciskei. The remaining bantustans occupy varying points along the road to 'independence'.

The differences in constitutional development of the different bantustans in part reflect their different political and economic development. KwaZulu, for example, *de jure* home of six million Zulu-speaking people, is divided into forty-four separate patches of land, which makes any kind of planning for development impossible. Its Chief Minister, Chief Mangosuthu Gatsha Buthelezi, has long resisted the state's attempt to foist independence on the poverty-stricken 'homeland' before it consolidates its landholdings. Building on his own position as a scion of the Zulu Royal family and a former member of the African National Congress, Buthelezi has been a master of the 'politics of the tightrope'.[19] By refusing 'independence', he initially created a role for himself as a champion of African rights, despite his position as a paid functionary of the South African state. At the same time as opposing the policies of the banned liberation movements, he has also proclaimed himself the true inheritor of the traditions of the ANC. Today he opposes the disinvestment campaigns of the 'radicals', and is outspoken in his defence of capitalist enterprise with which he is closely associated in Natal. At the same time he has created a new and divisive black trade union movement in Natal.

In 1975 Buthelezi established *Inkatha*, the Zulu Cultural Liberation movement. Its object was to inculcate a spirit of unity among the Zulu 'and all their African brothers in Southern Africa' and it was said to have 300 000 paid-up members by 1980. Since then it has lost much of its lustre, particularly outside Natal, partly because of its increasingly violent vigilante action against its opponents. While its leadership is drawn from the middle-class beneficiaries of KwaZulu patronage, it retains an enthusiastic following amongst rural Zulu. In 1986 Inkatha claimed a membership of one million, but these figures have to be seen in the light of the fact that membership is essential to gain access to any of the jobs controlled by the KwaZulu government. In the current struggles the organisation has taken overtly coercive action against students and youth and against the United Democratic Front. It was alleged to be behind much of the apparent quiescence in Natal and has been clearly implicated in the upsurge of violence since August 1985, with the connivance if not actual support of the police. As a leader, Buthelezi brooks no dissidence and does not scruple to use the threat of violence against his opponents. Nevertheless, perhaps because of his continued support for overseas investment in South Africa – contrary to the wishes even of his own urban supporters – Buthelezi has retained his image in the Western media as a 'moderate'.[20]

Buthelezi's preparedness to negotiate with whites in Natal and with big business gave rise in 1986 to the much discussed 'KwaNatal Indaba' which proposed a regional political solution. Seized upon by white reformists and a number of Natal business interests, it has been rejected – at least for the moment – by both the National Party and non-Inkatha blacks, who see in it yet another example of Natal's twentieth-century separatism. Given its power base, however, and its careful consolidation by the Zulu intelligentsia, Inkatha and the state through the twentieth century, Zulu ethnic nationalism is now a significant feature of the South African political landscape, and one which will have to be confronted in any future dispensation.

At the opposite end of the bantustan spectrum is KwaNdebele, a new geo-political entity which has sprung up in the last fifteen years as a result of government relocation policies, and which is an afterthought in terms of the bantustan strategy. Until the mid-1970s there was no provision of land or separate administration for the Ndebele people who were scattered on the white farms and in the other bantustans of the Transvaal. Today, as the state attempts to foist 'independence' on a clearly opposed populace through its local collaborators, 90 per cent of the half a million people in the demarcated area are recent migrants, and only about half of them are ethnically Ndebele. Unlike the situation in KwaZulu or the Transkei, the collaborating group have little popular legitimacy and their preparedness to accept 'independence' has led to bitter popular struggles, which, in turn, have led at least temporarily to the state's having to shelve its plans.

Each of the bantustans has its own particular regional and political characteristics. In most, however, apart from the bureaucracy and small middle class of traders, teachers and health workers, the majority of the people are women, children and old men outside formal employment. They are underfed and poorly housed, and largely dependent on remittances from absent migrants for their survival. It is no coincidence that over the past few years epidemics of cholera and typhoid have raged within their borders, and that infant mortality remains at very high levels.[21]

Welfare payments are dependent on ethnic identification and an acceptance of the bantustan authorities. Job opportunities, also dependent on the bantustan authorities, are few and far between. In 1979 it was estimated that a migrant from Lebowa who worked illegally in Johannesburg for nine months and spent the rest of the year in gaol for evading the influx control regulations was better off then if he or she had remained in the bantustan. Even if the time period was reversed, and he or she spent nine months of the year in gaol, the migrant would still be better off by 85 per cent than if he or she had remained in Lebowa. It is not surprising, under the circumstances, that large numbers of people have simply decamped from the bantustans to squatter camps on the outskirts of the cities, where they have some chance of finding work. The breakdown in influx control which resulted by the 1980s is a major reason for the state's withdrawal of the pass laws, and the new rhetoric of 'orderly urbanisation'.[22]

The extent of the corruption and brutality of the bantustan leadership, itself a product of the scarcity of resources and the absence of civilian checks on arbitrary rule, has even begun to concern the South African state. Despite its utility to whites who can point to this corruption as manifest evidence of the inability of blacks to rule themselves, the costs in both financial and political terms are becoming too high.[23]

For bantustan inhabitants, the fiction of independence has come to have a grim reality in the 1980s as the fact of 'independence' has come to control access to jobs and housing in the rest of South Africa. In the

1960s and 1970s black South Africans were divided into relatively privileged urban 'insiders' with rights to live and work in 'white' South Africa, and disadvantaged 'outsiders' who were rightless migrants. Today, as Colin Murray has pointed out, access to jobs and housing is even more highly differentiated:

> The life chances of individuals and households may be plotted on a complex grid of partly overlapping administrative barriers or on a proliferating hierarchy of relative insecurity. The boundaries which are most commonly manipulated and exploited are those which distinguish the following categories: migrants, commuters, urban 'insiders'; men, women; foreigners, citizens of 'independent' Bantustans; ethnic 'minorities', ethnic 'majorities' within Bantustans; 'squatters' legal or illegal on private or state land, inhabitants of self-built shacks inside or outside the Bantustans, municipal rent-payers (or rent boycotters); land-owners, tenants, sub-tenants inside the Bantustans.[24]

IV

For all the apparent success of social engineering in the 1960s and 1970s, cracks had begun to appear in the National Party's edifice of control by the late 1960s. Differences within the Party between the so-called *verligtes*, often identified with the Cape party, but also including individuals with interests in common with big capital, and the *verkramptes*, many of them harking back to the Strydom and Verwoerd era and marginalised by the rise of the new entrepreneurs, became more marked. In 1969, the formation of the Herstigte Nasionale Party (HNP – Reconstituted National Party) under Albert Hertzog symbolised the break-up of the apparently monolithic National Party.[25] At the same time, the eruption of the Black Consciousness movement signalled an end to the quiescence that had followed the banning of the black political movements.

The Black Consciousness movement represented the deeper strand of Africanism within African nationalism which can be discerned in its origins in the 1880s, but which has always been somewhat overshadowed, except in the PAC, by an ethos of Christian liberal multi-racialism, at least at leadership level. By the late 1960s it became more salient, perhaps influenced, as earlier generations of black activists had been, by black politics in the USA, the diminished contact between black and white as a result of apartheid policies and the racial consciousness encouraged by Nationalist policies (especially by the 'tribal' colleges and Bantu education). Not surprisingly, this restructured consciousness emerged among students – in the first instance those at Fort Hare and at Durban Medical School. In 1968–69 Steve Biko led black students in the break with the multiracial, but predominantly white and English-speaking, National Union of South African Students (NUSAS), to form the South African Students' Organisation (SASO) among university students. This had its counterpart in the high schools in the South African Students' Movement (SASM)[26] (see Chapter 3).

The break with NUSAS led a handful of white students to look for a new role – and perhaps was one reason why white students, radicalised by the international student upheavals, began assisting black working-class organisation.[27] In 1971 NUSAS set up Wage and Economic Commissions on its constituent campuses to give evidence to the industrial councils (established under the Industrial Conciliation Act) on black wages and conditions and their relationship to profits. The Wage Commissions drew attention to the widespread evidence that a substantial number of Africans were living below the poverty datum line. Between 1948 and 1970, wages of white factory workers had increased fourfold, from R864 to R3577 per annum; during the same period the black factory worker's wage had increased threefold, from R254 to R689. The wages of mineworkers and farm labourers were considerably lower: in 1973 the total wage bill for Africans – who constituted 90 per cent of the workforce in the gold and coal mining industry – was increased by roughly the same amount as that of white mineworkers, who constituted about ten per cent of the workforce.[28]

Poverty-wages, poor conditions and dissatisfaction over the lack of bargaining machinery led to a wave of strikes among South African workers, sparked first by strikes in the Durban docks towards the end of 1971. Strikes and work stoppages affecting a wide variety of industries followed, involving some 70 000 workers between mid-January and mid-October, 1973. Initially, the workers were treated with relative caution, both by the police and the courts. When the unrest spread to the mining compounds, however, this restraint disappeared. In September, 1973, the police fired on demonstrating miners at Anglo American's Western Deep Levels Mine at Carltonville, leaving twelve dead and numerous others injured.[29]

In response to the strikes and the worker strategy of not putting forward leaders and of calling rolling strikes, the state amended the old Bantu Labour (Settlement of Disputes) Act, bolstering plant-based

Works Committees and introducing liaison committees to which management was entitled to appoint half the members.[30] The state's attempt to undermine black trade unionism failed completely, however, and in the wake of the Durban strikes large numbers of workers flocked into revived working-class organisations and trade unions, often advised by old trade unionists of the 1950s (SACTU) as well as by white student activists. The success of the strike wave led the Black Consciousness movement to take an interest in workers for the first time.

Quite apart from the increasing challenge from black working-class organisation, the South African economy began to show increasing signs of weakness by the mid-1970s. In some ways this was a reflection of the international recession which followed the oil crisis, but it was also the result of deeper strains in the South African economy. By the 1970s, the South African economy had come to be dominated by a small number of very large firms. The extent of the centralisation and concentration of capital can be seen from figures cited by the 1977 Monopolies Commission. Five per cent of firms in manufacturing, the wholesale and retail sectors, transport and construction accounted for between 63 and 73 per cent of turnover. By 1982, the Anglo American Corporation, the Afrikaner controlled Sanlam group and Barlow Rand controlled over 70 per cent of the shares listed on the Johannesburg Stock Exchange. Of these, Anglo American, with over 52 per cent of the total, towered over the rest. It is difficult to overestimate Anglo American's stake in the South African economy: apart from its holdings in mining, it has substantial interests in the top companies in finance, property, manufacturing, construction, and plantation agriculture. The value of the assets held by the Anglo American Corporation and de Beers, which form part of a single group, surpasses that of the South African Railways and Harbours.[31]

As a result, in part, of this centralisation and concentration of capital and the massive import of machinery and equipment in the 1960s, South Africa was increasingly dependent on foreign investment, and once again faced a serious balance of payments deficit. At the same time, increased mechanisation also contributed to high unemployment rates, inflation climbed steeply, and the GDP dropped dramatically from the levels achieved in the 1960s. New technology led to a shortage of skilled and semi-skilled operatives whose ranks could not be filled by the white working class, and the absence of a sufficient internal market at a time when there were continued and increasing barriers on external markets led to considerable dissatisfaction among the business community. Even before this, the South African state had been involved in the search for external markets in Africa in an attempt to bypass the absence of a consumer market among its own low-paid black workers. Verwoerd had had his 'good neighbour' policy and Vorster had attempted a foreign policy of *détente*; as in the past, strategic concerns paralleled economic imperatives in determining these policies. None of these strategies proved particularly effective.

For workers, the expansion of capital intensive industry in the 1960s had resulted simultaneously in high levels of unemployment among the unskilled, the fragmentation of jobs for some of the more skilled workers, and a middle-level skills shortage. For both capital and labour there seemed to be an urgent need to rethink the job colour bar which protected white workers against black competition, and in the course of the 1970s most of remaining restrictions on employment fell away. An increasing number of Afrikaner businesses were now suffering from what became known as the 'skills shortage'. The formation of the HNP in 1969 now enabled Vorster to adopt more pragmatic economic policies, although he remained inclined to give the right-wingers still in his party their head on social and ideological matters.[32]

Initially, some of the white unionists were prepared to go along with the erosion of the colour bar, as most white workers were elevated into new supervisory and managerial roles, or given considerable salary rises. Even the conservative white unions advocated the rate for the job and promotion on merit, secure that their own members would continue to be protected. They were decidedly more ambivalent over the unionisation of black workers, an issue which was increasingly on the agenda by the late 1970s. The continued expansion of opportunity for whites came to an abrupt halt with the recession which began in South Africa in 1976 and deepened seriously after 1981. White workers who were hit by the elimination of the colour bar and whose jobs were lost in the reconstruction of industry began to form an increasingly vociferous element in the right-wing opposition to the National Party both within and outside Parliament.

For blacks, the recession was far more serious, given their much greater economic vulnerability. In the first instance, it put paid to their hopes of some improvement following the strike wave of 1972–73. In response to the strike wave, wages increased in certain sectors of the economy and in the urban areas African wages increased more rapidly than white. Thus, according to Lipton:

> from 1970–82, real wages for Africans in manufacturing and construction rose by over 60 per cent, compared with 18 per cent for whites; on gold mines real wages for Africans quadrupled, while those for white miners rose by 3 per cent; on white farms, real wages for Africans doubled between 1968–9 and 1976. As a result the white share of personal income declined from over 70 to under 60 per cent, while the African share rose from 19 to 29 per cent.[33]

Startling as these increases may at first appear, they should be set against rapidly increasing unemployment and the further deterioration of rural resources; in the 1970s, the ratio between the income of the urban and rural black wage-earners – 8 to 1 – was approaching that between black and white.[34] Although unofficial surveys of unskilled wages in Johannesburg showed a rise of around 20 per cent between June 1974 and June 1976, 80 per cent of Sowetan households still earned below what was defined as the effective minimum level of subsistence, while a quarter lived below the poverty datum line, then estimated at R130 a month for a family of six, and this was before the onset of the recession. Between 1970 and 1985, the proportion of Sowetans between the ages of 20 and 64 earning a wage declined from 67 to 46 per cent.[35] While there are regional differences, Soweto by no means represents the worst case.

Moreover, whatever the wage gains, urban conditions for Africans continued to deteriorate, as large numbers of impoverished bantustan inhabitants – now ignored by the labour recruiters – bypassed influx control mechanisms in their desperate search for employment. Existing dwellings became grotesquely overcrowded as the state put a brake on the provision of new urban housing and huge squatter settlements grew up on the outskirts of the cities. Transport, long a matter of contention, deteriorated even further.[36] Inevitably, discontent mounted among both workers and the unemployed. At the same time the relative success of the workers' strikes, the independence of Mozambique and Angola and the subsequent humiliation of the South African invasion of Angola inspired the Black Consciousness movement. It was the state's determination to impose Afrikaans on school students, however, in the context of a rapid expansion of high school numbers in urban areas, which provided the flashpoint.

V

From the early 1970s Vorster had reversed the earlier Verwoerdian policy of inhibiting the expansion of secondary schooling for Africans in the urban areas, in response to the demand from businessmen for trained black workers. This, together with the industrial unrest of 1972–73, had led to considerable expansion of educational opportunities and a rapid expansion of school building. At the same time, however, a decision to reorganise the year structure of African schools as part of the restructuring of secondary education resulted in a massive shortage of teachers and classroom space at the beginning of 1976. It was in this situation that Andries Treurnicht was appointed Deputy Minister of Bantu Education as a sop to the Afrikaner right-wing who opposed Vorster's somewhat more pragmatic economic polices.[37]

Under Treurnicht, the flexible policy on language in African schools which allowed for either English or Afrikaans to be used as the medium of instruction was reversed. The Minister now insisted on the use of Afrikaans as the language of instruction in half the subjects in black schools in so-called 'white areas'. The policy was opposed by the teachers, who were ill-equipped to teach in Afrikaans; by high-school students, who resented the attempt to cut them off from an international language and who saw English as an essential requirement for better paid and skilled employment; and by school boards who warned that its enforcement could lead to trouble. Nevertheless, the state pressed ahead with its policy of 'equal treatment' for both official languages.[38]

In May and June 1976, students from seven Sowetan schools boycotted classes over the language issue. Behind the student protest there was also a wider set of grievances over the nature of Bantu education – widely seen as 'education for servitude' – overcrowding in schools, double sessions and poor teaching. The number of students in secondary school had trebled between 1970 and 1975. Most had acquired their education at enormous sacrifice to their families yet they found on graduation that there were no jobs. After a series of minor affrays, on 16 June the police fired on an unarmed crowd of about 10 000 schoolchildren demonstrating outside the Orlando West Junior Secondary School, killing at least one pupil and wounding several others.

From Soweto the protests spread dramatically to most of the urban areas and some of the bantustans. While the main activity occurred in

Soweto (which remained the epicentre), Cape Town and Port Elizabeth, more than 160 African communities were affected, if only sporadically. Of the major urban areas, only Durban remained relatively quiet. Over the country, some 350 schools were attacked, including 95 in Soweto, 40 in the bantustans and nearly 200 coloured schools in the Cape. Inspired by events in Soweto and expressing solidarity with the schoolchildren there, students elsewhere were also responding to very specific local issues. Before this phase of protest had come to an end, between 600 and 1000 blacks had been killed, while large numbers had been wounded and detained. Several thousand young people began to flee the country to join the liberation movement in exile. Despite its coercive response, in order to restore control the state was forced to abandon its plans to enforce Afrikaans in schools.[39]

The police shootings of the schoolchildren unleashed deeply felt opposition to a wide range of state policies. Not only were parents bitterly resentful of police brutality; as we have seen, urban conditions were appalling and were fuelling African anger. Thus, Afrikaans was not the only issue arousing passionate discontent in the townships in 1976. Nor was it the only area where the state was forced to withdraw, at least initially.

Local administration constituted another such retreat in the face of African opposition. In 1972–73, the transfer of urban African administration from local authorities to 23 Bantu Affairs Administration Boards of the Department of Bantu Administration had greatly increased the presence of the state bureaucracy in African urban areas. In the case of Soweto this also meant that the tempering influence and modest financial assistance hitherto provided by the Johannesburg City Council were removed. From the outset the new Administration Boards combined higher rents with a deterioration in services. Between 1973 and 1976 the number of whites employed by the West Rand Administration Board rose from 950 to 1205, while the numbers of black employees declined from 7736 to 6648. Nearly half of the income of the Board went on salaries. Much administration was funded by money from rents and the sale of beer in municipal beerhalls. It is perhaps not surprising that during the upheavals, twenty-one offices of the WRAB were burnt out, and ten ransacked, while countrywide 250 bottle stores and beer-halls were attacked.[40]

More widely, drink was seen as a social evil which had to be rooted out – a strand of puritanism in the students' movement which was to recur in the consumer boycotts of 1985–86. In 1976 the Soweto Students' Representative Council called for the beer-halls, or *shebeens*, to stop operating because

> they were a cause of unhappiness in the black man's life . . . A number of lives have been lost because of the operation of these shebeens. Salaries have not reached homes because they were first opened in shebeens . . . Futures have been wrecked by the operation of these shebeens. Nothing good has ever come out of them. Many of our fathers and brothers have been killed in or out of them. Hundreds of our colleagues have become delinquents, beggars or orphans as shebeen kings and queens have become capitalists. We can no longer tolerate seeing our fathers' pay-packets emptied in shebeens.[41]

The destruction of the beerhalls and the loss of beerhall revenue may well have lain behind the decision by the Administration Boards in February 1977 that site rentals would be raised in the black townships. This was announced in Soweto in April 1977 by the West Rand Administration Board and led to widespread opposition, particularly when it was learnt that the black Urban Bantu Councils had known of and approved the proposal for some time without consulting residents. The Soweto Students' Representative Council which had led the protests in 1976 took the lead in opposing the rent increases and the Urban Bantu Council was put under such pressure that it was finally forced to resign by the beginning of June, 1977. The Community Councils as they were now known were seen as government creations and their elections boycotted. The state was also forced temporarily to suspend its rent increases. This retreat may have created the feeling that there should be no taxation without representation. The vacuum left by the collapse of the Urban Bantu Council was filled by the launching of a new non-governmental body sponsored by Soweto's civic associations, popularly known as the Committee of Ten. It was this Committee, together with the numerous civic associations which arose to oppose the Community Councils, that provided the basis for the formation of the United Democratic Front (UDF) in 1983 (see Chapter 5).

If drink and urban administration were issues which elicited broad community reaction across class divides, the students also came to realise the significance of ensuring specifically working-class support. At the beginning of August 1976, when the Soweto students called on workers to stay away from work they met with a considerable response, despite some evidence of earlier tensions between the students and workers. There was some evidence of strong-arm tactics, but the stayaway was none the less impressive: Johannesburg firms reported absenteeism of between 50 and 60 per cent. A second, three-day, stayaway called between 23 and 25 August 1976, was even more successful with reported absenteeism of around 70 per cent. The police were out in force and, according to Chief Buthelezi, it was they who were responsible for egging on Zulu hostel dwellers in Soweto to attack the strikers.[42]

It was subsequently claimed that the confrontation was the result of a misunderstanding, and Buthelezi intervened to end the conflict. Nevertheless, this episode seems to indicate the state's strategy of manipulating existing tensions and conflicts within the black population in its attempts to retain control. This was not new. There is evidence that in the 1950s the authorities used criminal gangs to disrupt community actions such as bus boycotts as well as ANC campaigns. Since 1976 it has reached a new sophistication, both externally in the support South Africa has given to dissident groups in the Front Line States, and internally in the use of black vigilantes.

The fomenting of internal divisions in order to 'destabilise' African political organisation was an immediate response by the state to the renewed protest signalled by the events of 1976, and one which was to be vigorously renewed in the struggles since 1984. Different sectors of the state and big business also produced more complex responses, however. For these interests, the upheavals of 1976 were the tip of an iceberg. Particularly ominous were the signs of a growing alliance between students and workers. Structural changes in the economy were already creating a demand for political and social change. Businessmen were concerned by the government's economic policies, and in particular the restriction on the training and use of skilled black labour. They asserted that the use of low waged, unskilled labour was limiting productivity and earnings for all South Africa's people, an argument that reflected the growing need of capital intensive manufacturing industry for an educated, skilled and politically neutralised working class.

VI

As it became apparent that the existing system was producing instability incompatible with the needs of industry, there was an intensified demand for reform from both local and foreign capital.[43] The nightly scenes of violence on Western television undermined the confidence of investors in the stability of the South African regime. From the very beginnings of its mineral revolution, South Africa had been heavily dependent on international investment. The links between local and foreign capital were intimate, although in the past it had been English-speaking capitalists who had the closest ties to overseas bankers and investors. By the 1970s, however, an increasing number of Afrikaner businessmen were also meshed into the international economy. Their voices now joined in the demand for reform, and for a brief period after P.W. Botha became Prime Minister in 1978, the state seemed responsive.

The relationship between big business and the state was epitomised by the widely acclaimed Carlton and Good Hope Conferences in Johannesburg and Cape Town in 1979 and 1981 respectively. Although some businessmen were later to feel that they had been 'set up' and 'naive', and that 'those conferences were nothing more than a forum for the propagation of government's policies', at the time business saw its relationship with the state as complementary. Even in the 1950s when Verwoerd took wide powers of labour control, the possibilities of exemption involved businessmen in intense and continuous negotiation with government, however uncomfortable these negotiations may have been.[44] As John R. Wilson, Shell's senior executive in South Africa told a conference of the corporation's staff in August 1986, the fact that it had waited so long to make a statement on apartheid arose from

> the notion that the political arena was something divorced from the business world; that the business of business is business, and not politics. Business leaders were oblivious of the extent to which co-operation between the state and business in fact repressed black aspirations. Business saw its role as maintaining long-term growth and profitability and looked to the state to be supportive of this goal.[45]

After the July 1985 Emergency, as the state showed itself unable to quell black resistance, some businessmen became disillusioned with Botha's reformism. They became 'acutely aware that the policies of government could, far from supporting, in fact defeat that goal' of long-term growth and profitability, and they tried to distance themselves from the state. Some of the most important, including Gavin Relly, chairman of the economically dominant Anglo American Corporation, even made their way to Lusaka to talk to the ANC in the hopes of dissociating capitalism from apartheid and ensuring their future whatever the political complexion of the state.[46]

Initially, however, under Botha, businessmen, including some who supported the opposition Progressive Party,[47] had been drawn into Cabinet Committees as 'experts' on economic matters and their recommendations not infrequently found their way into state policy. The language of technocratic rationality enabled their collaboration to be depicted as politically neutral. On the other hand, by labelling an issue 'political', the government was able to exclude capitalist participation from certain areas and reserve these for its own decision making.

The coming together of government and business in the late 1970s was spurred by the increasing number of Afrikaners who were now major industrialists and financiers in their own right and by the recognition that an increasing number of young blacks had come to identify apartheid with capitalism. As the Progressive Party saw it, the question of colour was 'a divide which disguised far more dangerous class divisions. The threat of revolution was no longer primarily a threat to white power, or to "Western Civilization", but to capitalism itself'.[48] If capital accumulation was to continue, a more incorporative political and ideological strategy was necessary.

For both the National Party leadership and businessmen, it became increasingly important to affirm free-market principles rather than state intervention as the basis of policy. As the old apartheid certainties came to be jettisoned in the face of the economic and political challenge of the 1970s, a new 'apolitical' language of technocratic rationality, based on the catchwords 'realism', 'pragmatism', 'reform', 'orderly urbanisation' and 'effective government' emerged. The destructive consequences of National Party policies were increasingly explained as the inevitable results of economic growth and industrialisation, to which experts could find solutions which were technical, non-ideological and therefore non-contestable. Closely connected was what was termed the 'total strategy' designed to overcome the 'total onslaught' which South Africa was said to be facing; this too was justified in view of the 'objective facts' as a 'rational necessity'. ' "Total strategy" is defined sufficiently widely to cover anything which the government or military experts deem a matter of "national security" ', whether military or civilian.[49]

The 'total onslaught' also allowed for changes in the *form* of state. Institutional reforms have greatly increased the power both of the head of state, and of cabinet committees which are no longer necessarily drawn from parliament. Since 1979 the power of the military has been greatly increased, with military men playing an important role as 'experts' on the cabinet committees and in interdepartmental meetings, and through the enlarged powers of the South African Military Intelligence Directorate. In 1979 a parallel system of government was established in the National Security Management System (NSMS). First set up to eliminate competition between departments of state, and as an answer to 'total onslaught', the NSMS now acts as an alternative to parliamentary and cabinet government. The 'main advisory and planning body' of the state's 'total strategy' became the State Security Council (SSC) which meets twice a week and includes key ministers and military and police chiefs. At local level, a network of some 500 Joint Management Committees (JMCs) bring together the security and police forces with business and black local government officials. The Joint Management Committees provide a civilian political base for the security forces and formulate strategies to combat opposition based on detailed local information.[50]

In the process of formation are Regional Service Councils (RSCs) which are planned to replace both municipal and provincial elected authorities. Through these changes even the limited democratic rights of the non-white population have been diminished. They have done little to provide forms of representation at either local or national level for unenfranchised Africans. As Posel has pointed out, given the anticipated opposition to the State President's reform programme of the late 1970s and early 1980s, it was 'not surprising' that there was an 'increased centralization of decision-making and withdrawal from the arena of party and parliamentary discussion'.[51]

United States political scientists have provided much of the vocabulary for 'total strategy'. The National Party's discovery that it has the capacity to become 'a model modernising oligarchy' owed much to the writings of Robert Rotberg of MIT. Even more significant has been Professor Samuel Huntington of Harvard who has argued that 'narrowing the scope of political participation may be indispensable to eventually broadening that participation'; an increasingly authoritarian state in his view may be indispensable to the reform of apartheid. As Joseph Lelyveld has pointed out, this begs 'the question of what it is that is being reformed. In South Africa the essential question about reform is whether it aims at eliminating, or simply renovating, the racial system'.[52]

Huntington's popularity is not accidental. His 'thesis' that reform has to be carried out from above, by an authoritarian oligarchy, has been cited with approval by the Commissioner of the South African Police, General Johan Coetzee, who has almost elevated it to 'a law of nature'. Although Huntington himself has recently complained that 'in the years since 1981, government did not follow many of my key prescriptions on the tactics and strategy of bringing about reform', his 1981 speech provided the state with both a framework for discussion of what he has called 'reform from above' and a language of legitimation for an increasing authoritarianism which pre-dated his address.[53]

Initially the military were in the forefront of those demanding reform, on the grounds that the external defence of South Africa depended on 'winning hearts and minds' internally. In the wake of the 1976 disturbances and responding to the wider changes detailed above, a flurry of Commissions were appointed. Of these, the most important were the Wiehahn Commission which called for the registration of black trade unions, the abolition of statutory job reservation, and the opening of apprenticeship to Africans; the Riekert Commission which called for greater mobility for urban Africans with section 10 rights; and the de Lange Report which recommended the provision of equal resources for the education of all racial groups. The commissions were a response both to the new political challenges to the state and the demands from business, including large-scale Afrikaner business, for a restructuring of the workforce. The National Party's response was hesitant and equivocal, as it looked anxiously to the reactions of an increasingly restive and vociferous element in its own political constituency. The objective of reform was manifestly not designed in any way to jeopardise white control. Nevertheless, the government was forced to make a number of concessions in its bid to expand and co-opt the black middle and skilled working classes and to incorporate coloureds and Indians.

The spread of the Black Consciousness movement among coloureds, especially at the segregated University of the Western Cape, was however a spur to fresh thought. In 1973 the government appointed the Theron Commission to enquire into the political, economic and social conditions of the coloured people. Published in June 1976, the report recommended far-reaching changes in the state's policies towards coloureds. Overall these were designed to incorporate coloureds politically and culturally. The recommendations went beyond what the government was prepared to contemplate at the time, despite the further evidence of coloured alienation provided by the school boycotts in the Western Cape in 1976. It was not until the 1980s that the Theron Commission recommendations had any effect, within the more general context of reformist strategy. Its recommendations that the Mixed Marriages Act and Section 16 of the Immorality Act be repealed were finally implemented in 1985, unlike its further suggestion that the Group Areas Act be modified. More momentous, in the event, was its proposal to allow coloureds direct representation in Parliament, at different government levels and in various decision-making bodies. This proposal was implemented in terms of the Constitution Act of 1983 which established the basis for a tricameral parliament. As will be seen, this limited reform dramatically increased the state's confrontation with the African population and was hardly greeted with enthusiasm by its intended beneficiaries.

From an African and working class point of view, the proposals of the Wiehahn Commission were to have greater effect. This Commission was a response to the growth of black unions since the strikes of 1972–73. Initially, the government responded to the recommendations of the Wiehahn Commission with a White Paper which proposed to divide workers into migrants without rights and the more skilled permanent workforce who were to be allowed registered trade unions. Registration, moreover, was meant as a way of controlling working-class organisation. To begin with, the unions were divided over how to respond to these proposals. They were all opposed to attempts to exclude migrant workers from the registered unions, and in the end the state was forced to concede the issue. In addition, however, while many of the general unions rejected registration on the grounds that it would lead to over-bureaucratisation, others argued that registration created new opportunities for organisation and that shop-floor organisation and the principle of workers' control would effectively prevent the bureaucratising of the unions and their co-option by employers and the state.[54]

These changes in the position of the black unions could hardly fail to anger white workers at a time when their wages were barely keeping up with inflation and their job security was being threatened perhaps for the first time since the 1930s. Over one-third of the economically active white population were employed in the state sector either as civil servants or in the parastatal corporations. Bureaucrats who saw their livelihood as dependent on the administration of apartheid were also resentful of the state's apparent jettisoning of the Verwoerdian project, particularly as there had been a dramatic decline in real public sector pay averaging 23 per cent in central government and 12 per cent in the provinces between 1974 and 1979.[55] Dissatisfied civil servants were in a position to obstruct the state's reformism effectively, as P. W. Botha realised when he became Prime Minister in 1978. Soon after his accession to the premiership, a number of measures to make the civil service more effective and more compliant were introduced. The Public Service Commission was instructed to investigate all departments, state agencies and legislative enactments. According to Marcel Golding, its 'hidden agenda . . . was to identify areas, and even personnel, which would obstruct the new direction the state was taking under the Botha government'. While some of the known opponents of the new strategy were forced into early retirement, the government hoped to secure the loyal support of the remainder through a variety of material benefits including salary increments, housing subsidies and loans and increased pensions. Nevertheless, their opposition to reform was sustained.[56]

Small farmers being driven off the land by drought and inflation were also becoming disenchanted with the big business profile of the National Party. Thus, the class and regional divisions among Afrikaners that had been largely absent since 1948 began to open up once again. The revived divisions were revealed by the formation of the Conservative Party under Dr Treurnicht in 1982, and the growth of a right-wing extra-parliamentary populism, epitomised by the formation of the Afrikaner Weerstandsbeweging (AWB) with its base in the northern Transvaal.

From the state's point of view, the other areas requiring urgent reform after the urban uprisings seemed to be in local government, education, health and housing. In relation to its white constituency, these areas may have appeared relatively safe by comparison with the measures which more directly affected the orthodoxies of the Verwoerdian apartheid. Reforms in these fields could be conducted within segregated townships and out of the normal purview of white politics. What the National Party did not foresee was the way in which all these spheres would become politicised for blacks as the state was seen to use welfare for purposes of social control and to concede too little too late. Its attempts to solve one problem almost invariably led to fresh confrontations with the alienated black population.

Thus the collapse of the Urban Bantu Councils in 1977 resulted in the creation first of 'community councils', and then, following their being discredited, Black Local Authorities. The object of these new Black Local Authorities was, as Riekert, by then Chief Director of the Western Transvaal Administration Board, saw it, 'to defuse pent up frustrations and grievances against administration from Pretoria'.[57] The state also hoped to transfer the responsibility for raising the finance to these new urban authorities which had somewhat enlarged powers compared to the old Urban Bantu Councils. As the Riekert

Commission put it, it was vital that 'Black communities . . . bear to an increasing extent a greater part of the total burden in connection with the provision of services in their own communities.'[58]

These ambitions were to be disappointed. The new councils were unsuccessful either in raising revenue or in achieving acceptance. Both the community councils and the black local authorities proved politically unviable. According to Jeremy Seekings:

> The councils were caught in an overwhelming contradiction. Their revenue largely comprised rent and service charges, and state funds were only available for housing construction at economic rates of interest. But increases in rents or charges were met with effective passive resistance from residents, either through a proliferation of shacks, increasing overcrowding, or through growing rent arrears. Revenue could therefore only be increased if 1) informal housing was controlled and/or taxed, 2) rents were increased, and 3) rent defaulters were evicted (and replaced by tenants who would pay the rent). But such action would remove any residual legitimacy that councillors enjoyed and could precipitate active resistance.[59]

Although initially the new councils were not rejected out of hand and local people were prepared to make use of them where possible, residents grew increasingly dissatisfied as local councils were forced to implement state fiscal policy. Allegations of council corruption and mismanagement became widespread, and

> corruption was accorded a symbolic importance. What had previously been seen as the appeal of patronage was transformed into the crime of corruption, as councillors crudely manipulated their control over trading licenses, bursaries for students and council funds in general, to favour themselves or their supporters.[60]

All over the country, since the end of 1984, large numbers of councillors and mayors have been attacked and killed, their property destroyed. Hundreds of councillors have resigned or, like many black policemen, have been forced to flee the townships and live in specially protected government compounds. Local government buildings have been attacked and only five of the thirty-eight Black Local Authorities were still functioning in 1986. This onslaught on local government is a major reason for the army of occupation which has been in the black townships since the declaration of a State of Emergency in the middle of 1985, and the proposal to establish multiracial Regional Service Councils as the new form of local government.

A further area which called out for attention after 1976 was the educational system which was in total disarray. The crisis in the schools, together with calls by businessmen for increased expenditure on African literacy and training, led to a massive increase in secondary and higher education, although as we have seen some of the expansion pre-dated 1976. Although the expenditure on white education is still seven times more than on black, the increase in the number of black students in secondary education, matriculation and university has been dramatic, as can be seen in Table 1.1.

Table 1.1 Expansion of African education since 1960.[61]

Year	*Secondary school*	*Matriculants*	*University*
1960	45,598	717	1,871
1965	66,568	1,607	1,880
1970	122,489	2,938	4,578
1975	318,568	9,009	7,845
1980	577,584	31,071	10,564
1984	1,001,249	86,873	36,604

This has led to further outbursts of anger as the growth in the number of matriculants has far outstripped the growth in the number of black jobs, a situation which was exacerbated by the recession. Since the late 1960s high black unemployment has been remarked on as a feature of the South African economy.[62] The 1981 National Manpower Commission recorded that 59 per cent of unemployed Africans were under the age of 30, and 66 per cent of Coloureds. As Colin Bundy has pointed out:

> In 1985, somewhere between 15% and 30% of the workforce was unemployed. Within this huge total, high school leavers have fared particularly badly. They have been thrust onto the labour market at precisely the moment that it is contracting; many are too highly educated for cheap or unskilled labour; and white collar openings are increasingly the preserve of those who manage to obtain tertiary education.[63]

In an attempt to defuse some of the growing urban discontent and co-opt the urban middle class, the government also set about trying to establish a class of urban householders with property. After decades in which the state had refused to recognise the rights of urban Africans to permanent residence and had whittled away their rights, it conceded leasehold tenure once more to people with rights under Section 10 of the 1945 Urban Areas Act. Once again the promises were simply to lead to further frustration. Ambitious housing schemes were proposed by the Urban Foundation for the black middle class, although as tensions rose against collaborators in the townships it became increasingly difficult for the small black petty bourgeoisie to enjoy their new property with any sense of security. In any event, the housing construction programme barely touched the needs of the black urban population. In 1982 the Manpower Services Commission estimated the shortage of black family housing units for the approximately ten million Africans in the urban areas as 560 000, yet in 1984 there were less than 421 000 family housing units in 'white' areas. The result has been fearful overcrowding, with twelve to twenty-four people sharing a unit, depending on how it is calculated, and huge squatter settlements in which vast numbers of people live in the most ramshackle conditions. In the Greater Durban area, for example, 1.25 million blacks out of a total of two million live in shacks.[64]

VII

In retrospect, the state's reformism in this form was short-lived and was made possible by a brief economic revival between 1978 and 1981, which provided the wherewithal both for the provision of some urban black welfare and to buy off white opposition. Essential to the reformist position was the assumption that the economy would continue to expand. In the past, white accumulation had been at the expense of blacks, and white well-being had been secured by transferring the costs of economic down-swings to the black population. As black militancy grew, this became more difficult. With renewed economic recession, and the increasing burden of military expenditure as a result of external pressure and the war in Namibia, the possibility of buying off the opposition, whether white or black, became more and more remote.

The increasingly disillusioned and impoverished black population met the limited reforms wrung out of the Botha government with anger. Although they may have been accepted by an earlier generation, the events of 1976–77 had marked a shift in the consciousness of the young in the townships. As early as June 1976, Mr Hlaku Rachidi, President of the Black Peoples' Convention, remarked that it would be difficult to restore the 'old order' in the townships.

> The authorities, the parents and the teachers are going to be faced with a new child. The kids have learnt a whole political lesson during the last week . . . They are rejecting the imposition of the whole White establishment and system, plus the norms and values of Whites. The BPC interprets this as black consciousness in the kids. It is gut reaction, not lofty philosophy, and it reflects and articulates the feelings of the people.[65]

The transformed consciousness went further than simply the youth, and had four main aspects: the radicalisation of substantial sections of the Christian churches; the complex network of new community organisations which came together in 1983 to form the United Democratic Front; the massive growth in the trade union movement which we have already partly discussed; and the revival of support for the outlawed ANC.

The church has long been an important factor in South African political life. For over a hundred years, the mission churches provided Africans with schools and education. As in other parts of Africa, the first African nationalists were Christians who accepted the universal doctrines of the church, only to be confronted by the very different reality of even the church's own practices in a colonial society. Leading members of the African National Congress from its earliest years to the present have been practising Christians impelled into politics by the South African situation.

Not all black Christians have been or are political activists. By far the vast majority belong to the independent African churches of which there are several thousand. The independent churches encompass a wide variety of religious and secular beliefs, ranging from the millenarian to the severely pragmatic. While the earliest to break away are often difficult to distinguish from their mission mother church in either theology or organisation, the prophetic Zionist churches or 'Churches of the Spirit' belong to the most impoverished and oppressed. One of the largest is the four-million strong Zion Christian Church (ZCC) which celebrated its 75th anniversary at the 'City of Morija' in the Northern Transvaal in 1985 in the presence of the State President. It would be wrong to dismiss either the ZCC or the smaller 'Churches of the Spirit' with their stress on biblical literalism as merely diffusing and defusing the emotional energies of their adherents into an apolitical escapism. As Jean Comaroff has recently pointed out, they represent 'an attempt, under pitifully restrained circumstances, to address and redress experiental conflict'. Through an analysis of the ritual and symbolism of the Spirit Churches, Comaroff shows their profoundly subversive character. Their rejection of both capitalism and the state may be indeed more thoroughgoing than that of either the black urban elite or the organised proletariat. Yet their vision cannot easily be incorporated by more radical political movements; nor can the practices of the 'Churches of the Spirit' transform their powerlessness.[66]

By the 1960s a small number of white Protestants were beginning to appreciate the sharpness of the contradictions confronting their black fellow-Christians in the mission churches. In 1960 the three Dutch Reformed Churches (DRCs), whose members largely supported the National Party, withdrew from the ecumenical World Council of Churches and the Christian Council of South Africa over the adoption of the Cottesloe declaration which maintained *inter alia* that no one who believed in Christ should be excluded from any church on the grounds of colour or race. The formation of the Christian Institute in 1963 led to an even sharper cleavage between the Dutch Reformed Churches and the rest of the Protestant churches. In the 1950s a number of DRC clergymen experienced doubts over the theological justification for apartheid as practised by Dr Verwoerd. Most were forced back into line and did not respond to the call from the ecumenical movement.[67] The most notable exception was the redoubtable Dr Beyers Naude who was invited to become the first Secretary of the Christian Institute and later of the radicalised Southern African Council of Churches (SACC).

Part of this radicalisation of the SACC – which was by no means reflected in the general body of the white religious community – resulted from the increasing number of black clergy in the Protestant churches. The development of black theology by a group of churchmen from within the heart of the Black Consciousness movement, influenced by Latin American liberation theology, was also important. Liberation theology also affected the stand of the Roman Catholic Church within South Africa, and the increasingly outspoken opposition to apartheid of the South African Catholic Bishops Conference.

The claims of the National Party that they were running the country along Christian national lines both provoked a response from those who saw apartheid as a heresy and provided a forum for their protest. By the 1980s a number of churchmen, including the Anglican Bishop (later Archbishop) Desmond Tutu and the Reverend Dr Allan Boesak, who became President of the World Alliance of Reformed Churches in 1982, were outspokenly defiant of government and playing a leading role in community politics. They and others like them were influential too in the founding of the United Democratic Front in 1983.

The United Democratic Front (UDF) grew out of the discrediting of the state sponsored Bantu Urban Councils and the collapse of black municipal government. This led to the emergence of new democratic political structures in the townships. The first was the widely representative Committee of Ten in Soweto which emerged in the power vacuum created by the events of 1976; it was supported by the Student Representative Council and the Black Consciousness organisations, and was followed by the establishment of civic associations in a number of cities. The banning of nineteen major Black Consciousness organisations in October 1977 did not slow the momentum: in May the following year, the Azanian Peoples' Organisation (AZAPO) was formed to fill the gap.

At the local level, literally hundreds of associations, street committees, church, youth and women's organisations, welfare groups and mutual aid societies sprang up to cope with the new urban situation. Again the phenomenon is not entirely new – as early as the 1930s, Ellen Hellman's *Rooiyard* revealed a network of mutual aid societies, and women have long been organised in church groups and prayer meetings – but the scale and creativity is surely unprecedented.

In 1983 the state's attempts to buy off coloured and Indian opposition through the establishment of the tricameral parliament opened up a new space for national organisations, the United Democratic Front and the National Forum (NF). Both bodies formed

> loose coalitions [which] took on the character less of organisations than of mechanisms for consultation and/or co-ordinated action between existing organisations. They brought together a wide variety of predominantly black political, community, labour, student, professional and pressure groups of varying strengths. Some organisations were to participate in both the UDF and NF.[68]

Of the two movements, the United Democratic Front was to prove the more substantial. It was formed in the first instance to boycott the elections on the grounds that the proposals excluded the major black population. Labelled 'progressive nationalists', its leaders maintain that, while the working class should lead the political struggle, 'all oppressed sections of the community had an overriding interest in the destruction of apartheid' and allowed white participation where whites identified with this national struggle. The Front brought together over 650 local organisations. Although there are clearly problems of coherence and control for an umbrella organisation bringing together so many and such diverse local associations, there can be little doubt of the continuities between the UDF and the banned ANC. Many of the political and economic demands of the UDF and the mass of affiliated organisations coincide with the ANC's political manifesto, the Freedom Charter, and its belief in a class coalition to engage in 'the broader national democratic struggle'. The UDF has repeatedly called for the ban to be lifted on the ANC and other political organisations, and has refused to negotiate with the South African government in the absence of 'recognised leaders of the people', who are in gaol or in exile.

Within the National Forum, AZAPO provides the driving force. AZAPO was reinvigorated when a number of Black Consciousness leaders, released from detention on Robben Island at the end of 1982, returned to head the organisation. Unlike the UDF, the dominant voice in AZAPO has been explicitly socialist. Its manifesto 'declared that the people's struggle was directed against "the system of racial capitalism which holds the people of Azania in bondage for the benefit of the small minority of white capitalists and their allies, the white workers, and the reactionary section of the black middle class" '. For AZAPO, the black working class is the 'driving force of the struggle', and it differs from the UDF in its reluctance to admit whites.[69]

The prominence given to the role of the black working class is a reflection of its increased centrality since the strikes of the early 1970s. Whereas in 1976 very few black workers were unionised, today a significant proportion has been organised into unions. This in turn is a reflection of the increased concentration of the workforce in factories. The small enterprises of the 1950s employing ten to twenty workers have given way to large-scale industries employing hundreds and sometimes thousands of workers. A substantial number of black women are also now employed in industry and, as is the case among male workers, their concentration on the shop-floor provides a real basis for unionisation.[70]

As Jon Lewis has pointed out:

> South Africa is one of the few countries where trade union membership and militancy have increased during the current recession. The new unions have challenged managerial prerogatives within the factories over such issues as the right to hire and fire at will, health and safety, the intensity of work, as well as wages. More recently, the unions have sought to defend their members' interests in the sphere of reproduction of labour – in struggles over rents, removals,

transportation, education, etc. As the present political and social crisis has intensified – in the townships, the schools and the factories – unions have begun to deploy their power in pursuance of political rights and national liberation.[71]

The establishment of the Federation of South African Trade Unions (FOSATU) in 1979 was evidence of the growing confidence of the black unions. By April 1979 it had twelve affiliates representing 45 000 workers. The Black Consciousness movement and independent unions were, at that stage, equally prominent, and perhaps included a larger percentage of recent migrants and migrant workers. Divisions in the unions related to the differentiated industrial experience in different regions: it is no coincidence that the FOSATU unions with their heavy emphasis on shop-floor industrial organisation were based in industries with a large, relatively homogeneous workforce, as on the East Rand and in Natal. In the Western Cape, where the workforce was far more fragmented, community issues provided a unifying factor around which general unions were better able to mobilise. In the Eastern Cape, with its long radical political tradition and cultural homogeneity, unions, confronted by the unremitting hostility of the bantustan governments of the Transkei and Ciskei, combined political and industrial demands. The decline of the motor industry in the Eastern Cape sharpened political perceptions and made a purely industrial strategy inappropriate.

By far the most important of these new black unions is the black National Union of Mineworkers (NUM) which was formed at the end of 1982 after more than one hundred years of the mining industry in South Africa. As the major earner of foreign exchange, the mining industry remains at the heart of South Africa's economy and this gives the mine workers a particularly strategic significance. Although the NUM was not the first attempt to organise African mine workers, previous efforts had been destroyed by a combination of state action and the opposition of the powerful Chamber of Mines, which adamantly resisted any recognition of black trade unions until recently, and which continues to view the NUM with hostility and suspicion. Within three years, the NUM had a membership of over a quarter of a million (out of a total workforce on the mines of over 500 000), and was representing miners' interests over a broad range of issues: wages, safety conditions and health. The ability of the union to mobilise its members was shown on 1 October 1986, when between 250 000 workers (according to the employers) and 325 000 (according to the NUM) observed a day of mourning for the 177 miners killed in the mining disaster at Gencor gold mine at Kinross near Johannesburg. As Phillip van Niekerk reported at that time, '. . . it was – by far – the biggest-ever stayaway in any one industry, and the most impressive response to a safety issue by the South African union movement'.[72] In the context of the international sanctions campaign and delicate wage negotiations in the mining industry, the Secretary-General of the NUM, Cyril Ramaphosa, warned that 'Management should take heed that the NUM is prepared to take up any issue be it wages, be it political issues, be it safety, and it could mobilise workers around any issue, virtually.'[73]

Pressed on the debate about sanctions, Ramaphosa, while not wishing to commit his executive, said that they would be discussing 'the whole question of sanctions and how the workers and the unions should respond' in the gold and coal mining industries. He even went so far as to say that 'the NUM would consider the possibility of cutting gold production' – an action which would undoubtedly weaken South Africa's capacity to withstand sanctions.[74]

The intensity of the divisions between many of the unions over the registration debate which had been dominant in the late 1970s and early 1980s had diminished by the mid-1980s, when the formation of the Confederation of South African Trade Unions (COSATU) brought together the largely industrial unions in FOSATU and the Council of Unions of South Africa (CUSA), most notably including the NUM and some of the independents, including those who were far more overtly political. Today some of the larger COSATU unions (e.g. the NUM and the National Union of Metalworkers of South Africa (NUMSA)) have adopted the Freedom Charter and a mooted Workers' Charter with more explicitly socialist aims.[75] Some of the Black Consciousness unions remained outside this new grouping, maintaining an 'anti-racist' stance. This is essentially a ban on white leadership, in contrast to the position of the COSATU unions which argue that it is up to workers to decide on their leaders.

As Denis MacShane has noted:

> The 12 years between the mass strikes in 1973 that was generally held to mark the rebirth of black trade union organization and COSATU's first convention have given workers and advisers time to deeply root themselves, debate strategy and tactics, develop leadership, and acquire the confidence that comes from long experience of struggle and, in particular, from winning victories rather than suffering defeats. There have been many setbacks and not a little

> repression, but the move from a powerless, atomized working-class in 1970 to the 500,000 plus strong COSATU Federation and the successful organization and militancy of workers in key industrial and service sectors of today is a remarkable success story for working-class organization anywhere in the world.[76]

Nevertheless, only some 1.5 million out of the twelve million economically active population have been unionised in South Africa, and not all of these are in the COSATU and Black Consciousness unions. Three other trade union groupings have remained outside the half-million strong COSATU: the extreme right-wing South African Confederation of Labour (about 100 000 strong) and the now defunct Trade Union Council of South Africa which represented some 300 000 black and white workers in single-race unions brought together in a highly bureaucratic 'multiracial' federation.[77] In addition, in April 1986 the Zulu cultural-political organisation Inkatha formed its own trade union movement, the United Workers' Union of South Africa (UWUSA). This was formed explicitly to counter the UDF and COSATU and their pro-disinvestment and socialist policies. Led by 'veterans of KwaZulu politics with management and business backgrounds and some white professionals', UWUSA also receives support from big business and the AFL/CIO in the United States of America.[78] Clashes between workers in Inkatha/UWUSA and the UDF/COSATU have led to a number of deaths and have opened up a very deep fissure between Africans in Natal.

The States of Emergency since 1985 have also taken their toll of the trade unions with whole regional committees being detained in some areas. After the period of liberalisation in the early 1980s, the unions have come under increasing repression, restriction and direct physical attack, with, for example, the sabotage of COSATU House in May 1987. The effects of sanctions have also put severe strains on the unions, despite their initial advocacy by COSATU. The recession, too, has taken its toll. Nevertheless, it is difficult to envisage the state's being able to roll back all the achievements of the past decade. Trade union organisations are clearly going to be of major significance in the future transformation of South Africa.

Accompanying the rise of internal political organisations and the emergence of the mass trade union movement has been the resurgence of the African National Congress, after a period in which its activities were little reported. The change over the past few years has been profound. Thus, in 1976, Tsietsi Mashinini, exiled President of the

Soweto Students' Representative Council, indignantly rejected ANC claims to have been behind the Soweto uprising, stating

> As far as the students in South Africa are concerned, the ANC and the PAC are extinct internally. Externally we are aware they exist. Internally they are doing their work, there may be some underground work they are doing which we are not aware of, but as far as the struggle is concerned they are not doing anything.[79]

As recently as 1984, Tom Lodge remarked on its 'low intensity military operations' within South Africa, and the 'unfavourable international environment' which it increasingly confronted.[80] Yet, within the last three years it has reconstructed a clandestine organisation within the country and has established its ideological hegemony through the widespread acceptance of its leadership role in the internal struggle. A wide variety of community and trade union organisations have adopted the principles of the Freedom Charter which was unbanned in 1983. By the end of 1985, businessmen, trade unionists, churchmen, and even some Afrikaner students had trooped to Lusaka to talk to the ANC, while the United Democratic Front roundly declared:

> Broad sectors of the population . . . have granted the ANC the credibility it truly deserves. . . It has generally come to be accepted that there can be no solution of South Africa's problems without the involvement of the ANC. . . Unbanning of the ANC must be seen as the first step in the process of resolving the problems in this country.[81]

At an international level, it has been equally widely accepted that there can be no internal solution without the full participation of the ANC, and world leaders have joined in the call for the release of the organisation's imprisoned President, Nelson Mandela. ANC leaders abroad have been received by the British and United States governments, both of whom had previously dismissed the organisation as 'terrorist'.

In part this transformation in the position of the ANC is a response to the increased visibility of the ANC as it has escalated the armed struggle from within, despite the closure of the Mozambiquan border as a result of the Nkomati agreement. There have been a mounting number of guerrilla attacks: from around thirty in 1983 to over 200 in 1986.[82] At the same time, the success of the ANC in exile in providing for the material needs of the waves of young exiles who have left South

Africa since 1976, and incorporating them politically, has also been a major factor behind its resurgence.

VIII

By the mid-1980s the problems confronting the South African state had become truly formidable as the black organisations challenged the stability of the social order without being able to transform it and as the state proved incapable of re-establishing its own authority except through increasingly coercive measures. The rejection of the constitution and the boycotting of the 1984 elections for the tricameral parliament proved a major setback to the reformist strategy. Only a very small sector of the coloured and Indian communities responded positively and the African population was further alienated. The Black Local Authorities which the state had hoped would offer Africans some political leeway were already in some disarray, as has been seen. Widespread anger against rent increases and corruption exploded first in the PWV triangle (Pretoria, Witwatersrand and the Vaal area) in August 1984, and spread to the Eastern Cape and then other urban townships in the form of highly successful rent and consumer boycotts. Schools boycotts meant that in some areas children were out on the streets for years at a stretch.

Street committees were often dominated by the youth who became the effective leaders of the boycotts. These radical youngsters came to be known as 'comrades' and adopted a socialist iconography. Alternative courts were set up to try alleged collaborators and came to settle local disputes. Many councillors were forced to resign and some even had to move out of the townships. As large numbers of police and then troops were sent in to 'restore order' in the black townships there were almost daily scenes of violent confrontation between the police and the youth. The armed force met sticks and stones with armoured cars, tear gas and automatic weapons. The funerals of those killed by police fire became political demonstrations. When, in 1985 on the anniversary of Sharpeville, the police fired on a procession of mourners near Uitenhage in the Eastern Cape, killing several people, this fuelled the mounting tide of black anger. Funerals begat funerals.

Although many of the young people who were in the forefront of the demonstrations were highly disciplined, there were excesses. Particularly disturbing was the use of the so-called necklace: a rubber tyre placed around the neck of the victim, filled with petrol and then set alight. These episodes of undirected and uncontrolled violence by so-called 'comrades' have to be seen as the product of the social dislocations created by the decades of apartheid policies. Broken families, the absence of both parents at work from the early hours of the morning until late at night, poverty and insecurity, high unemployment, juvenile delinquency and gangs among the young, were commented on by observers as early as the 1950s if not before. These features of township life were greatly exacerbated by the uprooting policies of the 1960s and 1970s, the increase in inordinately long journeys to work (often misleadingly termed 'commuting'), and the renewed influx of rural migrants into the towns as a result of the continuous impoverishment of the countryside, the severe drought of 1979–84, and the recession. The schools boycotts and the absence of any routine among the youth gravely increased the risks of social breakdown.

Large numbers of young people found their only outlet in semi-criminal and criminal gangs, again not a new feature of township life but one given a new lease of life by deteriorating urban and economic conditions. On many occasions, gangs found political demonstrations a fruitful site for their activities, while attempts by student activists in AZAPO and the UDF-affiliated organisations to incorporate and politicise the gangs for their own purposes often backfired. At the same time, the slogan 'no education before liberation' was leading to the emergence of a culturally deprived generation which rejected any form of discipline. In their confrontations with state and parental authority they had reached a 'no-win' situation, and there were those who were talking of a Khmer Rouge generation. By the beginning of 1986 concerned parents and community leaders had formed the National Education Crisis Committee in an attempt to resolve the impasse over schooling. They were backed by the ANC in their endeavour to persuade the youth that poor education was preferable to no education at all, and that the schools boycott was depriving them of an organisational base. In addition, they promised to provide alternative forms of education while demanding improvements to the system as a whole from government. The state has proved totally hostile to these efforts.

Given the turbulence in the townships, it is hardly surprising that conservative forces, horrified by the disorder, should have regrouped and used violence to reassert their control. In the circumstances, the South African state has found it easy to manipulate the divisions and tensions within the black community, and to use them to justify the declaration of the first State of Emergency in July 1985. It has been quick to seize on incidents of intra-community violence which have been portrayed by the South African media as 'black on black violence', the inevitable result of 'primitive black savagery'. Yet, as Nicholas Haysom has pointed out:

> The use of this label served to obscure the emergence of a pattern of extra-legal violence by right-wing vigilantes. By referring to all conflict in which both parties were black, as black on black conflict, the links between the conflicting parties and apartheid structures were buried.[83]

By the end of 1985 these black vigilantes had appeared in many parts of South Africa, directing their violence against opponents of apartheid, whether in the urban areas or in the bantustans, where they had the explicit backing of many of the bantustan authorities. Although not an entirely new phenomenon, their virtually simultaneous appearance in so many different parts of the country and the growing evidence of covert if not overt police backing for their activities, suggest that a strategy of deliberate destabilisation had been adopted by the state against what it regarded as its internal enemies, as it had already been adopted against its external enemies.

In the years since the 1976 Soweto uprising, the consciousness of South Africa's black population has been radically transformed. A new generation of political activists has lived through several major confrontations with the state. The expansion of the economy since the 1960s accelerated capital accumulation and its centralisation and this in turn gave rise to the concentration of more skilled urban workers both in urban communities and on the shop-floor. A vast army of industrial workers has been recruited into the trade union movement and their demands have become increasingly political. The combination of worker and community organisation has significantly laid down a challenge to the political and economic order. Even in the state-created and impoverished bantustans there have been increasing signs of resistance.

Throughout this period, the state has remained under the control of the Afrikaner National Party, and seems set to do so for the foreseeable future. Although its policies have remained acceptable to the majority of whites, the apparently monolithic structure it constructed in the 1950s and 1960s had dramatically broken up by the 1980s. Changes in the class structure of Afrikaners and the concessions the state was forced to make to blacks and to the now highly monopolised capitalist class fractured the National Party, though insufficiently to dislodge it from power. At the same time, the concessions made by the state were rejected by the major black organisations who call not for the reform of apartheid but for its total abolition. For the moment, then, South Africa has reached an oppressive stalemate. While welfare reformism from above cannot satisfy popular aspirations, neither can insurrection and 'ungovernability' topple the regime.

NOTES

1. Cited in G. H. Le May, *British Supremacy in South Africa, 1899–1907* (Oxford: Oxford University Press, 1965), p. 21.
2. The introductions in S. Marks and S. Trapido, *The Politics of Race, Class and Nationalism in Twentieth Century South Africa* (London: Longmans, 1987), and S. Marks and R. Rathbone, *Industrialisation and Social Change in South Africa. African class formation, culture and consciousness, 1870–1930* (London: Longmans, 1982) summarise the literature. See also F. R. Johnstone, *Class, Race and Gold. A study of class relations and racial discrimination in South Africa* (London: Routledge & Kegan Paul, 1976).
3. For an elaboration of this argument see Marks and Trapido, *The Politics of Race, Class and Nationalism*, op. cit. note 2 above.
4. See, for example, J. Cell, *The Highest State of White Supremacy. The origins of segration in South Africa and the American South* (Cambridge: Cambridge University Press, 1982). For Heaton Nicholls, see S. Marks, *The Ambiguities of Dependence in South Africa. Class, state, and nationalism in twentieth century Natal* (Baltimore: Johns Hopkins University Press, and Johannesburg: Ravan Press, 1986).
5. S. Marks and N. Andersson, 'Industrialisation, Rural Change and the 1944 National Health Services Commission', forthcoming in S. Feierman and J. Janzen, *The Social Basis of Health and Disease in Africa* (Berkeley: University of California Press, forthcoming).
6. T. Lodge, *Black Politics in South Africa since 1945* (Johannesburg: Ravan Press, and London: Longmans, 1983).
7. For recent reinterpretations of Afrikaner nationalism, see H. Giliomee and H. Adam, *Ethnic Power Mobilised* (New Haven and London: Yale University Press, 1979); A. du Toit, 'No Chosen People: the Myth of Calvinist origins of Afrikaner Nationalism and Racial Ideology and its History', *American Historical Review*, vol. 10, no. 4, 1983, pp. 920–52; D. O'Meara, *Volkskapitalisme. Class, capital and ideology in the development of Afrikaner nationalism, 1934–1948*, (Cambridge: Cambridge University Press, 1983); D. Moodie, *The Rise of Afrikanerdom* (Berkeley: University of California Press, 1975); and Marks and Trapido and Hofmeyr in *The Politics of Race, Class and Nationalism*, op. cit. note 2 above.
8. D. Posel, 'Doing Business with the Pass Laws: Influx Control Policy and the Interests of Manufacturing and Commerce in South Africa in the

1950s', unpublished seminar paper, Institute of Commonwealth Studies, London, 1987.

9. A. D. Wassenaar, *Assault on Private Enterprise* (Cape Town: Tafelberg Press, 1977).
10. This paragraph is based on Adam and Giliomee, *Ethnic Power Mobilised*, ch. 6, (op. cit. note 7 above), quotations from pp. 165, 167, and the mineral interests are on p. 172.
11. M. Lipton, *Capitalism and Apartheid* (London: Gower, 1985), p. 197.
12. This draws heavily on I. Goldin, *Making Race. The politics and econonomics of Coloured identity in South Africa* (London: Longman and Cape Town: Maskew Miller, forthcoming). See also I. Goldin, 'The Reconstitution of Coloured Identity in the Western Cape', in Marks and Trapido, *Race, Class and Nationalism*, op cit. note 2 above, pp. 156–91. G. Lewis, *Between the Wire and the Wall. A history of South African 'Coloured' Politics* (Lansdowne, Cape: David Philip, 1987) which also deals with the origins and development of coloured identity and politics was unfortunately available to us only after this chapter was completed.
13. M. Swan, 'Ideology in Organised Indian Politics, 1891–1948', in Marks and Trapido, *Race, Class and Nationalism*, op. cit. note 2 above.
14. For an account of the opposition in the 1950s see, for example, T. Lodge, *Black Politics*, op. cit. note 6 above.
15. Lipton, *Capitalism and Apartheid*, op. cit. note 11 above. p. 65 argues that the level of black wages rose in the 1960s and this explains their political quiescence; our proposition is based on the South African Institute of Race Relations (SAIRR), *Annual Survey, 1972*, pp. 232–8. See also SAIRR, *Annual Surveys 1964–70.*
16. See, for example, C. Murray, 'Displaced Urbanization: South Africa's Rural Slums', *African Affairs*, vol. 86, no. 344, July 1987, pp. 311–30; and A. D. Spiegel and J. S. Sharp, 'Relocation in Qwaqwa, Betterment in Matatiele: Resources and Responses', in Institute of Commonwealth Studies, *The Societies of Southern Africa in the Nineteenth and Twentieth Centuries*, vol. 14, collected seminar papers, 1984–6 (London, 1988). The neighbouring black 'resettlement' of Onverwacht or Botshabelo has seen population growth of similar magnitude, as has the rather larger area of KwaNdebele in the Transvaal.
17. Murray, 'Displaced Urbanization', op. cit. note 16 above, citing C. Simkins, *Four essays on the Past Present and Possible Future of the Distribution of the Black Population of South Africa* (Cape Town: South African Labour Development Research Unit [SALDRU], 1983), pp. 83–7. We have rounded the figures.
18. These figures have been drawn from Lipton, *Capitalism and Apartheid*, op. cit. note 11 above, pp. 85–109, and A. Callinicos, *Southern Africa after Zimbabwe* (London: Pluto Press, 1981), p. 83.
19. Marks, *Ambiguities of Dependence*, op. cit. note 4 above, ch. 4.
20. For popular attitudes to Buthelezi and Inkatha, see M. Orkin, *Disinvestment, the Struggle and the Future. What Black South Africans Really Think* (Johannesburg: Ravan Press, 1986), esp. pp. 37–44. For the 'vigilante' activities of Inkatha's amabutho (Zulu regiments), see N. Haysom, *Apartheid's Private Army. The Rise of Right-Wing Vigilantes*

in South Africa (London: Catholic Institute for International Relations [CIIR], 1986), pp. 80–99. For a man who constantly denounces the 'violence of the ANC', and is much praised in the Western media for his 'moderation', Buthelezi has done little, as Haysom points out, 'to denounce publicly' (or to curb privately) the campaign of terror perpetrated by 'Amabutho, identified with or led by Inkatha-associated personalities' (p. 99).

21. World Health Organisation, *Apartheid and Health* (Geneva: WHO, 1983), pp. 110, 126–8; C. de Beer, *The South African Disease. Apartheid health and health services* (London: CIIR, 1986), ch. 4.
22. According to J. Lange in *Financial Mail*, 12 October 1979, cited in S. Greenberg, 'State Against the Market in South Africa: Prelude to Crisis', in ICS, *Societies of Southern Africa*, op. cit. note 16 above, vol. 14.
23. See, for example, P. Laurence, 'The Graft-Cancer Spreads a Lot Further than Transkei', *Weekly Mail*, Johannesburg, 2–8 October 1987.
24. C. Murray, 'Displaced Urbanisation: South Africa's Rural Slums', in the original version of the paper cited above in note 17, and presented to the seminar on the Societies of Southern Africa, Institute of Commonwealth Studies (ICS), London, October 1986.
25. C. Charney, 'Class Conflict and the National Party Split', *Journal of Southern African Studies*, vol. 10, no. 2, 1984, pp. 269–82.
26. For an insider view of developments in the Black Consciousness movement, see the annual *Black Review*, 1973–76 (published by Black Community Programmes, Durban, and printed by Zenith Printers, Johannesburg, 1974–77).
27. D. McShane, 'Black Working-Class resistance in South Africa', *New Politics*, vol. 1, no. 1, Summer 1986, p. 43.
28. SAIRR, *Survey, 1973*, p. 242.
29. Ibid. 1973, pp. 285–6.
30. Ibid. pp. 242–3; J. Maree, 'The Emergence, Struggles and Achievements of Black Trade Unions in South Africa from 1973 to 1984', *Labour, Capital and Society*, vol. 18, no. 2, November 1985, p. 286.
31. D. Innes, 'Monopoly Capitalism in South Africa', *South African Review I* (Johannesburg: Ravan Press, 1984); see also D. Innes, *Anglo American and the Rise of Modern South Africa* (Johannesburg: Ravan Press, and London: Heinemann, 1983).
32. This is based on J. Hyslop, 'State Education Policy and the Social Reproduction of the Urban African Working Class: 1955–1976', unpublished paper, March 1986 (forthcoming in *Journal of South African Studies*). The shift in policy from the early 1970s is also borne out in Lipton, *Capitalism and Apartheid*, op. cit. note 11 above.
33. Lipton, *Capitalism and Apartheid*, op. cit. note 11 above, pp. 65–6, and Hyslop, 'State education', op. cit. note 32 above.
34. S. Greenberg, 'State Against the Market in South Africa: Prelude to Crisis', op. cit. note 22 above, citing J. Nattrass, 'Towards Racial Justice – What Can the Private Sector do?', SAIRR, 50th Anniversary Conference, University of Witwatersrand, July 1979, pp. 9–10, and 18.
35. *The Guardian*, 14 October 1986, cited in G. Dor, 'The Political Economy of Health in South Africa', unpublished MA thesis, University of

London, 1986.

36. M. O. Sutcliffe, 'The Crisis in South Africa: Material Conditions and the Reformist Response', University of Natal, Durban.
37. Hyslop, 'State Education Policy', op. cit. note 32 above.
38. For the events in 1976, and their origins, see A. Brooks and J. Brickhill, *Whirlwind Before the Storm. The Origins and Development of the Uprising in Soweto and the Rest of South Africa from June to December 1976* (London: International Defence and Aid, 1980); J. Kane Berman, *South Africa. The Method in the Madness* (London: Pluto Press, 1979); and B. Hirson, *Year of Fire, Year of Ash* (London: Zed Press, 1979).
39. J. Hyslop, 'State Education Policy', op. cit. note 32 above.
40. Kane Berman, *South Africa*, op. cit. note 38 above, p. 20.
41. Ibid. p. 112.
42. For the events at Mzimhlope, the role of the police and Buthelezi's ambivalent stance, see Brooks and Brickhill, *Whirlwind Before the Storm*, op. cit, note 38 above, pp. 215–25.
43. Cf. John R. Wilson, 'Change from a Shell Perspective', keynote address, Shell South Africa Senior Staff Conference, Cape Sun Hotel, Cape Town, 4–5 August 1986: 'Business today recognises that a sound economy presupposes a stable political system. Its attempts to reason with government are founded on this belief.'
44. D. Posel, 'Doing Business with the Pass Laws', op. cit. note 8 above.
45. John R. Wilson, op. cit. note 43 above.
46. *Weekly Mail*, Johannesburg, vol. 1, no. 14, 11–19 September, 1985, and vol. 1, no. 15, 20–6 September, 1985.
47. We have used the term Progressive Party for the major white opposition party which was known at different times as the Progressive Party, then the Progressive Reform Party, and now the Progressive Federal Party.
48. B. Hackland, 'Incorporationist Ideology as a Response to Political Struggle: the Progressive Party of South Africa, 1960–80', in Marks and Trapido, *Race, Class and Nationalism*, op. cit. note 2 above, p. 382. Cf. Harry Schwartz, Chairman of the PFP's federal executive in 1976:

> The problem of South Africa is not only colour; it is a potential conflict between capital and labour. This is why one has to convince the people who represent labour, who are the Black consumers, that there is place for them in the free enterprise system.

In the same year, Colin Eglin, now the leader of the party, argued in similar vein:

> Those who believe in the free enterprise system and who want to eliminate conflict will have to find ways and means of enabling black South Africans to share significantly in economic progress not merely as workers but as share-holders and partners and participants in the ownership of business in South Africa [cited in Hackland, pp. 381–2]

Cf. also P. Laurence, 'White Capitalism and Black Rage', *Weekly Mail*, vol.1, no. 14, 13–19 September, 1985: 'There is no doubt that there is a growing hostility towards capitalism amongst black youth. The reason is simple: capitalism is seen as the driving force behind apartheid.'

49. D. Posel, 'The Language of Domination, 1978–83', in Marks and Trapido, *Race, Class and Nationalism*, op. cit. note 2 above.
50. Anton Harber, 'Mr Botha's Other Government Waits in the Shadows', *The Guardian*, 3 October 1986; 'South Africa: A Total Strategy', *Africa Confidential*, vol. 27, no. 24, 26 November 1986.
51. Posel, 'Language of Domination', op. cit. note 49 above.
52. J. Lelyveld, *Move Your Shadow* (London and New York: Michael Joseph, 1985), pp. 67–9.
53. Ibid. fn. on p. 68. See also Samuel P. Huntington, 'Whatever Has Gone Wrong with Reform?', *Die Suid-Afrikaan*, no. 8, 1986, p. 20.
54. For the Wiehahn and Riekert reports see the special issues of the *South African Labour Bulletin*, vol. 5, no. 2, August 1979, 'Focus on Wiehahn' and vol. 5, no. 4, November 1979, 'Focus on Riekert'.
55. C. Charney, 'Class Conflict and the National Party Split', op. cit. note 25 above, pp. 269–82, 278.
56. M. Golding, 'Workers in the State Sector: the Case of the Civil Administration', SALB, vol. 10, no. 5, April 1985.
57. J. Seekings, 'Political Mobilisation in Black Townships in the PWV region of South Africa', unpublished seminar paper, 1986, p. 7, cited from S. Becker and R. Humphreys, *From Control to Confusion. The changing Role of the Administration Boards in South Africa, 1971–84* (Pietermaritzburg: Shooter and Shuter, 1984), p. 111.
58. Cited in Ibid. p. 3.
59. Ibid. p.6.
60. Ibid. p. 10.
61. Cited in C. Bundy, 'Street Sociology and Pavement Politics: Aspects of Youth and Student Resistance in Cape Town, 1985', *Journal of South African Studies*, vol. 13, no. 3, April 1987, p. 311. Compiled from statistics in the *Annual Surveys* of the SAIRR.
62. D. Innes, *South African Review I*, p. 189, quoting from C. Simkins, 'Structural Unemployment Revisited', SALDRU Fact Sheet 1, Cape Town, 1982.
63. Bundy, 'Street Sociology', op. cit. note 61 above, p. 312.
64. M. O. Sutcliffe, 'The Crisis in South Africa: Material Conditions and the Reformist Response', University of Natal, Durban.
65. *Natal Mercury*, 18 June 1976, cited in A. Rambally (ed.) *Black Review, 1975–6* (Lovedale, Eastern Cape: Black Community Programmes, Lovedale Press) p. 100.
66. J. Comaroff, *Body of Power, Spirit of Resistance. The culture and history of a South African people* (Chicago: Chicago University Press, 1985), esp. ch. 8.
67. J. Lazarre, 'Conformity and Conflict. Afrikaner Nationalist Politics in South Africa, 1948–61', Oxford University D.Phil. 1987.
68. H. Barrell, 'The United Democratic Front and National Forum; Their Emergence, Composition and Trends', *South African Review II*, edited and compiled by South African Research Service (SARS), Johannesburg, 1984.
69. Ibid., pp. 8–12.
70. Innes, *South African Review I*, op. cit. note 62 above, p. 181.

71. J. Lewis, 'The Trade Unions', *Monthly Review*, vol. 37, no. 11, April 1986, pp. 84–5.
72. 'Whatever the Figure, the Biggest Boycott', *Weekly Mail*, vol. 2, no. 39, 3–8 October 1986.
73. Cited in Ibid.
74. Ibid.
75. *Weekly Mail*, vol. 3, no. 24, 19–26 June 1987.
76. MacShane, 'Black Working-Class Resistance', op. cit. note 27 above.
77. Lewis, 'The Trade Unions', op. cit. note 71 above; K. Moodley and H. Adam, 'South Africa: Revolution, Repression, Reform', *International Journal*, vol. XLI, Autumn 1986, pp. 841–3.
78. P. van Niekerk, 'New Union Seeks US Aid', *Weekly Mail*, vol. 2, no. 22, 6–12 June 1986.
79. Cited in Alex Callinicos and John Rogers, *Southern Africa After Soweto* (London: Pluto Press, 1977), pp. 162–3.
80. T. Lodge, 'The African National Congress, 1983', *South African Review II*, pp. 21, 25.
81. P. Laurence, 'UDF Calls for ANC Unbanning', *Weekly Mail*, vol. 2, no. 22, 6–12 June 1986.
82. P. Laurence, 'A 75-year Thorn in the Flesh of White Power', *Weekly Mail*, vol. 3, no. 1, 9–16 January, 1987.
83. Haysom, *Apartheid's Private Army*. op. cit. note 20 above, p. 1.

2 The Outlawed South African Liberation Movements

Howard Barrell

INTRODUCTION

In African terms, South Africa is an enormously powerful and sophisticated state. In southern Africa, it is a veritable giant. This power, together with the particularities of South African society, guarantees a high casualty rate among those South Africans committed to a revolutionary route to democracy and the destruction of apartheid.

Historical precedents provided by other modern African national liberation struggles give only limited tactical guidance to South African revolutionaries. Indeed, conditions in South Africa have demanded of them an unusually high measure of tactical innovation and self-reliance – over and above the self-evident requirements of organisation, resilience and courage.

Seen against this background, the recent achievements of the pre-eminent South African "liberation movement", the African National Congress (ANC), are remarkable. Now seventy-five years old and outlawed for nearly three decades, this movement has risen in power and influence to the point where it can reasonably be said to be contending – though by no means yet decisively – as an alternative power to the existing state.

Conversely, the peculiarities of South Africa and a failure – in tactical terms – to address them adequately, help to explain the increased marginalisation of revolutionary groups other than the ANC. Principal among these is the Pan Africanist Congress (PAC) which, like the ANC, enjoys official accreditation as a 'liberation movement' from the Organisation of African Unity (OAU).[1] This marginalisation could of course prove ephemeral, but current indications suggest that it is likely to endure throughout South Africa's national liberation struggle.

SPECIAL FACTORS BEARING ON THE LIBERATION MOVEMENT

A comprehensive evaluation of the theoretical models of the various South African revolutionary groups is beyond the scope of this chapter. The differences between these 'theories of revolution' have, of course, an important bearing on what tactics are put forward – certainly at the level of rhetoric, if not always in concrete action. I propose, however, to follow a more empirical course: to review the recent visible performances of the two OAU-accredited portions of the liberation movement against the background of South Africa's peculiar characteristics.

The power and sophistication of both the indigenous state military/security complex in South Africa and its systems of social and political control (see Chapter 7 and 8), are unparalleled in any other modern national liberation context. Whatever its historical antecedents, the white power bloc in South Africa is patently resident; it is not in any primary sense an agent of an external colonial power. There is a close historical and contemporary dependency between the fact (and mechanics) of the political oppression of the black majority, and that majority's economic dispossession and exploitation. No third party readily exists to act as a mediator in the South African conflict – a role which Britain was able to play, constitutionally, between the government and nationalist guerrillas in the transition from Rhodesia to Zimbabwe. No neighbouring state has hitherto been able or willing to provide secure rear bases for guerrilla infiltration into South Africa, and none seems likely to do so openly in the foreseeable future.

The South African state has sought to further its military and economic dominance of the region and to reverse anti-colonial gains in the sub-continent (see Chapter 11). Only small areas of South Africa lend themselves to the classical African pattern of rurally based, 'bush' warfare waged by guerrillas. South Africa's relatively high level of industrial and infrastructural development has accelerated the growth of a (black) proletariat, which is clearly emerging as the single most important social and political force within the national liberation configuration (see Chapter 4). Demographically and politically, what little remains of a 'peasantry' in South Africa is of considerably less importance than in any other modern national liberation process. Moreover, a wide range of Western economic, political and strategic interests have traditionally identified white minority rule in South Africa as the local guarantor of their welfare (see Chapter 10).

Several important considerations for South African revolutionaries emerge from this cursory characterisation. First, they cannot simply rely on one form of political struggle – for example, guerrilla warfare. The pivotal role of the black majority in industrial production, together with their demonstrable (and increasing) organisational power has placed important weapons in their hands. Further, this ideological and organisational assertiveness combines to make organised workers realistically (rather than merely programmatically or rhetorically) the leading social force in national liberation politics. The advantages – indeed, the necessity – of building defensible and increasingly self-reliant political/military bases among the 'revolutionary constituency' inside the country are clearly defined. Demography and the distribution of organisational structures ensure that the main terrain of struggle in South Africa is urban, although certainly not exclusively so.

Western perceptions of their self-interest in South Africa and the region must be altered if the liberation movement is to avoid a potentially decisive intervention by the West on the side of the existing state, or some variant of it. Similarly, there is an added imperative to develop tactics to win over – or at least to neutralise as active enemies – elements from within the white power bloc, in order to encourage the state's isolation.

The extremities of the national liberatory task at hand do not allow for the luxury of class or ethnic sectarianism within or between revolutionary organisations. The national liberation movement must of necessity construct around itself a popular fighting alliance; an alliance of such strength that it can enforce the revolutionary option or, in the event of negotiations, successfully confront the government and its allies. The achievement of state political power must remain the primary objective; it is the *sine qua non* of transformation. Without it, the critical question of property relations cannot be adequately addressed. But it is the balance of class forces within the national liberation alliance which is achieved during the process of struggle that will most significantly influence the interests represented by the new state, and, hence, the nature and extent of the economic transformation it enacts over time.

In short, South Africa is a fairly advanced capitalist country and, one can reasonably assert, a sub-imperialist power of sorts. It also contains, however, strong elements of colonialism. This requires of revolutionaries that they wage an unusually complex struggle at a mass level for political and organisational unity.

THE ANC: OUTSIDE IN AND INSIDE OUT

Long the largest and most effective of the South African liberatory or revolutionary organisations, the ANC has, since the uprisings in Soweto and elsewhere in 1976, addressed these dynamics to considerably more effect than its counterparts. As a result it has, over years of revolt since 1984, provided the dominant tactical agenda. In contrast, its counterparts have been reduced largely to playing a spectator role – despite seemingly rash claims about their own activities. While hot on advice and squabbles on the terraces, they have been decidedly cool on action in the field of battle.

The foundation of the ANC's dramatic recent rise to public prominence has been laid over a number of years. It has regenerated an undeniable popular legitimacy among black South Africans and (for a liberation movement) an unusual reputation for moral rectitude. This latter is partly a product of history: the ANC exhausted what it saw as all available options of non-violent resistance before including armed struggle in its political strategy in 1961, one year after it was outlawed.[2] Decisions taken in the years since the banning, combined with the ANC's long-standing alliance with the South African Communist Party (SACP),[3] have put the two main tributaries of militant anti-apartheid politics within the ANC's political ambit. These are the nationalist and socialist streams. The movement has self-consciously constructed a broad 'national liberation alliance', uniting different ideological tendencies within its ranks around two main lodestars, the Freedom Charter and Strategy and Tactics.[4]

Despite grave internal reverses in the 1960s, the ANC managed to keep a (small) underground presence intact inside South Africa. Trials involving some of its internal activists in the 1960s and 1970s, as well as its joint 'Wankie Campaign' with the Zimbabwe African Peoples' Union (ZAPU) in 1967–68 in then-Rhodesia, testified to attempts at internal reconstruction and a residual combative will. The movement's leadership managed to overcome the debilitating effects of breakaways (by right-wing African nationalists) in 1959 and 1975; grave internal frustration and dissatisfaction at its first post-banning National Consultative Conference in Tanzania in 1969; as well as a challenge from the far left in the late 1970s. The relative maturity of its visible leadership – both in prison and in exile – was a major factor contributing to its survival during these crises. Throughout these bitter conflicts, the ANC was able to retain a degree of continuity and bedrock political unity – so much so that it was the envy of a number of liberation movements elsewhere.[5] Within its own structure, the ANC tended to concentrate on the mechanics of organisation and specialisation in its ranks. Diplomatically, it sought international support from governments which opposed apartheid, whether 'capitalist' or 'socialist', and attempted to avoid being instrumentalised in East–West power struggles. Militarily, it became combative after 1976 at a level which none of its counterparts has been able to emulate.[6] By 1984, the ANC had convinced much of its internal constituency and the world community of its 'seriousness' about achieving its primary goal – the ending of white minority rule, and the birth of a united, democratic and non-racial South Africa.

The ANC's survival through the bleak 1960s and early 1970s (albeit in a much-weakened form), had a cumulative – and pivotal – result for the movement. Its long-established traditions and symbols of resistance survived with it, and would be repopularised – to considerable effect – during the resurgence of militant internal resistance (see Chapters 3 and 5).

By the late 1970s, the ANC's ranks had swollen rapidly, and its central task was purposively to deploy these cadres against the government in a credible revolutionary offensive. The credibility of the offensive was still unclear in late 1987; and so it will remain until the ANC demonstrates that it has the will and means to contend *decisively* for national political power. It is worth re-emphasising the point that this contest will be against a state structure which can reasonably be described as the most powerful indigenous adversary to be confronted in any modern national liberation context.

Over the period 1972 to 1983, the ANC's External Mission (and in particular its military wing, Umkhonto we Sizwe [Spear of the Nation]), was the destination for waves of black militants leaving South Africa. Several hundred university students who left the country during the black campus revolts of 1972–74 injected new and gifted blood into the ANC's middle levels.[7] Most of the more than 4000 young black militants who left in the year following the 1976 revolt also joined the ANC.[8]

The mass influx into its External Mission in the 1970s gave the ANC – alone among South African liberation organisations – an important political potential: the capacity to embark on a campaign of 'armed propaganda' inside South Africa. It had lacked this capacity since the early 1960s, after which its central concern had been the rebuilding of its own decimated structures. The new offensive was designed, in effect, to prove to the ANC's domestic constituency that armed struggle was 'feasible' under South African conditions. In short, it was a campaign to legitimate the 'revolutionary option'.[9] Armed attacks on South Africa's Sasol oil-from-coal plants and the country's only nuclear power station[10] were among several high-profile guerrilla attacks, intended to reinvigorate the combative spirit which had characterised the 1976 revolt. This mood had flagged somewhat in the intervening years in the face of the security forces' massive repressive capabilities.

As the 1970s drew to a close, a wide range of independent anti-apartheid activists working legally inside the country, as well as members of the ANC's underground machinery and External Mission, were drawn into overlapping discussions on appropriate resistance tactics in the light of South African peculiarities and the contiguous victories and defeats of 1976.[11] Central to these debates was the realisation that millions of South Africans had to be involved *actively* in resistance if a transfer of power to the majority, or that majority's seizure of power, was to be achieved.

Furthermore, this active mass participation would be essential in protecting such a transfer, once effected. A high degree of mass unity would have to be forged around political, tactical and ideological issues – no easy task given the complexity of the South African situation. In order to achieve unity in action (and sustain it under conditions of extreme repression), unique organisational forms might have to be developed.[12]

THE ANC AND INTERNAL RESISTANCE

By 1983, the ANC stood on the verge of a potential breakthrough. Its External Mission and internal underground were in broad agreement with much of this body of sympathetic (though autonomous) activists working legally inside the country – what was needed was the construction of a united political front of opposition to apartheid.[13] The ingredients for such a front already existed. A wide variety of sometimes small worker, student, youth, community, women's, religious and other organisations had mushroomed throughout the country, and some degree of national organisational co-ordination had been achieved during a campaign against South Africa's 'Republic Day' celebrations in 1981. By 1983 this loose grouping agreed that the experience should be taken further, and that a single national alliance could be built. The solution of the multifarious problems experienced by these organisations depended finally on the same condition: an end to apartheid. Therefore, the front should provide a mechanism by which these disparate organisations could all address themselves to the issue of political power, in both its national and localised forms. In united action resided the potential for moving towards a relatively high degree of political and organisational unity; for articulating the most desirable form which political power should take; and, ultimately, to ensure its transfer to, or in the case of the ANC seizure by, the majority. Whites who shared these basic democratic perspectives, it was agreed, should be allowed to participate fully in the envisaged front.[14]

The result was the formation of the United Democratic Front (UDF) in August 1983. A parallel (and sometimes antagonistic) development was the launch of the National Forum, a smaller and still looser alliance of mainly black exclusivist organisations. The National Forum seemed a strained marriage between the rump of the Black Consciousness movement inside the country, and both pro-PAC and far-left elements.[15]

The immediate issue around which these alliances mobilised was the government's decision to introduce a new constitution. It was viewed by the two new resistance groupings as an attempt only to modernise, and thereby entrench, the pillars of minority domination. Under the new constitution, full black enfranchisement and democracy would depend, for the first time, upon the formal overthrow of the South African constitution itself; these aims could no longer be achieved, theoretically, by the mere amendment of racist legislation.

The formation of the UDF and National Forum stimulated considerable debate over how the central issue of state power should be addressed, and in particular over how a broad democratic alliance should relate to working-class organisation and interests. The importance of this debate was underlined by the decision of the country's best organised democratic trade unions (most of whom were affiliated to the then Federation of South African Trade Unions (FOSATU)) to remain outside the new alliances (see Chapter 4). In this process of debate, aspects of the ANC's political and theoretical traditions – particularly the ANC/SACP articulation of the conceptual distinction between the 'national democratic' and 'socialist' phases of revolution – came under close examination (and frequently attack) from both left and right. In succeeding years, as generalised confrontation with the government intensified, these debates appeared to indicate close attention to what forms of organisation were appropriate, rather than any deep-seated differences over the publicly declared strategic objectives of the antagonists. In this process, a significant synthesis of views appeared to become a real possibility.

As preparations for the formation of the UDF progressed, a long debate over the correct tactical perspective was coming to an end within the ANC's own ranks. The movement apparently ditched notions (which had until then survived in some quarters even in the face of overwhelming evidence to the contrary) that it could wage a guerrilla war along the same lines and with the same effect as in Angola, Mozambique and Zimbabwe. Instead, said sources within the ANC, the key to progress lay in what was termed 'the development of insurrectionary forces and tactics'.[16] Herein lay much of the explanation for the ANC's considerable subsequent advances. It began to arrive at a tactical formulation better suited to South African conditions than any African precedents could provide.

The new perspective made possible an offensive which was potentially more internally self-reliant. It still attributed a crucial role to guerrilla warfare, particularly in the urban areas but also in the countryside. However, a new stress was laid on the ability of black working people to paralyse the South African economy; on the capacity of the youth and other militant popular forces to inflict heavy damage on the organs of state administration and coercion; and on the ability of 'progressive' artists and intellectuals to undermine the ideological underpinnings of apartheid and promote alternatives. It provided a reasonably coherent model, under South African conditions, for what was described as 'people's war' – the full and protracted engagement of the widest possible spread of resistance and revolutionary forces in all political, economic, military and ideological modes of struggle for national liberation.

The first public sign of the change came in the ANC's traditional New Year's address to the people of South Africa in 1984, in a broadcast on 8 January on the ANC's 'Radio Freedom'. It called for an offensive against those institutions of the state by which apartheid is upheld. It also acknowledged the need, as a matter of judgement, to choose targets on a selective basis, and in particular to attack those parts of the administrative system where the state was most vulnerable.[17]

The slogan which emerged following the broadcast was 'Make Apartheid Unworkable! Make the Country Ungovernable!' The method was to isolate and destroy the vulnerable 'outposts of apartheid administration' in locales such as the segregated black townships and rural reserves. The means were to be insurrectionary forces and tactics: the use of boycotts, strikes, formal guerrilla forces, small informal combat units comprising militants, and the alienation and neutralisation of security forces detailed to protect these organs and institutions. Thousands of ANC pamphlets and tape recordings were distributed inside the country by underground ANC units in the first half of 1984.[18]

The signing of the Nkomati non-aggression pact between Pretoria and the Frelimo government in Mozambique in 1984 gave greater urgency to the ANC's attempts to popularise the new approach inside South Africa. The pact interrupted a major ANC guerrilla infiltration route, running from Mozambique through Swaziland and into South Africa. Subsequent expulsions of ANC members from Lesotho, Swaziland and Botswana further reduced the ANC's presence in neighbouring countries and, hence, its capacity to reinforce its struggle from abroad (see Chapter 11).

Despite the Nkomati setback, conditions for the new style offensive ripened with the approach of the coloured and Indian elections for the new tricameral parliament in August–September 1984. Africans' sense of national grievance was deepened by this constitutional entrenchment of their exclusion from central state power. Mass legal organisations' capacity for mobilisation against apartheid had improved greatly in the intervening year, and a new mood of solidarity and unity in action between the different sectors of the black population (and the minority of democratic whites) had emerged, reminiscent of the days of the ANC-led 'Congress Alliance' in the 1950s.

As mass unrest broke out in African townships south of Johannesburg a few days after the polls closed, the ANC's five Radio Freedom stations broadcast a call from Tambo's political secretary, Thabo Mbeki, encouraging an all-out national revolt.[19] As the revolt spread to other areas of South Africa over the next nine months, the ANC prepared for a National Consultative Conference (its second since it was outlawed in 1960). Held in Kabwe, Zambia, in June 1985, this conference drew extensively on experience gained inside South Africa, apparently related in part by members of the ANC's internal underground who were present at the conference. The conference endorsed the new tactical approach.[20] Disagreements and debates which did emerge within the ANC – largely over tactical issues – showed no signs of seriously affecting its unity. The frustration of a number of its guerrillas in camps in Angola (which had at times threatened to lead to mutiny), was also largely attenuated at the conference. The result was the manifestation of the ANC – at a crucial moment – as a united, combative organisation of some seriousness.

The cumulative result was that the ANC was able to set the intermediate objectives and tactical direction of the revolt in South Africa. Its leadership was acclaimed in mass displays by tens of thousands at hundreds of funerals of victims of police and army action across the country. It was, above all, the new level of organisational and ideological unity that was to provoke the most serious crisis ever faced by the state, evident at political, security and economic levels, and requiring the declaration of three States of Emergency in as many years.[21]

FROM 'UNGOVERNABILITY' TO 'PEOPLES' POWER

An important intermediate objective in the evolution of the ANC's insurrectionary model was the development of organs of popular self-rule in those black areas in which state administration had collapsed or been subjected to intense pressure. The basic unit of local 'self-rule' was the 'street committee' in the case of the townships, and the 'village committee' in the rural areas.

The formation and slow but steady growth of these committees was judged by the ANC to be a qualitative development of enormous importance – there was a sense of 'new ground' having been broken. The committees were potentially capable of involving millions of people in mass political activity, while at the same time not being quite as vulnerable to state pressure as the mass legal organisations. Because of their nature and (small) size, they readily lent themselves to clandestine forms of activity, and could promise a considerable growth in the distribution and power of underground networks. They made the maintenance of organisational and area security against state penetration potentially more manageable. Moreover, they were organs in which people could experience democracy within the 'struggle' itself. Their range of concerns could span from national issues to the day-to-day problems of individuals and families. As units of national political activism, these committees and those 'second-tier' structures developed to co-ordinate and aggregate their activities had the potential to develop into highly effective localised groupings. In sum, from the ANC's perspective these committees represented one form of internal resistance which could play a critical role not only in the intended victory over the government, but also in the future state's organs of democracy and its ability to defend itself.[22]

The new slogan became 'From Ungovernability to People's Power'. By early 1987, attention was necessarily focused on the need to develop 'people's self-defence militias', able to defend these organs of self-rule against attack. The longer-term objective was to build 'mass bases' in the townships and countryside, capable not only of some degree of self-defence, but also of providing launchpads for attacks on the citadels of state rule.[23]

These developments were uneven and, in many cases, ragged. However, a tactical perspective had taken root among the ANC's real and potential constituency, and had been acted upon. Despite the enormous cost in human life and suffering, the post-1984 period marked another (at least temporary) leap forward in the legitimation of the ANC's political option.

Concurrent with these developments in the period 1984–87, there was a considerable increase in the size and combat potential of Umkhonto we Sizwe under the leadership of commander Joe Modise, political commissar Chris Hani and the then chief of staff, Joe Slovo. The exodus of young militants into ANC guerrilla forces in the eighteen months following the September 1984 revolt exceeded that over the same period following the Soweto uprising.[24] In early 1987, Umkhonto we Sizwe's strength was estimated at some 10 000 guerrillas.[25] It now had the capacity, for the first time in its twenty-six-year history, to infiltrate considerable numbers of guerrillas into South Africa in combat and training roles. Significantly, this could now be done without denuding its capacity for renewal, located mainly in its training camps in Angola.[26] The ANC had the potential to embark on a qualitatively different guerrilla deployment from that of the 'armed propaganda' phase of 1976–83. In the third quarter of 1986, well-placed sources disclosed that some 500 formally trained ANC guerrillas were to work inside the country, mainly as 'officers' charged with reproducing their skills among, and leading combat units of, workers and youths.[27] In the first quarter of 1987, the same sources said this figure was 'out of date', thus implying that it was higher.[28]

According to the ANC's long-term tactical perspective, at some future point of serious crisis for the government, the movement could realistically hope to contend decisively for state power through a closely co-ordinated and well-timed combination of strike action by workers, mass political action involving combat units and people's militias, military actions by formal guerrilla units, and the neutralisation of key elements of the South African security forces.[29] The critical element would be the ANC's political-military underground: its ability to relate democratically to and co-ordinate a wide variety of legal mass organisations; to defend these structures; and to arm combat forces, both formal and informal. In terms of this perspective, 'people's war' was, according to some in the ANC, the 'gathering of forces for national insurrection'. Others in the ANC argued that partial and general uprisings would play a vital role in this unfolding 'people's war', adding that recent developments had shown that the possibility of a successful national insurrection as the culmination had begun to appear a feasible objective.[30]

The ANC leadership conceded that the real potential for such an outcome was, in 1987, still a good many years away. The state was far from breaking point. Nevertheless, they believed that a crucial tactical breakthrough had been achieved.[31]

THE ROAD TO LUSAKA

It was in recognition of this 'breakthrough' – or at least of an incipient shift in the balance of forces in South Africa – that a variety of interests attempted new interventions in the crisis. In most cases they sought out the ANC, in order to assess the movement at first hand.

Twelve months after the onset of the 1984 revolt, some of South Africa's leading white businessmen and newspaper editors, followed by leaders of the Progressive Federal Party (PFP), and later other (more publicity-shy) groups, travelled to meet the ANC External Mission. Behind the congenial and sometimes jocular atmosphere of the meetings lay, on the side of the white 'liberal' establishment, two pressing questions. First, how could the violence be stopped? Second, how could the way be opened to negotiations for a 'reformist' solution capable of safeguarding its interests?[32] That these implicit questions were posed to the ANC signalled an acknowledgement that the banned movement was a vital protagonist in the South African crisis.

Simultaneously, comparable questions were apparently occurring to some members of the South African government. These coincided with the mission to southern Africa of the Commonwealth Eminent Persons Group (EPG) and a considerable increase in diplomatic and economic pressures on the government to make major concessions to the black majority. In late 1985, Foreign Minister Pik Botha raised the possibility (with two FLS presidents) of releasing Nelson Mandela from prison and flying him into enforced exile.[33] In November 1985 another senior South African cabinet minister was reported to have sent feelers to the leadership of the ANC's External Mission through an intermediary. The key elements of the message were that the government acknowledged that it alone could not resolve the crisis into which the country had been plunged, and that the decision had been taken to release Mandela but the government was unable to implement it unless it could be assured of saving face and of not further inflaming domestic political emotions.[34] The implication appeared clear: some elements within the government were beginning to test the waters of a possible political solution to the crisis.

Mandela held that he and his jailed colleagues would not be drawn into any negotiations outside the framework of the ANC and the broad legal democratic movement inside South Africa. Release into enforced exile in one of the bantustans or a foreign country was unacceptable. The External Mission held that it would insist on concrete action from the government signifying that it was prepared to begin negotiations towards a 'united, democratic and non-racial country'; that negotiations on any other basis would not be entertained; that oblique 'signals' would not suffice; but that the government could create a climate conducive to 'talks about talks' were it to release all political prisoners unconditionally, lift the State of Emergency, withdraw troops from the black townships, release all emergency detainees and immediately terminate all security law trials.[35]

Behind this ANC position was the principle that it could not enter into any negotiations with the government unless it had been able to consult fully with imprisoned members of its leadership, as well as 'the legal democratic movement such as the political and trade union organizations'. Furthermore, the ANC maintained, any negotiations with the government had to be 'a matter of public knowledge'.[36] It seemed the ANC was demanding safe passage into South Africa for a National Executive Committee (NEC) delegation to consult a wide range of forces and personalities with which it considered itself aligned, before it would allow matters to proceed.

Press disclosure of this brief exchange of feelers elicited a bellicose response from the government. Deputy Information Minister Louis Nel charged that it was a fabrication by 'propaganda experts from behind the Iron Curtain'.[37] Hawks in the government, identified with P. W. Botha, reasserted their grip on policy – essentially re-emphasising 'security' considerations over diplomatic or political initiatives. The matter of the cabinet minister's feeler to the ANC was never satisfactorily explained,[38] and the glimmer of hope that a change of heart might be occurring within some government quarters was abruptly extinguished.

The continuing sorties to Lusaka and cabinet ministers' manoeuvres were of undoubted propaganda advantage to the ANC. In the view of the outlawed movement, however, their real importance lay in the fact that they suggested the presence of a highly significant crack (albeit hairline) in the unity of the white power bloc. Clearly, fundamental questions about what national political conditions (other than apartheid) could best guarantee white political and economic interests were now being asked in powerful circles. The Leninist axiom – that a split in the ruling class was a prerequisite for revolutionary success – was apparently not lost on the ANC.[39]

The ANC was uniquely placed to take advantage of this soul-searching among a sector of whites. It had self-consciously stated on a number of occasions that it was a 'national liberation movement' rather than a more narrowly conceived black nationalist organisation. But it had added an important qualification. It insisted that the main content of this national liberation struggle, overriding all others and governing all aspects of its activities, was the liberation of the most oppressed, exploited and numerous group in South Africa, i.e. the black African majority.[40] None the less, the ANC had sought, since the days of the Congress Alliance in the 1950s and particularly in more recent years, to ensure that there was the fullest possible participation in anti-apartheid activity of other racial groups, including whites. This principle of non-racialism, expanded upon at the 1985 Kabwe National Consultative Conference,[41] allowed the ANC an important measure of tactical flexibility in dealing with rising white anxieties.

In its meetings with white business, political, religious and other leaders from late 1985 onwards, it was able to conduct a skilful political offensive within the white bloc.[42] As an interim aim it was seeking, if not to win over, then at least to neutralise these whites as active enemies in the future. Ultimately, the objective was comprehensively to isolate diehard supporters of apartheid. To some PAC, Black Consciousness Movement of Azania (BCMA) and Unity Movement (UMSA) elements, however, such talks constituted a 'sell-out' in the making. The ANC countered by accusing these critics of showing little 'seriousness' about actually building conditions for the fundamental transfer of power.[43]

This response notwithstanding, the ANC was aware that the meetings carried attendant dangers. At times, it appeared to the ANC that it had become merely 'fashionable' for some members of the white establishment to meet with the group of men and women who (working under difficult conditions from tumbledown headquarters located down a littered alleyway in central Lusaka) were allegedly responsible for the country's most serious crisis since Union in 1910. The ANC leadership therefore made a conscious decision to weigh up the potential political gains of such talks against the 'distraction' they might cause from pressing issues inside the country.[44]

None the less, an important benefit accrued from these talks with white leaders. This was the creation of a new atmosphere, bordering on legality, which made it possible for the ANC External Mission to hold open, formal talks with leaders of a number of mass organisations working legally inside South Africa. Whether the ANC's underground had links with these organisations is open to conjecture. The most important of these were the UDF, the Congress of South African Trade Unions (COSATU), and the National Education Crisis Committee (NECC).[45]

After these meetings, the UDF and COSATU publicly acknowledged the overall leadership of the ANC in the political struggle in South Africa. A communiqué released at the end of the meeting between the ANC, its trade union ally, the South African Congress of Trade Unions (SACTU), and COSATU on 6 March 1986 was particularly important. It illustrated the ANC's continuing ability to draw on the major currents of both the nationalist and socialist tributaries of militant anti-apartheid politics. The three sides agreed that

> the fundamental problem facing (South Africa), the question of political power, cannot be resolved without the full participation of the ANC, which is regarded by the majority of the people of South Africa as the overall leader and genuine representative . . . [T]he solution to the problems facing our country lies in the establishment of a system of majority rule in a united, democratic and non-racial South Africa. Further, that in the specific conditions of our country, it is inconceivable that such a system can be separated from economic emancipation. Our people have been robbed of their land, deprived of their due share in the country's wealth, their skills have been suppressed and poverty and starvation have been their life experience. The correction of these centuries old economic injustices lies at the core of our national aspirations. Accordingly, [the three delegations] were united not only in their opposition to the entire apartheid system, but also in their common understanding that victory must embrace more than formal political democracy.[46]

This and subsequent meetings with COSATU and other union leaders enabled the ANC to ease tensions which had existed between some of its own supporters and proponents of the 'independent worker' tendency. The latter had sought (at least temporarily) to keep the organised formations of the black working class out of popular political structures like the UDF, while concentrating on the strengthening of union organisation.[47]

As these different sets of talks continued, the ANC emphasised a distinction between two 'categories' of anti-apartheid forces in South Africa. On the one hand, were the 'forces for change' – essentially those liberal or big business elements experiencing a new urgency about breaking with apartheid, but who had hitherto held back from involvement and identification with militant mass politics. On the other hand, were the 'revolutionary forces', both within and outside the ranks of the ANC, which the organisation regarded as the fighting detachments of insurrection and custodians of the objectives and form of post-apartheid society. Both required attention in the ANC's attempts to encourage an alliance, under its aegis, which would be capable of confronting the government in decisive political activity or in 'negotiations' (if they materialised).[48]

THE LIBERATION MOVEMENT AND INTERNATIONAL DIPLOMATIC GAINS

Rising domestic interest in the ANC had an echo in the arena of international politics. The crisis within South Africa led to an increase in pressures for Western economic disinvestment and political disengagement from the South African government. The Western international solidarity movement, painstakingly built up over three decades and for so long so painfully unsuccessful, became, in a short time, a potentially significant influence on Western policy towards South Africa. This solidarity movement tended, in the main, to look to the ANC for guidance. Traditionally, the ANC had made a distinction between the actions of a foreign government and the (sometimes contrary) sentiments of a substantial body of its people. The ANC had also long maintained – in the face of attacks in some instances – that the participation in international anti-apartheid solidarity activity was the right of a broad spectrum of people, from 'liberals' to 'socialists'. Participation was not a privilege to be confined to any small group of highly politically-conscious or militant activists. Fierce battles were fought over this issue in the British Anti-Apartheid Movement (AAM) in the mid-1980s, counterposing the movement's mainstream (which held similar views to the ANC) against a sectarian grouping originating in the Revolutionary Communist Group (RCG).[49] In the event, the victory of the mainstream position in Britain and elsewhere helped ensure that the call for sanctions and political disengagement could attract the support of leading Western establishment figures, as well as those of a more militant political hue. For the ANC, developments of this kind in Europe, and the 'Free South Africa' campaign in the United States were welcome.

Among previously hostile or dismissive Western governments a body of opinion emerged, suggesting that a new approach to the ANC might be necessary. Among Western governments, only the Scandinavians and Dutch had managed to achieve a comfortable mix of moral imperative and self-interest regarding South Africa. The ANC was deriving the bulk of its military aid from the Soviet Union and its Eastern Bloc socialist allies. China, too, was showing signs of growing impatience with the apparently sedentary PAC, and a concomitant interest in improving relations with the ANC.[50] Even if the ANC's legitimacy and support inside South Africa still far exceeded its somewhat limited organisational capacity, none the less the possibility had to be entertained that the movement might quite quickly transform that popularity into far-reaching organisational advances. This would have obvious implications for Western economic, political and strategic interests in southern Africa. The West had to come to terms with the fact that a revolutionary situation was developing inside South Africa. If the prospect of a revolutionary *victory* was still distant, it was no longer entirely fanciful. Further, if any grouping was the likely harbinger of such change, it was the ANC.

Essentially, two possible courses of action – not mutually exclusive – lay before the major Western powers. The preferred option was to assist in the promotion of a 'reformist' solution[51] in South Africa built around a 'moderate third force', able to interpose itself as a potential government between the indefensible and familiar crudities of National Party-style apartheid and the perceived political and economic threats posed by the ANC. But the South African government failed to respond positively to Western pressures for substantive reform, so necessary for the credibility of such a 'solution'. The government was even less receptive to attempts to forge an alliance from among its own ranks and elements situated mainly in white business circles and the intelligentsia – an alliance which might, with foreign backing, be able to wrest power from it.[52] The resounding National Party victory in the white elections of May 1987 (fought on the security issue), make this quite clear. Chief Mangosuthu Buthelezi and his Zulu-based (though nationally ambitious) Inkatha movement was an important element of any putative 'third force'. It had substantial organisational force in Natal, and was pro-capitalist. Buthelezi appeared, however, to be rapidly losing political ground to the ANC, and his political behaviour was often erratic.[53] The PAC was, in its weakness, likely to be manipulable, and was fiercely anti-Soviet. But the large-scale Western aid which would be needed to make it a real force, would in itself further undermine the PAC's legitimacy within South Africa's black populace. It seemed impossible, therefore, for the West to ignore the potential of the ANC.

The second option was to investigate the possibility of attracting elements of the ANC, particularly in its leadership, into a 'reformist' solution; or for so weakening the movement politically and organisationally that it had to forego the revolutionary option as well as any hope of achieving the full extent of its basic transformatory goals at any future negotiations. This involved advocating a break in the alliance with the SACP; calling for the abandonment of armed struggle and the disbandment of Umkhonto we Sizwe; and increased Western economic and intelligence involvement in neighbouring stages to enhance Western prospects of ensuring that these states would 'deliver' the ANC External Mission to negotiations on a Western timetable.[54]

In early 1986, British diplomats in southern Africa were reportedly instructed to 'get to know' as many ANC exiles as possible.[55] Other elements of British practice began to contradict the Thatcherite dictum that Her Majesty's government did not deal with organisations which employed armed struggle in pursuance of domestic political aims. In February, senior Foreign Office official John Johnson met members of the ANC NEC in Lusaka. Four months later, Tambo addressed a meeting of the Royal Commonwealth Society, met British MPs, and was officially received by Lynda Chalker, Minister of State in the Foreign and Commonwealth Office. In September, Tambo met British Foreign Secretary Sir Geoffrey Howe, and US Assistant Secretary of State for African Affairs, Chester Crocker. The latter meeting was a precursor to talks in January 1987 between Tambo and US Secretary of State, George Shultz.

Whatever its suspicions about the motivations of some Western governments in their changing stance towards the movement, the ANC sought to exploit the meetings for their propaganda and diplomatic advantages. The ANC was provided with a rare platform. It could put forward its vision of a post-apartheid society, and explain its reasons for resorting to armed struggle. It could serve notice of its refusal to indulge in 'anti-communism' within its own ranks, and point out that the Soviet Union had helped the movement for decades while major Western powers had been supplying arms to, and trading intelligence with, the South African government. It could encourage future support from the West provided that it was unconditional, and argue that the survival of apartheid in any variant was the greatest danger to Western interests in the region. Finally, the ANC could press its fundamental case: that apartheid could not be reformed, but had to be entirely replaced.[56]

Of all the foreign initiatives, potentially the most important was the mission of the Commonwealth Eminent Persons Group (EPG) in 1986.[57] The group was constituted at the 1985 Nassau Commonwealth Summit, and its brief clearly excluded any possibility of its becoming a 'mediator' between the South African government and its opponents. Rather, their task was to identify a platform on which, and a process through which, negotiations might commence in South Africa. Official 'mediator' or not, the EPG was nevertheless intended to modify, at least in the early stages, the likely 'two-sided', confrontational shape of any South African negotiating table. The EPG had been established as a compromise after Margaret Thatcher's stonewalling on the sanctions issue at Nassau – but it was Commonwealth Secretary-General Shridath Ramphal's interventions leading to the Lancaster House negotiations on Zimbabwe independence in 1980 that provided the real inspiration for the EPG efforts.[58]

Zambian President Kaunda and Zimbabwean Prime Minister Mugabe interceded with the ANC to facilitate a meeting with the EPG.[59] The ANC, weighing up the pros and cons, concluded that it should meet and co-operate with the EPG, despite its disappointment after the Nassau summit had failed to agree upon resolute anti-apartheid action. The movement's leaders had grave reservations, however, about the South African government's willingness or ability to bring any seriousness to bear on the issue of negotiations. There were also doubts within the ANC about the movement's readiness to confront the government over the negotiating table, and particularly, if things went awry, whether it would have sufficient reserves for the resumption of its revolutionary offensive. It became clear that the ANC perceived its role in such (hypothetical) talks as being at the head of a variety of anti-apartheid forces, including representatives of legal mass organisations. The government and its supporters would thus sit across a 'two-sided' table. The ANC would fight any attempts to 'drown' it in round-table negotiations where a proliferation of insignificant parties (such as those from the government-created bantustans) were introduced as supposedly autonomous entities. For the ANC, any negotiations would have to be clearly predicated on agreement between the sides that the ultimate objective was a united, democratic and non-racial South Africa. None the less, the ANC acknowledged that both sides could take a number of interim measures to create a climate conducive to 'talks about talks'.[60]

In the event, the ANC was not put to the test. Escalating government fears that the EPG's mission might bear actual fruit, given the ANC's conditional amenability to its efforts, resulted in a complete reversal in mid-May of the government's earlier, tentative co-operation with the EPG. In a calculated move, the South African Defence Force struck against what it said were ANC military and transit facilities in three Commonwealth countries – Botswana, Zambia and Zimbabwe. On the morning of 19 May 1986, the EPG mission lay in rubble – as the South African government had apparently intended it should. No ANC members were killed in the raids; all casualties and fatalities were non-South Africans; and only two (publicly known) ANC properties were hit.[61] The ANC felt that its pessimism about the EPG effort had been vindicated. The ANC believed that it had shown that it was 'reasonable' and, further, provided that they were about the total dismantling of apartheid, amenable to negotiations.[62] The net result was the further diplomatic isolation of the South African government, which had shown itself to be intransigent.

Soon after the EPG left South Africa, the ANC broadcast its most explicit call yet for the development of insurrectionary forces and tactics among its supporters inside the country, using the slogan 'From Ungovernability to People's Power'.[63] Its engagement in diplomacy returned to more traditional patterns; attempts at exploring avenues for a 'negotiated settlement' were off the agenda.

Notice of the South African government's intention to make its most intensive efforts ever to quell resistance came a month after the raids. In early June 1986 the government imposed the second State of Emergency in two years, this time covering the entire country. Legal mass internal resistance was largely forced to employ quasi-underground methods.[64]

In September and October, the ANC NEC and top operational officials met in Lusaka over several weeks to assess the situation in South Africa. They concluded that the organisation should do all in its power to escalate the insurrectionary offensive inside South Africa. No other way to end apartheid presented itself. There was no reason to change its 1961 decision on the necessity for armed struggle. It was to be war.[65]

LIVING IN THE MARGINS: THE PAN AFRICANIST CONGRESS

The PAC, and other organisations in exile advocating a revolutionary option, found themselves increasingly marginalised over this period. Whether the action was insurrectionary, military, political or diplomatic, their contribution both individually and collectively hovered between the slight and the insignificant.

Inside the country, those of their supporters in the Azanian People's Organisation (AZAPO) and its offshoots, the Cape Action League (CAL), the National Forum and the trade union movement, formed a fractious alliance.[66] Their different tendencies, both within and outside the country, tended to derive a conscientious comfort from elaborate and often sectarian Africanist or socialist formulations of the South African problem and its solution. Their capacity for concrete action around a common programme was minimal.[67] Their habit was generally to define themselves primarily in contradistinction to the ANC, UDF or COSATU rather than in terms of conflict with the state. Psychologically and organisationally they failed to make the transition from being splinter or adjunct groups to potential contenders for state power. The successes of the ANC, UDF and COSATU were presented, by means of a most tenuous logic, as the product of a conspiracy between the South African government, communists, the ANC, journalists and liberals.[68] Their failures were rationalised by reference to the same conspiracy theory. The objective of this conspiracy was said to be the betrayal of the legitimate nationalist or socialist aspirations of the oppressed.

The causes of their marginalisation, however, lay in their failure to grapple with real South African conditions. They showed little capacity to transform elemental rage at black oppression and exploitation into programme and action. In the process, moreover, they proved largely incapable of any coherent tactical address on how – practically – to take the struggle against apartheid forward.

None the less, these groups did represent significant (even if, over the period under review, apparently rather small) constituencies inside

South Africa. If the chronic organisational and political problems that have beset them since the mid-1960s were to be solved and a mature leadership were to emerge, the basis could be built for an important intervention in the South African conflict. There is no guarantee, as a number of their critics allege, that these organisations' particular brands of politics ensure their perpetual marginalisation. Furthermore the ANC has not yet achieved in international forums the status of 'sole and authentic representative' of the South African people – a status accorded to the South West African Peoples' Organisation (SWAPO) of Namibia. Rather, through the OAU's recognition of the PAC there exists a shell in which a meaningful counterpart to the ANC could yet emerge and tap the sources of international backing on a large scale. The importance of the PAC, other black exclusivist, or Trotskyite groups in South Africa lies, therefore, in their potential rather than in their performance hitherto.

The PAC has been bedevilled by internal rivalries and splits for many years. Their aetiology was more often to be found in personality disputes or individual ambition than in ideological or political divergences. These chronic internal problems, which broke out again in late 1986, seriously sapped the PAC's energies and denuded its ranks.

At the PAC's consultative conference in Arusha, Tanzania in 1978, the then chairman Potlako Leballo had outlined his organisation's understanding of 'people's war' in South Africa in terms more rhetorical than analytical.[69] Since then, the PAC had not put forward a detailed revolutionary programme or tactical perspective. So far as Leballo's posture went, the essence was guerrilla infiltration in the rural areas, and the mobilisation and arming of the oppressed in those areas along quasi-Maoist lines. The quite literal objective was to seize the land. Opinion has long been divided on the extent to which this emphasis on repossession of the land is PAC-speak for seizure of the 'means of production' and, with it, state power. What the intermediate tactical objectives were supposed to be in terms of this outlook have appeared as much of a mystery to those inside the PAC as to those outside its ranks.[70]

The PAC's internal difficulties reached a peak in the period 1978–79, when Leballo expelled and alienated relatively effective PAC members grouped around his former guerrilla commander Templeton Ntantala. This group eventually numbered around eighty. Leballo's actions apparently constituted an attempt by him to seize complete control of the organisation following the serious illness and death inside South Africa of Robert Sobukwe, President of the PAC.

Leballo was himself later deposed and replaced by a presidential triumvirate comprising Vus Make, David Sibeko and Elias Ntloedibe; Sibeko was assassinated by a group of Leballo loyalists; Leballo was expelled from the PAC itself; there was a spate of defections from the PAC to the ANC in Tanzania; and Vus Make took effective control while Ntloedibe subsequently concentrated on business interests in Botswana. Thus, at the time when it most needed to do so, the PAC was unable to formulate a coherent initiative to suit new conditions in the post-Soweto period.

The release from prison in 1980 of John Pokela, after thirteen years on Robben Island, provided the PAC with the option of having a leader unsullied by the bitter infighting which had characterised their twenty years of exile. Within weeks of his arrival in exile in 1981, Pokela was propelled into the chairmanship. Make agreed to step down as *de facto* chairman. Pokela made it his central task to reunite the organisation. One of his first acts was to rehabilitate the Ntantala Group, on the secretly agreed understanding[71] that Ntantala himself did not get a seat on the Central Committee for a long period and that his group completely disbanded itself within the PAC. By this time some African governments had made it clear to the PAC that it could face OAU derecognition as a liberation movement if it continued in such disarray.[72]

But Pokela, a modest and somewhat timid man, was only partially successful in the task he had set himself. Just a year after his accession to the chairmanship, Henry Isaacs, a former president of the Black Consciousness aligned African Students' Organisation (SASO), who was the PAC's relatively effective United Nations representative, resigned his post and membership of the Central Committee. Isaacs released a long and detailed indictment of ineptitude, corruption and continuing factionalism under Pokela's leadership.[73] In late 1982, physical clashes broke out between different PAC factions in Lesotho.[74] The Dar es Salaam-based Central Committee had decided to replace its Lesotho representative Naphtalie Sidzamba, an 'independent' who had also complained of continuing factionalism under Pokela. The Central Committee went about it in a way which resulted in a number of Sidzamba's supporters being detained briefly by the Lesotho authorities for allegedly supporting South African-backed Lesotho dissidents.[75] The following year, the PAC's assistant administrative secretary and a member of the Central Committee, Benny Sondlo (accused by his PAC detractors of being the 'epitome of corruption'[76]), was murdered in Tanzania. Ntantala was fired as PAC chief representative in Zimbabwe. From 1980–83 there were also persistent difficulties in PAC settlements in Tanzania, with Tanzanian security forces having to be called in on more than one occasion to quell mutinies.[77] More than one hundred PAC exiles left the organisation, either to apply for registration as ordinary refugees with the United Nations High Commissioner for Refugees in Tanzania, or to defect to the ANC.[78]

Once again, as the rebuilding of mass legal anti-apartheid forces was underway inside South Africa, the PAC had crippled itself. If it indeed had the will to intervene formatively, it apparently lacked the ability to do so. Pokela's leadership had, however, provided some stability in comparison to the Leballo years. His death by natural causes, on 30 June 1985, was a serious blow for the PAC.

At a special Central Committee meeting in Harare on 15 July 1985, Johnson Mlambo, a relative unknown who had just completed twenty years on Robben Island and who had served briefly as PAC foreign secretary since arriving in exile, was elected Pokela's successor. On Robben Island, Mlambo had earned the respect of inmates from other organisations. Prior to his jailing, he had been a branch chairman of the PAC in the township of Daveyton outside Johannesburg.[79] Again, it had been necessary to choose a man of limited experience whose most important qualification was that he was untainted by factional squabbles in the External Mission.

Under Mlambo, the internal problems continued. Make, who had now been passed over twice as chairman, became increasingly alienated.[80] Administrative secretary Joe Mkwanazi became the target of allegations from a variety of enemies in the leadership questioning his handling of PAC resources – charges he energetically denied.[81] In addition, the ANC received more membership applications from disenchanted PAC members in the FLS as well as in Europe.[82] Yet again, as South Africa experienced its most serious and sustained revolt, the PAC External Mission was largely paralysed.

The rise to power in Zimbabwe of Mugabe's Zanu (PF) party had created highly favourable conditions for the potential rehabilitation of the PAC, which had enjoyed a close relationship with it in exile.[83] Once in government, Zanu (PF) pursued the diplomatically correct policy of parity between the ANC and PAC, in line with the equal formal status accorded to them by the OAU. But there was evidence of a more natural sympathy with the PAC, and a number of ruling party officials expended some energy to help the PAC to unravel its organisational problems in the first few years after Zimbabwe's independence.[84] By the end of 1986, however, the PAC appeared to have substantially squandered these highly favourable conditions. It seemed that a number of Zimbabwean leaders now despaired of it, questioned its seriousness, and concluded that a closer and warmer relationship should be forged with the ANC.[85]

Matters again came to a head in the PAC at the end of 1986. An eighteen-page document from a section of the internal leadership of the PAC was delivered to the External Mission.[86] The document threatened open mutiny. Mlambo claimed in a statement from Dar es Salaam that the document was a fake, but the route by which it reached some journalists and the ructions it caused within the PAC left little doubt that it was genuine.[87]

The memorandum stated that, inside South Africa the PAC was 'virtually absent'. The PAC had 'failed to defend the people'. The return to the country of a senior PAC military man, Enoch Zulu,[88] arrested by South African security forces eight months earlier, and the infiltration of a handful of other PAC guerrillas had been ill-conceived. There were 'no receiving structures for such operations'. The authors feared that their organisation 'was losing control'. There was a 'sad lack of co-ordination between the External Mission' and the authors. There was a 'yawning gap in military activity of the PAC inside the country'. There was no effective flow of information about the PAC to non-members and, worse, between members themselves. Some members of the Central Committee had engaged in behaviour that had been 'very disappointing, embarrassing and at times downright distressing'. The memorandum bemoaned the 'unexplained and evidently baseless and humiliating removal of comrade Vus Make from the Central Committee' a few months earlier. It deplored the fact that Mlambo had been elected chairman of the PAC without reference to the authors. It accused Mkwanazi of 'negligence', of holding secret meetings with Buthelezi, and of possible involvement in corruption.

The memorandum ended with a series of demands and threats. Mkwanazi should 'be removed forthwith' as administrative secretary. The Central Committee should be totally restructured. No appointments should be made to a new Central Committee before a meeting between the delegation bearing the memorandum and chairman Mlambo, scheduled to be held before 15 December 1986. The External Mission should immediately cease working with individuals inside South Africa who did not have the approval of the authors.

If these demands were not met, according to the document, 'the internal movement' would 'select ten committed members to take over the PAC administration abroad', a press conference would be called to denounce the former External Mission leadership, and the OAU and African governments would be informed of the reasons for this course of action. Further, if 'unexplained deaths' continued in PAC camps, the authors would 'hold the chairman and members of the military commission responsible'. If 'anything unbecoming' happened to Make or the delegation carrying the memorandum, the same would apply. Finally, the demands were 'not negotiable'.

Tension between different PAC factions in the FLS reached breaking point shortly after delivery of the document. The support for Make and condemnation of Mkwanazi touched an open wound. In February 1987 at least one African government felt compelled to take stern action to prevent a serious outbreak of fratricidal PAC violence.[89] A series of extraordinary meetings was held to try to iron out differences. Rank and file members were addressed by members of the leadership who, in some cases, received humiliating receptions.[90] Michael Muendane, a former PAC chief representative in the United Kingdom and the manpower secretary, was sacked in early 1987, dismissed from the central committee, and suspended from all PAC activities for a year. Muendane had long been a Make supporter on the Central Committee. The same fate befell Ike Mafole, PAC education secretary; and Vus Nomodolo, the then chief representative of the PAC in the UK, resigned from the Central Committee but remained a member of the organisation.[91] Nomodolo had a reputation for independence through the years of factionalism. PAC secretary for foreign affairs Gora Ebrahim said that the PAC Central Committee was, after the purge of people seeking to 'destabilise' it, now more 'action orientated'.[92]

Quite what its capabilities for taking action were, however, remained unproven. Reliable estimates of the PAC's formal guerrilla strength, some twenty years after it began developing a guerrilla army outside the country, were of less than 450 men and women under arms located mainly in Tanzania and Libya.[93] To disclosure of this figure, the PAC response was that it was conducting a 'people's war' and that the 'oppressed population of Azania [the PAC's name for South Africa] is more than 450'.[94] This argument could only be meaningful if the organisation demonstrated that it was capable of a tactical address to the task it had proclaimed for itself. Until such time, or in the possible event of an action oriented alliance with the rump of Black Consciousness and other groupings, the PAC appears doomed to remain a tragic figure of modern exile politics. In late 1986 and early 1987, PAC sources in the FLS claimed that they had returned a few score guerrillas to South Africa, but said that most were believed to have been picked up almost immediately by South African security forces.

Squabbles of the kind affecting the PAC are not uncommon given the insecurities and vagaries of revolutionary exile politics; and the damage they wreak is not necessarily irreversible. Zimbabwe's Zanu party, for example, also suffered some serious internal difficulties, but was able to stage a remarkable comeback.[95] The crucial factors in Zanu's renaissance appear to have been that it was able to ensure the dominance of a leadership of undoubted political acumen and discipline; it was able to formulate tactics appropriate to Zimbabwean conditions, above all to root its cadres firmly and often indistinguishably among its constituency; it demonstrated its will to engage the enemy in battle; and it seized and exploited opportunities when they presented themselves (such as base facilities in Mozambique).[96] Prospects for the PAC's salvation, on each of these counts, looked bleak in 1987.

THE ANC AND THE GOVERNMENT BACKLASH

In January 1987 the politburo and central committee of Zimbabwe's ruling Zanu (PF) party invited the ANC to two days of talks in Harare. The ANC delegation was led by Tambo, and included Mbeki, Modise and Hani among others. The changing situation inside South Africa was discussed and various perspectives on the regional crisis exchanged. Both sides concluded that a new warmth had begun to characterise their relationship, and that the earlier awkwardness between them was something largely of the past.[97]

President Botha's announcement of a whites-only general election for 6 May again placed the focus where the ANC wanted it: on the issue of state power in South Africa. The movement attempted to regroup its own and allied forces, which had been dealt heavy blows by successive States of Emergency. It also recognised an opportunity to carry forward its tactical objectives. The ANC wanted to demonstrate by every conceivable method that apartheid and its proponents were responsible for the national crisis, and that the election itself was incapable of producing a solution. Instead, in the ANC's view, the election constituted an attempt by the government to build the basis for a restructuring and further modernisation of white minority domination.[98] The ANC was among the organisations to call for work stayaways on May Day and election day, which were among the most successful ever.

As the ANC celebrated its seventy-fifth anniversary on 8 January 1987, its tacticians declared optimistically that 'state repression' – though so greatly intensified – did not demand a 'retreat' of the kind which had been necessary after the movement was outlawed in 1960. In early 1987, the ANC considered the time to be ripe for a considered, gradual escalation of its offensive. Tacticians argued that a 'spirit of hot engagement' among the mass of people could be sustained and extended, and that government forces could be tellingly stretched.[99] The ANC's declaration of 1987 as 'The Year of Advance to People's Power' reflected this outlook.

A vindication of this analysis seemed to hinge on a number of essentially subjective factors: the ANC's ability to transform itself into a far more adaptable organisation, able to initiate and respond more quickly than its sometimes cumbersome bureaucracy seemed to allow; morale within its ranks; the ANC's ability to rid itself of pockets of remarkable indolence in some of its structures; the quality and extension of the mechanics of mass legal and underground organisation; sufficient innovation and imagination to tap new sources of weaponry on a massive scale for people inside the country; sufficient infiltration of formally trained guerrilla units, and the development of popular militias to defend organisations; the will and ability to strike blows against the state to shatter the latter's image of invincibility; the further consolidation and extension of its brand of ideological and organisational unity inside the country; and the further isolation of its fighting enemy.

Above all, the quality of the ANC's formal political and military underground machineries inside the country would be decisive. The ANC claimed that there was a widespread realisation within mass legal organisations of the need to adopt conspiratorial methods. The ANC was insistent, however, that the mass legal movements should be maintained, expanded, and stabilised – in line with the principle that all forms of struggle be employed in combination in order to build 'the political army of the revolution'. ANC operational leaders reported, in early 1987, that they were increasingly getting on top of problems associated with consolidating and extending their underground network – notwithstanding incidents such as the abduction and subsequent interrogation by South African security forces of three relatively senior ANC officials in Swaziland in late 1986 and early 1987. The operational officials also reported that their units were encountering a considerable growth of opinion among ordinary people inside South Africa that armed struggle was now 'necessary', as opposed to being merely 'feasible'. Numbers of people who had previously baulked at the prospect were now allegedly demanding weapons and training. ANC guerrilla units inside the country were not encountering any trained combatants from other organisations such as the PAC.[100]

As 1986 progressed, the government had shown signs of developing a relatively coherent response to ANC tactics, over and above the conventional activities of its own formal security forces and intelligence establishment. It was reported to be using 'vigilante' groups, comprising conservative or easily mustered lumpen black elements, to conduct 'reigns of terror' against anti-apartheid activists and to demoralise their political bases.[101] In effect, these vigilante groups constituted counter-militias. In addition, the government created area Joint Management Committees (JMCs) in both black and white areas, linked into the State Security Council (SSC).[102] Their role was to co-ordinate security forces, provide on-the-ground intelligence and assessments and, wherever possible, to mobilise against insurrectionary activity. Thus, in effect, these 'JMCs' constituted area counter-undergrounds.

CONCLUSION

Severe repression by a government of its most vociferous political opponents need not necessarily be inconsistent with a control-reform strategy. For repression can contribute substantially towards creating the space for reform. Furthermore, political antagonists can be guided in their behaviour in the period immediately prior to possible settlement talks by a keen awareness that they are unlikely to win at any negotiating table much more than the victories they have scored, or the positions they have held, on the political-military battlefield itself. In a national liberation struggle, negotiations are most often only the conduct of the political-military warfare on different terrain; and no rational party enters a particular battleground – one on which it is not compelled by circumstance to fight – unless, on the basis of its calculations, the new terrain promises either a reasonable chance to cement its gains or to take forward its objectives, at least slightly.

However, the South African government had, by October 1987, not yet prepared any serious or intelligent political reform initiative of a kind which might prove capable of significantly undermining either the ANC's unity, its domestic support, or its commitment to the revolutionary option. The government's concentrated action against internal resistance forces, which included in the latter half of 1987 the arrest of numbers of ANC underground organisers in the Western Cape and Transvaal regions, the blows it continued to strike against the ANC External Mission, as well as the major Western powers' veto of proposals for far-reaching international sanctions against it, could all be said to have given the government much of the space it might need in which to mount a formative political manoeuvre. Yet the most the Botha government offered publicly was the establishment of a National Statutory Council which offered less than token representation in the organs of central government to the black African majority. The NSC's only likely participants were discredited individuals involved in the government-created township councils or bantustan hierarchies. Indeed, the eventual establishment of this council had the potential to inflame seriously, at some point in the future, the wound of the 1984 constitution and to precipitate a new round of perhaps still more bloody, and serious, insurrectionary activity.

Furthermore, neither side had yet been compelled by weakness, or by a divided and still hesitant international community, to enter into negotiations. In fact, neither side showed any real sign that, at this stage, it saw in negotiations the promise of substantial advantage for its objectives. The government had not initiated any campaign to prepare its white constituency for possible talks with the ANC or an alliance of militant anti-apartheid forces. Rather, it vilified in more strident terms than before, and threatened action against, those who continued to seek contact with the ANC. For its part, the ANC continued a skilful political campaign to contest the middle ground of South African politics, which included attempts to win over liberal whites. Although this was not inconsistent with preparations for possible negotiations, the campaign appeared to be motivated by broader political-military considerations than the likely requirements of possible future settlement talks alone. In the short- to medium-term, both sides appeared still to see direct physical or insurrectionary engagement as the terrain on which their objectives could still best be served.

The anticipated Western attempts to undermine the ANC's revolutionary posture and to thrust it into a 'reformist' compromise appeared still to be limited. The FLS had also not yet significantly pressurised the ANC towards negotiations – as had been the experience of the Zimbabwean liberation movement in 1979. Thus the ANC had not yet been subjected to the same stresses and strains which other national liberation movements in other contexts had experienced when obliged to confront the real prospect of a negotiated or, worse, 'reformist' solution. How the ANC would cope with these – when or if they took real effect – would have an important bearing on any outcome in South Africa.

None the less, in the latter half of 1987, it appeared that the major Western powers might have begun a potentially important re-evaluation of their tactics in the region. In the case of South Africa itself, their fear that the SACP's (and other socialists') position in the ANC-led alliance might become substantially stronger the longer a credible settlement was delayed prompted some conservatives in Western foreign policy and intelligence establishments to advocate a more activist role in pressurising the South African government towards meaningful compromise.[103] Their analysis held that if a putative ANC government took over in the short- to medium-term, it would inherit an intact state structure, as well as an institutional and military balance of forces, overwhelmingly hostile to many of its transformatory objectives. On the other hand, lengthy delays in achieving a compromise settlement might lessen these constraints on a future majority government. Western warnings along these lines were issued to the Botha government.

Both the government and the ANC had also to consider the possibility that the two superpowers might collaborate on a 'peace plan' for the region after the replacement of Ronald Reagan by a US President and administration less simplistically or aggressively anti-communist. Tambo had in fact raised the issue of possible US-Soviet co-operation on the region during his talks with US Secretary of State Shultz in January; and officials of the two superpowers had later in the year exchanged perspectives on the suggestion.[104] This possibility of co-operation gained some respectability among Soviet and Western analysts in 1987.[105] Among other things, it relied on a prediction that one likely outcome of a then-inconclusive re-examination of Soviet foreign policy doctrines occurring under Soviet Communist Party General Secretary Gorbachev would be a more flexible application of traditional Leninist support for national liberation revolutions. Basically, the argument held that, relatively speaking, neither superpower had considerable strategic interests in the region; neither superpower favoured direct military intervention; nor did either stand to benefit substantially from continued regional conflict. Conditions therefore favoured flexibility on both sides, and made possible the drafting of joint Soviet-US guarantees to the main actors in the region's proliferation of serious conflicts – all of which appeared to centre on the South African conflict itself. A leading Soviet analyst on African affairs suggested that such co-operation might begin with joint US-Soviet efforts to end 'South African destabilisation of its neighbours'. This could, among other things, make the Cuban troop presence in Angola unnecessary which, in turn, could open the way for Namibian independence under UN Resolution 435. At this point, according to the argument, the prospects might be considerably improved for co-operation towards settlement of the South African conflict itself.[106]

Similar thinking characterised some of the debate at the Vancouver Commonwealth Summit in October 1987, where the British stress fell on the need to strengthen the Front Line States' abilities to defend themselves against South African destabilisation. This implied, for some, an attempt to re-define what had hitherto (certainly since the Bahamas Summit in 1985) been the major presentation of the regional conflict, namely a portrayal which centred on the internal South African struggle. A major reason for this attempted re-definition was obviously Britain's reluctance to impose economic sanctions on South Africa or to fall in line with the majority Commonwealth call for far-reaching and united international action against Pretoria. Given that Britain was already, by the time of the Vancouver meeting, providing military aid to a number of states in the FLS grouping, this emphasis on defence posed no challenge to Mrs Thatcher's positions on South Africa. This new emphasis could, indeed, draw Britain into the kind of approach to the region being suggested by some Soviet and US analysts. Furthermore, there were obvious potential advantages to the Western bloc in having Britain very well placed in the armouries of South Africa's neighbours.

Indications that Western tactics could evolve from inertia towards concrete and meaningful pressure on the Pretoria government may have been among the factors which again prompted a South African cabinet minister to attempt, in July 1987, to open up contact with the ANC, this time in the person of Tambo. An intermediary who attended the talks in the Senegalese capital, Dakar, between an ANC delegation and elements mainly from the Afrikaner intelligentsia, reportedly conveyed the unnamed cabinet minister's wish through an ANC delegate to Tambo (who was not in Dakar). According to Tambo,[107] however, attempts by the ANC to get further information about the attempted contact failed; and there had been no follow-up to the message by late September. Western pressures may also account for the unconfirmed report of a visit to Lusaka, also in the latter half of the year, of a senior officer in South Africa's Directorate of Military Intelligence.[108] Details of his mission were not made public. Tambo, however, rejected speculative reports that talks or contacts had opened up between the South African government and the ANC.[109]

The government's declaration – in the run-up to the Commonwealth summit in Vancouver – that it was considering the release from prison of Govan Mbeki (and, possibly, of other ANC leaders) may have been a response to the same pressures. Such releases offered the South Africa government a number of potential gains. First among them was the likely favourable response in the West. Second, it could monitor closely the political effect of these releases, and the mechanics employed to effect them, with a view to calculating the likely consequences of a subsequent release of Mandela and other top ANC leaders still physically capable of playing an activist political role. Third, it might allow the South African government to posture as willing peacemaker. That is, it might enable Pretoria to argue that its imposition of a State of Emergency and suppression of the ANC, UDF, COSATU and other forces had made possible these releases; hence, if the ANC and others were restrained by the West and FLS, further releases or 'reforms' were possible. Fourth, it might also provide Pretoria with more space for manoeuvre in its attempts to broaden its political base among blacks, by presenting the releases as the result of demands from black people co-operating with it, and by removing an obstacle between some blacks and their participation in government-created structures.

The 'war' between the government and the ANC continued inconclusively at low intensity in late 1987. Neither side had yet released its full capacity for violence. This was particularly true of the South African government with its awesome formal military-security power. Yet, under the constraints imposed by the domestic and international climates, neither appeared ready or equipped for a decisive political-military breakthrough in the short term.

Government pressure on the ANC External Mission took a variety of forms. ANC officials reported the discovery of several South African plots in the two-year period to September 1987 – aimed, among other things, at the assassination of selected ANC leaders. The intention (in at least one case[110]) was allegedly to pass such an assassination off as the result of tensions within the ANC, in the hope of threatening the organisation's unity. Pressures on the FLS and other neighbouring states to expel or exercise tight control over the activities of exiles made the business of reinforcing the internal struggle from across foreign borders increasingly difficult for the ANC. The movement's headquarters in Lusaka remained highly vulnerable to attack and were further threatened by alleged South African attempts to undermine the hitherto remarkable political stability of Zambia,[111] which had survived serious economic problems over a protracted period. In states immediately bordering South Africa, notably Swaziland, highly successful security force operations apparently aimed at the assassination or abduction of ANC exiles suggested that a new grade of intelligence was now available to Pretoria. In July 1987, the ANC suffered the costly loss of its capable military logistics commander, Cassius Make, who was also the youngest member of its NEC. Make was the eleventh ANC member in Swaziland killed in the eight months to July. In addition to the three senior ANC officials kidnapped earlier, a further three alleged ANC members or supporters were abducted to South Africa over the same period. It was in response to Make's assassination that the ANC detonated a large car bomb outside a military headquarters in central Johannesburg on 30 July.[112]

South African attempts to break the broad political and organisational unity of the ANC continued along two main lines. The first was to try to encourage the development of anti-communism within its ranks. The second was apparently to attempt to foster tensions between the different ANC generations by, *inter alia*, portraying the older generation as unnecessarily cautious and, ironically, by agitating for a less discriminating approach to armed struggle through the direct targeting of (white) civilians in guerrilla attacks as a matter of policy. The latter device raised a particularly interesting debate within ANC circles. The dominant position to emerge in early 1987 was that resort to terrorism in its literal sense, consciously as a tactic in itself, was an 'empty radicalism'. Among other things, such actions could hope at best to drive an embittered white minority to the negotiating table. Rather, the central objective of armed struggle was to increase the insurrectionary capacity of the ANC's broad constituency and to make possible a seizure of state power.[113]

Such an outcome looked a far-off prospect in late 1987. The ANC had hit on a tactical formulation which appeared to make patent sense in terms of South African peculiarities. It had shown itself capable of spearheading a far-reaching offensive which had temporarily rocked the foundations of minority rule. But it patently still lacked the practical tools and techniques of organisation, the security proficiency, the military capacity, the discipline and the sense of purpose to mount an offensive (alone or in alliance) capable of forcing a 'revolutionary' outcome in South Africa. On that capacity would also hinge its ability to avoid being manipulated into a settlement of a kind which might mean substantial compromise to its transformatory objectives.

Although the warlike postures struck by both sides could, in late

1987, not be said to exclude the possibility of a negotiated settlement – and such talks themselves could be spread inconclusively over many years – the bleak prospect was that 'rivers of blood'[114] might still have to flow before that bridge was properly built; if ever it was.

NOTES

1. They might be said also to include the Black Consciousness Movement of Azania (BCMA) and the Unity Movement of South Africa (UMSA), two small groups not enjoying OAU recognition as liberation movements. BCMA, consisting of a few score members situated mainly in southern Africa and Europe, has provided a fertile recruiting ground for the ANC in particular, the PAC and UMSA. Formed in the late 1970s by those relatively few Black Consciousness adherents who did not join the ANC or PAC, it has been in decline since then. UMSA, also very small in size, has been affected by repeated fractures around the finer distinctions of left-wing theory and has limited organisation. Neither BCMA nor UMSA has a formal guerrilla capacity.
2. In addition, the ANC's development of armed struggle has been consciously gradual. Initially, it hoped that a limited campaign of sabotage in the 1960s might alter white minds about repression, and it decided to exhaust this option before proceeding to any more ambitious armed project. See Nelson Mandela's statement from the dock, 20 April 1964, recounted in N. Mandela, *The Struggle is My Life* (London: International Defence and Aid Fund, 1978).
3. This long-standing *de facto* working alliance achieved some formality at the ANC's first National Consultative Conference (after its banning) in 1969 in Morogoro, Tanzania.
4. See these documents in *ANC Speaks: Documents and Statements of the ANC.*
5. The ANC has, since 1958–59 (when a group of Africanists around Robert Sobukwe broke away to form the PAC), suffered two breakaways. In 1975, eight senior ANC members formed the ANC (African Nationalist). Later, in the 1970s, a smaller group of white intellectuals, suspended from the ANC, formed the Marxist Workers Tendency of the ANC. Neither eventually had a significant impact on the ANC's organisational or political unity, and each failed to develop an organisational strength of its own.
6. Figures for ANC guerrilla incidents rose from twenty-three in 1977 to 118 for the first six months of 1986, according to Tom Lodge in 'State of Exile: The African National Congress of South Africa, 1976–86', *Third World Quarterly*, vol. 9, no. 1, January 1987. Other groups registered only a handful of incidents over the same period.
7. ANC sources. None of this generation has yet risen to the top level of leadership, namely the National Executive Committee, though this appears likely within the next few years, probably at the next consultative conference of the ANC due by June 1990.

8. ANC sources.
9. This formulation comes from ANC sources.
10. The Sasol plants were attacked in June 1980, whereas the Koeberg Nuclear Power Station was mined in December 1982. ANC sources told the author that the organisation had also been responsible for a fire which destroyed most of the electrical circuitry alongside the main reactor building a few months earlier, but the South African government would not concede sabotage in this first incident.
11. Sources in the ANC and legal democratic mass organisations inside South Africa. This similarity of focus appeared more a happy congruence than a conspiracy.
12. Sources in the ANC and legal democratic mass organisations. Again, congruence rather than conspiracy.
13. Ibid.
14. For a fuller description of this process, see H. Barrell, 'The United Democratic Front and National Forum: Their Emergence, Composition and Trends', *South African Review: II* (Johannesburg: Ravan Press, 1984).
15. National Forum sources.
16. ANC sources.
17. Reprinted in *Sechaba* (ANC's journal), March 1984.
18. The author was among many in various parts of South Africa to receive this series of duplicated leaflets. Their relative typographical crudity indicated production by internal underground units of the ANC.
19. Radio Freedom broadcasts from Lusaka and Addis Ababa monitored by the author in Gaborone, Botswana, in September 1984. ANC officials later confirmed that the message was also broadcast over the other three Radio Freedom stations in Antananarivo, Luanda and Dar es Salaam. Interviews with black activists in 1983 and early 1984 indicated a fast-growing Radio Freedom listenership and the existence of 'clubs' for this purpose.
20. ANC sources. The ANC also agreed on the need for far-reaching changes in its operational structures which would better enable it to take forward this insurrectionary offensive. These changes, which institutionalise a close relationship between political and military formations at most levels and which assert the primacy of the political, were still being implemented in early 1987. For a fuller description of the tenor of the conference, see H. Barrell, 'ANC Conference: All for the Front', *Work in Progress* 38, Johannesburg, August 1985.
21. The first state of emergency, covering thirty-six magisterial districts, was declared on 21 July 1985 and lasted until 7 March 1986. The second, covering the entire country, was declared on 12 June 1986. Immediately upon expiry of the second emergency, a third was declared on 11 June 1987.
22. ANC sources.
23. ANC sources. The ANC National Executive Committee's 8 January 1987 'Address to the Nation', broadcast over Radio Freedom stations and later distributed in pamphlet form puts forward the same interim objective.

24. ANC sources.
25. ANC sources whom the author considers reliable. Other estimates of the ANC's guerrilla strength are available in Lodge, 'State of Exile: the African National Congress of South Africa, 1976–86', op. cit., note 6 above.
26. This is the assessment of ANC military sources, as well as former commanders of other non-South African liberation movements in the region with whose judgement on this point the author agrees.
27. ANC sources.
28. Ibid.
29. For a clearer and fuller outline of the ANC's tactical perspective see the interview with ANC official Ronnie Kasrils, 'People's War, Revolution and Insurrection', in *Sechaba*, May 1986. See also the interview with Umkhonto we Sizwe political commissar Chris Hani, '25 Years of Armed Struggle', in *Sechaba*, December 1986.
30. ANC sources.
31. Ibid.
32. Both ANC sources and other participants in these talks. By the term 'reformist' in relation to the ANC is meant a solution which entails either a significant compromise to the ANC's current demands for one person one vote, a unitary state and fully democratic representative government, or significant abrogation of the objectives outlined in the Freedom Charter. The ANC's insistence on unencumbered majority rule and the economic clauses of the Freedom Charter were areas on which some members of the white liberal establishment and others sought compromise.
33. Front Line State official sources.
34. A number of other journalists, among them Allister Sparks (*Washington Post*, 23 November 1985), came across similar information at this time, although this excluded an exchange of feelers between the South African government and the External Mission of the ANC. Sparks wrote of the South African authorities having discussions with imprisoned ANC leader Nelson Mandela about the possibility of releasing him, adding that the government was 'trying more seriously than before' to find a suitable way of doing so.
35. ANC sources.
36. Ibid.
37. See *The Star*, Johannesburg, 26 November 1985.
38. Allister Sparks, writing in the *Weekly Mail*, Johannesburg, 6 December 1985, provided perhaps the best available explanation. He suggested that a 'small but influential' lobby for Mandela's release existed within the ruling National Party around Justice Minister Kobie Coetsee; that this lobby had been active in preceding weeks; that Nel's overstatement reflected an angry reaction by President Botha to the activities of the pro-release lobby; and that the pro-release lobby had been 'stymied for the moment' by a hardline military-security group around then Law and Order Minister Louis le Grange. Later, as the EPG mission gathered momentum, Allister Sparks (*Observer Foreign News Service*, 6 February 1987) wrote, in response to renewed speculation that Mandela would be

released, that some government elements saw his liberation not as a precursor to negotiations but as a tactic which might 'demythologise' Mandela among blacks, cause a resultant decline in the popularity of the ANC and bolster the political image of Chief Buthelezi and the politics of compromise. Mandela's release might also have the result of neutralising the EPG's demands on the government, create a favourable impression in the West and help to prevent economic sanctions.

39. ANC sources.
40. See 'Strategy and Tactics of the ANC', in *ANC Speaks: Documents and Statements of the African National Congress.*
41. At the Kabwe Conference, delegates decided to remove the two remaining restrictions on full participation in the ANC by non-black Africans. So-called coloureds, Indians and whites could now formally belong to the internal ANC, whereas previously they had been constitutionally restricted to membership of the External Mission alone. This restriction had, in practice, been honoured more in the breach than in the observance. In addition, the old bar on non-black Africans being elected members of the National Executive Committee was removed. Following this change, the conference elected Reg September and James Stuart, Mac Maharaj and Aziz Pahad, and Joe Slovo members of the NEC. For a fuller account of the conference, see Howard Barrell, 'ANC Conference: All for the Front', op. cit. note 20 above.
42. See Howard Barrell, 'The ANC and Business: The Tactics of Talks', *Work in Progress*, 39, Johannesburg, October 1985.
43. Sources within these organisations.
44. ANC sources.
45. In fact, the ANC met with the prime movers in the development of the NECC a few months before its formal launch in March 1986.
46. Joint communiqué of the three organisations, 7 March 1986, telex copy received from ANC Headquarters, Lusaka.
47. ANC sources. In fact, the ANC and SACTU were highly impressed with some leading individuals at some stage identified with the 'independent worker' position, and with whom they had (wrongly, they concluded) previously imagined themselves to be in conflict.
48. ANC sources.
49. The row within the British Anti-Apartheid Movement and other disputes led, among other things, to the suspension from the ANC of David Kitson, who had been released from prison shortly before the expiry of a twenty-year sentence for ANC activities.
50. Both ANC and PAC sources. An indicator of improved ANC-Chinese relations are the visits by ANC delegations to China led by ANC president Oliver Tambo in 1983 and ANC secretary general Alfred Nzo in 1986.
51. What follows immediately is, essentially, the author's own argument which he considers is amply demonstrated by the evidence and the Western Powers' responses to other modern national liberation processes.
52. The alliance around Corazon Aquino is construed by some to be an example of this type of intervention – in the case of the Philippines, intended to out-manoeuvre the National Democratic Front and New

People's Army. The 1987 white general election result in South Africa showed that the white electorate was not willing to endorse, not yet anyway, the kind of 'Third Force' potential represented by some defectors from the ruling National Party who stood as independents in what was effectively a tacit alliance with the liberal Progressive Federal Party.

53. Comparable opinion surveys suggest a continual decline in black African support for Buthelezi and Inkatha both in Natal and at a national level. In 1977, Buthelezi and Inkatha were the political choice of 78 per cent of black Africans in Durban, according to Theo Hanf *et al. South Africa: The Prospects of Peaceful Change* (London: Rex Collings, 1981). By 1981, Buthelezi and Inkatha were polling 48 per cent support among black Africans in metropolitan Natal, according to L. Schlemmer, 'The Report on the Attitude Surveys', ch. 3 in *The Buthelezi Commission* (Vol. 1) (Durban: H. & H. Publications, 1982). By September 1985, there was 33 per cent support for Inkatha and Buthelezi among black Africans in metropolitan Natal, according to Mark Orkin, *Disinvestment, The Struggle and the Future: What Black Africans Really Think* (Johannesburg: Ravan Press, 1986). Orkin put the combined black African support in metropolitan Natal for the compatible political visions of Archbishop Desmond Tutu (9 per cent), Nelson Mandela and the ANC (21 per cent), and the UDF and other pro-disinvestment groups (11 per cent) at 41 per cent. Nationally, Orkin established Buthelezi's urban black African support at 8 per cent. In 1986, a survey by the *Sunday Times*, London, 3 August, gave Buthelezi 5 per cent of national urban black African support, against Nelson Mandela's 64 per cent. Buthelezi's extraordinary sensitivity to criticism has been one basis on which some observers and politicians have questioned his political behaviour.

54. In much the same way that the Zimbabwean liberation movements, Zanu and Zapu, were 'delivered' to the Lancaster House conference and kept bound to its provisions in 1979–80. Liberation movement delegates to the Lancaster House conference disclose that their desire to continue to prosecute their war and to bring the Muzorewa–Smith government to the point of collapse was overruled by Front Line States, who in a number of cases cited Western pressure as their reason.

55. Western diplomatic sources, Harare.

56. ANC sources.

57. See the lucid and readable account of the EPG's efforts in *Mission to South Africa: The Commonwealth Report* (Harmondsworth: Penguin, 1986).

58. Front Line State political sources.

59. According to EPG joint chairman and former Australian Prime Minister Malcolm Fraser in conversation with a group of South African businessmen, subsequently quoted to the author.

60. ANC sources.

61. The inaccuracy of these attacks was confirmed to the author by independent observers in the affected areas, among them representatives of the International Committee of the Red Cross and the UN High Com-

missioner for Refugees.

62. ANC sources.
63. It was also distributed in pamphlet form inside South Africa.
64. Between the imposition of the second state of emergency in June 1986 and March 1987, the Detainees' Parents Support Committee estimated that 25 000 people had been detained under the emergency regulations for various periods. See *SA Barometer*, Vol. 1, no. 1. The DPSC also reported in a telephone interview with the author that of a sample of 4160 emergency detainees between June and October 1986 whose organisational affiliation could be established, 53.8 per cent were from the UDF and affiliate organisations, 17 per cent were from COSATU, 1.7 per cent were AZAPO members, and 2.14 per cent were from the CUSA–AZACTU trade unions (since renamed NACTU).
65. ANC sources.
66. National Forum sources, 1973–4. Since then the tensions between the distinctly nationalist and Africanist tendencies, on the one hand, and the strong rhetorical emphasis on socialism by others have continued, resulting in a number of National Forum leaders seeking a closer individual relationship with the UDF.
67. A possible exception is the CUSA–AZACTU trade union grouping, renamed the National Council of Trade Unions (NACTU) in 1987.
68. PAC literature in particular regularly refers to this alleged conspiracy. Mention of it is usually combined with claims that the PAC was responsible for the Soweto uprising of 1976 and the genesis of the 1984 revolt in townships south of Johannesburg. One more recent example of this is the PAC's official organ, *Azania News*, vol. 22, no. 6. Another is a pamphlet 'June 16th Tenth Anniversary: Land Is The Basis For All Economical And Social Changes – There Is No Compromise', distributed in Zimbabwe in 1986.
69. Accounts of the speech given by PAC members present at the consultative conference are that it was grandiose in conception though thin on specifics.
70. The author's opinion is derived from interviews with PAC members.
71. PAC sources.
72. Front Line State official sources, confirmed by PAC sources.
73. The author was among a number of journalists to receive copies of Isaacs' indictment.
74. PAC sources.
75. The explanation of the cause of the fracas comes from PAC sources.
76. PAC sources.
77. Ibid.
78. PAC and ANC sources.
79. ANC and BCMA sources on Mlambo's character. On his past position in the PAC, a PAC press statement, issued in Harare, 16 July 1985, by PAC Administrative Secretary Joe Mkwanazi. (Duplicated copy).
80. PAC sources.
81. Ibid.
82. ANC sources.

83. Whereas the PAC had aligned itself with Zanu, the ANC's alignment had been largely with Zapu.
84. PAC and Zanu (PF) sources.
85. Zanu (PF) sources.
86. The author received a copy of this typed document from PAC sources in early 1987. It is entitled: 'Memorandum. From: The Internal Wing (Movement) of the Pan Africanist Congress of Azania (PAC). To: The External Mission of the Party'. It is dated 16 November 1986. Whatever PAC failings this document enumerates, it does indicate the existence of some PAC underground presence inside the country serious about making some progress.
87. PAC chairman Johnson Mlambo denied the validity of the document in a statement carried by *The Herald*, Harare, 5 February 1987.
88. According to the indictment in the case against Enoch Zulu, he was arrested by South African police in the Bophutatswana bantustan on 10 April 1986.
89. The Zimbabwe government detained several PAC members for a short period to avoid violence. It gave full support in the conflict to Mlambo's leadershp.
90. PAC sources.
91. PAC sources; *The Sunday Star*, Johannesburg, 22 March 1987; *The Sowetan*, Johannesburg, 23 March 1987, in which PAC finance secretary Joe Moabe confirmed the suspension of Muendane and Mofole and Nomodolo's resignation.
92. Ebrahim in a press statement from Dar es Salaam, 23 March 1987, in which he confirmed Moabe's version.
93. PAC and Front Line State official sources.
94. Ebrahim's press statement, 23 March 1987.
95. David Martin and Phyllis Johnson succeed in bringing out some of Zanu's internal difficulties as well as the key factors in its rise in *The Struggle for Zimbabwe* (London: Faber & Faber, 1981).
96. Ibid. The author considers the leadership of Robert Mugabe and Josiah Tongogara to have been particularly noteworthy.
97. Zanu (PF) and ANC sources.
98. ANC sources.
99. Ibid.
100. Ibid.
101. See N. Haysom's *Mabangalala: The Rise of Rightwing Vigilantes in South Africa.* Occasional Paper 10. Centre for Applied Legal Studies, University of the Witwatersrand, Johannesburg, 1986.
102. See *The Star*, Johannesburg, 17 March 1987, for an interesting account of the role of these JMCs.
103. Western diplomatic sources, Harare.
104. Interview with Tambo, Harare, Zimbabwe, 26 September 1987, jointly conducted by journalists Mono Badela, David Niddrie and the author.
105. Proceedings of a conference on 'Regional Security in Southern Africa' in Harare, Zimbabwe, 8–10 June 1987, hosted jointly by the International Institute for Strategic Studies, London, and the University of Zimbabwe's Department of Political and Administrative Studies. See also Howard

Barrell, 'Soviet Policy in Southern Africa', *Work in Progress*, 48, June 1987.

106. Ibid.
107. Interview with Tambo, Harare, 26 September 1987.
108. FLS official sources.
109. Interview with Tambo, Harare, 26 September 1987.
110. See *The Chronicle*, Bulawayo, 15 April 1987, for Kaunda's allegation.
111. The author considers Zambia's degree of political stability to mid-1987 to have been remarkable in view of the serious security and economic problems it has endured through the conduct of five national liberation struggles in the region (Angola, Mozambique, Namibia, South Africa and Zimbabwe).
112. ANC sources.
113. Ibid.
114. Words taken from an ANC song.

3 'The Soldiers of Luthuli': Youth in the Politics of Resistance in South Africa

Shaun Johnson

INTRODUCTION

In the black township of Alexandra in April 1986, an elderly resident stood watching a group of teenagers erect a roadblock of burning tyres at the end of his dirt road. They were attempting to prevent police and army vehicles from entering the township, then in the throes of an uprising. 'This revolution', he said, 'it is a child'.[1]

In the same month, a Johannesburg newspaper editor wrote:

> [Black] South Africa has experienced a cultural revolution, a metamorphosis in values and conventions of the profoundest type . . . Young people have experienced an unprecedented moral ascendancy. They are known universally as 'the youth', the legion of black teenagers who for the last two years have provided the shock troops of a nationwide popular insurrection. This has been a children's war.[2]

These observations reflected one of the most striking features of the rebellion which swept across South Africa from 1984 to 1986 – the centrality of young blacks in extra-parliamentary resistance. Although the uprising involved all sectors of the black community, including the range of mass organisations affiliated to the United Democratic Front (UDF), the trade unions, and myriad local structures (see Chapters 4 and 5), it appeared at times that 'the youth' were both the motor of the rebellion, and its outriders. Loosely referred to as 'the comrades', militant youngsters not only bore the brunt of vicious street fighting against the security forces, but they often directed community resistance. By the time Alexandra erupted, the revolt was so widespread, and the militancy of the youth so unremitting, that many began to believe the collapse of white rule was imminent: freedom lay 'around the corner'.

That this was folly was proved in June 1986 by the most comprehensive government clampdown on extra-parliamentary opposition in South African history. Overt signs of the insurrection (and in particular its youth component), disappeared from view as the state reimposed its control over the townships. Some commentators concluded that the period of youth prominence had been something of an aberration.[3]

I will argue that the importance of the 'youth factor' in resistance has in no way diminished, but that it is changing in nature. The ascendancy of the youth is intertwined with the development of a system of racial capitalism in South Africa, and the changing fortunes of resistance to it. I propose to trace the development of the 'youth component' through this history; the organisational and ideological forms it has taken, and the phases through which it has passed.[4] In examining its strengths and weaknesses, it will be suggested that although the youth movements are beleaguered in 1988 they are on some levels more sophisticated than ever, and will remain at the interface between state power and black aspirations.

But who are 'the youth', and why have they evolved into a distinct category within resistance? Much of the history of black youth activity in South African politics revolves around black schools and universities. Students (or graduates) and pupils have provided much of the impetus and framework for youth activism. As it has developed, however, a far wider range of young people has been embraced: the 'youth component' has sub-components of its own. Its members do not constitute a 'class', but comprise young workers, professionals, students, pupils and unemployed people alike. In its broad sense, the category includes children of pre-school age through to young adults.[5] 'Youth', in this context, refers to an attitude of mind as much as it does to age.[6] It connotes the most energetic, volatile and impatient elements of the black communities.

At a general level, there are several factors which tend to encourage radicalism in 'youth politics'. Colin Bundy has provided a useful overview of theoretical writing on the subject, as well as examples of other societies in which the youth component has played an important role in times of crisis or transition.[7] Principally, he isolates the sociological notion of generational conflict giving rise to a *generational consciousness*.[8] This unifying consciousness can transcend differences of age, class and race, and its growth is likely to be accelerated when a society is in crisis.

In the case of South Africa, black youth – African, Indian and coloured – experience both acute social problems and constant political upheaval:

> [All] the youth share a particular background – subject to political and national oppression and exploitation. This is manifested at all levels of life . . . in the schools, in the factories, and in the townships. [This is] the nature of the society we all live under.[9]

Extreme poverty, little prospect of eventual employment, and an intense politicisation of society provide potent conditions for the growth of a generational consciousness in South Africa. And its translation into action is facilitated by the fact that

> [We] have few economic restrictions. Often [youths] don't have a family to take care of. They have nothing to lose and a future to gain, hence they are always politically active. [And] the youth are at a particular point of human development where they are receptive to ideas . . . This makes us a more conscious sector of the community . . . and more militant . . . The youth can take ideas and exploit them and use them, whatever the implications.[10]

Demographic factors also play a part. Fully half of the South African population is under twenty-one, and more than 40 per cent of Africans are under fifteen, increasing at three times the rate of whites.[11] In arithmetical terms alone, this youth-to-adult ratio raises the potential influence of young blacks. A further special ingredient is black education, which is grossly inferior to that for whites, but which has been expanding rapidly in response to economic and political necessities. Schools have become laboratories and fortresses of resistance, providing raw political education to the pupils passing through them,[12] and deeply influencing the youth outside.

These and other factors combine to mould a distinct if heterogeneous political constituency. Its expansion and entrenchment underpins the laconic comment of the young black activist who said: 'You don't have to shout too loud to get the youth involved in the struggle.'[13] But it is also an admixture, in Bundy's suggestive phrase, of 'precocity and immaturity',[14] releasing the courage and energy of youth, but also its callowness: hence the youth component can have positive and negative effects on the progress of extra-parliamentary resistance.

PART I: THE EMERGENCE OF THE 'YOUTH COMPONENT' OF RESISTANCE

Youth in the development of popular resistance

A discernible 'youth consciousness' within resistance organisations was evident in the 1940s, spearheaded primarily by young university graduates. However, conditions for the political involvement of school-aged youth were also being laid in the sphere of black education during this period.

In the 1920s and 1930s individual 'youthful militants' had a distinct influence on black political and trade union organisation.[15] But an independent, separately organised political voice of black youth first emerged with the formation of the Youth League of the African National Congress (ANCYL) in 1944. The invention, in the main, of graduates of the university of Fort Hare, the ANCYL counted among its founders such resistance luminaries as Nelson Mandela, Oliver Tambo and Anton Lembede, and set about devising its own programme of action and support base.

The younger generation of militants in the ANCYL succeeded in revitalising the almost moribund ANC, injecting a note of impatience and confrontation, and overseeing the installation of sympathetic older leaders in positions of power. Several Youth Leaguers were themselves elected to the national executive. These self-styled representatives of 'South African youth' set the agenda and forced the pace of resistance politics, establishing a niche for the more radical younger generation within the liberation movement. Through the Youth League, younger activists participated in the campaigns of defiance and civil disobedience of the 1950s.

Although the black youth of school-going age had no such unified consciousness or political presence as yet, they were the objects of developing grievances. At the formation in 1912 of the South African Native National Congress (forerunner of the ANC), the education of black children[16] featured prominently in a list of complaints against the government. Again, in the 1944 document *African Claims*, the ANC called for control of African schools to be ceded gradually to the black community, and for eventual compulsory schooling for South Africans of all races. In the same year black parents organised and monitored the first school boycotts in the Transvaal, in protest against the dismissal of teachers who opposed inferior education.[17]

In 1953 the Nationalist government introduced the Bantu Education

Act, which sought to address both a growing economic need for black workers with basic literacy skills, and a concern that 'mission schools' were inculcating in their pupils a desire for equality with whites. Bantu Education was designed to prepare black children for an economically useful role in white South Africa while setting a ceiling on their levels of achievement and aspiration.

The ANC's annual congress of 1953 proposed a boycott of black schools to coincide with the passing of their administration to the government. On 12 April 1955 pupils stayed away from classes in Witwatersrand townships in Benoni, Germiston, Brakpan and Alexandra 'after the ANC Youth League, volunteers and mothers visited the schools'. The boycotts spread to Soweto and beyond, eventually involving as many as 10 000 black children.[18] In May 1955, an 'anti-Bantu Education' campaign was a major component of the ANC's larger 'Resist Apartheid' campaign.

Throughout the first half of the century black education was an element of the evolving policy of segregation in South Africa, and it was taken up by black political leaders within the context of their generalised campaigns of opposition. The politicisation of black schoolchildren and youth by the ANCYL had begun in the 1940s, and was stepped up in the 1950s. An older generation of black youth had staked their claim to political influence through the ANCYL, and all the necessary elements were present for the development of a similar generational consciousness amongst their school-aged counterparts.

With the declaration of South Africa's first State of Emergency,[19] and the banning of the ANC and the breakaway Pan Africanist Congress (PAC) in 1960, a decade of relative black political quiescence descended, in which widespread internal resistance activity all but disappeared. As leaders (notably the erstwhile Youth Leaguers) were jailed and structures decimated, the black majority lapsed into an exhausted political silence. Hopes which had been raised in the 1950s now receded as the government, buoyed up by an economic surge, appeared invincible. Although sporadic protests continued in the schools, many black schoolchildren were brought up in township homes in the 1960s by disillusioned and fatalistic parents, most of whose struggle to support their families left them with little energy or enthusiasm for political activity.

Nevertheless, renewed youth militancy surfaced in the late 1960s, and the impetus came once again from black university students. Under the policy of apartheid, ethnically based universities and colleges had been established to ensure the separation of races at the educational as well as other levels of society. The 'Extension of Universities Act' had in fact closed the doors of the established 'white' tertiary institutions to all but a handful of blacks. The bulk were forced into 'bush colleges', so named by their students because of their geographical locations (many were in rural areas) and the low standard of facilities. Thus marginalised and obviously discriminated against, Africans, Indians and coloureds at these institutions began to revive a spirit of resistance.

Student leaders like Steve Biko laid a tentative framework for organising black youth, utilising the inchoate philosophy of 'Black Consciousness' (BC). This was a different style of politics to the non-racial, inclusive axioms which had informed the campaigns of the ANC and its 'Congress Alliance' in the 1950s. Rather than drawing on the Freedom Charter, Black Consciousness owed much to both the exclusivist 'Africanism' of the PAC and black American Civil Rights leaders. Black Consciousness was essentially a spontaneous philosophy which developed along with the movement itself, and as such, its overarching legacy lies in its regalvanisation of black militancy rather than its specific ideological content.

In 1968 Biko was instrumental in engineering a black breakaway from the predominantly white National Union of South African Students (NUSAS), forming the South African Students' Organisation (SASO). SASO embraced all 'non-white' university students, and preached a credo of black unity, black self-reliance and 'psychological liberation'. The overcoming of feelings of racial inferiority, it was believed, was an essential precursor to contesting for power. Biko and his supporters struck a responsive chord among young black intellectuals, touring the country and popularising their ideas in a journal. They also reintroduced the politics of public protest, illustrated by the 'Viva Frelimo' rallies of 1974 which celebrated the independence of Mozambique and once again conjured up a vision amongst young blacks of eventual political freedom in South Africa.

As with the ANC some twenty years before, organised youth had a catalytic effect on other elements of the black community. A rash of Black Consciousness oriented organisations emerged, notably the Black Peoples' Convention (BPC) in 1972, made up of adult leaders. (It is held by some commentators that members of the ANC operating underground were instrumental in bringing SASO and the BPC together.) There was, however, an important practical difference between the agitation of the Black Consciousness students and their forebears in the ANCYL. The new militants did not have their primary effect on the older generation alone. Their agitation also operated – self-consciously – in the opposite direction. More extensively than ever before, children of school-going age were recognised as a potential political constituency in their own right, and the South African Students' Movement (SASM) was formed in 1972 as a school-based counterpart to SASO.

The number of black schoolchildren in the urban areas had more than doubled in the ten years since 1960 as the demands of industry and commerce for trained labour grew. Schools sprouted in the townships, and the educational boom brought problems of overcrowding, inadequate facilities and impossibly large pupil-teacher ratios. As the black school-going population continued to increase by roughly 100 per cent every five years from 1970 onwards, its potential as a political force grew apace. In the early 1970s, particularly in Soweto, nascent structures emerged in the schools allowing for the election of pupil representatives, and paving the way for the first experiments in united action by the pupils.

The militant proselytising of Biko and his colleagues imbued in their younger counterparts in SASM a sense of rebellion and self-assertion – the beginnings of a generational consciousness. By the early 1970s a new generation of children was beginning to cohere and evolve; to believe in itself and its right and ability to fight for something better, vague as that notion was.

Soweto 1976 and the birth of a new generation

This process culminated in the Soweto uprising of 16 June 1976, which saw the black school-going youth catapult themselves to the forefront of militant opposition to apartheid – over the heads, even, of their mentors in the universities.

The events of 16 June were the unintended result of a series of *ad hoc* decisions made by a very young and patchily organised pupils' movement. The process itself reveals all the elements which contributed to the 'take-off' of the youth factor: principally the growth of a powerful, aggressive, but as yet untested generational consciousness, fuelled by widespread economic and social grievances, and the absence of political channels for its articulation.

It is useful to revisit the experiences of an individual leader of the Soweto march to illustrate the shaping of this first generation of pupil-activists. In 1972 Daniel Montsisi, a thirteen-year-old pupil, joined his local school branch of SASM. His political awareness, like that of his contemporaries, was vague – informed primarily by day-to-day experience of police harrassment in the township. ‘Pass raids’, for example, then still common, made a great impression on black schoolchildren:

> Even at the football fields on Sundays, at the train stations, police would move around in vans and sweep the whole township. Not to mention in town [Johannesburg] – say, at the library – you were always avoiding the police. It was a terrible experience for a youngster. It caused revulsion amongst young people, made them politically conscious, and it made me eager to get involved in these new student organisations.[20]

In the absence of adult-led black resistance, Montsisi’s generation seized on the message of black student leaders at the universities. Impromptu political discussions took place in and out of the schools, the text for debate often being the *SASO Bulletin*, the Black Consciousness journal. In 1974 Montsisi was elected branch president of SASM at Sekano–Ntoane high school in Soweto. The organisation was top-heavy, ‘with leaders more politically advanced than the mass of students’,[21] and membership scattered unevenly around the country. With no historical antecedents, SASM was still feeling its way forward, but it was tapping ‘very strong – if undefined – anti-apartheid sentiments at grassroots level. As we started to mobilise kids, we found that the response was tremendous.’[22]

Pupil leaders themselves received a rapid education in the mechanics of resistance organisation, especially after the state began to show an interest in SASM. Montsisi, already a prominent figure at the age of fifteen, had to go into hiding for the first time:

> Many activists were being detained, and I fled to the Orange Free State. I told my parents I was going to visit my granny. When I came back after a few weeks they told me the police had been looking for me, and I acted shocked. My parents didn’t know the extent to which I was involved.[23]

Youth leaders were, at this early stage, outstripping the older generation in their militancy, and beginning to act independently of them. SASM met with resistance from black teachers. Most teachers supported the conservative, apolitical Students’ Christian Movement (SCM), and were wary of SASM’s fiery lunch-time gatherings in their schools. For a time Montsisi and his vice-president were banned from discussing politics at school, but by 1976 SASM had attracted a sufficient following to defy the authorities. In this ascendant mood, SASM convened a meeting of its general council in May 1976. There the single issue which sparked the June uprising was identified. Sporadic protest boycotts were already occurring in Soweto against the proposed introduction of instruction in Afrikaans as well as English in urban black schools.

The grievance itself was real enough: most of the already pressurised teachers were themselves not proficient in Afrikaans; the language was regarded as a 'symbol of the oppressor'; and English increased the youngsters' (already slim) chances of finding employment. But SASM's decision to take 'some action' against the ruling plumbed a far deeper well of resentment among newly organised black pupils.

At a meeting in a Soweto church hall on 12 June, SASM leaders resolved to organise a protest march. On 15 June, leaders reported back to their members and agreed to march the following day. When some 10 000 pupils took to the streets the next morning, most of them dressed in school uniforms, mass protest was reborn. Had the march passed off peacefully, the children's initiative would have been significant, serving warning that an impatient generation was prepared to 'go it alone' if their parents remained inactive. However, after peripheral exchanges between pupils and security forces, police opened fire on the marchers: one pupil died immediately and several were wounded, leading to uprisings and boycotts as far afield as Cape Town. When the wave of confrontation ended, between 600 and 1000 black people had died, many of them children.

The violence had a great effect on the political consciousness of the SASM leaders and tens of thousands of children who had been drawn willy-nilly into the uprising. According to Montsisi,

> No-one expected the response of the government to be so harsh and brutal. Suddenly we were carrying wounded people, even corpses. There was no time to think; people were doing things they would never have had the courage to do otherwise – they were thrust into a totally new situation which left an impression that will never go away.[24]

Hardly a member of the Soweto community was left untouched by the transition from rhetoric to confrontation. The uprising also shook the white establishment with a vigour not seen since the Sharpeville shootings of 1960. A relatively small section of the black youth of

South Africa, organised as a distinct component of resistance, had almost unwittingly presented a vista of the political potential of the vast pool of angry, politicised young blacks.

SASM leaders now faced the problem of what to do with the militancy they had unleashed. On 2 August Soweto branch leaders decided to form a student council to represent all schools in the township. Tsietsi Mashinini, the principal spokesman of the rebellion, was installed as first president of the 'Soweto Students' Representative Council' (SSRC). Within a month he had been forced to flee South Africa, and by January 1977 Montsisi was at the helm of the new organisation.

There had been total unity among the pupils during the 'anti-Afrikaans' campaign. Lacking a coherent political philosophy or manifesto, the SSRC now needed to provide new forms of action for its agitated, volatile constituency. For the first time, pupil unity began to fray as debates emerged over correct tactics and means of organisational consolidation – although not yet over ideology. The pupils were evolving into a distinctive political movement, with all its attendant complexities.

In 1977 pupils split over whether to write examinations, or boycott them in honour of colleagues who had died or fled into exile. The SSRC thought it safest to let schools decide the issue on an individual basis, and organised a 'ceremonial burning' of Bantu Education textbooks in an attempt to restore unity. Although some scuffles broke out between pro- and anti-boycotters, the SSRC managed to maintain overall cohesion.

By the end of 1976 and early in 1977, organised pupils began to move, unevenly, from purely educational grievances to defining their position in broader resistance to apartheid. Leaders turned their attention to those black workers who were organised, and to the community. The SSRC called, with marked success, on workers to stage a stayaway in solidarity with the pupils. The initiative was particularly significant in the light of clashes which had taken place between the youth and migrant workers during the Soweto uprising. In 1977 Soweto pupils organised a rent boycott as part of a campaign against the Urban Bantu Council (UBC), and successfully canvassed the support of parents. Planned rent increases were dropped after a pupil-led march on Council offices, and the UBC eventually resigned *en bloc*. This paved the way for the formation of the unofficial, highly popular 'Committee of Ten' in Soweto, one of the earliest experiments in black 'alternative government'.

The pupils had thus demonstrated, to themselves as well as their parents, that they could act in a disciplined fashion, applying pressure on behalf of the community. In addition to appeals to workers and parents, hundreds of teachers had been influenced by the pupils' resistance, and resigned in support of their demands for equal education.

During 1976 the state's response to the youth-led uprising had centred on immediate containment. A year later the security police moved to the forefront, seeking to root out student and pupil leaders and ensure that there would be no repetition of the rebellion. Thus Black Consciousness leaders at the universities were detained, and on 10 June 1977, Montsisi and ten other pupil activists were arrested. Biko died in detention on 12 September, and in October all the major Black Consciousness organisations, including SASO and SASM, were banned. Black children were back at school, and the momentum of the youth-led revival of resistance was, quite literally, arrested.

After spending more than a year in solitary confinement, Montsisi and his colleagues were charged in September 1978, and convicted of 'Sedition' and 'Terrorism' after a trial lasting some nine months. In May 1979 Montsisi was sentenced to eight years on Robben Island, four of which were suspended.

What happened to Montsisi in his teenage years is an illustration, extreme but valid, of how many thousands of black children – an entire generation – received the rudiments of a political education in the 1970s. Generational consciousness was beginning to take on organisational forms, and black adults would have to redefine their own actions in terms of this new reality. The youth had proved that direct, mass resistance was possible, but had also learned that the state had the capacity to put down sporadic, isolated rebellions. The first divisions within organised youth had surfaced. The spasm of defiance had highlighted the need for more than just militancy in youth organisation: strategies, tactics, ideologies and alliances would have to follow.

Black Consciousness, COSAS, and the rediscovery of the past

SASO, SASM and the SSRC[25] were no more by the end of 1977. The principal leaders were either in jail, in exile, or dead. The way was clear for the establishment of new movements drawing on the experiences of 1976. An immediate task would be the construction of a unifying ideology.

The basic ideas and slogans of Black Consciousness had been popular in the Soweto uprising. After the dust had settled, debates began over the significance of this Black Consciousness influence for the ANC and the 'Congress tradition' which, some felt, had been eclipsed.[26] It was an important period of reflection, for any new manifestations of youth organisation would have to set down ideological markers. While there were important similarities between the rhetoric of Black Consciousness ideologues and earlier 'Africanist' leaders, this had not indicated a rejection of the ANC by the pupils of 1967–77. Indeed, in so far as the children of Soweto had been aware of the history of black resistance, the names of Luthuli and Mandela of the ANC were invoked along with those of Sobukwe of the PAC and Lembede, one of the spiritual 'fathers' of Africanism.[27] More importantly, the children were adamant that the resurgence of militancy was of their own making, and not engineered by the liberation movement in exile. Mashinini made this plain in 1976, and Montsisi expressed incredulity at the fact, that during his detention and interrogation in 1977,

> the security police were convinced that the students had been working with the ANC, that it could not have been a student initiative. They couldn't conceive of pupils planning and executing a demonstration on their own. To them it had to have come from radicals and communists outside the country.[28]

In fact, because of the generalised political inertia of the 1960s, it is unlikely that many of the children were even aware of the specific contents of the ANC's 'Freedom Charter'; still less the dissenting pronouncements of the PAC. The uprising had been spontaneous – a product of historical conditions, certainly – but not orchestrated. Conditions were now ripe for youth leaders to delve systematically into the history of South African resistance and to define themselves in terms of it.

As relative calm reasserted itself in the townships by 1978, two divergent ideological tendencies began to take shape in black politics (see Chapter 5). Crudely put, these were to divide between those who sought to take resistance forward under a reconstructed Black Consciousness banner, and those who moved toward the politics of a broad, inclusive anti-apartheid Front reminiscent of the 1950s – the (Freedom) 'Charterists'. New forms of youth organisation reflected these divisions.

The Azanian Peoples' Organisation (AZAPO) was formed in 1978 as a successor to the proscribed Black Consciousness structures, espousing and attempting to develop the Black Consciousness philosophy. It launched a student wing, the Azanian Students' Organisation (AZASO), made up of university students. AZAPO and AZASO were stepping into a new organisational vacuum in the townships, and there was at this stage no obvious conflict between the new groups and the ANC tradition. Much energy was consumed in the new youth movement in ideological debate as leaders sought to extract and codify a political philosophy from the short history of Black Consciousness. In particular, they began to address the question of socialism in a future South Africa, as well as the role of 'sympathetic whites' in the black liberation struggle.

At about the same time, a process of reclaiming and repopularising the history of the ANC, always latent in the townships, gathered pace – spurred on by young blacks (see Chapter 5). In 1979 the Congress of South African Students (COSAS) was launched, aiming to draw black pupils into a national structure. Although COSAS' conveners were products of the Black Consciousness period, the organisation was crucially different from any youth groups of the past ten years. In styling itself a 'Congress', it was self-consciously identifying itself with the Congress tradition, and it looked for political guidance not to the recent past, but fully a quarter of a century back. COSAS was the first mass organisation since the crushing of internal resistance to embrace the Freedom Charter of 1955. The guiding principle of the new organisation was that the ANC was the 'authentic liberation movement' of South Africa, and that the youth militants should plan their future activities as a continuation of that tradition.

There followed an extraordinarily pervasive reintroduction of ANC history and symbols into black community life, and it had a profound effect on numbers of post-Soweto youth militants. The Freedom Charter, then still a proscribed document (it was 'unbanned' in 1984), provided the focus for countless informal meetings and discussions around the country. A nationwide 'Free Mandela' campaign, aggressively promoted by COSAS in 1980, contributed to the saturation of some townships with the iconography of the ANC. The ANC itself stepped up its guerrilla campaign, receiving massive publicity after the bombing of the strategic SASOL oil-from-coal refinery in July 1980. A popular song implied the extent to which apparently substantial numbers of youths seemed to revel in the escalation of ANC sabotage activity:

> There is Sasolburg / The Supreme Court / Warmbaths /
> Koeberg / Pitoli going up in flames

We are going there, the Umkhonto boys have arrived
We are going there, Hayi, Hayi, We are going forward
Don't be worried, the boys know their job
Let Afrika return![29]

The growth of Freedom Charterism in youth politics received another decisive fillip, ironically, when the state sent numbers of young activists to Robben Island, thereby providing a direct link between the new generation and leaders of the liberation movement who had been jailed before the youngsters were born. Montsisi's experience is once again representative of a wide-ranging phenomenon:

> The Island was a political education for me. Firstly, we developed a deep comradeship through discussion with the older leaders, and a deep respect. Before I went to the Island my understanding of the Freedom Charter was not thorough. There I had the time to look back at history . . . It was like putting together pieces of a jigsaw puzzle which had been missing all along. We delved into our history. We discovered that we young people were not the first to take up the fight against apartheid, but a new part of a developing process.[30]

The re-entry of these 'veterans' of both Soweto and Robben Island into youth politics had an inestimable effect on the sophistication and credibility of the new organisation. COSAS soon overshadowed other youth groups. It allowed for pivotal student involvement in initiatives like the Anti-Republic Day protests of 1981, and in a variety of consumer boycotts, rent strikes, and solidarity action with trade unions.[31] Its formation, according to Montsisi, signalled 'the rebirth of progressive politics in South Africa. Before that people spoke about the Charter, about Mandela, in whispers. COSAS paved the way for a new phase of resistance politics, in which the youth would have a much higher level of political consciousness than ever before.'[32]

These new youth structures were developing against a background of greatly heightened extra-parliamentary activity. In 1978 and 1979 black schooling had proceeded with few disturbances, although the absence of boycotts in no way suggested a depoliticisation of the pupils. Indeed, in 1980 black schools were once again in turmoil. On this occasion a boycott in coloured schools in the Western Cape spread to Indian and African areas. As Bundy has noted, the general political maturation which had occurred in the years since 1976 was reflected in the 1980 boycotts which 'In some respects . . . looked like an action replay of Soweto. But there were significant differences. Hundreds of black teachers came out in public and organized support of the boycotts . . . Youth demands were integrated more explicitly with the broader political fight.[33]

Many people died in the course of the boycotts, and there were frequent clashes with security forces before the stayaways could no longer be sustained and the classrooms were refilled. Finnegan's account of the period, based on his experience as a teacher on the Cape Flats, indicates the extent to which pupil leaders were attempting to present their educational struggle as an integral part of resistance.[34] The militancy of 1976 was replicated, but the widespread political 'awareness' sessions held in place of regular lessons indicated a deeper grasp of and concern with political ideology and strategies.

While direct action in the schools was being revived at the beginning of the 1980s, youth activists were hardening in their loyalties to either the Charterist or Black Consciousness approaches. At an AZASO conference held at Wilgespruit in 1981 these differences surfaced publicly within the organisation. A majority of Charterist delegates defeated Black Consciousness aligned leaders, committing the organisation to the Freedom Charter and co-operation with COSAS, and confirming the dominance of 'united front', non-racial politics among organised youth. In the following year most black pupils were back behind their desks, but political activity proceeded at a furious pace. Localised 'student congresses', loyal to COSAS, emerged in many townships, providing a sub-structure for the national pupils' organisation. The now buoyant COSAS convened a national conference in 1982 which assessed the gains made by pupil and student structures since 1976, and looked for ways of increasing the influence of youngsters in the revitalised resistance scenario.

Here, for the first time, school based activists pinpointed the need to cast a wider net in recruiting and channelling youth cadres. Citing the history of the ANC Youth League,

> COSAS leaders noted that many activists who had operated from the schools had dropped out either because of financial pressure, or hostility from the school authorities and the state. At the same time, over the years, many COSAS activists had completed school and were left with no organisational base in the community. Then there were the unemployed youths, as well as young workers, young married couples . . . people who shared the interests and aspirations of COSAS but could not belong to it.[35]

The formation of 'youth' structures was thus mooted to accommodate this more broadly defined category of young people. COSAS members would be free to participate in the new organisations, which would work in close co-operation with the educationally based structures. It was left up to individual townships and regions to establish their own 'youth congresses' as they deemed appropriate, but it was clear that the political cynosure would be the Freedom Charter.

The idea took off unevenly but quickly, and soon many townships had structures catering for 'students' and 'youth'. The mushrooming of youth organisation coincided with, and to an extent provided the impetus for, the rapid growth of like-minded community organisations catering for a range of interests, including civic associations, trade unions, church and women's groups, sports clubs and professional bodies.[36] In 1983 these structures came together in the broad-based umbrella resistance movement of the 'United Democratic Front'. Black Consciousness and left-wing groups opposed to the Front coalesced in the National Forum. As one commentator has noted:

> The formation of the UDF and National Forum marked a turning point in the political complexion of popular opposition. These popular organizations rode the crest of a groundswell of localized agitation. They represented a new correlation of social forces that had grown up in the townships. The inability or unwillingness of the white minority regime to fundamentally address the visible grievances that had sparked the Soweto uprising alienated and angered growing numbers of township residents.[37]

Against this background of militancy, the ideological divergences which had been gestating since the revival of extra-parliamentary resistance were codified and given organisational trademarks. The youth adherents of both movements would now be clearly allied to national organisational superstructures which, although they shared the aim of fundamentally transforming South African society, embraced different visions and tactics.

Youth in the UDF and National Forum

On its formation in August 1983, the UDF comprised several hundred affiliate groups. The bulk of these were student and youth organisations.

COSAS catered for black school-goers; the now Charterist AZASO organised black students at tertiary level, while 'progressive' whites worked with them through the National Union of South African Students (NUSAS). The youth congresses completed the web of Charterist youth structures which now spanned South Africa.

The structure of the UDF lent itself to decentralisation and encouraged localised initiatives. The national leadership established some regional youth portfolios, youth officers being charged with overall 'coordination' of the youth constituency, but in practice this only extended to occasional statements of broad policy and the facilitation of contact between youth groups from different areas. Thus a central reference point was created, but in fact the hundreds of thousands of politicised young blacks created a momentum of their own, and the formation of a youth or student congress in one township would spark another nearby in a roller-coaster effect.

On an ideological level, the UDF's approach was clearly dominant in the townships soon after its formation. Young blacks were drawn by both the weight of the ANC tradition and the obvious vitality of UDF-affiliated youth groups in their own areas. The presence of many former Black Consciousness figures in leadership positions in the UDF youth structures encouraged further support, and provided an historical explanation for the transition to the Charterist camp. The former SASM leader Montsisi was one example. On his release from Robben Island he joined SOYCO, and was soon elected to the youth portfolio on the UDF's national executive. With his resistance 'credentials', he was in a strong position to articulate the Charterist attitude toward their Black Consciousness rivals; essentially acknowledging that Black Consciousness had been an 'important phase' in the rekindling of resistance, but insisting that it had outgrown its usefulness and was now anachronistic and divisive:

> BC [Black Consciousness] refracted conditions at a particular time. The formation of the UDF marked a new era in resistance, and those of us who had analysed our history after our important but highly unco-ordinated actions in 1976, realised that it was a logical progression for BC to lead into the progressive movement. The problem is that some activists of the 1976 era regarded BC as the exclusive possession of a particular political faction, essentially in opposition to the authentic peoples' movement. In 1976 there was no sense amongst us of being in competition with that movement.

> Unfortunately some people still say: we are the political organisation, we have the particular leadership and programmes, we have a particular flag and so on.[38]

Those groups which did not make the 'transition' and came together in the National Forum, included several youth structures. The largest was the Azanian Students' Movement (AZASM). Following the Charterist takeover of AZASO in 1981, Black Consciousness diehards, angry at having been pushed into the political background by the phenomenal growth of UDF student and youth congresses, set out to make a comeback. 'Black consciousness faithfuls found themselves politically homeless', the Black Consciousness publication *Awake Black Student* announced, 'after the up to then BC AZASO abandoned the BC ideology for something "more contemporary" [the Freedom Charter]':

> This act constituted an inexcusable abrogation of responsibility to the legacy of SASO. The BC faithfuls began anew, to organize themselves as Black students, because of their unique position in relation to the historically evolved social and national peculiarities of the Black people in this country.[39]

Thus AZASM was launched in the Transvaal in July 1983. Its areas of relative strength lay in the Western Cape, parts of the Eastern Cape, the Orange Free State and the Transvaal. AZASM saw 'BC [as] the unquestionable ideology that will usher the Black oppressed masses into the new envisioned order',[40] and angrily rejected the 'broad front' approach of UDF structures. Black Consciousness was itself changing from its early constructions, moving away from the stress on 'psychological liberation' and beginning to impose, somewhat unevenly, a socialist timbre on to its ideology. The rump of Black Consciousness adherents operated in AZAPO and AZASM, styling themselves 'anti-racist' as opposed to 'non-racial', and excluding whites from membership 'at this stage of the struggle'.

The injection of an element of socialism into the new Black Consciousness facilitated the National Forum alliance with left-wing groups opposed to the Charterists. These groups, strongest in the Western Cape, drew on traditions of 'non-collaborationism' and 'anti-liberalism'. The Forum – more of an annual 'platform' than a structured national organisation – brought a range of groups, including youth and student structures, under the ideological roof of the 'Azanian Peoples' Manifesto' of 1983, an alternative to the Freedom Charter.

AZASM entered into a fraternal relationship with small, left-wing, largely coloured-based youth groups such as the Students of Young Azania (SOYA) in the Cape, and Action Youth in the Transvaal. A further political tendency was represented by the Azanian National Youth Unity (AZANYU), whose ideology was most reminiscent of the Africanism of the PAC.

Critics of the Forum-aligned youth movements pointed to the 'intellectualism' of their approach, their emphasis on ideological debate rather than confrontation with the state, and their lack of a 'mass base'. Forum leaders responded by attacking the 'populist' strategies of the UDF groups, warning against 'politicisation by slogans' which would create thousands of politically unsophisticated youngsters, and challenging the 'sacrosanct' position of the ANC. Forum youth leaders took a 'long view' of the struggle against apartheid, committing themselves to political education 'at grassroots level' in preparation for some point in the future when 'objective conditions' would favour decisive action.[41] The period 1983–84 was a critical time of expansion and preparation for the youth movements, particularly those aligned with the UDF. On one level, the youth component of resistance made tremendous organisational strides, translating a spreading militant generational consciousness into structures – however rudimentary – in schools and townships throughout South Africa. The youth were poised to play a political role far surpassing that of 1976. On another level, however, the organisational expansion marked the formalisation of differing and potentially hostile political tendencies within that youth component. Further, although the youth structures proclaimed loyalty to national superstructures, the mechanics of such alliances had yet to be tested, particularly regarding the question of ultimate authority and accountability within the resistance movements.

PART II: THE 'YOUTH REVOLT' OF THE 1980s

Schools, comrades, and the 'insurrection'

An unprecedented popular rebellion against the South African state began in the second half of 1984, and it took on a variety of forms. Its outstanding feature, however, was the prominence of the separately organised black youth, both in reactive campaigns against government initiatives such as the tricameral parliament, and in enactive campaigns to establish popular, alternative structures of control over township life.

The onrush of internal militancy came despite the signing of the 'Nkomati Accord on Non-Aggression and Good Neighbourliness'[42] between South Africa and Mozambique in March 1984. Many commentators believed that Pretoria's success in forcing Maputo to deny sanctuary to the ANC would halt the dual growth of ANC popularity and 'revolutionary consciousness' in the townships. In fact, the militant youth interpreted the pact as a challenge to intensify their own efforts while the ANC adapted to the setback. A township song reflected the youths' acceptance of this responsibility – to the extent, even, of implying that they could themselves deliver 'liberation' to the banned movement:

> When there's roll-call of our heroes,
> I wonder if my name will be on that roll,
> I wonder what it will be like
> When we sit with Tambo
> And *tell him* about the fall of the Boers.[43] (Emphasis added.)

In those days of 'insurrectionary' politics, in addition to leaders in their teens and early twenties and thirties having graduated as political veterans, the deep-seated spirit of militancy had seeped down to much younger children. This was expedited by the conditions of 'civil war' which enveloped many townships. Senior youth leaders noted the phenomenon:

> The militancy was more intense [by 1984] than it had ever been. The four or five year-old playing on the streets of Soweto played games involving the struggle, singing about Mandela, about Tambo, chanting slogans. They were coming up to imitate their brothers and sisters, being politicised by the situation itself. I would ask them – these very young fellows – what is the struggle?, and they would say the struggle *ke ntwa*! The struggle is fighting! It is shocking the extent to which children turned into daredevils. Soldier meant only teargas to them, policeman only enemy target. There was such a great contrast with the young whites, still playing with toys and pestering their mothers for popcorn and ice-cream.[44]

The spark which lit the insurrectionary fires in 1984 came, as in 1976, from the black schools. In 1983 and 1984 COSAS had evolved a composite strategy of educational and political demands. The former were to be enshrined in the 'Education Charter' campaign, in which pupils would be canvassed for their vision of an equitable system of education. The latter were integrated with the demands of other sectors of resistance. COSAS president Lulu Johnson made this explicit: 'Before they are students', he said, 'students are members of their communities. The schools and the community are inseparable.'[45] The implication that educational reform – however radical – would not suffice without fundamental change in the society, represented a qualitative shift in the nature of the school-based youths' consciousness. According to a Cape educationist and National Forum political activist:

> The Education Charter became a national campaign . . . linking activities all across the country and vastly improving the level and quality of organisation. It was picked up and improved upon by other youth organisations and acted as a catalyst. This, together with the increasingly direct political demands of the youth groups, put the government in trouble both in the medium- and long-term because it faced a new generation of schooled youth, youth almost immune to suggestions of collaborationist politics with the government. A few years ago [in 1976] they might have been satisfied if a few concessions were made. Now they were talking about a total reorganisation, not only of education, but a transformation of society.[46]

As early as January 1984, high school pupils in the township of Atteridgeville near Pretoria staged a boycott under the banner of COSAS, in which they focused on educational grievances such as the excessive use of corporal punishment and the sexual harassment of schoolgirls by teachers.

With more than a million African children now undergoing secondary schooling (compared to less than 50 000 in 1960),[47] facilities were hopelessly inadequate and achievement ratios in rapid decline – and this despite increasing government expenditure.[48] Six Atteridgeville high schools were eventually closed by the authorities in 1984. This was the first manifestation of the mood of confrontationism which bubbled close to the surface in hundreds of African, coloured and, to a lesser extent, Indian schools. By May, more than 200 000 pupils were 'on boycott' in support of a COSAS campaign which now included demands for, among other things, democratically elected student representative councils, and an end to 'politically motivated' expulsions of pupils and teachers. More Transvaal schools became embroiled, and the boycotts spread to townships in the Eastern Cape.

Meanwhile, protests against elections for the coloured and Indian houses in the new tricameral parliament had drawn in hundreds of thousands of township dwellers, young and old, and clashes with the police were frequent. A marked economic downturn had increased material hardship; strike activity had escalated, and the government found it increasingly difficult to administer the townships through their black proxies, the Community Councillors. Youth leaders and their organisations played prominent roles in a variety of non-educational campaigns, and commentators began to recognise their influence in activism *beyond* the schoolyards.[49] By the end of 1984, it was estimated, close to a million black pupils and students had taken part in mass protest action.[50] These vast numbers were a source of encouragement to UDF and other national leaders, but also some cause for concern: while the school-aged youth were increasingly influencing broad resistance activity in the townships, the adults had little if any say over actions in the schools.

When South African Defence Force (SADF) troops were ordered into Sebokeng township in the Vaal Triangle in October 1984, the incipient signs of civil war became reality. In the ensuing months, hundreds died or were injured in clashes with police and soldiers, and thousands of young blacks – exhibiting extraordinary courage – began to employ 'guerrilla-style' tactics, improvising petrol bombs, ambushes and roadblocks, and learning to communicate and convene meetings clandestinely.[51] Besides bullets, teargas and whips, many youth leaders experienced police detention for the first time.

While the street battles, by their very nature, involved the youth in increasingly unco-ordinated, uncontrolled and localised activities, some leaders recognised the need for support from other sectors of resistance. At the instigation of COSAS and some youth congresses (the fruits of calls for broad-based youth organisation), [52] a highly successful two-day stayaway was organised in the Transvaal in co-operation with trade union and community groups. In pamphlets COSAS told workers 'Our struggle in the schools is your struggle in the factories. We fight the same bosses' government, we fight the same enemy.'[53] The seeds of a coalition between COSAS, UDF-aligned community groups and the trade unions were sown at this time.[54]

Black schooling resumed in 1985 with the momentum of the rebellion unchecked and the demands of the youth unchanged. In March the government implicitly recognised the power of the schoolchildren by declaring the propagation of boycotts illegal. It was too late to reverse the trend: boycotts flared in hundreds of schools as the rebellion took on new forms and spread to new areas. By July the government was forced to declare a State of Emergency in thirty-six magisterial districts. It failed to restore order in the now chaotic black educational system: indeed, a boycott of secondary schools in the townships surrounding Cape Town began on 29 July. Less than a month after the imposition of the Emergency, the government banned COSAS outright – the first proscription of an organisation since October 1977. At the time of the banning, journalists estimated that the organisation represented more than half of the six million black students in the country.[55] The closure of 'affected' schools continued, notably in the Western Cape, where 464 schools shut in September following a spate of boycotts and public rallies.[56] 'The entire educational framework for coloureds was shut down in an attempt to deny pupils their classrooms and school grounds as rallying points and organisational bases.'[57]

The state's attempts to 'depoliticise' the schools took different forms according to local conditions. In Soweto, pupils were herded back to school at gunpoint. In the Eastern Cape *dorp* of Graaff Reinet, police extracted lists of boycotting pupils from black principals, and drove them – in police vehicles – from their homes back to school. A strict curfew was imposed on the township's children. In August, police and SADF soldiers corralled some 800 schoolchildren in a Soweto police station in an effort to dissuade them from boycotting. About half of those arrested were under the age of thirteen, and several were as young as eight.[58]

Black schools remained profoundly unsettled throughout 1985, and in many areas education broke down totally.[59] Among other effects, this added tens of thousands to the ranks of full-time juvenile and adolescent activists whose sole activities were in pursuance of the 'struggle'. 'Liberation before Education' became the clarion call for these inveterate boycotters, and pamphlets appeared proclaiming 1986 as 'The Year Of No School'.

A breakdown of those detained 'highlighted the youthfulness of the most dedicated participants in the revolt.'[60] Even before the Emergency, students had made up the largest category of detainees held under the Internal Security Act. But in the short weeks between the declaration of the Emergency and the banning of COSAS, a further 500 members of the organisation were arrested. It was estimated that two-thirds of the more than 2000 people arrested between July and late August were children under the age of eighteen, the majority being either COSAS members or UDF student and youth congress cadres. Senior police officials warned they 'would not rest' until remaining members of COSAS were rounded up, blaming them for fomenting continuing 'unrest, boycotts and violence' from underground.[61] Pupil leaders still at large announced their intention to continue their agitation, and a range of new organisations and committees sprang up almost immediately to replace COSAS. Said Jabu Khumalo, the Congress' last administrative secretary:

> [The government] is repeating the very same mistake they made when they banned organisations in 1960 and 1977. They thought people would stop organising. But this is not 1960. It is 1985 . . . They can only really ban the name of the organisation. COSAS is the students and the students are COSAS . . . I don't want to say that we will defy the ban. But students are going to carry on doing and saying the same things.[62]

Despite this defiance, the changed conditions had a profound effect on the matrix of organisational structures and their attempts to channel youth resistance. As one analyst has noted,

> intensified repression . . . generated a shift in the co-ordinates of the popular struggle. The mass detentions, killings and the numbers forced underground deprived many organisations of their leadership and severed the ties that had linked political groups in a loose but coherent organisational network.[63]

Youth groups found the relative freedom of organisation they had enjoyed, substantially eroded. Strictly democratic internal procedures had become an article of faith for the majority of youth organisations, and were largely adhered to. But now, regular open meetings, elections, report-backs, codes of discipline and the like were seen by many to be an 'unaffordable luxury' in circumstances of blatant repression.[64] Campaigns were decided upon by leadership coteries, and 'instructions' were delivered by couriers rather than debated and endorsed in meetings. Where contact within and between the student and youth congresses continued, it was restricted to secretive communication between leaders. The exigencies of the Emergency dislocated large numbers of excited, angry youth activists from their leaders and from a necessary process of political education and development.[65]

In addition, the growth of direct, responsible alliances with other community groups – a process seen by many leaders as essential in keeping the youth militants under the broad discipline of the resistance movements – was stunted. The state offensive led to accentuated regional differences and a loss of overall co-ordination within the popular movements. The vigour of the youth was undiluted, but while some campaigns bore the hallmarks of careful planning and strategic vision, a growing number were ill-considered and poorly canvassed. The inherent dichotomy of the youth component of resistance – precocity and immaturity – lay exposed.

In this atmosphere in 1985 the phenomenon of 'the comrades' gained common currency. A generic, ill-defined term, it came to be used to refer to practically any black youngsters engaged in resistance. The term was commonly used in both the student and youth congresses, whose members addressed each other as 'comrade', by which they meant 'friend in the struggle'. In the same way that youth activists were sometimes referred to as 'young lions', 'the comrades' became a catch-all phrase for young militants who were

> at the forefront of the confrontation between the state and the people . . . on the education front and in community campaigns . . . for planning and execution it was the young people who put up posters, organized meetings, went from house to house. In the formation of street committees, defence committees, they were in the forefront and most visible. They were also the first to be detained, the first to be shot.[66]

Increasingly, it was only the 'daredevil' comrades who continued to engage in overt resistance, regardless of the risks. As a result, some came to regard themselves alone as 'leaders of the struggle'.[67] In consumer boycotts (a preferred method of community campaigning under Emergency conditions), many over-zealous or undisciplined 'comrades' took it upon themselves to enforce compliance by brutal means.[68] This earned them the derogatory title *abosiyayinyova*, or thuggish, lawless youths. In addition, gangs of apolitical *tsotsis* (hoodlums) exploited the political legitimacy of the comrades by extorting money from township residents, ostensibly for political campaigns, but in fact for their own enrichment. Dubbed the *com-tsotsis*, they damaged the inchoate relationship of trust and mutual respect which had been nurtured between the youth and adults.

The state and its allies in the black communities promoted this image of the comrades, aided by the emergence of perhaps the most gruesome invention of the South African conflict – the 'necklace'. Soon after twenty-one mourners were shot dead by police while walking to a funeral in the Eastern Cape township of Langa in March 1985, a Community Councillor was assassinated by the 'necklace' method: the placing of a rubber tyre, filled with petrol, around a victim's neck before setting it alight. The 'comrades' and the 'necklace' came to be regarded as synonymous in many quarters. Speculation grew – and not only in government circles – that elements of the new generation of youth activists were out of control.

As consumer boycotts and stayaways spread, so reports of 'comrades' excesses' became more frequent in the turmoil of 1985 and early 1986. Although the incidents were isolated and certainly did not reflect the activities of the vast majority of organised youth, many black adults were alienated by what they saw as the unbridled power of the youth in township life. These older township residents faced a dilemma. They had come around to supporting youth activism, but objected to some of its manifestations. The attitude of Linda Twala, a popular figure in Alexandra, reflected this succinctly when speaking to the author in May 1986:

> These kids have changed many things, the truth is that. Like now we are not going to carry the *dompas* – it is because of the children. But there are some things I don't like. A child is a child. I am an elderly person. Children are right to battle for freedom, but they must respect older people. People's courts are not the right way. Children can't discuss their fathers' problems. These comrades, they need us too. We will pay if we misdirect them now.

The brief ascendancy of 'peoples' courts' was crucial in this process. Conceived as an alternative form of judicial dispensation, they were a further attempt to seize control of township life from the state. In theory, street committees would elect representatives to a local 'peoples' court', which would pass judgement on issues ranging from the ownership of a puppy, to marital disputes and political offences. Necessarily held in secret (and self-evidently illegal), the courts were shrouded in controversy. Supporters emphasised the 'rehabilitative' approach of the 'judges', drawn as they were from the local community rather than the white establishment. Opponents pointed to the courts' arbitrary nature and susceptibility to abuse, dubbing them 'kangaroo courts' and accusing some 'magistrates' of passing the death sentence on alleged informers, or *impimpis*.

Other phenomena called attention to widespread psychological brutalisation among the youth. In urban townships in particular, even that degree of 'normal' family life which had been possible in a situation of dire poverty and exploitation, was further pressurised. It was not uncommon for child activists to live in bands without adult supervision, substituting the security of political hierarchies for those of the family.[69] Still others became 'street children', turning to glue sniffing and other forms of drug taking, promiscuity and indolence.[70] According to one clinical psychologist and political activist, there was

> very little normality in the lives of politicized children. No good familial relationships, no normal schooling, no integrated existence. Norm restraints were non-existent. There is a very short gap between being the victim of brutality, and beginning to commit it oneself. Distinctions between right and wrong, killing and not killing, attacking and defending, become blurred . . . Personalities begin to fracture.[71]

This process reached a peak in August and September 1985 amid countless allegations of police brutality against black children and township residents. For those removed from the mayhem of the townships to the isolation of the cells, the psychological effects were equally direct. Allegations persisted that school-age detainees were being held in solitary confinement for lengthy periods, interrogated in the absence of lawyers, and even tortured. The security police, it was held, sought thus to break the grip of student and youth groups in the townships; to scare activists into deserting their organisations, perhaps even becoming informers; and to extract intelligence about the mechanics of youth activism and its links with other resistance forces.[72] The Detainees Parents' Support Committee, an organisation which monitors detentions and provides assistance to detainees' families, claimed that only a small minority of the child prisoners were involved in youth organisation at leadership level.[73]

Systematic brutalisation fed yet another debilitating trend: for the first time, violent clashes began to occur between the overwhelmingly dominant Charterist youth groups and those in the National Forum camp.[74] Although it was contended that such internecine violence was orchestrated by *agents provocateurs*, much of it was clearly spontaneous, thus enabling the state to promote an image of what it termed 'black-on-black' violence in the townships.

In spite of these grave problems, the youth movements were buoyant in terms of numbers and morale at the end of 1985. Almost six months of Emergency rule had failed to stamp out the popular uprising, and diverse youth organisations embracing school-goers, university and college students[75] and the township youth in general, survived. But it seemed the influence of the organisational structures and leaders had been outstripped in many areas by an undirected, often suicidal, street militancy. This was predicated upon a simple belief: that the Emergency proved the state to be losing control, and that wave upon wave of street revolt would cause it to topple. Arguably for the first time in South African history, vast numbers of young blacks believed that 'liberation' was imminent. This faith was typified by a young (female) activist on the East Rand, who said: 'Mandela told us many years ago it was no easy walk to freedom. But now we are there. Freedom lies only months away.'[76] Township 'freedom songs', one of the most potent and pervasive forms of whipping up support and politicising the youth, reflected this apocalyptic belief. At a meeting of the Alexandra Youth Congress (AYCO), leaders sang:

Do not believe them when they say it is far
It is coming today, it is coming tomorrow
This drought will be broken
For us it will be that the rains have come
Do not believe them when they say
We do not know why we are dancing[77]

AYCO members responded: 'Botha, will you fight for it? We will fight for it!' There was now no hesitation among many activists in proclaiming allegiance to the leaders of the banned ANC, and even to its military wing. At a funeral for victims of police shootings held in the African township of Guguletu near Cape Town on 7 September 1985, 'Banners and slogans openly implored the ANC to supply weapons to the townships. "Tambo, we are ready", one banner said. "Give us AKs".'[78] For the first time, police acknowledged that they were frequently coming under fire in the townships. The notion of a decisive, armed uprising was taken seriously by many youngsters. Triumphalism was in the air. One 'freedom song' ended with the words:

We're going to take over, take over
take our country in the Mugabe way
Run away, run away, Botha
Umkhonto has arrived
We are the soldiers of Luthuli,
Led by Mandela,
Even if it is bad we are going
move aside and give us way[79]

Although cautionary notes were sounded by senior youth leaders, the mood of the rank and file was infectious. Adults noted it with a mixture of awe and trepidation. The *Sowetan* newspaper commented:

> Let there be no illusions about this: the youths in the townships are in an unstoppable mood of anger and have seeming disregard for their lives . . . most parents and a number of very respectable leaders are aware that they have lost control of the anger expressed by township children.[80]

Archbishop Desmond Tutu highlighted the strain of martyrdom which was running deep among the youth, saying 'We've got a new breed of children. They believe that they are going to die . . . and the frightening thing is that they actually don't care.'[81] This was even reflected in the *noms de guerre* which became fashionable among young comrades. In one striking instance a boy aged about fourteen, active in the youth congress of the Crossroads squatter complex in the Cape, styled himself 'Comrade I-will-Die'. He explained: 'It means I am a brave comrade. I am brave in the struggle. I fight for our people. I say I-Will-Die-We-Will-Live. There are many of us and we want to fight for freedom, and some we die, but we know the people will live. This apartheid it is going.[82]

The 'rebel' Afrikaner priest Nico Smit, ministering in one of the flashpoint Pretoria townships, warned an audience of whites that what had evolved was nothing less than

> a youth revolution . . . a civil war in the townships with soldiers patrolling the streets while young people control the community . . . The elderly people may be confused, but the youngsters know what they want: liberation has entered their minds and they are obsessed to be liberated. They will die for it if they must.[83]

In the fervour of the rebellion, the notion of 'liberation' itself was very imprecise, and demanded little political rigour from its champions. In so far as the 'street warriors' articulated it, their rhetoric increasingly included denunciations of 'capitalism' and 'imperialism' along with 'apartheid'. But it was usually enough, in activists' argot, to denounce 'the system', an 'almost infinitely malleable term that was at once a sneering epithet and a catchall phrase referring to white authority and all its offshoots.'[84]

In many townships, comrades spoke of 'liberated zones'; areas in which official administration had broken down and, they believed, the security forces could never again assert the authority of the state.[85] As an outward sign of this usurpation of power, comrades began to construct 'peoples' parks'. Reclaiming waste sites in the ghettoes, they planted grass and flower-beds, fashioning 'sculptures', benches, fences and goal-posts from wrecked cars and township flotsam. Each park was given a name, prominently displayed. 'Mandela Park' was the most popular, although many resistance leaders were thus honoured, and other parks bore more obscure titles such as 'Kissing Park', 'Club Maseru' and even, simply, 'Our Park'.

The parks, according to their architects, were intended to demonstrate to black adults as well as the state that the comrades had a vision of the future and a role in improving township life, beyond just battling the security forces. The parks represented, at one level, an attempt to come to terms with – even invent – self-initiative and democratic activity by people who had never been allowed to experience it. They were an assertion of self (a slogan in one Soweto park read 'People with their own STYLE'), and an indication of the extent to which generational consciousness now embraced the notion of an impending transfer of power.

Upheaval in the townships continued into 1986, with the youth component of resistance bigger but more amorphous than ever. Levels of political sophistication fluctuated wildly from region to region, and even within groups in particular townships. Detained youth leaders had certainly been replaced in their organisations, but often by inexperienced activists, 'generally younger, more radical in outlook, more militant in practice'.[86] The 'decentralisation' of popular resistance made it more difficult for the state to crush, but it also made the youth component more difficult to guide. In its worst manifestation, according to one leader, the youth movement had become

> one big frustrated organism with a lot of energy at its disposal but faced with a confused direction . . . and finding the only option to be to face things head on. When you have huge numbers not properly politicised, you often see mob responses, and there are great dangers in that.[87]

Ten years on from the Soweto pupils' revolt, 'the youth', now greatly expanded, were still the most prominent promoters of resistance activity, and their raw power was an irremovable feature of South African political life. This was accepted by adult community leaders:

> One lesson community organizations and others have learnt is that the youth are a joint and equal partner in all processes of community life. They emerged [in 1985] as a group not to be talked about but to be talked to.[88]

But their direction and role in organised resistance activity was indeterminate. The virtual breakdown of black education had completed a process whereby the fulcrum of youth militancy shifted from the confines of the schools to the *terra incognita* of the streets. The situation begged the intervention of the increasingly influential trade union movement and adult-based community organisations.

Alliance building, internecine strife, and clampdown

By the end of 1985, resistance leaders were increasingly emphasising the need for a process of alliance building,[89] reflecting 'the feeling within the broad popular movement . . . that student activism had perhaps lost its vision'.[90] Adult and youth leaders who did not subscribe to the belief in 'imminent liberation' identified the 'indefinite' school boycotts as a great threat to the prosecution of the anti-apartheid struggle. Politically, disunity and indiscipline dissipated the power of youth action, and alienated black adults. Socially, successive generations of illiterate and innumerate children would augur badly for future leadership, and would exacerbate many of the problems of township life.

A challenge to the shibboleths permeating school-based youth organisation emerged when Soweto parents began to voice their disquiet in August 1985. In 1976 many parents had simply opposed the actions of their children: now they sought a role in shaping tactics to further the children's aims. The attitudes of 'normally apolitical residents of the township were changing', according to one commentator,[91] encouraged by the increasingly high-handed actions of the security forces in the schools and on the streets.

In October 1985 the Soweto Civic Association (SCA) convened a meeting at Diepkloof Roman Catholic Church. Township parents flocked to the hall to discuss ways of engineering a return to the classrooms with the approval of the boycotting pupils. The meeting illustrated the depth of feeling among a broad spectrum of parents that they were being 'left behind' by the children. The 'conditions' for supporting a return to school set out by the meeting were indicative of the political influence which pupils had brought to bear on their elders. The rump of COSAS' original demands were endorsed. The 'Soweto Crisis Committee' was formed and demanded, among other things, the withdrawal of troops from the townships, the release of detained pupils, and prior consultation with government departments on educational issues. Parents accepted that they 'should take more responsibility in matters affecting their children',[92] and that they and community leaders had failed to involve themselves adequately in the educational struggle.

By December 1985 the *ad hoc* parents' committee had become the 'Soweto Parents' Crisis Committee' (SPCC). Although more militant pupils were hostile toward, or at least wary of the initiative,[93] the fledgeling organisation aroused tremendous interest among black parents in communities throughout South Africa. A broad meeting was convened in Johannesburg in the last week of December, attended by 312 delegates and some 300 observers, representing more than 160 organisations, including the UDF, National Forum, and trade union groupings. Parents agreed to withdraw from official school committees and governing councils, and to create in their stead localised 'Parents' Crisis Committees' to work with teachers and pupils. The conveners argued for a 'tactical return' to school and a thoroughgoing reassessment of indefinite or wildcat boycotts. Specific demands should be agreed upon, it was suggested, and the schools used as organisational bases while the response of the authorities was awaited. The case for basic education, even under an inferior system, was powerfully put by the SCA's Nthato Motlana.[94]

After seven hours of intensive deliberation it was agreed that pupils should stage an orderly return to school, while a list of demands was presented to the educational authorities.[95] A further meeting would be held after four months to assess developments. Three SPCC representatives would work with parents from other regions toward the establishment of a national parent/pupil/teacher structure. The SPCC meeting gave rise to report-backs in dozens of townships in all four provinces, attended by tens of thousands of parents. On 7 January 1986, 30 000 people (a large proportion of them adults) crammed into a stadium in the Eastern Cape to discuss the return to school. The meeting, organised by the newly-formed Port Elizabeth Crisis in Education Committee, stood in marked contrast to a gathering held precisely a year before, where only a handful of parents had been present to hear some 5000 schoolchildren resolve not to return to class.[96]

Because of the chaotic state of black education after fifteen months of boycotts, the SPCC requested that the educational authorities delay the schools' reopening. This was refused, and the SPCC unilaterally set 28 January – two weeks later than usual – as the date of return. To the surprise of the government, and indeed of many SPCC supporters, the vast majority of boycotting pupils honoured the call, thus conferring great legitimacy upon the SPCC. Primary school attendance was at 100 per cent after only a few days, and secondary schools filled up rapidly. The initial SPCC success marked a new, nascent phase in the politics of youth resistance, in which the principle of disciplined alliances had been introduced in practice.

However, resistance leaders were soon reminded of the extent to which the student organisations had relinquished control over some of their more militant constituents. Gangs of youths who opposed the return disrupted classes in Soweto and in the Eastern Cape. The SPCC faced the challenge head-on, calling them 'peddlers of division', '*agents provocateurs* and political megalomaniacs', and urging 'disciplined students' to eschew 'opportunism, adventurism and pseudo-radicalism'.[97] They were supported by officials of the UDF-affiliated Transvaal Students' Congress (TRASCO) – one of several regional federations – and AZASM.

Although the return to school held initially, it was soon rendered unworkable. Clashes occurred at several township schools in January. Police and soldiers were accused of 'herding pupils into classrooms' with *sjamboks* (whips) in the Cape Town coloured township of Athlone, and Thabong in the Orange Free State.[98] The 'orderly return' began to crumble in the face of shootings, detentions, and spontaneous localised boycotts. An 'uneasy calm' prevailed at the end of January, but a month later the SPCC admitted that attendance was deteriorating sharply. Leaders accused the government of intransigence and provocation. The authorities had responded to only one of the original demands, announcing on 23 January that 'basic stationery' would henceforth be supplied free of charge to black pupils. The move received a muted welcome, but was soon overshadowed by police bans on SPCC meetings in Soweto and the Indian township of Lenasia.

The SPCC's credibility survived, even though the schools were once again in ferment by March. The parents' 'planning committee' evolved into the 'National Education Crisis Committee' (NECC), and this set about convening a national gathering to assesss government responses and provide a clear policy on the fast-disintegrating return to school. During the build-up to the conference, scheduled for Durban over the Easter weekend, it was recognised in quarters as unlikely as the Afrikaans press that the NECC held the key to 'order' in the black schools.[99] And the Johannesburg *Sunday Star* pointed to the significance of the alliance beyond education:

> there is growing [black] political unity. The days are over when demands for real change were the domain of young people . . .

> There can be no doubt that parents and teachers are with the children . . . the decision of the [NECC] conference will be as binding as law, and perhaps more so. For millions of blacks will respect the decision more than they respect the laws of a parliament in which they have no say.[100]

A range of groups shared an interest in the success of the conference. Most importantly, the resistance movements regarded it as a litmus test for the desired alliance between adults and the youth. More than 100 schools were now affected by boycotts and stayaways, involving up to 80 000 pupils. The lifting of the State of Emergency on 7 March had been interpreted by many youth militants as an admission of failure by the government. A complete breakdown of black education was once more imminent. If that were to happen, many feared, the youth movements would become a wholly uncontrollable force – the 'loose cannon' of resistance.

The educational authorities, maintaining a low profile during the run-up to the conference, privately acknowledged that no amount of coercion could reimpose true stability in the schools. A triumph for the 'return to school' policy would thus be a windfall for the Department of Education and Training (DET) as well.[101]

'Black Education's Easter of Reckoning',[102] as much a coming together of all sectors of resistance as a purely educational gathering, began amid high drama. The original venue was withdrawn only days before the conference. As frantic efforts were made to find an alternative, some 1500 delegates including parents, teachers, pupils, trade unionists and political leaders,[103] streamed into Durban from all corners of South Africa. Several were attacked and harassed by unknown assailants, and as delegates gathered for registration, two busloads of armed blacks – many of them allegedly uniformed members of the Inkatha Youth Brigade[104] – bore down. Delegates defended themselves, and in the ensuing mêlée two of the attackers were killed.[105]

By the time the conference got under way in the Indian township of Chatsworth, emotions were at fever pitch. 'Comrades' from the youth movements acted as marshals, patrolling the grounds of the Rajput Hall in case of invasion. The agenda was truncated: regional reports which were to have been orally delivered and debated were collected earlier in the day, and the conference moved directly to the central question, deliberating *in camera* through the night. The result was a call for a return to school, despite the fact that the government had not responded satisfactorily to the earlier ultimatum. This was an indication of the store set by resistance leaders on the 'redisciplining' of the school-based movements, and of the strength of the NECC alliance. The strategic maturity underlying the decision was reflected in the conference's keynote speech, in which it was asserted that 'a cross-roads had been reached in the struggle', and that united community action had to outweigh maverick youth militancy:

> We will not defeat apartheid while the youth alone carry on the struggle against Bantu Education or other aspects of racist rule. We will not win while our ranks are split by teachers who have not yet thrown in their lot with the democratic movement. We will not win while parents remain alienated from the demands of their children . . . To cast aside unity at this time is to weaken our shield and blunt our spear.[106]

In the euphoria which followed the apparent promise of tranquillity in the classrooms, few white commentators grasped the real import of the new tactics, which were aimed at nudging the fulcrum of youth militancy away from the streets and back to the schools. In fact, as the Johannesburg *Weekly Mail* noted,

> The resolution to return to school is more accurately described as a switch of strategy . . . schools [will] be used as marshalling yards to regroup and press forward for the withdrawal of troops from the townships, the release from detention of students and teachers and the lifting of the ban on COSAS. The combative spirit . . . was manifest in several resolutions . . . [which were] evidence not of 'moderation' and 'reasonableness' . . . but of a fine honing of strategy.[107]

As with the inaugural SPCC meeting, the resolution did not pass without dissent from diehard pro-boycotters and others sceptical of the alliance's authority. Angered by the curtailed discussion period, and harbouring misgivings about their ability to implement the resolution at their own schools, several hundred pupil delegates publicly aired their doubts. But the majority returned to school. At the end of the first week of the new term, black schools had an average attendance rate of 80 per cent, with variations in some regions.[108]

Despite this second victory for proponents of 'methodical [resistance] progress, consolidation of gains rather than hasty, ill-considered action',[109] the pattern set in January 1985 soon reasserted itself. Boycotts flared in disparate areas, usually in response to security force action. In Vosloorus on the East Rand, a stayaway began to mark the funeral of an alleged ANC insurgent. In a Heidelberg township a youth wearing a UDF t-shirt was shot, sparking a boycott. The NECC, clearly worried by mid-April, called on the DET to address the list of educational grievances or face plummetting attendances. The DET responded by suspending several schools in April and May. Troops invaded schools; pupils burned textbooks; clashes led to injuries and deaths which in turn prompted boycotts and funerals and even more deaths. Black schooling was sucked, once more, into the vortex.

What had taken place in the early months of 1986 was not, however, to be judged simply on the numbers of pupils back behind their desks. On those grounds the NECC initiative had failed. The long-term significance lay in the *legitimacy within resistance* which had been established for the adult/youth alliance. School-based youth leaders had accepted the principle, and would attempt to promote it through their organisational structures. The collapse of education was almost inevitably dictated by conditions; when those conditions changed, the basic agreement which underpinned the alliance would be given its head.

To some extent, the message of unity and mutual responsibility was also feeding into the non-school-based structures of the youth movement. At a meeting in Alexandra township in March 1986, for example, the organising secretary of the local youth congress told 'comrades':

> Our parents . . . say there must be unity between teachers, parents and youth . . . If we alienate our parents, the authorities will arm our parents to kill us. And we will have to kill them. I can see this situation if we do not change . . . Do not cause unnecessary problems. Do not cause unnecessary death. We are tired of mourning. We are tired of funerals. We are the people who are fighting for peace.[110]

But a violent stalemate – costly both physically and politically – was developing as it became apparent that the edifice of white rule was not about to crack. Bloody feuds escalated between youth organisations on the one hand and township gangs or 'vigilantes' on the other. Vigilantes fought activists in well-known townships like Crossroads and Alexandra, but also in more remote areas: Leandra, Mpumelelo, Thokoza, Lindelani among others. Children as young as twelve were forced to seek refuge in mission stations and in the mountains. Equally ominously, rivalry between resistance groups became increasingly violent. In many townships 'the popular movement turned inward, in effect creating phantom adversaries and striking at available targets of opportunity'.[111] In Soweto in April and May 'territorial disputes' between supporters of the SOSCO and AZASM left many dead. Fratricidal disputes fed on themselves, with 'revenge' killings becoming more common and providing fertile ground for *agents provocateurs*. Many activists with impeccable 'anti-apartheid credentials' – including, in several cases, lengthy spells in prison – were killed by rival activists.

The situation spiralled so quickly that resistance leaders, both internal and external, were prompted to make public appeals for an end to the internecine violence; it appeared to be 'an almost unilateral acknowledgement that the township unrest was at least on occasion slipping out of control'.[112] Turmoil on the streets and in the schools left communities battle-weary and enervated. Beneath the defiant action, imagery and rhetoric of the youth revolt, a malaise was taking root. The editor of the Johannesburg *City Press*, Percy Qoboza, argued evocatively in April 1986:

> If it is true that a people's wealth is its children, then South Africa is bitterly, tragically poor. If it is true that a nation's future is its children, we have no future, and deserve none . . . [We] are a nation at war with its future . . . For we have turned our children into a generation of fighters, battle-hardened soldiers who will never know the carefree joy of childhood. What we are witnessing is the growth of a generation which has the courage to reject the cowardice of its parents . . . to fight for what should be theirs, by right of birth. There is a dark, terrible beauty in that courage. It is also a source of great pride – pride that we, who have lived under apartheid, can produce children who refuse to do so. But it is also a source of great shame . . . that [this] is our heritage to our children: The knowledge of how to die, and how to kill.[113]

The statement encapsulated the dual elements characterising the youth component of resistance in the first months of 1986: their demonstrated courage and resilience, and the apparent lack of direction of their sacrifices. As preparations began for a massive commemoration of the tenth anniversary of the Soweto uprising, it was unclear whether the youth would engage in maverick activity on 16 June, or if the nascent alliances would bear fruit.

In fact, the situation was wholly pre-empted by the government. Having failed to steer two swingeing security bills through the tricameral parliament, the State President declared a new, national State of Emergency on 12 June. Although hydra-headed, the measures were predicated on the simple principle of reimposing law and order which the earlier, selective Emergency had failed to achieve. This meant a concerted attempt at eradicating, rather than just silencing, the disparate structures of popular resistance. Student and youth groups were particularly badly hit, and thousands of activists were detained. Powers conferred on the security forces, including an indemnity from prosecution for any actions taken under Emergency regulations, allowed police *carte blanche* in dealing with the troublesome youth.

Those youth activists who escaped the security dragnet scurried for the cover of the 'underground', which swelled to bursting point. Youth congress leaders fled their own townships, becoming 'internal refugees'[114] and leaving organisations in disarray. The political initiative seized by the government 'marked the end of one phase of the popular struggle and the beginning of another.'[115] Peoples' courts and parks disappeared, and many street committees were rendered moribund.

Inter-organisational consultation was severely hampered as mass meetings became impossible. Of the 22 000 people detained in the first five months of the Emergency, it was estimated that 40 per cent were under the age of eighteen. Most were aged between thirteen and eighteen years, although cases were reported of children under nine being jailed. At the height of the clampdown, some 250 minors were being detained each week in what was judged to be 'the greatest wave of repression and violence unleashed by the state against the people of South Africa'.[116] Some 79 per cent of all detainees were said to be members of the UDF, 16 per cent from the trade union movement, and four per cent allied to the National Forum.

The 16 June demonstration of youth force did not materialise as planned. Although there was an extremely successful stayaway from work and schools – abetted, ironically, by the 'sealing off' of Soweto and other townships – great shows of street strength seemed of the past. The resistance movement, and in particular its youth component, had reached a point at which it would have to adapt its methods, or concede defeat.

The retreat 'underground', SAYCO, and a turn to the unions

Youth leaders had been given a taste of clandestine operation during the Emergency of 1984–85. In June 1986 the retreat 'underground'[117] was on a massive scale. The government's measures had the potential of finally severing the organisational head from the extemporising body of the youth movement. But some organised youth resistance of this type did survive, albeit in an altered form. In Alexandra township in August, for example, representatives of the local youth and student congresses were able to convene a secret meeting, where they told a journalist:

> We must admit it is very hard. We are operating under very trying conditions . . . The security police . . . even roam the streets at night now and go to the *shebeens* [bars] . . . Our organisation is underground . . . we are holding meetings underground . . . we can't move around freely, but we are still organising the youth. We just arrange a meeting point and move from there to a venue . . . Our support is still strong. People [had been] mobilised and conscientised and the next step was to organise them, to get them into structures. Now we are having to talk to people about the clampdown and how it affects the struggle.[118]

Few of the young activists were able to live in Alexandra, entering the township only when it was considered relatively safe, and politically essential. One leader, describing this twilight lifestyle, said 'we call it *double-up*. You walk sideways so no-one can see you'.[119] On one level, the Emergency was forcibly enrolling activists in a new school of politics. As the *Weekly Mail* noted:

> What is crystal clear is that the major effect of the Emergency has been to teach the activists a new mode of 'underground' operation. They have long since learnt to live in hiding – and expect to do so indefinitely . . . Having grown used to this 'underground' organisation, these activists are unlikely to re-emerge in a hurry. And that is likely to be the major – and most lasting – effect of the Emergency.[120]

Perversely, the Emergency was encouraging a reappraisal of exclusively confrontationist, 'populist' youth tactics which resistance leaders themselves had been having great difficulty in promoting. The demonstration of the state's power was sufficient to disabuse young militants of notions of impending victory, and to stamp out some of their more heavy-handed pursuits in the townships. They had now to look at the resilience, capabilities, and shortcomings of the structures they had created. Focused political activity and collaboration with other sectors of resistance was no longer a theoretical ideal, but a practical necessity for survival.

Unprecedented repression had another bizarre spin-off, welcomed by resistance leaders. The inter-organisational conflict which had reached a peak prior to the Emergency, began to decline. Although internecine killings continued, the temperature of the conflict fell as rival activists fled from their common enemy. In one celebrated instance, activists from the Soweto Students' Congress (SOSCO) were placed in a communal cell in Johannesburg Prison at Diepkloof with members of AZASM's Soweto branch. The Charterist/Black Consciousness conflict between the two groups had been among the worst manifestations of fratricidal violence, and several attempts at convening 'peace meetings' had failed. Now, forced to live cheek-by-jowl, the warring comrades hammered out a 'tactical alliance' – to the astonishment of the adult prisoners. Saths Cooper, convener of the National Forum and president of AZAPO, claimed he witnessed these developments from his own cell in Diepkloof. On his release, he argued that the fundamentally altered conditions under the Emergency offered a unique opportunity for resistance unity and increasingly sophisticated tactics:

> In [a] perverse sense, the Emergency has been a blessing. It has forced common ground between different factions. They have had to acknowledge that they've got something in common and that the luxury of attacking each other – even verbally – cannot continue. People must learn from this Emergency and from past mistakes . . . leaders must stand up and be counted now . . . I believe that with more maturity as a result of this common hardship, they will come to their senses . . . until we achieve that, the state will continue to make the inroads we have seen.[121]

He argued further that the Emergency could have a salutary effect on the *nature* of extra-parliamentary resistance: 'as all structures are taking a heavy knock on all sides of the political spectrum, this will necessarily lead to a tactical reassessment by different organisations. It would be almost foolhardy to persist in the same types and levels of activity which result in activists being . . . available for arrest as cannon-fodder.'[122] There would, he said, be a shift away from protest politics represented most commonly by the mass funeral-cum-rally, towards less conspicuous 'grassroots' organisational work. 'Local labour, sporting and cultural work will be re-emphasised. Many activists will find new homes, new ways of doing things, making their individual contributions . . . Organisation will become more local and less public.'[123] This change would affect youth politics more than other sectors of resistance.

The youth movements had no choice but to alter their activities in response to the clampdown: in a sense, the potential benefits in terms of professionalism and discipline which accrued from the move underground were imposed rather than achieved. But a more deep-seated shift was taking place at the level of their strategic conception of their role in resistance. In the heady days of 'insurrectionary' politics, this area was left underdeveloped. Attempts at a parent/pupil alliance had addressed the question, but in a limited and episodic fashion.[124] More importantly, while there had been isolated instances of formal co-operation with trade unions and innumerable statements of fraternal loyalty to 'the organised working class',[125] the youth/union relationship had never been rigorously defined, let alone applied. A new popular slogan, 'From Mobilisation to Organisation', was intended to stress the need for millions of 'mobilised' youths to understand, through their organisational outlets, where they stood in relation to other sectors of resistance in what was going to be a protracted struggle.

The clampdown thrust the question of the role of the working class, in particular, to the fore. The incremental politicisation of the ascendant labour movement is dealt with in Chapter 4. Its importance for youth politics lies in the fact that, for a complex of reasons, the unions emerged in the aftermath of the Emergency in a relatively stronger position than other elements in the resistance movements. 'The main leadership in the black community . . . shifted to the unions . . . Their strikes [rapidly] became politicized and turned into mobilizing points for wider action in the townships.'[126] The role of primary resistance-catalyst had belonged to the youth for a decade. Now it was being ceded, at least in part, to the unions.

For the beleaguered youth structures, the implications of this historical shift outweighed all others. Youth leaders had asserted, since the early 1980s, that young militants were in the 'forefront' of resistance in so far as they stimulated action and invariably shouldered the bulk of the practical work in implementing various campaigns. But to this was added the rider that

> this should not be mistaken with the view that we are the *vanguard* of the struggle. That role belongs to our own working parents. The youth can be in the forefront of the confrontation between the state and the people, but working parents are the vanguard as they have the power to break the economy of the country . . . they are the decisive force in the liberation struggle.[127]

In the style of youth resistance politics which characterised the period 1984 to mid-1986, this intellectual construct was never put to the test decisively. Now the notion of 'workers-as-vanguard' changed from being an ideological tenet to a demonstrable fact. If the youth movement in its various forms was to continue to play a central role in resistance, its organisations would have to make their acceptance of the 'leading role of the labour movement' a day-to-day reality. Youth organisation was embattled and dispersed – the labour movement, although under equal pressure, was increasingly unified and resilient. Thus the process of necessary organisational adaptation demanded by the youth retreat underground coincided with a far more serious approach to the question of operational alliances.

The new importance of accountability and proper canvassing before embarking on campaigns was tellingly illustrated by the experience of the 'National United Action' initiative toward the end of 1986. In an attempt to rally resistance forces, UDF, NECC and COSATU leaders hurriedly announced a national campaign of unified action. After much fanfare, it fizzled out due to lack of support from organised workers who were used to debating such measures thoroughly before agreeing to implement them. The impatient youth movements drew a lesson from this, admitting that it was a mistake to expect solidarity action from the unions without properly consulting them and gaining their approval at shop-floor level. 'Youth were made aware that workers [had a specific] process of discussing things . . . discussions between workers, shopstewards and the youth [were essential].'[128]

Among youth *leaders* at least, the distinction between youth as forefront and workers as vanguard was progressively elevated. Increasingly, in youth meetings, pamphlets and other ephemera, a Marxist analysis of the future of the liberation struggle was posited. The following construction is typical of the period:

> We have found . . . that there have been two basic classes throughout the history of mankind . . . The youth are not a class, but most fall into the broad category of the working people. We are mindful of the fact that class struggle between workers and capital is an ongoing phenomenon, even here in South Africa. So we will align ourselves with the workers who represent the most progressive future . . . The youth and the workers are not in competition as far as the future goes . . . we see it as one of our tasks to strengthen the working class.[129]

However, accepting a secondary position in the 'resistance hierarchy'

> [would] not circumscribe our independence as the youth. We can't allow the militancy of the youth to be watered down . . . we can

> revolutionise other structures and struggles. But we will retain our independence, and won't pursue compromise politics.[130]

It is too early to judge the effects of these shifts. However, initiatives at the level of organisation at the end of 1986 and early in 1987 do suggest a trend toward tactical maturity on a scale not yet seen in the history of the youth movement.

Most important was the underground launch of the South African Youth Congress (SAYCO), the country's largest-ever youth grouping. Following the 1982 COSAS conference, where 'youth' as opposed to 'student' congresses had first been mooted, an *ad hoc* committee was charged with investigating the feasibility of creating a national youth co-ordinating body. At Wilgespruit in January 1984, this responsibility passed to the thirty-six youth congresses then in existence. In November of the same year, five fledgeling regional youth structures met in Lenasia township to discuss the formation of a (as yet unnamed) 'national youth organisation'. In Durban on 10 and 11 January 1985, a further meeting agreed after some debate on a 'disciplined federal structure' for the national organisation, and adopted the traditional colours of the liberation movement.[131] However, many delegates reported that their organisations were not fully prepared, and local youth congress leaders were told to go back and canvass their constituents in anticipation of a future launch. The 'National Interim Committee' undertook meanwhile to encourage the growth of more youth congresses, especially in the rural areas. Several workshops ensued, both at township and regional levels. These efforts were interrupted by the July 1985 State of Emergency, which 'brought activities to a standstill'.[132] A meeting in the Western Cape in April 1986 revived the initiative, but the national Emergency imposed three months later led many observers to believe that the long-gestating national youth body would be still-born.

In fact, preparations were speeded up after the June 1986 Emergency, providing concrete evidence of the ability of youth activists to adapt to – and even, to an extent, profit by – semi-underground conditions. By November, after consultation with the UDF and student/pupil groups, the Interim Committee announced that a 'national youth organisation . . . the voice of the young men and women of our country, channelling the militancy of the youth in a progressive political direction',[133] would soon be launched under the proposed title of the South African Youth Congress (SAYCO). 'The youth', said the Committee, '. . . must strengthen the leadership of the working class, forge relationships with progressive trade unions, civics and other groups within the democratic movement and add their muscle and ideas'.[134]

While conceding that 'severe repression . . . in which the youth have often been key targets . . . affected interim [regional] co-ordinating structures',[135] the Committee claimed that some 600 youth congresses were functioning nationwide, and that a draft constitution and draft policy statements had emerged from discussions in regional workshops. The new organisation would affiliate to the UDF, attempt to have the Freedom Charter endorsed, and exclude Black Consciousness groups. By December, secretly-formed regional structures were in operation in the eastern Cape, western Cape, northern Transvaal and southern Transvaal, and preparations were advanced in Natal, the northern Cape, and Orange Free State. Several hundred thousand youths were already represented in the regions, and despite the strictures of the Emergency, SAYCO was to be launched early in 1987.[136]

Officials of the Southern Transvaal Youth Congress (STYCO), interviewed in December, indicated that the SAYCO activists had debated the change in tactics in some depth:

> Before the first State of Emergency, we were organising publicly, through rallies and open meetings. With the crackdown, many of us were detained and killed. We learned the lessons . . . and have adopted a new, semi-clandestine way ever since . . . [we are] a legal organisation, operating legally . . . [the secrecy] has been forced on us by the state.[137]

Even more significantly, a direct connection was drawn between this 'new style' of youth organisation, and an improvement in relations between the 'comrades' and the wider black community. Although critical of the media for 'exaggerating' reports of 'comrades' excesses', STYCO officials conceded that the youth movement had lost support through such actions. 'Now', they said, 'we are working more closely with our parents and brothers and sisters.'[138]

SAYCO was launched in great secrecy on 28 March 1987 in Cape Town. The organisers spun an intricate web of disinformation to prevent police from discovering the venue, changing the location three times immediately before the event. Few of the more than 100 delegates knew the real venue, and were moved about in small groups by marshalls. Journalists chasing rumours fared less well, some ending up in Durban as the meeting began hundreds of miles to the west. The launch of the half-million strong organisation, now comprising nine regional delegations, went undetected and was over within a few hours. Under the slogans 'Freedom or Death – Victory is Certain', and 'Every Youth a Combatant!', SAYCO emerged as the most overtly militant mass youth organisation in South African history, but it was a militancy tempered to some extent by clarity about specific tasks, and a new stress on discipline.

At the launch, a representative of the Cape Youth Congress (CAYCO) told delegates that the formation of SAYCO was a 'historically determined event . . . realising the initiatives and efforts of the (now banned) COSAS'.[139] Although it had been '. . . realised under very difficult conditions, trials and errors, fights and disagreements . . . from today we as the South African youth are a force to be reckoned with . . . The women, the workers, the students, all sectors are looking to the youth today'.[140]

SAYCO listed its principal objectives as unifying and politicising all 'progressive' youth, irrespective of race; encouraging the youth to join trade unions; and ensuring that women participated fully in the activities of the youth movement. Its resolutions included the now standard set of demands to the government, calling for the lifting of the State of Emergency, the withdrawal of troops from the townships, the unconditional release of Mandela and other political prisoners, and the unbanning of the ANC.[141]

Furthermore, SAYCO pledged to be part of a 'class alliance . . . of organisational unity led by the working class [involving] a principled working relationship with all progressive workers, community, women and student organisations with principles similar to ours'.[142] Of nine specific campaigns enshrined in a 'programme of action', seven demanded direct co-operation with other resistance sectors, chief among these being COSATU-led initiatives. COSATU itself sent a representative to speak at the launch: he suggested practical means of co-operation between unions and local SAYCO affiliates, including youth attendance at shop stewards' councils, and joint campaigns to unionise the unemployed – many of whom were youths. His speech ended with the slogan 'Forward to the worker and youth alliance!'[143] SAYCO's first president pursued the theme:

> Thousands of our working youth, student youth, and unemployed youth have taken their rightful role in the forward trenches of our national democratic struggle . . . The struggles of the past three years have clearly demonstrated the dynamic role . . . of the youth . . . [but] a clear understanding flows from the realities of national

> oppression and exploitation that while the youth continues to play a dynamic and energetic role in our struggle, it must accept . . . working class leadership of the . . . struggle. . . We have come together as the *youth detachment* of the democratic movement at a time of unprecedented state attacks.[144] (emphasis added)

SAYCO's size alone made it a milestone in resistance organisation – it was by far the largest single affiliate of the UDF. It was also important in terms of its structure and personnel. For the first time, a broad *youth* structure assumed the primary position within the youth movement, displacing student and pupil organisations. SAYCO's executive was dubbed the 'Class of '87' in a pointed comparison with the 'Class of '44' leaders of the ANC Youth League. SAYCO president Peter Mokaba was a twenty-five year old activist from the Northern Transvaal, and a veteran of Robben Island and several spells in detention. His ten colleagues were similarly seasoned. In terms of organisational capacity, ideological clarity and potential influence – SAYCO was the most ambitious and professional youth initiative to date – it was heralded as representing a 'coming of age' of the youth component of resistance.

The difficulty in assessing the permeation and permanence of these shifts is exacerbated by the fact that a clandestine organisation's performance can often only be judged through the prism of its own leaders' assessments. There have, however, been signs of concerted efforts to put the principles of alliance politics into practice. Local SAYCO cadres played a role in the Soweto rent boycott, and joined the UDF and COSATU in endorsing a variety of resistance campaigns. Reports of SAYCO participation in shop stewards' councils (or 'locals') began to filter through, and SAYCO publicly encouraged COSATU to adopt the Freedom Charter. In June 1987, Mokaba was invited to address the COSATU conference in Johannesburg, where he reiterated and clarified SAYCO's understanding of the new phase of resistance:

> We in SAYCO greatly appreciate the steadfastness and honesty of this workers' weapon [COSATU] . . . and [the fact that] the fighting alliance between us and COSATU is seen by both . . . as a necessary condition of struggle . . . [We] urge COSATU and its unions to begin now at once to build conscious worker participation at the core of our [United Democratic] Front . . . From COSATU locals [local committees] in which we so much wish to participate and turn into sites of struggle . . . this must become the first phase of building against apartheid and imperialism.[145]

Without rejecting their former organisational structures, the leaders of the youth movement were envisaging a new approach to youth organisation. Individual youth and student congresses in the townships would no longer be as important as they had been as *separate entities*. The definition of alliances appeared to be shifting from notions of separate organisations choosing to act together when the need arose, to a concept of single localised structures in which the youth would be ordinary participants. The pivot of these embryonic organs would be the 'locals'. If successful, this would signal a decisive harnessing of the youth component into broad resistance and a genuine regrouping of extra-parliamentary opposition – the dreamt-of progression from 'mobilisation' to 'organisation'.

In one sense at least, the strategy would have immediate costs for the youth movement. 'Membership' would take on a new meaning. Whereas in 1985 attendance at local mass meetings and participation in street battles were sufficient to make youngsters fully-fledged participants in the youth movement, much more discipline and commitment (as opposed to mere courage) would be required of the young blacks of 1987. Grassroots work no longer involved simply mobilising a community for a particular campaign; it demanded painstaking, inconspicuous politicisation with few visible or immediate results. For some of the youth at least, a drift away from politics – and possible recidivism – was inevitable. For others, particularly those wedded to 'immediatist' action, the changed conditions would convince them to leave the country to join the ANC's military wing rather than participate in the 'long view' activities of SAYCO.[146]

By mid-1987, the complexion of the 'youth revolt' had altered considerably. Its bedrock – militant generational consciousness – remained intact and had spread widely over the past decade. But balances of power and forms of operation differed. One of the most striking characteristics was the overwhelming dominance of the Charterist groupings. Not only in youth structures like SAYCO, but also in the student- and pupil-led organisations, the Congress tradition held sway.

An indicator of this trend was a decision by AZASO, the Charterist organisation for black students at tertiary institutions, to drop the anomalous 'Azania' from its title in December 1986. At a national conference – also held in secret – AZASO renamed itself the South African National Students Congress (SANSCO), thus falling directly in line with other UDF structures. Although it did not presage any ideological shift, the change in nomenclature was of great symbolic significance, reflecting a high degree of organizational confidence – somewhat surprisingly given the harshness of the State of Emergency. For AZASO to risk losing the media and membership notoriety of a well-marketed trademark in favour of ideological consistency is, among other things, an indication that the organization believes it has so far outstripped its rivals (like AZASM) that it need not be concerned about their exploiting it.[147]

Although National Forum-aligned youth and student groupings continued to function, they had been overshadowed. There is some validity in the contention of their leaders that the influence of the ideas of these groups permeate far beyond organisational affiliations. In terms of visible action, however, Forum groups had difficulty in rebutting consistent allegations that they were little more than 'easily excitable and well-read intellectuals'[148] whose efforts were dwarfed by SAYCO, SANSCO, and the myriad UDF-affiliated youth/student structures. Ironically, much of the 'anti-populist' content of the Forum groups was now mirrored in the changing strategies of the UDF youth affiliates, but this did not signal significant *rapprochement* between the rival formations. Charterist youth leaders tended more and more to ignore the other camp, even when Black Consciousness loyalists launched the Azanian Youth Organization (AZAYO) in 1987 as an apparent rival 'national structure' to SAYCO.[149]

While school-based organisation was somewhat overshadowed by SAYCO's debut, progress was also made toward national co-ordination in the educational sphere. Despite the unrest in the black schools which had sputtered on in 1987, aggravated by new, draconian security measures,[150] the refusal of the DET to address the pupils' central demands, and the detention of the NECC's leadership, student congresses were able to maintain some measure of co-ordination through the National Students' Co-ordinating Committee (NASCOC), a political descendant of COSAS, which allied itself to both SAYCO and SANSCO. This organisational triumvirate completed the Charterist dominance of all forms of youth organisation.

CONCLUSION

The fortunes of the youth component of resistance in South Africa will continue to ebb and flow with those of the omnibus anti-apartheid struggle, but also in response to the *sui generis* dynamics of youth organisation. The extent to which gains in organisational sophistication and tactical maturity can offset the setbacks inflicted by the state remains to be seen. It can confidently be predicted, however, that the development of the youth movements into a wholly disciplined, far-sighted and controllable component of resistance can be neither smooth nor linear. A few certainties demonstrate this truth: activists still have much to learn about operation 'semi-underground', and will be forced deeper into hiding; internecine strife persists; despondency at the lack of immediate successes ensures that 'comrades' excesses' recur from time to time; the whirlwind of psychological brutalisation will be reaped within a very few years; the insolubility of the crisis of black education under apartheid will weigh heavily on adult leaders; 'vigilanteism' and the use of 'hit squads' will exact a bloody price from the black youth.

But these factors – and the many others which could be cited – cannot alter the essence of the revolt of black youth: the irrevocable entrenchment of a militant, specific generational consciousness on a scale perhaps unequalled in any other political struggle. What has developed in South Africa is a Children's Crusade of sorts, and the question to be asked is not whether it will continue, but in what form, and to what effect. Leaders of the myriad youth organisations have proved their capacity to achieve unity, act democratically, devise imaginative structures in response to changing conditions, and, above all, to make sacrifices. They have shown their willingness to develop their own political awareness and recognise the seniority of other components of resistance, particularly the trade unions. I believe that they will proceed, haltingly, toward a position of prominence in the resistance movements equal to that of 1984–86, but as a much more manageable and mature grouping – and hence they will be more effective in the pursuance of their declared aims.

The composition of 'personnel' in the youth sector of resistance changes constantly, as activists grow older and feed into other structures. Their replacement is certain, however, and is likely to lead to even more pronounced levels of political commitment as the struggle in South Africa drags on. Those who dismiss this contention would do well to consider the implications of events in a township called Tumahole in April 1986. There, township children of primary school age decided that their *fellow activists* in the secondary schools were not sufficiently militant; the juveniles bypassed the adolescents, forming gangs called the '14s', and operating on their own initiative.[151]

One of the most popular slogans of the youth movements is 'Long live the spirit of *Asijiki*'. *Asijiki* is an evocative Zulu phrase, meaning 'we do not turn back'. It aptly describes the political commitment – the 'obsession to be liberated' – of millions of young blacks in the schools, universities, factories and the streets of South Africa. UDF patron Allan Boesak contends that if nothing else, 'South Africa has a government that is afraid of children'.[152] And the children themselves believe they have power:

We bold enough to question
We brave enough to fight
We strong enough to challenge you
for what we know is right
We are the young and the strong
And we are the writings on the wall[153]

NOTES

1. Author's interview with residents, Alexandra, April 1986.
2. *City Press*, Johannesburg, 20 April 1986.
3. See, for example, 'Comrades Crushed', the *Independent*, London, 21 April 1987.
4. There are inherent limitations to this approach, which should be conceded at the outset. First, an attempt to provide a national overview of the youth phenomenon within the confines of one chapter results in regional particularities not receiving the attention they deserve. Some over-generalisation is inevitable. Second, in focusing on the *organisational* manifestations of the youth component of resistance, great stress is placed on the initiatives and consciousness of leaders at the expense of the rank and file. The question of the – undeniably large – numbers of black youth who do *not* choose to become politically involved, but seek other outlets, is not addressed here.
5. The structures which have emerged to give organisational coherence to this otherwise amorphous grouping usually include age-limits in their constitutions, but in practice these are not applied. In this context, it should be noted that the inferior educational system for blacks produces a student body which is significantly older and more mature than its white counterpart. As Brewer has noted, 'The social category of "youth" for Africans in South Africa has extended barriers at the top end.' J. D. Brewer, *After Soweto. An Unfinished Journey* (Oxford: Oxford University Press, 1986), p. 73.
6. This was put to the author in several interviews with youth leaders – notably by Roseberry Sonto (president, Cape Youth Congress), Cape

Town, May 1986; and Daniel Montsisi (UDF Youth Officer and Executive member, Soweto Youth Congress), Johannesburg, May 1986, June 1986.

7. C. Bundy, 'Street Sociology and Pavement Politics: Aspects of Youth and Student Resistance in Cape Town, 1985', *Journal of Southern African Studies*, vol. 13, no. 3, 1987, p. 305. I have drawn widely on this article in this chapter.
8. Ibid. Generational consciousness is 'analogous to class consciousness and national consciousness'. Members of a 'social generation,' by 'grappling with a distinct set of social and historical problems . . . develop an awareness and common identity'.
9. Interview with members of the National Interim Committee of the South African Youth Congress (SAYCO), *State of the Nation*, South African Students' Press Union (SASPU), Johannesburg, April 1987.
10. Ibid.
11. Figures cited in *Weekly Mail*, Johannesburg, 1 August 1986.
12. See, for example, M. Bot and L. Schlemmer, *The Classroom Crisis: Black Demands and White Responses* (Durban, University of Natal, Centre for Applied Social Sciences, 1986) p. 16. 'Our analysis suggests that African education in South Africa, as it is presently structured, has a complex relationship to black political consciousness. It probably generates . . . frustration at high school, which is rapidly evolving into a revolutionary consciousness.'
13. SAYCO National Interim Committee interview, op. cit. note 9 above.
14. Bundy, 'Street Sociology and Pavement Politics', op. cit. note 7 above, p. 318.
15. Bundy refers in particular to the 'youthful militants of the ICU' (Industrial and Commercial Workers' Union), and the 'radicals who formed the Independent ANC'. Bundy, ibid., p. 310. Another form of youth organisation was represented by the Young Communist League (YCL), which acted as an adjunct to the Communist Party of South Africa (CPSA), then still predominantly a white party.
16. The history of black education is treated in this chapter only in so far as it relates directly to the growth of youth organisation. There are several specialist studies on the subject. See P. Christie, *The Right To Learn* (Johannesburg: Ravan Press, 1985), and Detainees' Parents' Support Committee, *Abantwana Bazabalaza: A Memorandum on Children Under Repression* (Johannesburg: DPSC, 1986), Appendix 3(a), pp. 171–212.
17. *Speak* community newspaper, Johannesburg, April 1986.
18. K. Hartshorne, 'Post-apartheid Education: A Concept in Process', address to McGraw-Hill Seminar, Johannesburg, 18/9/86. The African Education Movement (AEM) was launched at this time, 'perhaps the first attempt by the people of South Africa to take control of their own education', but eventually collapsed – along with the school boycotts – in the face of a threatened state 'lock-out' of boycotting pupils, as well as 'bannings . . . and police raids'. (DPSC, op. cit. note 16 above, p. 83).
19. In the 1960 State of Emergency, 1500 people were detained, and a further 12 000 prosecuted, mainly for pass law offences. See DPSC, op. cit. note 16 above, p. 4.

20. Montsisi interviews, op. cit. note 6 above.
21. Ibid.
22. Ibid.
23. Ibid.
24. Ibid.
25. The banned SSRC had been replaced by the Soweto Students' League (SSL), but the latter never achieved the prominence or influence of its progenitor.
26. See for example J. Kane-Berman, *The Method in the Madness* (London: Pluto Press, 1978) and Baruch Hirson, *Year of Fire, Year of Ash* (London: Zed Press, 1979).
27. Montsisi interviews, op. cit. note 6 above.
28. Ibid.
29. Quoted in J. Frederikse, *South Africa: A Different Kind of War* (Johannesburg: Ravan Press, 1986) p. 184.
30. Montsisi interviews, op. cit. note 6 above. There was another important, and even more direct link with the exiled liberation movement, as numbers of youths crossed the borders of South Africa after the Soweto uprising to join the ANC's military wing, Umkhonto we Sizwe (Spear of the Nation).
31. DPSC, op. cit. note 16 above, p. 9.
32. Montsisi interviews, op. cit. note 6 above.
33. C. Bundy, 'Schools and Revolution', *New Society*, London, 10 January 1986.
34. W. Finnegan, *Crossing the Line: A Year in the land of apartheid* (London: Hamish Hamilton, 1987).
35. Montsisi interviews, op. cit. note 6 above.
36. M. Murray, *South Africa: Time of Agony, Time of Destiny. The Upsurge of Popular Protest* (London: Verso, 1987) p. 195.
37. Ibid., p. 197.
38. Montsisi interviews, op. cit. note 6 above.
39. *Awake Black Student*, publication of the Azanian Students' Movement (AZASM), March 1985.
40. Ibid.
41. Author's interview with Xolisile Mnyaka, vice-president of AZASM, Johannesburg, May 1986.
42. For details of the Nkomati Accord see Murray, op. cit. note 6 above, pp. 55–7.
43. Frederikse, op. cit. note 29 above, p. 184.
44. Montsisi interviews, op. cit. note 6 above.
45. *Weekly Mail*, Johannesburg, 6 September 1985.
46. Author's interview with Dr Neville Alexander, Cape Town, May 1986. See also Bot and Schlemmer, op. cit. note 12 above, p. 13: 'the conflict in the schools appears to be shifting from a protest over rights and opportunity to a struggle for control'.
47. Statistics cited by Bundy, 'Schools and Revolution', op. cit. note 33 above.
48. See Bot and Schlemmer, op. cit. note 12 above, pp. 4, 12. 'Hartshorne has calculated that for every 100 [African] pupils who commenced

school in 1973, 64 survived as far as standard two, 46 as far as standard five, 26 as far as standard eight and only 10 survived to write the final senior certificate in 1984. Even worse, for the past five years, out of each 10 survivors in standard ten, only one gained matric exemption, four obtained a senior certificate and five candidates failed.'

49. See for example the *New York Times*, 21 October 1984: 'Student leaders have apparently come to view themselves as the cutting edge of community protest.' Certainly, the youth were central in the formation of street committees, the basic unit of township resistance and the linchpin of attempts to evolve popular, non-governmental structures – the so-called 'organs of peoples' power' (see Chapter 5).
50. Murray, op. cit. note 36 above, p. 249.
51. On 11 September, in response to the dramatic escalation of street clashes, the Minister of Law and Order extended the longstanding ban on outdoor political meetings to include indoor gatherings in twenty-one magisterial districts.
52. COSAS' call for the formation of 'youth congresses' had already achieved some success by January 1984. Present at a conference attended by regional COSAS representatives, were leaders of several youth congresses then in existence. These included the Port Elizabeth Youth Congress (PEYCO); the Cape Youth Congress (CAYCO); the Soweto Youth Congress (SOYCO); the Alexandra Youth Congress (AYCO); and the Saulsville-Atteridgeville Youth Organisation (SAYO). The conference encouraged the formation of more township-based youth groups, in preparation for a regional youth infrastructure to complement COSAS' own organisational framework. It was suggested at this meeting, for the first time, that a national co-ordinating body for all the South African youth congresses should be the ultimate aim.
53. Bundy, 'Schools and Revolution', op. cit. note 33 above.
54. DPSC, op. cit. note 16 above, p. 9. 'Parents came out in their tens of thousands to support their children on 5th and 6th November 1984 . . . This student/parent alliance enabled the students to build on the gains they had recently made.'
55. Ibid., p. 8.
56. On 26 October, the Emergency was extended to eight magisterial districts in greater Cape Town.
57. Bundy, 'Schools and Revolution', op. cit. note 33 above.
58. Murray, op. cit. note 36 above, p. 334.
59. Ibid., p. 374.
60. Ibid., p. 334. During the full nine months of this Emergency some 11 500 people were detained, more than 2000 of them aged between eight and sixteen. These figures do not include people detained in areas falling outside the Emergency restrictions. (DPSC, op. cit. note 16 above p. 13.)
61. *Weekly Mail*, Johannesburg, 6 September 1985.
62. Ibid., 31 August 1985.
63. Murray, op. cit. note 36 above, p. 307.
64. Author's interview with activists, Transvaal, December 1985.
65. Ibid. The problem created by committed but politically unsophisticated

youths promoting campaigns which were unwise or insufficiently canvassed had been noted by commentators even before this time. Swilling, for example, referring to the Eastern Cape stayaway of March 1985, pointed to the tendency of unemployed, radical youths to 'confront all forms of authority without always getting approval from community organisations'. Mark Swilling, 'Stayaways, Urban Protest and the State', in *South African Review III* (Johannesburg: Ravan Press, 1986).

66. Montsisi interviews, op. cit. note 6 above.
67. This was conceded by several youth leaders. A Transvaal activist's comments were typical: 'With the first Emergency, many of our leaders were detained, and local groups had to keep working, often in isolation. In some, a trend developed in which they identified themselves, the youth, as leaders of the struggle.' *Weekly Mail*, Johannesburg, 12 December 1986.
68. In Alexandra township, for example, elderly women returning from white shops in Johannesburg – which had been placed 'out of bounds' by boycott organisers – were forced to drink the cooking oil they had purchased. These and similar incidents were widely reported in the South African Press, contributing to the monochromatic image of 'the comrades' as being composed only of 'thugs'. Reports of some comrades' own attempts to stamp out these activities did appear, but were far less frequent and prominent. An exception was a feature article entitled 'The Robin Hood Comrades', in the *Sunday Star*, Johannesburg, 21 September 1986.
69. Author's interview with activists, Alexandra township, April 1986.
70. See M. Nash (ed.) *Problems of Township Children and Youth.* Report of a seminar organised by the Townships Liaison Project of the Black Sash (Cape Western) (Cape Town: Black Sash, 1986), and DPSC, op. cit. note 16 above, 'Street Children in South Africa', pp. 142–60.
71. Author's interview with Saths Cooper, convener of the National Forum and president of AZAPO, Johannesburg, August 1986.
72. Murray, op. cit. note 36 above, pp. 334–5. It was estimated by the ANC that among youths reporting to ANC structures in neighbouring states in 1986, a startling six out of ten were informers.
73. DPSC, op.cit. note 16 above, p. 25. See ibid., pp. 114–41 for a comprehensive account of 'the social and psychological effects of detention and repression on children and families'.
74. It was suggested in numerous interviews with youth leaders that a contributory factor to the fratricidal violence was frustration among 'less sophisticated cadres' at their inability to strike telling blows against the security forces. The potential for violence which had developed was thus, in many cases, turned inwards against 'easier targets' – i.e. activists within rival youth groupings.
75. Considerable protest activity took place on many university campuses during this time. For example, police raided the Universities of Cape Town (UCT) and the Western Cape (UWC) in August at the height of rallies calling for the release of Mandela. The University of the North at Turfloop was in constant turmoil, eventually being occupied by troops and subjected to strict curfews.

76. Author's interview with activists, Transvaal, January 1986.
77. *Sunday Star*, Johannesburg, 16 March 1986.
78. Murray, op. cit. note 36 above, p. 345.
79. Frederikse, op. cit. note 29 above, p. 48.
80. *Sowetan*, Johannesburg, 28 February 1986.
81. The *Star*, Johannesburg, 18 April 1986.
82. Author's interview with activists, Cape Town, 1986.
83. The *Star*, Johannesburg, 18 June 1986.
84. Murray, op. cit. note 36 above, p. 376.
85. By October 1985 more than 200 black local councillors, including twenty-seven 'mayors', had resigned. The state's system of black local government was in disarray, with very few 'town councils' able to operate normally. However, the ephemeral nature of the 'liberated zones' was illustrated, often with some pathos, in the aftermath of the June 1986 Emergency. In Alexandra township, for example, an area which had been described to the author as a 'liberated zone' in April, was transformed by June into a military staging post.
86. Murray, op. cit. note 36 above, p. 373.
87. Cooper interview, op. cit. note 71 above.
88. Reverend Molefe Tsele in the *Weekly Mail*, Johannesburg, 20 December 1985.
89. Montsisi interviews, op. cit. note 6 above.
90. Murray, op. cit. note 36 above, p. 403. Curtis Nkondo, president of the (UDF-aligned) National Education Union of South Africa (NEUSA), put the argument succinctly: 'If [the students] do not go back they will fail to organise themselves and will not be able to work as a coherent force . . . If they are not together they will be easily manipulated and divided by the system.' Ibid., p. 404.
91. *Weekly Mail*, Johannesburg, 30 August 1985. Although many parents resented the fact that their children were spurning educational opportunities which they themselves had never enjoyed and for which they had made great financial sacrifices, the courage and organisational ability of the youth increasingly impressed them. This emerged in numerous interviews with parents conducted by the author. See also Sam Mabe, *Sowetan*, Johannesburg, 12 June 1986: 'Of late parents who were . . . sceptical of the childrens' action are now in the forefront of the search for a better and more acceptable system of education.'
92. *Upbeat* magazine, Johannesburg, 1 November 1986. A typical example of the atmosphere prevalent among parents was provided in a newspaper report in January which told of a 'Mrs M. Mphane' making an impromptu speech in which she said 'We have accused our children of taking the law into their own hands. Where were we when they did so?' She went on to urge parents to 'involve themselves directly in the educational struggle'. The *Star*, Johannesburg, 6 January 1986.
93. The *Star*, Johannesburg, 9 December 1985.
94. Ibid., 6 January 1986.
95. The demands included the unbanning of COSAS and the development of 'relevant' curricula – an initiative which came to be known as 'peoples' education'. (See DPSC., op. cit. note 16 above, p. 99). For a

full list of the demands, see Ibid., pp. 97–8.

96. *Weekly Mail*, Johannesburg, 27 March 1986.
97. The *Star*, Johannesburg, 30 January 1986 and *Weekly Mail*, Johannesburg, 31 January 1986.
98. The *Star*, Johannesburg, 16 and 22 January 1986.
99. See for example *Die Vaderland*, Johannesburg, 7 February 1986: 'A new alliance for peace and order has been established . . . the SPCC deserves most of the credit.'
100. *Sunday Star*, Johannesburg, 23 March 1986.
101. Government spokesmen were well aware that the return to school had been agreed upon 'so black pupils could be more effectively organized politically', but they nevertheless welcomed the decision. *Sunday Tribune*, Durban, 6 April 1986.
102. *Weekly Mail*, Johannesburg, 27 March 1986.
103. The National Forum refused to send delegates, charging the NECC with having been constituted by an 'extremely sectarian, undemocratic and manipulative process'. (Author's interview with executive members of the Forum, Johannesburg, April 1986). Nevertheless, the Forum resolved to support those resolutions it found politically acceptable.
104. The Inkatha Youth Brigade (IYB) operates, like its parent movement (discussed in Chapters 1 and 12), outside the folds of mainstream resistance, and hence falls beyond the scope of this chapter. It is worth noting, however, that the black youth of the IYB manifest a different type of generational consciousness to that underpinning the UDF and National Forum youth structures. Whereas the militant actions of the latter since 1976 had a catalytic effect on the national resistance organisations, the IYB is a creation of, and is under the strict control of, the parent organisation – and in particular its president, Chief Mangosuthu Buthelezi, Chief Minister of KwaZulu. Although the IYB is constitutionally charged with 'playing a vanguard role' in Inkatha, it is in fact a tightly structured, highly professional and scrupulously loyal *adjunct* of the organisation. A generational consciousness has been instilled in, rather than evolved by, the Inkatha youth. The Brigade was launched in 1977, and claims a membership of half a million – making it, for a time, the largest single youth grouping in South Africa. The IYB initially concentrated its energies on teenagers, but its parameters now stretch to pre-teens and people up to forty years old. Together with the paramilitary Inkatha Youth Corps, the IYB is in essence a weapon to be deployed by the Inkatha leadership at any time. Beneath similar anti-apartheid pronouncements, the Brigade's policies run counter to the campaigns of the mainstream youth resistance movements at every turn, and often result in physical conflict with rival youth groups. Rather than alliance with UDF or Forum youth structures, the IYB has held joint meetings with the Afrikaner youth organisation *Jeugkrag* (see Chapter 6). The IYB is an important youth structure in South Africa, but is essentially restricted to the KwaZulu/Natal region. It is able, through its organisational sophistication and resources, to impose its will (which is that of Inkatha) within its geographical sphere of influence. Nationally, however, it has little or no influence, and has no prospect of becoming a

threat to SAYCO, for example. However, the tremendous hostility which has built up between IYB rank and file and the youth of the UDF and Forum in Natal bodes ill for future generations in the area. (Sources: author's interview with Musa Zondi, National Chairman of the Inkatha Youth Brigade, Durban, March 1986; Interview with Ntwe Mofole, National Organiser of the IYB, Ulundi, August 1986; Peta-Ann Teague, 'A Study of Inkatha yeSizwe's Approach to the Youth, with Specific Reference to the Movement's Youth Brigade', unpublished honours dissertation, Faculty of Arts, University of Cape Town, 1983; Speeches and resolutions of the Annual General Conference of the Inkatha Youth Brigade, Ulundi, 30 August 1986.)

105. Buthelezi strenuously denied involvement in the attack, denouncing the 'political motives' of the educational conference. (*Sowetan*, Johannesburg, 8 April 1986). He was also reported as saying 'If there were Inkatha youths with Inkatha uniforms involved in the eruption of anger, why must I be blamed for their behaviour? The NECC itself came here to court anger.' (*Weekly Mail*, Johannesburg, 4 April 1986) NECC spokesman Molefe Tsele said it was 'self evident' that it had been an Inkatha attack, especially in view of the fact that the buses had been hired in the name of a senior Inkatha official. (The *Star*, Johannesburg, 4 April 1986). At the NECC conference itself, Buthelezi was declared an 'enemy of the people'.
106. Zwelakhe Sisulu, 'Peoples' Education for Peoples' Power', keynote address to the national consultative conference of the National Education Crisis Committee, Durban, 29 March 1986.
107. *Weekly Mail*, Johannesburg, 4 April 1986.
108. The response was weakest in the Western Cape, where a boycott which had begun before the NECC conference continued.
109. *Weekly Mail*, Johannesburg, 4 April 1986.
110. *Sunday Star*, Johannesburg, 16 March 1986.
111. Murray, op. cit. note 36 above, p. 392.
112. Ibid., p. 425.
113. *City Press*, Johannesburg, 20 April 1986.
114. See DPSC, op. cit. note 16 above, pp. 32–4.
115. Murray, op. cit. note 36 above, p. 430.
116. DPSC, op. cit. note 16 above, p. 5, p. 13.
117. For a discussion of the differences between 'underground' resistance operation, such as that undertaken by ANC guerrillas within South Africa, and 'semi-underground', legal activity such as that of the UDF, see Chapter 5.
118. *Weekly Mail*, Johannesburg, 29 August 1986.
119. Ibid.
120. Ibid.
121. Cooper interview, op. cit. note 71 above.
122. Ibid.
123. Ibid.
124. Under Emergency conditions, the NECC initiative was seriously hampered. Ninety per cent of the Committee's top leadership were arrested by the end of 1986. The principle of the alliance remained alive,

but was not easily translated into meetings and discussions.

125. As Bundy has noted, 'certain objective factors make a common cultural identity between youth/student and organized worker consciousness relatively attainable in South Africa. There is . . . common racial/ national oppression . . . the enforced propinquity across social divides . . . of various strata within ethnically demarcated ghettoes. There is the widespread phenomenon of "first generation students", linking within single families the solidly proletarian and the potential petty bourgeoisie. And finally there is the lived experience of many students: many who complete high school or enter tertiary education can do so only by interrupting their schooling with periods of wage labour.' Bundy, *Street Sociology and Pavement Politics*, op. cit. note 7 above, p. 324.
126. Tom Lodge, quoted in *The Observer*, London, 24 May 1987.
127. Montsisi interviews, op. cit. note 6 above.
128. SAYCO National Interim Committee interview, op. cit. note 9 above.
129. Ibid.
130. Ibid.
131. Ibid.
132. *Saspu National*, Johannesburg, November–December 1986.
133. Ibid.
134. Ibid.
135. Ibid. Several key members of the Interim Committee were in detention.
136. 'Massive Youth Group to Come Out of the Shadows', *Weekly Mail*, Johannesburg, 12 December 1986.
137. Ibid.
138. Ibid.
139. Speeches and resolutions of the South African Youth Congress (SAYCO), Cape Town, March 1987. *State of the Nation*, Johannesburg, April 1987.
140. Ibid.
141. Ibid.
142. Ibid.
143. Ibid.
144. Ibid.
145. Address by SAYCO president Peter Mokaba to the Congress of South African Trade Unions (COSATU) conference, Johannesburg, June 1987.
146. A resurgence of this trend had been evident at the height of 'insurrectionary' activity. Murray has claimed that more youths went into exile between July 1984 and January 1986 than had left during the 1976/77 uprising. On average, four out of five of these joined the ANC. (Murray, op. cit. note 36 above, p. 397).
147. *Weekly Mail*, Johannesburg, 12 December 1986.
148. Ibid.
149. AZAYO was launched in 1987, but its influence and size could not be assessed at the time of writing as the organisation had not engaged in any significant campaigns.
150. DPSC., op. cit. note 16 above, pp. 102–103.
151. *Weekly Mail,* Johannesburg, 25 April 1986.

152. DPSC., op. cit. note 16 above, p. 102.
153. Extracts from a poem in *Arise! Vukani*, Magazine of Action Youth, Johannesburg, March–April 1986.

ACKNOWLEDGEMENT

Besides the members of the Study Group, I am especially grateful to the following people for their comments on this chapter – not all of which, sadly, I have been able to address: Colin Bundy, Graham Watts, Kate Maxwell, Howard Barrell, Gerda-Marie Kenyon, Kumi Naidoo.

4 The Trade Union Movement in the Politics of Resistance in South Africa

Phillip van Niekerk

INTRODUCTION

The three-week-long strike by some 300 000 black miners in August 1987 cast an international spotlight on South Africa's labour movement. Almost fifteen years of slow building had produced an organisation of oppressed South Africans capable of a very real expression of power. The fact that the strike was over wages and that the state – on the whole – stayed out, 'depoliticised' it to some extent. That it took place in such a strange arena (the South African mining industry, virtually a state-within-a-state with a private army), meant that it could hardly be held to reflect what was happening in the labour movement as a whole. Yet such a strike, in such a country, could not occur without a political dimension.

The performance of the union was watched with keen interest. To an otherwise unenfranchised population, union strength is an important lever of power. When black workers take industrial action it is because they have a deep sense of deprivation and injustice. Their ability to hold out for so long, and to return to work in such a disciplined manner (even without a major wage increase), contributed to making the National Union of Mineworkers' (NUM) strike a watershed event. The duration of the strike was proof of the growing maturity of the union movement. Though smaller in scale, earlier disputes at the 'OK Bazaars' and South African Transport Services (SATS) had lasted even longer than the mine strike. Another major dispute, involving postal workers, was still unresolved after the return of the miners.

The growing muscle and self-confidence of black unions during 1987 was combined with their increasing importance within broad resistance organisation. By late 1987 this had prompted a response from the state, as the government threatened new legislation to crack down on 'revolutionaries' in the union movement, and fuelled speculation about a formal clampdown. Informally, two bombs wrecked the headquarters in Johannesburg of the Congress of South African Trade Unions (COSATU) in May. COSATU's Community House in Cape Town was blown up in August, and the federation's property was destroyed in other regions.

That the state did not deal with the unions 'formally' – through 'traditional' bannings or detentions – was an indication of the survival of elements of its 'reformist' ideology, aware of an international audience and insisting that industrial relations be 'a matter for employers and employees'. It was also a sign that by 1987 the union movement had such deep roots in the factories and mines that the state could not simply clamp down in the manner to which it was accustomed – at least without provoking a real fight. Yet fourteen years previously, only a handful of Africans had been members of trade unions.

THE 'POLITICS OF CONTROL'

When workers at the Coronation Tile and Brick Company went on strike on 9 January 1973 – launching the Durban strikes and heralding the renaissance of black unionism in South Africa – they chanted: 'Man is dead, but his spirit still lives'. They were describing the condition of their lives. Not only were they without the vote, but they had pitifully little control over any aspect of their lives. They were, to all intents and purposes, dead – stripped of their humanity.

From these origins in 1973, the emergent union movement has had to address itself to two kinds of politics. First, there was the 'national liberation struggle' and how and where the unions fitted in to it. Second, there was the 'politics of control' – of black workers struggling and winning for themselves some say over their own lives at the point of production. In the decade after the Durban strikes, this was the most fundamental aspect of the task of the union movement. Factory by factory, every struggle over unfair dismissals, retrenchments and wages pushed back the frontier of control and won gains for black workers. It was often an uneven struggle against hostile employers; a racist state whose laws prevented black workers from participating in the industrial relations system; police who were often deployed and used violence against strikers; and a conservative, largely white-established union movement – especially the Trade Union Council of South Africa (TUCSA). TUCSA attempted to set up 'parallel' unions and co-opt black workers into a system which was not of their own making, not geared towards their own interests, and in which whites would retain control.

When the government liberalised the labour laws in 1979, following the publication of the report of the Wiehahn Commission of enquiry into labour legislation, the hardy nucleus of a trade union movement already existed. The six years of struggle had forged the bedrock principle of the movement – its ideology of worker control. Thousands of trained shop stewards, educated primarily in the 'school of struggle', were the cornerstone of the labour movement which was now ready to take off.

'WORKERISM' AND 'POPULISM'

In terms of the 'politics of control', the union movement in South Africa was always in essence 'political'. But on the national level, there was much debate about how to slot into the broader 'liberation struggle'. By the early 1980s, emerging federations and a number of individual unions were jockeying for support. When the United Democratic Front (UDF) was formed in 1983, only a small section of the union movement affiliated to it.

The largest federation, FOSATU (Federation of South African Trade Unions), embraced rapidly growing unions in a number of sectors: steel and engineering (MAWU – the Metal and Allied Workers' Union); automobiles (NAAWU – National Automobile and Allied Workers' Union); transport (TGWU – the Transport and General Workers' Union); chemicals (CWIU – the Chemical Workers' Industrial Union); textiles (NUTW – National Union of Textile Workers); paper (PWAWU – Paper, Wood and Allied Workers' Union); and food (SFAWU – Sweet, Food and Allied Workers' Union).

At first FOSATU shied away from overt political involvement. The Federation feared state repression, believing that they had to build up structures on the shop-floor before confronting the state. This fear had been underlined by a series of bannings of union leaders in 1976 – a serious setback to the fledgeling movement.

Second, they feared that the interests of the working class could be subsumed by the national democratic struggle. Some FOSATU leaders considered this to have been the 'error' of the South African Congress of Trade Unions (SACTU), in its alliance with the largely middle-class leadership of the African National Congress (ANC) in the 1950s. The repression of the 1960s not only outlawed the ANC, but also virtually wiped SACTU off the factory floors. FOSATU was criticised in turn for its narrow, factory based focus and branded by many in the political movements as 'workerist'. Much of the early organisational and theoretical bases of FOSATU had been laid by (white) former university students, whose involvement in groups such as the 'Wages Commissions' was critical to the lift-off of unionism in the mid-1970s.

The second largest grouping was the Council of Unions of South Africa (CUSA), which differed from the non-racial FOSATU in that it insisted on 'black worker leadership' in the unions. Formed in 1980, CUSA was strong in certain sectors, including transport (TAWU – Transport and Allied Workers' Union); food (the Food, Beverage Workers' Union); and chemicals (SACWU – the South African Chemical Workers' Union). CUSA also established the National Union of Mineworkers (NUM) after the wage strikes of July 1982 alerted them to the presence of a huge section of unorganised workers. Guided by its general secretary Cyril Ramaphosa, the NUM soon became the first black union since 1946 to penetrate successfully the mining industry. It was soon to become the largest single union in the country.

CUSA affiliated to both the United Democratic Front (UDF) and the Black Consciousness oriented National Forum in 1983. This apparently even-handed, self-consciously non-sectarian approach to the various anti-apartheid tendencies did not amount to much in concrete terms, however. CUSA never associated itself with the so-called 'UDF unions', which were far more narrowly committed to the UDF/Freedom Charterist camp.

Of these 'UDF unions', one of the most important was the South African Allied Workers' Union (SAAWU), with its strength concentrated in East London and Durban. From 1980 to 1982 it was the fastest growing union federation in the country, and also the most overtly 'political'. Along with a number of smaller general unions such as the General and Allied Workers' Union (GAWU), which affiliated to the UDF in 1983, SAAWU represented a political style starkly different to that of FOSATU. These unions were identified as 'populist', due to their willingness to organise through mass rallies and charismatic leadership. SAAWU's president was a former furniture salesman, Thozamile Gqweta. He was a high-profile public figure, in contrast to the hundreds of shop stewards – little known outside their own factories – who were emerging as the leadership of FOSATU.

The populist unions, though strong in particular areas, were unable to match the industrial muscle of FOSATU's affiliates, and faced constant state repression. In East London – one of the most militant centres – a combination of intransigent employers, the Ciskei bantustan government and the security police (who viewed SAAWU as the internal wing of SACTU and the ANC), succeeded to some extent in smashing the union. Gqweta was severely tortured on at least three occasions. However, these unions pioneered a political involvement which the mainstream of the union movement was later compelled to follow. Most of the bigger COSATU affiliates – the NUM and the National Union of Metalworkers (NUMSA) – hold mass rallies and involve themselves politically in a manner reminiscent of SAAWU in the early 1980s.

There were several important unions based in Cape Town which were not affiliated to any of the federations. These included the General Workers' Union (GWU) which organised dockers at the four major ports; and the Food and Canning Workers' Union (FCWU), a SACTU survivor which had been almost moribund before being revived in the mid-1970s. Both these unions had the input of a combination of old SACTU organisers and young, left-wing, white students.

In 1979 and 1980 the Cape-based unions mobilised community boycotts in support of workers in disputes with the Fattis and Monis and red meat companies, respectively. In so doing they pioneered links between trade unions and community and political organisations – and acquired the reputation of being 'political' unions, not simply at the level of rhetoric, but through hard struggle and alliances. In this sense they foreshadowed the political direction of COSATU by more than six years.

In the early 1980s, unions like the FCWU and the GWU were closely allied to SAAWU in East London, but their solid shop-floor basis moved them steadily closer to FOSATU, especially after 1982. Along with FOSATU, they opted not to affiliate to the UDF – stressing 'worker independence'.

A CHANGE IN THE WIND

FOSATU's political caution began to dissipate in the face of the revival of militant resistance, most graphically illustrated by the 'Vaal Triangle uprising' of September 1984. The unprecedented explosion of black anger throughout the country which followed could not help but affect the unions – whose members' homes were, after all, in the burning ghettoes. A key turning point was a 'stayaway' in November 1984 (in protest against the military invasion of Sebokeng), which paralysed the Witwaterstrand for two days and in which 800 000 workers participated. FOSATU and CUSA unions actively supported the stayaway, in alliance with the UDF and other community organisations. Union leaders, including CUSA general secretary Piroshaw Camay, were detained.

The conditions for such co-operation were laid by a consumer boycott at the 'Simba Chips' factory in which community groups – in particular the Congress of South African Students (COSAS) – backed members of FOSATU's SFAWU. It was the most important 'solidarity boycott' since those in the Cape in 1979 and 1980, and the workers were eventually reinstated. But regular, disciplined co-operation between unions and community based organisations was still more an ideal than a reality. There was union involvement in the township rebellion of 1985, particularly in providing experienced leaders for the community. In some instances, however, the level of union involvement was minimal; in others there was even friction between the organisational structures.

In March 1985 FOSATU unions, along with several others, refused to support a stayaway in the Eastern Cape, arguing that they could not take such a decision without consulting their members. The stayaway had a tragic finale in the 'Langa massacre' in which twenty-one people were shot dead by police.

THE BIRTH OF COSATU

The formation of COSATU in November 1985 introduced a new dynamic into political unionism in South Africa. It was founded with a signed-up membership of more than 450 000 workers. COSATU drew together the FOSATU unions; the UDF unions; several large independent unions such as the Commercial, Catering and Allied Workers' Union (CCAWUSA); the Cape based unions, the FCWU and GWU; and the increasingly important NUM, which broke away from CUSA.

COSATU's first president was Elijah Barayi, a mineworker from the West Rand who had been a member of the ANC Youth League in the 1940s and 1950s. The first general secretary was Jay Naidoo from SFAWU. Like Barayi, Naidoo was considered more 'political' than

FOSATU's previous general secretaries, who had been regarded by some as 'workerists'. The first vice-president was FOSATU's former president Chris Dlamini, who had been instrumental in moving FOSATU towards political militancy on the East Rand. COSATU's political direction was conditioned by the circumstances into which it was born; a State of Emergency and widespread rebellion in the black ghettoes. From its very inception, COSATU announced its intention of becoming a pivot of the struggle against 'apartheid and capitalism'.

The basic principles of the Congress, as set out in its constitution, committed it to a 'united, democratic South Africa, free of oppression and economic exploitation . . . [which] can only be achieved under the leadership of a united working class'. Resolutions passed at its inaugural conference supported disinvestment and sanctions; opposed the bantustan system; and called for the termination of the Emergency, the withdrawal of the military and the police from the townships; and the unconditional release of all political prisoners and detainees.

UNIONISM OUTSIDE COSATU

Despite its achievement of unprecedented trade union unity, COSATU failed to unite all the emergent unions under one banner. CUSA, which differed from the non-racial FOSATU and COSATU in its insistence on 'black worker leadership', stayed out. A smaller federation, the Azanian Confederation of Trade Unions (AZACTU), representing Black Consciousness and Africanist strands in the union movement, also opposed the principle of non-racialism, and declined the invitation to join the Congress.

With COSATU making most of the running and attracting most of the attention, CUSA and AZACTU began to forge a closer relationship. In the latter months of 1986 they united in one federation, which eventually became the National Council of Trade Unions (NACTU). CUSA's Piroshaw Camay retained his position of general secretary in the new confederation. Hailed as a 'labour giant', NACTU claimed an initial membership of more than 400 000, but although several CUSA unions (notably SACWU) were relatively strong, CUSA–AZACTU in its new incarnation was not in the same league as COSATU. Figures compiled by labour consultants Andrew Levy and Associates at the time of the CUSA–AZACTU launch in September 1986 revealed that in the period that COSATU unions were responsible for industrial action costing half a million working days, CUSA–AZACTU was responsible for some 22 000. These statistics notwithstanding, NACTU is a force within the union movement which cannot be ignored.

With the COSATU leadership moving quickly into the Charterist camp and broadly identified with the ANC, NACTU met with the Pan Africanist Congress (PAC) leaders in Dar Es Salaam in August 1987. Thus, more than ever, the union movement appeared to mirror the political divisions within the liberation movement.

Rivalry between COSATU and NACTU, however, has not turned into conflict on the shop-floor, as is the case between COSATU and the United Workers Union of South Africa (UWUSA). The latter grouping was launched on 1 May 1986 by Chief Mangosuthu Buthelezi, Chief Minister of KwaZulu and President of the Inkatha movement, at a rally attended by 70 000 people at Durban's King's Park Stadium. UWUSA was created as a rival to COSATU, spurred on, no doubt, by a scathing speech by Barayi in which he attacked the homeland system and Buthelezi in particular. (In Natal, FOSATU had attempted to co-exist with Inkatha, though the relationship was always uneasy. When COSATU threw its weight behind the national democratic struggle, Inkatha members in the unions found themselves having to make a direct political choice for the first time.)

While UWUSA has not had much impact on conventional industrial relations, a horrifying wave of violence on the shop-floors and in the townships of Natal has followed in its wake. The deaths of eleven Hlobane coalminers in May 1986, of a Food and Allied Works Union (FAWU) shop steward at Jabula Foods on the East Rand in June 1986, and of two MAWU shop stewards at BTR Sarmcol near Pietermaritzburg in December 1986, served as ugly testimony to this new trend. The widespread detention of COSATU leaders in potential UWUSA growth areas prompted speculation that the state was actively attempting to create 'space' for the Inkatha aligned union. UWUSA is pro-'free market' and anti-disinvestment (thus diametrically opposed to COSATU), and so has obvious attractions for some employers – including at least one major mining house. The fact that the NUM had to exempt its Natal region from the recent national strike is a clear indication of the inroads made by UWUSA. As KwaZulu becomes an increasingly important labour pool for the mines – at the expense of foreign states like Lesotho, as well as the other homelands – UWUSA could extend its influence in the mining industry.

Several important industrial unions operated independently of COSATU, NACTU and UWUSA. These included ex-affiliates of TUCSA, a middle-of-the-road grouping formed in the 1950s which had moved to the right in the 1970s, and was in a state of terminal decline by the beginning of 1986. The political chasm between TUCSA and the forerunners of COSATU and NACTU was reflected in its indecision over whether to support President P. W. Botha's 'new constitution' in 1983, and the fact that its president, Robbie Botha of the Mine Surface Officials' Association, once ran for parliament as a National Party candidate.

TUCSA continued to lose affiliates in 1986, eventually opting to disband – thus leaving the field open to what its president had described only five years previously as 'our minuscule rivals'. Its demise left a number of substantial unions without a home, and one of them – the Motor Industry Combined Workers' Union (MICWU) – merged to form NUMSA and so joined COSATU in 1987. In addition, two erstwhile TUCSA members were poised to link up with COSATU's National Union of Textile Workers during 1987.

On the far right, the rump of the once-powerful white labour movement remains under the umbrella of the South African Confederation of Labour (SACOL), whose membership has declined to below 100 000. Its only really important constituent is the Mine Workers' Union (MWU), which is fighting a rearguard action to maintain the privileged status of the white mineworker. The MWU's general secretary, Arrie Paulus, was elected to parliament as the (Conservative Party) member for the mining town of Carletonville in May 1987 – just in time, ironically enough, to see racial 'job reservation' disappear from the statute books.

COSATU's EARLY POLITICAL DIRECTION

By 1986 these other movements were sideshows in the main theatre of trade unionism. COSATU was unquestionably the leading player. COSATU's formation coincided with a recognition by union leaders that the struggle in the townships could not be ignored by workers' organisations. To have any say in the shaping of this struggle, the unions had actively to involve themselves in it. In response to the challenge, COSATU's leadership began to tread the tricky path of 'alliance politics' with the myriad anti-apartheid groupings and the liberation movements.

FOSATU and other unions had been wary of affiliating to the UDF precisely because there was support for different political tendencies among their members. For instance, FOSATU had Inkatha members in Natal; a large proportion of members of CCAWUSA were supporters of the Azanian Peoples' Organisation (AZAPO); and the Cape Town Municipal Workers' Association (CTMWA) had long-standing links with the Non-European Unity Movement (NEUM). At FOSATU's 1982 congress, general secretary Joe Foster mooted the formation of a political party of organised labour – a logical extension of the notion of 'working class independence'. Many 'workerists' supported the notion that the union movement should *reject* affiliation to established parties, and should establish their own political wing. However, the prominence of the ANC, the UDF and its allies in the struggle against apartheid made the creation of a new political centre unthinkable to many workers – both in terms of *realpolitik* and the shop-floor sentiment of the majority of union members. There appears to have been a decision soon after the formation of COSATU to seek alliances with the broad democratic movement – including exiles, the UDF, and in particular its youth affiliates (see Chapter 3).

At a meeting in Lusaka in April 1986, COSATU issued a joint statement with the ANC, accepting the ANC as the leading force in the liberation struggle of which COSATU was an 'integral part'. Internally, COSATU linked up with the UDF for national campaigns, thus setting the stage for new debates about its political direction. This direction was to cause tensions within the Congress, notwithstanding the fact that its largest constituent union (the NUM) supported it. The general political climate strengthened COSATU's industrial muscle as worker militancy grew despite massive unemployment, deep recession, and growing repression. In fact, workers broke records for industrial action in 1986; they occupied their factories and, crucially, entered the largely uncharted terrain of political struggle. New, politicised, forms of industrial action emerged: factory sit-ins, underground sit-ins by miners, and – instead of subsiding – industrial action increased in several sectors following the declaration of the State of Emergency on 12 June.

On the day of UWUSA's launch, COSATU (with the UDF), flexed its muscles as an estimated two million workers staged a May Day stayaway. An equivalent number stopped work on 16 June – Soweto Day – illustrating the capacity of South Africa's black workers to take action alongside political groups.

A ROCKY ROAD

COSATU experienced major teething problems in 1986. Several regional structures battled to launch themselves in the face of ideological and other disagreements, while unions in only two sectors – food and transport – met the deadline for COSATU affiliates to merge into a 'single national union per industry'. Some general unions continued to resist incorporation into industrial unions.

By mid-1987 the metal unions had merged into COSATU's second largest affiliate, NUMSA. Concurrent attempts at merger in the retail sector were, however, unsuccessful when the largest branch of CCAWUSA walked out of the founding conference. A loose alliance of 'workerists' and Black Consciousness supporters were resisting, in particular, the adoption of the Freedom Charter. The 'populist' versus 'workerist' debate continued to rage within sections of the labour movement (more so within than among unions), with a more complex pattern of union debate emerging. One union, the NUTW, actually split over what was characterised as a 'workerist-populist' conflict. A new union, the Textile and Allied Workers' Union (TAWU), emerged after mediation attempts by COSATU failed.

The State of Emergency influenced the developing relationship between the unions and the UDF. The UDF and its affiliates were the main targets of repression, but hundreds of unionists were also detained. The failure of the 14 July stayaway, called to protest against the Emergency, was indicative of the difficulties of mobilisation under the strictures of the clampdown. It was also a warning against the hasty calling of union action without proper consultation with the rank and file. On the regional, industrial and legal levels, however, the union movement showed that its deep organisational roots assured its ability to respond creatively to the Emergency. The grassroots 'politics of control' proved more enduring than the national alliance, which was more easily silenced by the bannings of rallies, funerals and open dissent. COSATU unions such as CCAWUSA, the NUM and CWIU embarked on rolling strikes demanding the release of union leaders.

The strikes took employers by surprise and put pressure on them to wield their influence with the government, attempting to secure the release of union leaders, as well as a measure of protection for the unions. The first major court challenge to the State of Emergency came from the metalworkers. In attempting to have the Emergency nullified in the Natal Supreme Court, MAWU succeeded in having some press curbs overturned.

1986 was a rough year for union activists. A number were killed, attacked, driven into hiding or detained for long periods. It was feared that during 1987 the state could crack down even more severely, using new forms of repression – especially the 'vigilante' attacks which had already been employed on a limited scale, rather than taking the risk of an all-out confrontation. At the same time there was a concern that the growing militancy of workers, the frequent stayaways, and union support for sanctions, could prompt an 'employer backlash'. Sanctions – virulently opposd by employer groups – are supported by both COSATU and NACTU.

THE SEARCH CONTINUES

In a statement distributed by pamphlet to members at the beginning of 1987, COSATU reaffirmed its belief that the base of its power lay in the workplace: 'We must ensure that every workplace has strong, democratic structures and active members. We must not allow our differences to undermine our unity in action.' The statement indicated that COSATU was willing to look critically at some of its own actions:

> We have made some progress – but not nearly enough. Too often we stood back while our comrades have struggled along against the bosses and the government. Too often we stood back and watched while our comrades were detained – even though we have resolved to fight every attack on our organisation with united action. And when we did take decisions for strong action – like the 14 July action against the Emergency or the 1 December action against the killings of our MAWU comrades – some problems and divisions in our movement weakened our protest. This is bad comrades. We must build our structures, our unity and our ability to mobilise more strongly and seriously – so that we can take action on what we decide, instead of just having resolutions on paper.

Apart from the call for a 'living wage', COSATU saw its tasks during 1987 as building mass united action; organising the unemployed; building worker self-defence; building democratic community and youth organisations; and organising farm workers – the last having remained largely without protection under the country's labour legislation. The most telling political statement in the document was that:

> COSATU workers are leading the struggle to build street committees in the townships. Like our unions in the workplaces, street committees will give us the democratic organisations and unity and strength to fight for all the things we need – including control over

every aspect of our lives through our own democratic organisation under the leadership of organised workers.

COSATU's political direction has continued in 1987. The unions are today the most radical force for the transformation of South African society – on democratic principles – but, for this transformation to be achieved, political allies are essential. National 'alliance politics' have become increasingly difficult in the atmosphere of repression which characterises South Africa, but the union movement has undertaken to pursue the ideal at all costs.

COSATU's endorsement of the Freedom Charter in 1987 was an important indication of the federation's identification with the broad anti-apartheid alliance, led by the ANC. As the struggle unfolds, however, debates about the specific details and conditions of the alliance will emerge. Because of the 'illegality' of the exiled organisations, much of the substance of alliance politicking can be expected to occur behind closed doors. Open political struggles appear most feasible on a regional level. Here, the politics of alliance spring from the politics of control, which workers have learnt on the shop-floor and carry home to their communities. This involves linking up with the youth congresses, the churches, and other local grassroots organisations.

At its second congress in July 1987, COSATU resolved that while it would not affiliate to any political organisation, it would establish 'disciplined alliances' with community organisations which were 'mass-based, democratic and non-racial, [with] a proven record of struggle and principles and policies compatible with COSATU'.

The response to the Emergency pointed to one of the most significant political developments in the union movement in recent years: the emergence of unions which cut across the 'workerist-populist' divide in that they are both industrially strong and politically effective. These unions prefer to define themselves as 'socialist', though the term is left unclear as to whether it implies 'social democracy' or 'Soviet-style' centralised socialism. The most advanced example of such 'workerist-populist' unionism is to be found in NUMSA, which has taken the lead in a number of political struggles while simultaneously mobilising workers on a combination of wage-related and community issues. NUMSA's leading role in resistance to the removal of some 10 000 people at Oukasie location in the Western Transvaal is a case in point. The union's militancy has had a high cost: NUMSA general secretary Moses Mayekiso, a leading figure in the community battle in Alexandra, was detained on 14 June 1986, and is presently facing charges of high treason. Joyce Modimoeng, wife of MAWU's organiser in Brits, David Modimoeng, was killed by a bomb in May 1986; several striking Sarmcol workers, including the chairman of the workers' committee and the daughter of a shop steward, were brutally murdered in December 1986; and the homes of Mayekiso in Alexandra and those of a number of NUMSA members in the Inkatha heartland of Northern Natal have been attacked.

Apart from the May Day and 16 June stayaways – which are now routinely successful – COSATU and the UDF joined together in calling for two days of protest to coincide with the all-white election in May 1987. More than a million workers responded, voting in the only way they knew how in South Africa – with their feet. However, it was the campaign for a 'living wage' – called by COSATU in 1987 – which prompted most of the activity on the ground. It is in this complex context that the NUM strike must be viewed.

THE NATIONAL UNION OF MINEWORKERS

When Cyril Ramaphosa first led a small delegation of workers to the Chamber of Mines, he had the distinct impression that the employers regarded him as an 'adventurer'. 'They probably felt that we did not know what we were letting ourselves in for, and they did not believe that the workers in the industry could be unionised', he said.

That was in 1982 – before the NUM shattered many of the myths (built up over a century) held by an industry which had been kept virtually free of black unions. Five years later, what would have been inconceivable to the employers at the first tentative meeting occurred: a sustained, organised and legal strike disrupting nearly half the country's gold and coal production. It was the most important trial of strength between a black union and employers in South African history. For the past five years the union had been steadily changing the balance of power in the industry, and it was widely speculated that by 1989 they would be in a position to stage an effective national action. That the strike went ahead perhaps two years early – and with more than half the industry still not unionised – contributed to the inconclusive outcome of the 1987 strike. 'We did not win and the Chamber did not lose', said Ramaphosa after the strike was called off.

The Chamber may well have decided in 1987 to 'dig in', believing it had to put brakes on the growth of the union before it was too late.

It was undoubtedly an unpleasant surprise to them that a strike of such a scale, longevity and discipline could ensue.

The long haul from powerlessness to posing a serious challenge to the might of the mining houses has involved sophisticated strategies and counter-strategies by the NUM and the Chamber of Mines. To understand these dynamics, one has to recognise the extraordinary strategic skills of Ramaphosa – once a student activist, detainee, and lawyer, whose name is now synonymous with South Africa's black miners. The scorn and contempt with which Ramaphosa believed the Chamber officials to be viewing him persisted for two years after their first meeting, while the union rapidly took root. The NUM succeeded where other unions trying to gain a toehold in the mining industry did not, because it was prepared to use a wide range of tactics – among them legal action. The union attended safety enquiries and won reinstatement for unfairly dismissed workers, for example. This provided a shield for the union, which could win perceptible and well-publicised victories even while numerical support was still thin. 'That was to us a very good organising tactic to show the workers that there was an organisation that was concerned about them', according to Ramaphosa.

But the crucial test of the NUM's ability to serve the workers' interests were the annual wage negotiations, where the union was effectively bargaining for *all* black miners although representing only a tiny proportion of them. In the first annual talks in 1983 (in the heyday of 'Chamber paternalism'), the union agreed to a wage increase which the Chamber had already decided to implement. Ramaphosa vowed that the débâcle would not be repeated.

In the following year's wage talks, the union fashioned a strategy which was to transform labour relations on the mines. It took the fight to the Chamber, drawing out the wage negotiations – through dispute, to conciliation board, to strike ballot. As the pattern of brinkmanship (framed within legal procedures) emerged, the Chamber was still trapped in the paternalism of the past; and too contemptuous of the NUM to take the organised black miners seriously.

It was only at the eleventh hour – and after a massive show of support in a strike ballot – that Anglo American offered a slightly improved deal. For the first time, a mining house had unwillingly conceded something to a black union. In 1985 the Chamber was more sensitive to the threat posed by the NUM, and began to devise counter-strategies. The union committed a classic error: it played its weakest card, calling its Goldfields and Gencor members out on strike, while allowing a separate settlement with Anglo American, hence neutralising its strongest base.

The NUM demonstrated its ability to mobilise support in the day-long strike by some 320 000 workers on 1 October 1986, called to mourn the 177 miners killed in an underground fire at the Kinross mine. However, both union and management appeared powerless to prevent ethnic 'faction fighting' on gold mines where more than 100 workers died at the end of 1986 and the beginning of 1987.

Patterns similar to those of previous years emerged in the negotiations of 1987. But the union appears to have digested some crucial lessons. It did not allow the possibility of a divisive offer to emerge: this was achieved by keeping its wage demand at 30 per cent, putting another separate Anglo American deal out of reach. In 1987, to the surprise of many in the industry, the brinkmanship ultimately carried the dispute over the precipice and into a massive legal strike.

Apart from NUMSA, the NUM – now the country's largest union claiming some 300 000 members – has developed to the extent where it is often difficult to draw a line between 'industrial' and 'political' issues. At the union's congress of September 1985 (which set the tone for the COSATU launch), Ramaphosa seemed to be steering the NUM in a political direction. For the first time in South African history, black miners, isolated from the townships in single-sex men's hostels, began to be sharply keyed-in to the political climate in the townships. This is particularly true of the coal mines around Witbank.

In 1987, the NUM embarked on a new challenge to the mining houses: it declared war on the migrant labour system. This followed a landmark conference in March 1987, where the union declared that this would be the year in which mineworkers would take control of their lives 'on every level'. NUM president James Motlatsi called on workers to dismantle the migrant labour system and the union geared itself up to negotiate the dismantling of the system of migrancy with the mining bosses. In April, black miners at Anglo American's Witbank collieries defiantly moved their wives or girlfriends into the single-sex hostels with them.

THE STATE HITS BACK

COSATU House in central Johannesburg was bombed on 6 May 1987 – the night that the extreme right-wing won almost 30 per cent of the vote in the all-white election. The attack followed two security force raids on the building in previous weeks, and a steady stream of government invective against COSATU and its 'political direction'. Attacks on COSATU property became commonplace. The Johannesburg newspaper *Business Day*, commented at the time:

> The bomb explosions bore the hallmarks of paramilitary skills. The explosions were sufficiently devastating to make the buildings unfit for use without creating visible images of Beirut; both occurred in the wee hours; both were executed with apparent care to avoid casualties. Plainly, even in a country accustomed to the use of explosives they were not the work of amateurs.

The May attack took place during the SATS strike – a crucial conflict between a quasi-state employer and a COSATU affiliate. The shootings and mass dismissals of SATS workers and other attacks on unions pushed the trade unions and the government close to all-out confrontation.

The government is clearly aware that the trade union movement is the best organised and most deeply entrenched form of internal opposition to the system. Where township based organisations have borne the brunt of repression under the State of Emergency, the unions have fared relatively better.

The state's strategic aims – importantly, to crush street committees and quell the township revolt – have been (at least partially) successful. The state's security apparatus was all originally targeted at the townships, though there is now evidence of some focus on the union movement as well.

The state has regularly interfered in labour relations through security force action, and (self-evidently) through apartheid structures such as the migrant labour system. But, however imperfectly, the doctrine of 'self-governance' between employers and unions has created space and relegated the state to a peripheral role in labour relations. This space has proved a curiously double-edged sword. It has left COSATU more exposed, and also with more expected of it. Both the SATS strike and state reactions to the escalation of labour unrest in 1987 have revealed that the state is divided in its response to the unions.

There is without doubt a large, security oriented grouping which would favour an all-out confrontation to cripple the unions, or at least force them to retreat from the political arena. The Minister of Law and Order, Adriaan Vlok, has warned trade union leaders whose activities are not 'in the interests of the country' that the security forces will take action against them. In a public statement, Vlok accuses COSATU of 'the polarisation, politicisation, organisation and mobilisation of the worker to plan for a so-called living wage campaign'. He draws a parallel with the ANC's theme 'Advance to People's Power', asserting that the labour terrain is an 'ideal area in which to reach the masses': 'Repeated pronouncements by the organisation's leaders are known: they say that the trade unions must be used for this goal [People's Power]. Certain events surrounding the recent strikes, especially the rail strike, must be seen in this light.'

Yet the Director-General of the Department of Manpower, Piet van der Merwe, placed a completely different interpretation of the SATS strike. Having repeatedly quoted the high rate of usage of the official dispute settling machinery as proof of success of the labour dispensation, he saw the root of the problem in the fact that the public sector was excluded from this machinery. 'One must', he said, 'weigh up the pros and cons of the government either providing for reconciliation machinery in its own legislation or adopting the Labour Relations Act.' He pointed out that 50 per cent of all strikes in the private sector ended within one day.

Those subscribing to this school of thought are also mindful of employers' concern that the heavy hand of the state could mean that they will have to bear the brunt of the political struggle in their factories. Differences of opinion could also explain why both SATS and the Post Office authorities allowed their respective strikes to drag on, before firing workers. (When, in 1982, a few hundred GWU members went on a go-slow strike in the Port Elizabeth docks demanding that SATS deal with them, it was only a matter of hours before they were fired and deported to the bantustans.) When the 1987 SATS dispute erupted, SATS had just been through its own 'Wiehahn Commission', and was clearly hesitant about how to deal with the escalating problem. The fact that they were willing to reinstate one Andrew Nendzandza – whose dismissal had sparked the strike – was unprecedented, as the workers at the Port Elizabeth docks would testify. But by then the long-standing grievances of the SATS workforce poured out and larger demands came to the fore – not least the call for recognition of the South African Railways and Harbours Workers Union (SARHWU).

At the same time the government – wary of the reaction of the more than 100 000 white voters employed on the railways should it be seen to be giving in to the demands of black workers, particularly over recognition of a COSATU affiliate – faced a sharp dilemma. In the end, the brutal intervention of the security forces prevailed, propelling the dispute towards full-scale confrontation, while at the same time serving warning of their repressive capabilities and preparedness. The mine strike, as has been shown, revealed similar divisions.

The complex relationship involving the unions, employers and the state is rapidly shifting, although its ultimate direction is indeterminate: it could be characterised by increasing state pressure on the unions, or an acceptance of their role as responsible actors in the industrial relations process. Certainly, it could be a confusing admixture of the two. For some employers at least, the manner in which the miners' strike was resolved is regarded as a positive step. One such optimist is Bobby Godsell, Anglo American's industrial relations advisor, and their chief spokesman during the strike, who commented at the time:

> What I think is encouraging is this is an unusual fascist state in which you can have free and independent unions using the ultimate weapon in a vital industry with the employers going along with that and with the state not interfering . . . This puts us in a small club of third world countries in which this could happen. The state are playing this game according to liberal democratic rules.

A few days later Community House in Cape Town was bombed and *Business Day* suggested that the emergence of Argentinian-styled death squads was almost certain. Clearly, the seemingly 'enlightened' stance of some individuals in government is not shared by the entire ruling party. Antagonism between the state and the union movement has reached such a pitch that it is impossible to envisage a let-up in the 'informal' attacks – vigilantes and bombs. A formal attack, possibly in the form of a treason trial of COSATU leaders, is equally likely.

5 Internal Resistance in South Africa: The Political Movements

Kumi Naidoo

INTRODUCTION

The resistance movements in South Africa have shown an increased maturity in recent years, and this has found an echo in a corresponding maturity in the modification of the apartheid system itself. The contention here is that most of the 'reforms' brought about by the South African government have, in one way or another, been primarily provoked by resistance activity. The tricameral parliament and the newly proclaimed National Statutory Council (NSC) – the major components of the new dispensation at a national level – reflect the state's increasingly 'sophisticated' responses in attempting to contain the emergent wave of resistance.

Extra-parliamentary resistance in the 1980s takes on a variety of forms, all closely inter-linked. Trade union organisation and youth structures are dealt with in Chapters 4 and 3. This chapter focuses on the mass *political* movements and should be read in conjunction with the previous two chapters. While the state offensive has certainly weakened the internal resistance organisations, their increased sophistication and the degree of popular support which they command should ensure their survival – although they will necessarily alter in form.

MASS LEGAL RESISTANCE, 1977–85

On 17 October 1977, history repeated itself for South Africa's legal extra-parliamentary opposition. The government outlawed nineteen above-ground, predominantly Black Consciousness-aligned organisations. South Africa's rulers, it seemed, hoped to re-establish the political vacuum which had characterised much of the 1960s and early 1970s, following the banning in 1960 of the African National Congress

(ANC) and the Pan Africanist Congress (PAC). However, the Black Consciousness movement resurfaced in 1978 with the formation of the Azanian Peoples' Organisation (AZAPO), and various forms of rudimentary resistance organisation had begun to take root by 1980.

By early 1983 there existed youth, student, women's, civic and workers' organisations at different levels of development, depending on factors such as regional location, resistance history and the availability of skilled leadership. Co-ordination among these various fronts of resistance at a regional and national level was rather haphazard. It took on various forms, depending largely on the extent of organisational development and regional particularities.[1] This is not to suggest that co-ordination of mass legal resistance was totally absent – indeed, diverse alliances were being fostered. As early as 1979 a consumer boycott of the Fattis and Monis company necessitated co-operation and co-ordination at a national level. A year later the Release Mandela Campaign (RMC) provided a further example of national co-ordination. Again in 1981, a nationwide consumer boycott against the British-owned Wilson Rowntree Company followed a labour dispute involving members of the South African Allied Workers Union (SAAWU). In addition, the regime's twentieth anniversary Republic Day celebrations in the same year resulted in widespread protest activities. Both campaigns saw close co-operation among various sectors of organisation in townships throughout the country.

By 1980 it was possible to discern a movement away from the orthodox Black Consciousness ideology, which was predominant in the 1970s and a concomitant identification with the ANC's Freedom Charter[2] by many of these nascent resistant structures. The ANC declaration of 1980 as the year of the Freedom Charter, the relatively successful military offensive at the SASOL oil-from-coal plant, and the national Release Mandela Campaign, were among the factors that aided this process. At a meeting in Johannesburg in 1983, which facilitated the re-launch of the Transvaal Indian Congress (TIC),[3] Dr Allan Boesak, the President of the World Alliance of Reformed Churches, called for the establishment of a 'united front'[4] to oppose the government's current constitutional proposals. This call was followed by the launch of the National Forum (NF) in June 1983, representing some 200 organisations – mostly sympathetic to the ideological position of the Black Consciousness movement. At this gathering the Azanian Peoples' Manifesto was drafted, identifying 'racial capitalism' as the principal source of oppression in South Africa, and committing its supporters to the ideal of an 'anti-racist Socialist Republic'. The initiative failed to harness the support of the majority of emerging organisations which, in response to Boesak's call, were already planning the launch of a 'United Democratic Front' (UDF).

On 20 August 1983, approximately 15 000 people from community-based civic associations, church and women's groups, trade unions, youth and student organisations, sporting, cultural, and professional bodies launched the UDF at the Rocklands Civic Centre in Western Cape. The gathering adopted a UDF Declaration and, while not officially endorsing the Freedom Charter, alluded to it warmly. Support for the Congress tradition led by the ANC was further manifested by the election of Nelson Mandela as the UDF's first patron, and the repeated chanting of 'Viva Tambo'.[5] Western Cape UDF leader Trevor Manuel drew a direct comparison between the gathering at Kliptown in 1955, and the launch of the UDF in Rocklands. Delegates were reminded that 'klip' was the Afrikaans word for 'rock': the implication was clear that many participants (both leadership and rank-and-file) regarded the UDF as the legal rebirth of the tradition of 'Congress' politics within South Africa.

Both the UDF and National Forum attempted to broaden and strengthen their support bases through campaigns and high-profile gatherings. The UDF fared markedly better, precipitating a groundswell of popular support. Both movements focused extensively on the government's 'reform' proposals. The UDF quickly consolidated its local structures, and on 21 January 1984 launched a 'Million Signature Campaign'.[6] The Front outlined its priorities for 1984 in a New Year's message, calling for a strengthening of affiliate organisations; unity building; campaigns against the New Constitution, the Koornhof Bills,[7] removals and military conscription; and the implementation of the Million Signature Campaign to illustrate the extent of opposition to the regime.[8]

The UDF's political baptism centred around the campaign to discredit the 'tricameral elections'. In this it enjoyed huge success, despite attempts by the state to discredit and hinder it, and its relative inexperience in the mechanics of national co-ordination. The Anti-Election Campaign contributed to the popularising of the Front and enhanced organisation, especially in the coloured and Indian areas, many of which had been barely touched by mass resistance activity in previous years. Within these communities the UDF called on residents to take 'direct' action against the tricameral elections, challenging election candidates to 'face the people' at UDF-organised meetings. The strategy succeeded in involving many thousands of supporters at a grassroots level. In the aftermath of the elections, the UDF was able to claim a significant victory on the grounds of massive non-participation by the coloured and Indian communities.

The UDF was further popularised, ironically, by the detention of its high-profile leadership in Natal and the Transvaal. In a skilful manoeuvre, six senior UDF leaders sought refuge in the British Consulate in Durban, creating an ideal platform for presenting the UDF case to the international community, and embarrassing the state.

A second early UDF success took the form of a work 'stayaway' in the Transvaal in November 1984. The organisation gave notice of its ability to cement working relationships with the major trade unions (see Chapter 4). In the Vaal Triangle 'uprisings' of September 1984, UDF affiliates played a role in the (largely spontaneous) protest, imbuing it with a measure of organisational coherence. New UDF-aligned organisations sprang up in areas affected by the resistance activity. The protest, initially focused on high rents and other 'bread and butter' grievances, quickly developed into a wide-ranging uprising which prompted the imposition of a selective State of Emergency in July 1985.[9] There was a clear shift in the nature, quality and content of internal resistance from 1984 onwards.

The fires of discontent raged throughout 1985. The UDF found itself exposed to increasing detentions, treason trials and general harassment from the state. Mass funerals became commonplace, allowing the iconography of the ANC to re-emerge in the townships through flags, banners and songs proclaiming allegiance to the banned liberation movement in defiance of the Internal Security Act. The youth, many in UDF-affiliated organisations, were increasingly engaged in militant confrontations with South African security forces. The Congress of South African Students (COSAS), the largest and most dynamic affiliate of the UDF (see Chapter 3), was eventually banned in August 1985 as the popular struggle continued to broaden its horizons and some activists spoke of the 'imminent collapse' of the regime.

The State of Emergency appeared to have caught the UDF off guard, reversing some of the organisational gains made in 1984. Many activists were detained or forced into hiding. In anger and frustration, resistance leaders – seriously underrating the power of the state – proclaimed that the State of Emergency would neither deter nor hinder them. However, resistance organisation was thrown into disarray by the clampdown. This success notwithstanding, the state overestimated its own ability to bring the burgeoning resistance to a swift end. As the wave of popular protest continued, the government extended Emergency restrictions to the Western Cape. Many deaths occurred, including those of children, and as a result militancy in the coloured community was accelerated. A typical activist's comment at the time was that the South African Defence Force (SADF) had 'accomplished in a day . . . what we've been trying to do for years'. At the end of 1985 local government had collapsed in many regions, and some 'comrades', as the young activists had come to be known, were attempting to usurp state control. Some activists began to recognise the need for a strategy of replacing official control with popular 'alternative' structures, and the importance of increased organisational discipline.

While the UDF had established itself as a national mass movement of resistance, the National Forum's visible presence and campaigns against the state paled by comparison. During 1983 and 1984, some Forum affiliates campaigned to persuade Indians and coloureds not to vote in the elections, but they never co-ordinated any major national campaign. This is reflected in academic commentary on the organisation, which invariably focuses on Forum conferences and the ideological standpoints emerging therefrom.[10] The National Forum had envisaged undertaking national campaigns – for example, an 'Isolate the Traitors' campaign after the 1984 elections for the tricameral parliament – but these have failed to materialise.[11]

A negative feature for resistance in this period was growing conflict between ideological tendencies, involving in particular AZAPO (the predominant organisation within the National Forum) and the UDF. AZAPO, which has persisted with a more or less conventional application of the Black Consciousness philosophy (though there has been strong class content injected into their analysis) does not allow white participation in its organisation. The UDF, a multi-class alliance, stresses non-racialism in all levels of its organisation. Many former leaders of the Black Consciousness movement are prominent in the UDF arguing that Black Consciousness was a necessary phase in the development of the struggle and that changing conditions necessitate a more enlightened approach. Some of these former Black Consciousness luminaries spent many years with leading members of the ANC on

Robben Island (dubbed by some 'the University') where there was much discussion and debate.

The divisions between the UDF and AZAPO received international attention during the visit of Senator Edward Kennedy to South Africa in 1985 when AZAPO supporters demonstrated vigorously against him. Uncharacteristically, the state tolerated many of these demonstrations and sought to exploit the ideological divisions, playing the one movement off against the other. In addition, the state banned the UDF from receiving overseas funding while letting AZAPO off the hook. As the confrontations between the movements continued to claim casualties, leaders on both sides urged calm and restraint, arguing that their supporters should not lose sight of the 'real enemy' – the state.

The period was also extremely important for the trade union movement. Apart from the 'Unity Talks' that were to yield the Congress of South African Trade Unions (COSATU) at the end of 1985, it was also the period when the union movement was beginning cautiously but decidedly to move away from the exclusivity of the shop-floor and enter the terrain of overt political struggle (see Chapter 4). To an extent this shift was necessitated by the dynamics of the mass rebellion then enveloping large parts of South Africa. Many trade union activists were involved in community struggles, and many workers found their children operating in the forefront of resistance. It was becoming increasingly difficult for the unions to eschew a direct political role in confrontation with the state.

New tools and forms of resistance were developed in the period 1983–85. Most prominent was the consumer boycott, which placed business leaders at the interface of government recalcitrance and black defiance. The tactic was highly successful in Port Elizabeth, prompting the local Consumer Boycott Committee co-ordinator, Mkhuseli Jack, to commend it to other communities engaged in resistance.[12]

Both the UDF and National Forum were fledgeling structures, undergoing a process of ideological and organisational development under conditions of resistance which they could neither fully predict nor control. There were marked differences in their approaches. At an ideological level, the UDF combined various structures united primarily by their opposition to the government's constitutional proposals. It would be incorrect to assert that all their affiliates were firm supporters of the Freedom Charter and the ANC's Congress tradition. Similarly, while Black Consciousness was the dominant unifying ideology in the National Forum, other (leftist) tendencies operated within the structure.

Beyond ideological considerations, there were important differences in organisational development between the new formations and what had preceded them. The ANC had constituted itself as a national liberation movement first, subsequently establishing subsections such as youth and women's leagues. The process was reversed in the case of the UDF. At its launch, no national youth or women's organisations were yet in existence – their emergence was facilitated by the Front itself. Nevertheless, several similarities were present. It has been argued that, broadly speaking, 'The nationalist movement . . . was still afflicted by the same split which had prevailed since the 1940s, between the ANC/Charterist camp and the Africanist/black-consciousness camp.'[13] The ANC tradition was powerfully reincarnated with the mass legal opposition often relegating opposing forces to a marginal role in resistance to the state.

The crisis which manifested itself within South Africa in the early 1980s cannot be fully understood without reference to the effects on the South African economy as a result of the international economic recession. Economic factors have played a decisive role in fuelling discontent and its translation into organised resistance. According to one academic analyst,

> The community council system, the role of the security forces, the state's political reforms, and the emergence of black extra-parliamentary political organization are central aspects, for example, in understanding the origins of the present crisis. But what also needs to be recognized is that the crisis has been triggered and reinforced by the deteriorating material conditions being experienced by the black majority. Economic factors have also played an important part in reducing the ability of the state to manage the crisis. In particular, the growing costs of Verwoerdian apartheid when coupled with the post-1980 recession and the loss of investor confidence, have provided severe constraints on the options available to the apartheid regime.[14]

An examination of the roots of organisational formations within the black communities confirms that poor housing, transport, employment and education feed directly into black protest. In Natal, for example, the Joint Rent Action Committee (JORAC) and the Joint Commuters Committee (JCC) – both aligned to the UDF – were formed in response to popular material dissatisfaction.

THE NEW EMERGENCY: AN ANALYSIS OF 1986/7

Believing itself to have contained mass resistance by early 1986, the government lifted the partial State of Emergency on 7 March. In preceding months the banning of the UDF had often appeared imminent. In defiant mood, the UDF's Transvaal General Secretary, Mohammed Valli, declared that the state would find it 'much more difficult to weaken'[15] the UDF in the event of further clampdowns. Murphy Morobe, acting as UDF Publicity Secretary since the detention of Patrick 'Terror'[16] Lekota in 1985, claimed further that the Front had been able to adapt its form of operating in some measure in response to the first Emergency. It was clear, however, that the UDF had suffered greatly as a result of widespread detentions and the fact that many of its leaders had been forced into hiding. However, the time spent 'underground' provided an opportunity for reassessment and reappraisal, and as leaders re-emerged, tactical and organisational changes were anticipated.

While the UDF was geared to take full advantage of the lifting of the Emergency, it was clearly not going to function as before. The Front attempted to decentralise its activities, primarily for reasons of security, but also in response to the development of numerous regional differences, necessitating localised initiatives and creativity. For example, the role of Inkatha in Natal posed specific problems for local UDF structures. Co-ordination at a national level was therefore de-emphasised in favour of the regions.

Resistance in the sphere of education was prominent in 1986, as in previous years. It marked the tenth anniversary of the Soweto uprisings and there were sustained calls for a total boycott of black education. The UDF was instrumental in the formation of the National Education Crisis Committee (NECC), which brought together parents, teachers and pupils in an attempt to devise a unified policy on school boycotts and the educational struggle in general (see Chapter 3). The NECC conference held in Durban in March evidenced remarkable progress in the process of alliance-building between different sectors of resistance. Not only did it address itself to engaging the 'comrades' in high-level decision making, it also consolidated the concept of 'People's Education' as an alternative to state curricula. Pupils were persuaded to return to the schools, and to use them as centres of resistance. The decision made it more difficult for the government to accentuate and exploit tensions between parents and youth.

The National Forum had participated in earlier meetings which led to the birth of the NECC, but it refused to attend the Durban conference (see Chapter 3), agreeing, however, to support resolutions which they considered acceptable.[17] By its absence, the Forum excluded itself from the most prominent initiatives in the educational sphere.

Campaigns to mark May Day 1986 reflected the complexities confronting the internal resistance organisations in South Africa. Despite the state having banned numerous COSATU rallies (planned jointly with the UDF), it was the most successful commemoration of the May Day demonstrations in the country's history. In the view of a leading journalistic commentator, the UDF's role in organising these rallies helped the Front to maintain a visible presence in mainstream politics, and assisted it to 'effectively shed its image of being a middle-class organisation that dictates to the workers'.[18] Those unions outside the COSATU federation and more inclined toward the Forum were unable to match their rivals' show of strength. But while both tendencies were hampered in their efforts by the state, the Inkatha movement was launching a rival federation, the United Workers Union of South Africa (UWUSA). State-controlled television gave extensive and sympathetic coverage to UWUSA's launch, highlighting its antagonism to COSATU (see Chapter 4).

The lifting of the first State of Emergency was preceded by the collapse of a major treason trial involving twelve UDF leaders of national stature. This was a decisive fillip for the Front. Shortly thereafter, the UDF publicly refused to meet Dr Chester Crocker, the US Assistant Secretary of State for African Affairs, because of the Reagan Administration's policy of Constructive Engagement toward the South African government. This illustrated the UDF's preparedness to assume a political profile in the international arena, notwithstanding the fact that its primary focus was on internal activity. Furthermore, at the NECC conference UDF affiliates adopted a resolution condemning Western powers for 'collusion with the Botha regime'.[19]

Early in 1986 the UDF made a conscious effort to expand its influence within the white community and emphasise its seriousness about non-racialism. The theme was pursued with the launch of the militant South African Youth Congress (SAYCO) in April 1987, which registered its intention to organise in the white communities as well as the townships. The principle of non-racialism applies equally in other sectors of resistance such as the trade unions and women's organisations. National workshops resulted in the UDF's 'Call to Whites Campaign', involving a series of public meetings in white areas around South Africa. At one of these gatherings Dr Frederik van Zyl

Slabbert, former leader of the white parliamentary opposition (who had resigned from parliament, calling it 'irrelevant'), appealed to 'democratic whites' to involve themselves in extra-parliamentary politics. For the first time, whites were exposed to an alternative perspective about the UDF from people within their own ranks. Slabbert went on to establish the Institute for a Democratic Alternative for South Africa (IDASA), an extra-parliamentary think-tank, which drew acrimonious attention from the state for its arrangement of a meeting in Dakar, Senegal, in mid-1987 between members of the ANC and Afrikaner intellectuals.

On its formation, the UDF was at pains to emphasise that it was not an 'internal wing' of the ANC, although it shared much of the liberation movement's political outlook. Such a distinction was, in any event, politically essential if the UDF was to operate legally in South Africa. Over time, however, and in the wake of visits to the ANC by church, student and business leaders and the massive popular support for the organisation in the townships, the UDF was able to adopt a less cautious stance. In a reference to increasing internal support for the ANC, a member of the National Executive Committee of the UDF, Curnick Ndlovu – himself recently released after serving over nineteen years on Robben Island – observed that suddenly 'all roads lead to Lusaka'.[20] This new atmosphere was evidenced by a meeting between the UDF, represented by Reverend Arnold Stofile[21] and three others[22], and the ANC's Thabo Mbeki and Mac Maharaj. Some members of the UDF delegation were arrested on arrival back in South Africa – in telling contrast to the businessmen and clergymen who had been left untouched by the government.

With hundreds still incarcerated under the first State of Emergency, the UDF continued to call for the release of all political prisoners. A Durban 'Release Mandela Campaign' rally necessitated the UDF engaging in a legal battle to gain permission to hold the gathering. After the second, national, State of Emergency was declared on 12 June 1986, the courts were to become a major area of legal resistance and every loophole in the Emergency regulations was challenged, yielding some short-term gains. The UDF's style of resistance since its inception centred on high-profile mobilisation. Changing conditions led to a discernible strategic shift, encapsulated in the slogan 'From mobilisation to organisation'.

On 12 and 13 June, hundreds of activists from various organisations, including some high profile trade union leaders, were detained. This led to spontaneous illegal strikes at several centres as workers demanded the release of union leaders. The Commercial, Catering and Allied Workers Union (CCAWUSA), for example, was severely disrupted by such detentions. The managements of several companies, fearing a further breakdown in industrial relations, began to pressurise the government to release trade union leaders. While some unionists were released, those that were integrally involved in community organisations remained in custody. It was clear that the clampdown was aimed largely at those activists straddling the union/community structures.

During the current Emergency (which was extended by the State President on 11 June 1987), both the regional and national executives of the UDF have had to meet in secret and rely on a clandestine network for passing on information among affiliates. The fact that the organisation has not yet fully mastered this type of 'semi-underground' operation was graphically illustrated when the police discovered several 'secret' meetings, and subsequently arrested leaders. The UDF leadership has been compelled to close ranks further and, as a corollary, the 'inner circle' of leadership has grown smaller. A side-effect of this process of forcing a legal organisation 'underground', according to one UDF leader, was that the state, through its own actions, had now to fight an 'unseen enemy'.

A digression is necessary at this point to draw a distinction between 'underground' and 'semi-underground' methods of resistance. Since its banning, the ANC has functioned as an underground organisation. Under the Emergency, the UDF remains a legal organisation, but has had to retreat 'semi-underground'. There has been much speculation as to why the government has eschewed a comprehensive proscription of the organisation. It would appear that the state finds itself in a dilemma. Ideally it would prefer to dispense with the UDF through legislation – which is well within its powers – and enter into a process of 'negotiation' with manipulable black 'leaders'. However, there are possible strategic considerations behind the government's continued tolerance of the UDF's existence, and these deserve some attention.

First, the UDF acts as a 'safety valve' for black discontent. It militates against a mass exodus of activists into the ANC's internal underground. Should the state ban the UDF, it could expect to swell the ranks of the ANC – creating yet more 'invisible enemies'. The UDF also serves as a barometer for measuring genuine black sentiment. Elements within the state may also wish to retain the option of eventual negotiation with a representative organisation like the UDF. Prior to the imposition of the Emergency, it might have been argued that one of the reasons preventing the outlawing of the UDF was a fear of international repercussions. Of late, the government's actions and pronouncements have given the lie to this theory.

The UDF finds itself occupying a terrain somewhere between legality and illegality. The scope for legal resistance has been dramatically curtailed, yet many UDF affiliates proceed with 'above-ground' programmes, and these have an inherent value which cannot be replicated underground. Activists have fashioned a new *modus operandi*, lying low and functioning when opportunities present themselves. Leaders regularly surface for important public occasions: for example, acting national publicity secretary Murphy Morobe surfaced to address the second national COSATU conference. He was, however, detained a few weeks later. Overall the number of public gatherings held by UDF affiliates has declined drastically, and it is likely that the trend will continue.

There have been concomitant signs of growing organisational sophistication even under the general repressive conditions that prevail. One of the most important has been the development of 'People's Committees'. As a concept, this dates back to the 1950s and Nelson Mandela's 'M-Plan', drafted in anticipation of a state clampdown, and the first concerted attempt to decentralise the activities of the ANC. The M-Plan was never fully implemented because of the debilitating effects of South Africa's first State of Emergency, declared in 1960. The concept itself survived, however, and re-emerged after September 1984. As resistance spread nationally and the ANC called for apartheid to be made 'unworkable' and the townships rendered 'ungovernable', the notion of alternative township structures resurfaced. The government lost control of several townships as community councillors were forced to resign – many fleeing their homes. Conditions were ripe for the development of 'organs of peoples' power'.

In a major assessment, after several months of experiments with various local township committees and structures, newspaper editor and influential political leader Zwelakhe Sisulu cautioned against overestimating the advances that had been made:

> It is important that we don't misrecognise the moment, understand it to be something which it is not. We are not poised for the immediate transfer of power to the people. The belief that this is so could lead to serious errors and defeats. We are however poised to enter a phase which can lead to transfer of power. What we are seeking to do is to decisively shift the balance of forces in our favour. To do this, we have to adopt the appropriate strategies and tactics,

> we have to understand our strengths and weaknesses, as well as that of our enemy, that is, the forces of apartheid reaction.[23]

Sisulu was attempting to dispel illusions of impending victory. More significantly, he was setting the seal on a strategic shift among resistance leaders from promoting 'ungovernability' to implementing 'people's power'. It was not enough to make the townships uncontrollable. If the resistance movement was to intensify and mature, new, democratic and effective control had to be imposed to replace state control. The central task was to create 'self-governing areas' or 'semi-liberated zones', where people could exercise power 'by starting to take control over their own lives in areas such as crime, the cleaning of the townships and the creation of people's parks, the provision of first aid and even in the schools.'[24]

In some areas, 'peoples' courts' also sprang up. In an apparent attempt to render the police less effective, activists encouraged residents not to report township crime to the police, but to 'disciplinary committees' or 'people's courts' run by the community itself. Their functions ranged from 'crime control' to the politicisation of residents about the local authorities and the broader political struggle. These makeshift 'courts' – also referred to as 'forums' – could be convened at any time.

According to a UDF activist from the township of Mamelodi, near Pretoria:

> The main aim [of the 'courts'] is rehabilitation, to re-educate the wrongdoer and make him a better person. You have to see this from our point of view. The community must be the judge and must see that justice is done. It has reaped tremendous rewards. Many people who opposed us have been converted and now work with us – even policemen.[25]

In many documented cases petty thieves were sentenced to community tasks, such as painting and watering the 'people's parks'. But, it appeared, corporal punishment was also meted out: a person found guilty of rape would receive punishment of approximately thirty lashes.[26] The 'peoples' court' phenomenon excited widespread criticism, particularly but not exclusively in the white communities, and the state exploited it effectively to undermine the credibility of the community activists. The most damaging allegation was that the 'necklace method' of punishment was employed at these courts. That there were excesses is generally accepted, but strenuous efforts were apparently made to combat this. However, the 'courts' were clearly illegal, and were not sanctioned by the UDF – rather, they developed spontaneously within certain communities.

It was also increasingly obvious that some 'opportunistic and unruly' elements were 'using the political struggle for their own ends'. This was noted by the General Secretary of the Mamelodi Youth Congress, Mike Seloane, who told reporters: 'We decided to launch an operation clean-up in June last year to weed out criminals and hooligans using the political struggle for their own ends.'[27]

The 'street committees' met about once a week, ensuring that political decisions were relayed throughout a particular community. Executives of street committees would then sit on 'district committees'. In Mamelodi, for example, the district committee plus five delegates of all other 'progressive organisations' combined to form 'area committees'. The area committee then served as a civic association. The intermediate structure between the street committee and the district committee is sometimes the 'block committee'.[28] 'Village committees' were to serve as rural equivalents. By August 1987, however, it was observed that: 'The violence had subsided and most townships are "governable" again. The alternative structures which were being built up have been smashed in most areas with the exception of Soweto.'[29]

What then was the relationship between the UDF and these various forms of 'people's committees'? The committees are essentially informally constituted, but democratically elected structures within the townships. Their members include youth, student, women's, trade union, and civic activists of the UDF. Many of those active in the people's committees – 'organs of people's power' in activists' shorthand – see them as ANC-aligned or even as part of the ANC itself. The ANC views the development of these committees as the 'people's state in the making'.[30] Alex Mashinini, writing in *Sechaba*, the ANC's official organ, argues that the creation of people's committees 'signifies that for the first time after many decades of struggle, the organised material force necessary for the destruction of the apartheid system has become a reality in South Africa'.[31]

While recognising the need for the execution of various administrative tasks (like refuse collection), he cautions that there is a need for vigilance, lest one plays 'into the hands of the enemy and opportunist elements'. The thrust of the argument is that these structures are political organs and must be developed as such.

> That they have to perform certain administrative tasks is functional to their essence, which is political. To guarantee their political purpose and to avoid their asserting themselves in an administrative sense only, it is important that certain political and strategic perspectives be considered.[32]

In the Eastern Cape township of Port Alfred the power of the organised civic associations necessitated the local government structures engaging the UDF-affiliated civic associations in joint decision making over questions of the budget and they were also able to exercise effective control over the schools in the township for a period. The growth of alternative structures was a major contributory factor to the re-imposition of the State of Emergency. According to the London-based International Defence and Aid Fund (IDAF): 'Both in the interval between the two States of Emergency and in introducing the second State of Emergency the government identified the establishment of "alternative structures" as a major concern and their destruction as an objective.'[33]

This is borne out by the detention of large numbers of grassroots activists. People's committees were considerably weakened, but not obliterated. The state continues to devise new methods of pressurising the structures, notably through the use of 'kitskonstabels' and, allegedly, vigilantes. The fortunes of these committees – representing, as they do, attempts at building democracy at grassroots level – have great bearing on the development of resistance, and an envisioned 'post-apartheid' society. Resistance leaders already note the possibility of the emergence of counter-revolutionary groupings in the future, and set great store by these localised structures.

The Emergency notwithstanding, the UDF continued to call for the unbanning of the ANC, and launched a campaign to this effect in June 1986. The campaign reached its apex on 8 January 1987, the 75th anniversary of the ANC, when the Front placed full-page advertisements in several national newspapers calling for the unbanning of the exiled movement.

The latter months of 1986 were marked by successful stayaways and consumer boycotts, spearheaded by the UDF. In December the organisation called for a 'Christmas against the Emergency' and received support from more than twenty religious, youth and community groups. The campaign urged people to 'abstain from merrymaking', and to light symbolic candles. On 12 December, six months after the Emergency's imposition, further detentions followed, these under

Section 29 of the Internal Security Act.[34] The campaign proceeded, coinciding with a month-long consumer boycott in some regions.

The most obvious setbacks suffered by the UDF in 1986 included detentions, threats of detentions, and restriction orders on detainees once they had been released. The latter differed from previous banning orders in that they were less comprehensive, but they nevertheless curtailed the activities of important leaders. Furthermore, several activists died in the wake of the emergence of right-wing 'vigilantes'. 1986 also witnessed the death in detention of Peter Nchabeleng, the UDF's Northern Transvaal President. Nchabeleng was detained at the height of mass resistance in the rural areas of Sekhukhuneland.[35] These protests indicated the UDF's growing penetration of the rural areas – a source of great concern to the state. In Leandra in the Transvaal, the murder of UDF leader Chief Ampie Mayisa was yet another serious blow to the Front in their attempts to offset their concentration in urban regions. In the wake of these killings, the UDF declared for the first time that it was finding it increasingly difficult to ignore calls from its affiliates for a revision of its policy of non-violence.

The state attacked the UDF on another front in 1986, declaring it an 'affected organisation', thus depriving it of foreign funding. Court appeals succeeded in having the order declared invalid, although the government immediately gave notice of an appeal of its own.

The National Forum's activities in 1986 centred around its major affiliate, AZAPO. In the Western Cape, some National Forum affiliates co-operated with UDF structures, but this remained an exception rather than a rule. The Forum itself was preoccupied with internal discussions in this period: the then convener of the Forum, Saths Cooper, noted this at the time, saying: 'We have to make a very detailed assessment of our previous positions and approaches. Right now there is a lot of intense discussion going on about method.'[36]

As with the UDF, some weaker AZAPO branches disintegrated as the threat of detentions forced leaders into hiding. AZAPO's most significant offensive was waged in the homeland of Lebowa, where the organisation instituted civil claims against the homeland police, but was forced to withdraw them after the Lebowa government hurriedly passed legislation to indemnify their police from prosecution. On 5 April a prominent AZAPO member and journalist, Lucky Kutumela, died only hours after his arrest in Lebowa.[37] In its public pronouncements, AZAPO advocated an alliance of 'the true forces of the left' in resistance. This was interpreted by some as a step towards opening its ranks to white activists, although this has not materialised. It was a period of intense fluidity within the National Forum, further complicated by the controversial departure of its powerful leader and Robben Island veteran Saths Cooper, who left South Africa to take up a scholarship in the United States.[38]

AZAPO Publicity Secretary Muntu Myeza intimated to journalists that Cooper had been 'expelled' because of his acceptance of the scholarship from 'an imperialist country'. It was widely speculated that Cooper had decided to further his academic career at this time because of growing disillusionment with the political direction of the organisational custodians of Black Consciousness, AZAPO, and his wish to avoid embarrassing the group by resigning publicly. Cooper and other AZAPO leaders insisted that he had neither resigned nor been expelled, but had 'stepped down' for academic reasons alone. The Cooper controversy saw a cooling of relations between AZAPO and the (predominantly Western Cape based) left-wing affiliates of the National Forum, who respected Cooper's leadership and vision.[39]

AZAPO frequently found itself pre-empted by UDF campaigns, and lent its support to some of them, notably the Soweto bus and rent boycott. Similarly, the NECC call for a return to school in 1987 was endorsed. This selective support approach also applied to AZAPO's relations with trade unions in the pro-UDF – and overwhelmingly dominant – COSATU federation.

1987: CONTINUING EMERGENCY, CONTINUING RESISTANCE

The visible intensity of community resistance substantially subsided in 1987. The 'comrades' were no longer the presence that they had been on the streets, but were developing new strategies of resistance (see Chapter 3). The South African Youth Congress (SAYCO) was launched in secret in March; it is the largest affiliate of the UDF, claiming a membership in the region of half a million.[40] SAYCO's debut was followed by the clandestine formation of the UDF Women's Congress and the re-constitution of the Release Mandela Committee (RMC) as a national organisation.

The UDF also had some noteworthy international contacts. Lynda Chalker, a Minister of State in the British Foreign Office, met Archie Gumede, one of the Front's national presidents, in London in February. Internally, the UDF proceeded with community campaigns:

in April the massive rent boycott received a boost, followed by two days of 'national protest' on 1 and 2 May. In response to the 'whites-only' general election, the UDF, COSATU and the NECC co-ordinated a two-day stayaway, the largest general strike in South African history.[41]

The increasing importance of the trade union movement in internal resistance politics has been one of the most notable features of 1987 (see Chapter 4). While successfully engaging in labour disputes on the shop-floor, the unions' political profile has been incrementally raised. The six-week strike by South African Transport Services (SATS) workers is a prominent example of the phenomenon. Workers called on the management of the state-owned enterprise to abolish racism in their employment practices, recognise the union, and pay wages for the duration of the strike. Strong, practical support from the black community organisations bore witness to the growing links between organised labour and other sectors of resistance. This was replicated in the subsequent national strike by mineworkers, one of the greatest displays of trade union sophistication and power ever seen in South Africa. Given the beleaguered state of the political structures of internal resistance, the demonstrated maturity and resilience of the trade unions – coupled with their willingness to engage in political activity – is a critical source of encouragement for a grouping like the UDF.

Despite the intense repression that was still prevalent at the beginning of 1987, the UDF was able to hold a National Working Committee (NWC) meeting from which emerged the slogan 'Defend, consolidate and advance'. This gathering, which took place in Durban in May and involved some 150 delegates, decided to adopt the Freedom Charter later in the year. By the time of the UDF's fourth anniversary it was clear that the movement had made enormous advances in its short history. The National Forum appears to have been less able to handle the repressive climate due to the lack of mass popular support and lack of infrastructure; no 1987 national gathering had been announced by September.

RESISTANCE IN THE RURAL AREAS AND HOMELANDS

Throughout the history of extra-parliamentary resistance in South Africa, the rural areas have proved exceptionally difficult for urban-based movements to draw into their organisational structures. This difficulty is exacerbated in the 'independent homelands'. This is not to suggest that rural people do not have a rich history of resistance, indeed they have – but much of it has been spontaneous and has lacked efficient organisational expression. Poverty and unemployment are worse in these areas than in the urban townships, and the repressive activities of homeland 'governments' often surpass even those of the South African security forces. While the UDF and trade unions are 'legal' in 'white South Africa', for example, they are banned in many homelands. Similarly, the Freedom Charter, now legal in South Africa, is a proscribed document in the Transkei. Protest campaigns and attempts to build alternative structures in these areas thus confront special difficulties.

Many of these difficulties involve relatively mundane practicalities: the non-availability of venues for community meetings, difficulties in publishing pamphlets, shortages of skilled speakers, and a general inexperience in dealing with security force repression in its diverse forms – all serve to make the work of the rural activist more problematic. An additional complicating and problematic factor is the necessity for dealing sensitively with traditionalist and conservative elements within the community.

Following the declaration of the Emergency by Pretoria, the South African government extended it to the so-called 'non-independent' homelands. Repressive powers were increasingly conferred on the administrators of these territories during 1986, particularly through a set of decrees issued in March. The 'non-independent' homelands were given powers to ban organisations, restrict meetings, censor publications prohibit 'actions furthering the aims of banned organisations', and to remove and restrict people.[42]

Nevertheless, resistance to certain homeland authorities accelerated in 1986. Selected examples will suffice to illustrate this trend. In 1985 a former student leader and community health worker in the Transkei, Batandwa Ndondo, was killed by Transkei police in front of several witnesses. Transkeian authorities prevented students from the University of Transkei (UNITRA) from holding commemorative services, thus prompting demonstrations and mass arrests. The funeral was held under severe restrictions, with only an ordained priest being allowed to speak. Some 200 mourners were arrested, and after several months in detention were banished to remote parts of the Transkei.[43]

Resistance organisation at UNITRA consequently shifted 'semi-underground'. AZASO (now SANSCO), the UDF-affiliated tertiary student organisation, was banned on the campus and its activists targeted by the homeland authorities. Resistance was fuelled by the expulsion from the Transkei of two students in May 1986. An armed attack on a police station in the 'capital', Umtata, on 29 July raised the political temperature. Even those groups which are cautious in their opposition to Transkei's rulers, such as the Transkei Council of Churches, have faced severe repression. A Catholic priest from the United States was expelled from the bantustan in March 1987. On arrival in Zimbabwe, Father Casimir Paulsen told reporters he had been treated badly before his departure.[44] Detention conditions in homeland prisons are often worse than in those under white administration.

Collaboration between homeland police forces and the security branch of the South African Police is well documented. After his detention by Transkeian police, Dr Zola Dabula alleged in May 1987 that he had been interrogated by six policemen from East London, outside the bantustan.[45]

A detention list issued by the Transkeian authorities in May 1987 revealed that ninety-seven people were jailed 'for offences related to furthering the aims of the ANC, five . . . for offences relating to terrorism, one for unlawful distribution of pamphlets and one for offences relating to sabotage'.[46] The statement indicates the extent to which the Transkeian authorities perceive a threat from the ANC, rather than the UDF.

Large-scale protests have taken place in Ga-rankuwa, Mabopane and Winterveld in Bophuthatswana, another of the 'independent' homelands. Activism has focused on a variety of issues. The Huhudi Civic Association co-ordinated a rent boycott; a Brits community vigorously resisted incorporation in the homeland; a bus boycott was successfully implemented in Ga-Rankuwa; school protests resulted in many detentions; police fired on a crowd gathered in Winterveld to hear the local police commandant speak. Even those parties which function within the homeland system cannot operate freely. Late in 1986, twenty-four members of Bophuthatswana's Seoposengwe Party were detained and their meetings banned.

Rural resistance was most prominent in 1986 in the 'non-independent' homeland of KwaNdebele. Since 1983 the central government has forcibly settled thousands of people in the area, and incorporated land bought from white farmers into the territory. Land and population trebled over a short space of time. 'Independence' for the tiny, impoverished and overpopulated homeland was planned in 1986. Residents of Moutse in the Northern Transvaal vigorously opposed incorporation into the bantustan. Opponents of 'independence' included bantustan officials, 'MP's' elected to the Lebowa 'parliament' and youth organisations affiliated to the UDF. Pleas were made to Western governments, delegations travelled to Pretoria, and community resistance became widespread.[47]

KwaNdebele's incumbent leaders responded to the opposition by developing a well-armed vigilante group known as the 'Mbokotho'. On 1 January 1986, vigilantes abducted 261 people and subjected them to torture, leaving at least twenty-two residents dead.[48] Similar action took place in the township of Ekangala, where a local 'Residents Action Committee' was co-ordinating opposition to incorporation into KwaNdebele. Concerted resistance, often spearheaded by militant youth working in co-operation with sympathetic traditional leaders, forced the South African government to postpone plans for 'independence' in 1986.

Popular sentiment in the area was increasingly aligned to the UDF, which increased its stature in the rural areas through structures such as the KwaNdebele Youth Congress (KWAYCO). In September 1987 the Congress of Traditional Leaders was formed. UDF-aligned, this organisation has the potential to reshape and invigorate rural resistance.

In mid-August many of the anti-independence leaders were released from detention,[49] but were re-detained within three months. A joint initiative between South African and homeland police succeeded in reversing the momentum of the anti-independence movement by May 1987. In the aftermath of the white election in South Africa, independence for KwaNdebele was once again mooted. Collaboration between central and homeland authorities was clearly demonstrated by the detention in Johannesburg of the new leader of the anti-independence alliance. The central government has wavered on the issue of independence after the election and it appears to be lacking clear direction as far as the 'homeland' policy is concerned.

Security trials have become commonplace in the homelands. In the Ciskei, for example, the UDF's Border Secretary General, Reverend Arnold Stofile, was sentenced to eleven years in prison. The charge sheet was arbitrarily changed to aid the prosecution during the trial, indicating the lengths to which homeland authorities are prepared to go to contain the influence of the resistance movements.

Increasing militarisation within the homelands is a further concern for resistance activists. In Bophuthatswana, a para-military initiative for youth attending schools in the homeland, the National Cadet Movement, has been established. Youth camps also supply political training to encourage antagonism toward the ANC and UDF, particularly its youth organisations. The trade unions face heightened difficulties when employers locate enterprises in homelands, relying on the authorities to quash worker militancy.

VIGILANTES: INTERNAL DESTABILISATION AT WORK

The term 'vigilante' has a special, wide meaning in South Africa.[50] Essentially, it refers to elements within the black community who engage in violent activity against members of all sectors of resistance. Vigilantes have, of late, become one of the greatest threats posed to the resistance movements (see Chapters 1 and 12). In many cases it is clear that vigilante groups have been fostered directly by state security forces; in others their genesis is more complex, involving disputes over political authority and patronage, among other factors. Vigilante groups became prominent in the second half of 1985, although they had a variety of historical antecedents. In 1976, for example, Zulu migrants clashed with students in Soweto, and during the school boycotts of 1980 *impis* of the Inkatha movement played a crucial role in crushing the boycott in the Durban township of KwaMashu. But 'vigilanteism' reached new heights as resistance activity accelerated in the 1980s.

Some commentators stress internal divisions in the black communities as the primary motivating force for the vigilantes:

> The growing influence of urban radicals provoked local power struggles with conservative vigilante groups determined to assert their own supremacy over the townships . . . They drew their support from local councillors, township officials, teachers, church elders, small township capitalists like shop, shebeen and taxi owners, and street gangs, all with reason to fear and resent the activities of radical groups on their homeground.[51]

The writer quoted above goes on to say that in many areas the vigilantes acquired 'the tacit approval of the police'.[52] While all these elements are true in themselves, this emphasis implicitly underplays the role of the state in actively creating forms of vigilanteism. According to another commentator,

> vigilantes were blacks who had a political or economic stake in the system, who disapproved of the comrades and who were prepared to do the government's dirty work for them by killing the radical

> activists. Establishing direct links between the vigilantes and the government is of course difficult; but if the authorities were not actively directing the vigilantes, they seemed to be taking advantage of their actions.[53]

The latter construction, although more accurate, remains inadequate in the face of a wealth of evidence of state complicity. In 1986, for example, one Abraham Zwane confessed that he had functioned as a police operative after being arrested for drug offences. As a paid informer, he aided the police in a series of arson attacks in which several people died. Zwane was caught after a group of vigilantes, including himself, acting under the direction of five policemen, petrol-bombed the homes of seven activists in the Transvaal townships of Thokoza and Katlehong.[54] According to Martin Murray, 'A flood of allegations, including reliable eyewitness accounts, pointed to police support for vigilante activities.'[55]

Several South African newspapers have implied – guardedly but clearly – that direct state involvement is beyond doubt. *Umsebenzi*, the underground publication of the banned South African Communist Party, popular in many townships, has dubbed the vigilantes 'Black Mercenaries'. The publication offers some speculation about the conditions which encourage the phenomenon, highlighting the existence of a large recruiting catchment area comprised of poverty-stricken unemployed people.[56] Certainly, there is an element of dissatisfaction in some sections of the black community, fuelled by 'excesses' which occurred at the height of the township uprising. But the extrapolation of this phenomenon into a simple notion of (what the state calls) 'black-on-black' violence in which the state plays no active role results in a dangerous misunderstanding of the present and future potential of vigilante action in weakening the internal resistance movements.

There are several categories of vigilantes (see Chapter 8): for example, some are linked to the homelands and rural areas, and others to the urban townships. Among the best known and well-organised are the *impis* associated with the Inkatha movement who are active in the Natal region. In 1986 Natal courts intervened to restrain various Inkatha members from committing acts of violence against NECC, COSATU and UDF-affiliated organisations.[57] More revealing was the fact that some of those brought before the courts were senior aides to KwaZulu Chief Minister and Inkatha President Mangosuthu Buthelezi. One such was Thomas Shabalala, who admitted controlling an army of 208 vigilantes who were paid via a protection tax levied by Shabalala on local residents of the impoverished squatter settlement of Lindelani.[58] In March 1987, after the gruesome killing of children in the UDF-affiliated KwaMashu Youth League, members of Shabalala's army (who were also members of Inkatha) were arrested. Local Inkatha leaders levied R2 from residents to pay for bail. The residents resisted: 'scores of Lindelani squatters refused to pay R2 contributions per household towards the bail for six local men who were charged with the horror slaying of KwaMashu pupils'.[59]

Further evidence of Inkatha linked vigilante action emerged in a statement revealing details of attacks against UDF and COSATU-aligned organisations in the Durban township of Claremont.[60] Khohlwangifile 'Twist' Ngema was a local Inkatha leader in charge of the 'Amabutho' vigilantes. In confessing his involvement, he told reporters: 'We are no longer prepared to be used as cannon fodder, forcing the community into accepting Jamile's [a senior Inkatha official's] leadership. My message to the comrades is: "let's unite and join forces".'[61]

In 1987 legal action was brought against senior Inkatha members for complicity in the murder of COSATU followers in Natal, and for an attack on the inhabitants of the Mpophemeni township. Inkatha and KwaZulu officials were arrested after the attacks, but released without charge. For many observers, the incident confirmed unequivocally the high-level co-operation between the KwaZulu police, South African Police and Inkatha.[62] In June 1987 Buthelezi was given control of several police stations by Pretoria.[63] The move followed a public request by Buthelezi to the South African Minister of Law and Order, Adriaan Vlok, to 'untie my [Buthelezi's] hands'. UDF leaders have predicted a resultant increase in violence against their members in the area.[64]

Vigilantes present the UDF, COSATU and other resistance organisations with a seemingly insoluble problem. They cannot respond to the organised violence in kind, for the 'blind eye' approach of the police to the vigilantes would certainly not be extended to them. Despite the UDF's call for the formation of township 'defence committees', these cannot compete with the organisation, resources, or latitude enjoyed by the vigilantes. It is now not uncommon to hear township residents expressing the belief that only underground Umkhonto we Sizwe guerrillas can protect them. Nevertheless, a national campaign against vigilantes was proposed at the UDF's national conference in June 1987.

> While recognising the vicious character of these death squads, the conference concluded that the ultimate solution must be a political one. The UDF plans to isolate these death squads from our communities and re-educate those vigilantes who have been politically misled.[65]

In addition to the vigilantes, township activists have come under acute pressure following the creation of so-called 'kitskonstabels' (instant constables). Black recruits are given three weeks of training as policemen, and then armed. The explicit objective of the scheme was to take on the community activists.[66] Of late, both vigilantes and 'kitskonstabels' (see Chapter 8) have been seen wearing the same two-piece blue overalls.[67]

These developments reflect a government trend to translate a major constituent of its foreign policy to the internal arena. The policy of destabilisation of neighbouring states has been applied to the various forms of internal extra-parliamentary resistance which have developed over the last decade. Surrogate forces fighting in Angola and Mozambique are finding their mirror images within South Africa. The seeds of counter-revolution appear to have been sown.

FRONTS OF RESISTANCE: WOMEN'S AND CULTURAL ORGANISATION

Various components, or fronts, make up the internal extra-parliamentary resistance movements. The labour and youth components are dealt with in other chapters. In this section I will briefly examine the relatively under-analysed, but important developing front of resistance represented by women's organisation. This will be followed by some discussion of culture in the context of resistance activity.

Since 1980, small, localised structures re-emerged to cater for women around the country. Identifying the gender, class, and racial oppression to which black women are subject, the structures sought to provide for united political action by women as a distinct grouping within the black communities. The fledgeling structures were developing organisationally but were largely unco-ordinated, even as late as 1986. At various workplaces the growing trade union movement was also beginning to address itself to the issues facing women. Plans proceeded for the revival of the Federation of South African Women (FEDSAW), which had played a major role in organising women in the 1950s but was now moribund. However, the proposed re-launch of FEDSAW was superceded in the early months of 1987 by the creation of a national UDF Women's Congress.

Launched in May 1987, the Women's Congress claimed a direct role in the national political struggle, while concentrating on specific issues confronting women, such as legal inequities. The organisation saw itself as being within the tradition of the ANC Women's League of the 1950s. Thus the new Congress adopted the Freedom Charter and the ANC's Women's Charter. Resolutions emerging from the Women's Congress indicated the explicit linking of general and specialised issues: they called for the unconditional release of detainees, especially children, and pledged to work with COSATU in establishing women's rights within the trade union movement. In an address to COSATU's congress in July 1987, UDF acting publicity secretary Murphy Morobe told delegates: 'We have still not taken the organisation of women as seriously as we should, if we hope to advance.'[68] Some evidence has emerged to suggest that such sentiments have been translated into concrete activity. Already, in the course of COSATU's Living Wage Campaign for example, special attention has been given to the position of women. COSATU told members: 'Until men and women equally share domestic duties, a 40 hour week will help women even more than men . . . women need to join the struggle, but often do not have time to go to meetings to put their views and take up leadership positions.[69]

The realities of day-to-day life for black women militate against their equal participation in the internal resistance organisations, and it is this area which the new Congress is attempting to confront. It is worth noting that the population profile of the homelands (largely comprising elderly people, children and women) accentuates the possibilities for a prominent role for women in resistance in these areas.

Affiliates of the UDF Women's Congress have already undertaken some political initiatives, notably regarding the protection of children. In the Durban township of Chesterville, for example, the Natal Organisation of Women (NOW) staged all-night vigils in 1986 to prevent attacks on their children by a vigilante group calling itself the 'A-Team'. The image of physical resistance being male-led has gradually shifted as increasing numbers of women (although still a small proportion) join the military wing of the ANC. Theresa Ramashamola, from the Sharpville township in the Transvaal, presently faces the death sentence, and other women like Thandi Modise and Marion Sparg are serving lengthy sentences for military activities against the system.

The women's front of resistance is weaker than others. Nevertheless, it is making tremendous progress given the objective conditions. The formation of the UDF Women's Congress is an indication of expanding forms of resistance organisation, even under Emergency conditions. The UDF Women's Congress intends to play a pivotal role in incorporating women who are outside the ranks of the UDF in a revived FEDSAW in the near future.

The constraints of the State of Emergency and the difficulty of holding mass rallies has encouraged a concerted focus by the resistance organisations on 'culture' as a means of politicisation. COSATU has been prominent in promoting this process, arguing that culture plays a key ideological role in society, and the federation has committed itself to 'the building of a working class culture'. To this end COSATU has established a National Cultural Unit. Its co-ordinator, Mi Hlatshwayo, has explained the beliefs underlying the COSATU initiative:

> In South Africa, because we are undergoing an exploitative period, it is even more important to record what is taking place. That is why so many poems in South Africa are about oppression. They cry about something. Culture should go far beyond documentation and it has to make known the vision of a new South Africa. Culture must be a mirror and a media. It is from this mirror that we catch a glimpse of the new liberated society, free of oppression and exploitation.[70]

These developments were not restricted to already politicised elements such as COSATU. A South African Musicians' Union emerged to provide an organisational structure for artists opposed to apartheid, and to ensure unified action. The importance of the latter was highlighted by the participation of several black musicians in a government sponsored (and highly lucrative) propaganda song which caused deep rifts in cultural and political circles.

The formation of the UDF aligned Congress of South African Writers (COSAW) indicated further progress in the politicisation of culture by the resistance movements. COSAW included among its patrons ANC figures like Govan Mbeki, Mongane Wally Serote, and the late Alex La Guma. COSAW argued that 'Art cannot exist in isolation from the interplay of the political and economic, intellectual and technological aspects of society.'[71] Contending that 'apartheid capitalism' had given rise to the development of 'two distinct cultures', COSAW saw the 'dominant culture' manifesting itself through overwhelming control of the 'means of production'. The 'dominated culture', they held, was characterised by 'economic exploitation and political repression'.

The impact of these organised 'cultural wings' of resistance has yet to be tested. As with the developing women's front, however, some early successes have been registered. The Sarmcol Workers' Co-operative (SAWCO), for example, formed after striking workers were sacked by the British-owned BTR Sarmcol, have presented their case nationally and internationally through their play 'The Long March'. Over the years, various student organisations have experimented with culture as a mechanism for organisation, and this seems set to spread to other sectors of resistance.

FORMS OF RESISTANCE IN THE COLOURED, INDIAN AND WHITE COMMUNITIES

Resistance within the two minority black communities, while integrally linked to national extra-parliamentary opposition, takes on some different forms to that witnessed in the African townships. Both the Indian and coloured communities are favoured by legislation compared to the majority African community, and have not experienced the same degree of exploitation. This is, of course, a manifestation of the overarching strategy of 'divide and rule' which informs government policy. However, resistance in the Indian and coloured areas is long-standing and is influenced by varying material conditions and degrees of oppression.

The larger coloured community has played a prominent role in resistance, particularly in the Western Cape. In most areas there are structural fronts of resistance to give the national movement a non-racial character. For example, the Cape Youth Congress (CAYCO), an affiliate of SAYCO, is very popular in the coloured townships of the Western Cape. In 1984 the coloured community efficiently resisted attempts by the state at co-option by implementing a massive stayaway from the polls for the tricameral elections. A similar campaign succeeded in Indian areas, but as a whole the community has not engaged in resistance activity to the same degree as Africans and coloureds. In Natal, where the majority of the community resides, the Natal Indian Congress (NIC) – a founding affiliate of the UDF – feeds into the national resistance movement. Although the most popular structure within the Indian community, the NIC has neither consolidated mass support nor an adequate organisational infrastructure. However, many Indian civic organisations, and youth structures affiliated to SAYCO participate in national resistance initiatives.

Marginally improved living conditions between the African, coloured and Indian communities play a role in determining the nature of resistance within each community. As a corollary, differing political relations with the state influence levels of anti-apartheid organisation and militancy. The increasingly troubled economy and a concomitant rise in unemployment levels tend to dilute the effects of these discrepancies, however, as greater material dissatisfaction is bred across the racial spectrum. In Natal, for example, 'advice centres' have been established for township residents experiencing a deterioration in living conditions. These structures are aligned to the UDF, providing another link to the national non-racial movement.

The white extra-parliamentary opposition, although limited to a fraction of the white community, is an important element in internal resistance, notably in its affirmation of the non-racial philosophy of the dominant resistance movement. Those whites who have chosen to participate fully in the extra-parliamentary opposition have found themselves subject to detention and other forms of state harassment. An important initiative within the white community is represented by the End Conscription Campaign (ECC) which consistently challenges the imposition of compulsory military service for white males. Operating in an extremely hostile environment, the organisation has suffered severe repression. Other predominantly white organisations such as the Black Sash[72] and IDASA, which function outside the confines of Parliament, have small memberships but play important supportive roles for the 'front-line' black resistance organisations. There has also been church-based resistance to apartheid rule from within the white community, and progressive white students are organised in the UDF aligned National Union of South African Students (NUSAS).

SOCIALISM, THE FREEDOM CHARTER, AND INTERNAL RESISTANCE

Since the emergence of the UDF and National Forum, divergent ideological trends within mass legal resistance have become sharply focused. Their roots are to be found in the lengthy history of the resistance movements, particularly in the 1950s, but have never been as clearly accentuated as they are in the mid-1980s.

The passing of the Suppression of Communism Act in 1950, and the repressive climate it created, made activists operating legally in South Africa wary of open ideological identification with 'communism' and 'socialism'. Certainly, at an organisational level, frank commitment to socialist principles was out of the question. In the current, vastly heightened atmosphere of resistance, socialist sentiment (broadly defined) has experienced a widespread re-emergence among leaders and rank and file members of the different sectors of resistance. In 1983, the National Forum adopted a socialist programme, and AZAPO itself had invested much of its energies in debates over socialism for several years.

However, the trade unions were the major vehicle for the popularisation of elements of socialism as an integral part of their programme for liberation. Both COSATU and the National Council of Trade Unions (NACTU) openly propound a socialist solution for South Africa, although its specific nature is yet to be defined. The UDF, like the ANC, does not argue overtly in favour of socialism, taking the view that in the 'present phase of the liberation struggle' all anti-apartheid forces, including liberals, must be accommodated. Many leaders and affiliate groups are clearly socialist inclined, but work in a tactical alliance with colleagues holding different views.

At this ideological level, one of the most distinctive features of 1987 was the degree of support harnessed around the ANC's 1955 Freedom Charter. As the popularity of the ANC itself burgeoned, its manifesto was increasingly accepted by a wide range of resistance formations, extending even to little-known church groupings like the Catholic Students Association (CASA). It also narrowed the gap between the mass legal resistance and the exiled, banned movement. COSATU has adopted the Charter, as has the UDF and its major affiliates like SAYCO. The pervasiveness of the 'Congress Alliance' tradition is an extraordinary phenomenon, given its practical eclipse after 1960 (see Chapter 1).

STILL NO EASY WALK TO FREEDOM: INTERNAL RESISTANCE AND THE FUTURE

In 1988, the future of the UDF, still the predominant political movement of internal resistance, is uncertain. Finding itself under unprecedented pressure from the state, the Front is attempting to consolidate its forces and evolve effective new methods of resistance. At the level of popular support, it is wholly intact. The challenge is for it to devise imaginative means of channelling and using that popular militancy. With so many of its leaders imprisoned or 'on the run', it remains far from achieving this goal. The state may not be able to recreate the pervasive quiescence it imposed in 1960 – the extent of mass discontent and a concomitant identification with the ANC and the UDF in 1987 is not comparable to the earlier period – but it will be weakened if it remains unfocused for a lengthy period.

The increasing political prominence of the trade unions signals hope for organisational structures like the UDF. For a time the Front may have to 'piggy-back' on the still functioning union movement, while it attempts to regroup. This political reality is recognised by the state, which gives it another reason for increasing pressure on the unions. The major Treason Trials which have been effectively used by the state to remove key UDF leaders from circulation could quite plausibly be applied to the union movement. Diverse, increasing state pressure is the only certainty which the resistance movements can currently identify.

The UDF will, from necessity, continue to function at a semi-underground level. It is likely that further clandestine organisational launches will take place: for example, preparations for the formation of a national co-ordinating structure for township civic associations are reportedly well advanced. With the options for legal, open protest action so severely curtailed – and likely to be further restricted in future – these types of structures still have to prove that they have alternative modes of resistance to offer. Legal loopholes and unevenness in the application of laws will continue to be exploited, but will require more and more ingenuity. The resistance organisations have proved beyond doubt that they are capable of such ingenuity, and have displayed enormous courage in confronting the state, even at great cost.

The government's strategy of mass detentions, while exercising a disruptive influence on resistance structures, has enjoyed little success in forcing activists out of politics once they are released. It is obvious that spells in prison have the opposite effect in most cases, turning sometimes inexperienced, angry militants into seasoned political veterans. This has, among other things, encouraged a process of introspection and a wider acceptance that simple militancy will not achieve immediate victory for the resistance movements. The triumphalism which characterised the period 1984–86 has dissipated, and has been replaced by a widespread acknowledgement of a long political struggle lying ahead.

Similarly, the internecine violence which has dogged the internal resistance organisations has subsided in the face of massive repression. A 'closing of ranks', even if temporary, is much easier to envisage in 1987 than in previous years. This is not to suggest a total disappearance of such conflict – its ideological basis has not changed – but it is a political gain none the less. In contrast, the 'vigilante' and 'hit squad' phenomena will undoubtedly become more prominent, taking on new and more sophisticated forms.

There is no evidence to suggest that the State of Emergency will be lifted in the foreseeable future. Repressive conditions are likely to worsen, and this is a reality which all sectors of resistance – and the political organisations in particular – are forced to confront. Spontaneous uprisings will be met with unbridled force. Formations like the UDF are therefore concentrating increasingly on raising the political consciousness of their constituents as opposed to encouraging insurrectionary activity. The conditions which gave rise to the resurgence of resistance in 1984 still obtain, but the state has ensured that it cannot manifest itself in the same form. The task of the political organisations of resistance is to adapt – organisationally – to this changed political terrain. While Mandela's cautionary phrase 'No Easy Walk to Freedom' still remains apposite, the immediate challenge facing the beleaguered internal resistance movements is to ensure that the march does not grind to a complete halt. It is against this background that their initiatives in the coming months and years must be judged.

NOTES

1. In the East London area, for example, the South African Allied Workers Union (SAAWU) worked closely with the local community in explicitly political campaigns.
2. The Freedom Charter was drawn up in 1955 by the 'Congress Alliance', between the African National Congress, the South African Indian Congress, the Coloured Peoples' Organization, and the Congress of Democrats. The document was 'unbanned' in 1983.
3. The TIC is a longstanding ally of the ANC.
4. Dr Neville Alexander, a leading figure in the National Forum and Cape Action League (CAL), had called for the formation of a united front in 1982. His call did not receive the attention which Boesak's later statement commanded.
5. The author was present at the launch of the UDF.
6. *Race Relations Survey 1984* (Johannesburg: South African Institute of Race Relations, 1985).

7. The 'Koornhof Bills' outlined 'local government' proposals for the African community.
8. *Evening Post*, Port Elizabeth, 5 January 1984.
9. The selective State of Emergency initially included thirty-six magisterial districts.
10. Na-Iem Dollie, 'The National Forum', in South African Research Services (ed.), *South African Review III* (Johannesburg: Ravan Press, 1986), pp. 267–77.
11. Ibid.
12. 'Witness to Apartheid', television documentary produced and directed by Sharon Sopher.
13. M. Meredith, 'The Black Opposition', in Jesmond Blumenfeld (ed.), *South Africa in Crisis* (London: Croom Helm, 1987), pp. 77–89.
14. M. Sutcliffe, 'The Crisis in South Africa: Material Conditions and the Reformist Response', in *Geoforum*, vol. 17, no. 2, 1986, pp. 141–59.
15. *Weekly Mail*, Johannesburg, 14 March 1986.
16. Lekota acquired the nickname 'terror' for his proficiency on the football field.
17. *Weekly Mail*, Johannesburg, 16 April 1986.
18. Unpublished notes. The author is grateful to Sefako Nyaka for supplying information used in the chapter.
19. Resolution Number 8 of the conference of the National Education Crisis Committee (NECC), Durban, 30 March 1986.
20. Address to a meeting at the University of Durban-Westville, 1985.
21. Reverend Stofile was sentenced to eleven years imprisonment in 1987 by the Ciskeian authorities.
22. Raymond Suttner, Mohammed Valli and Cheryl Carolus were detained upon returning to South Africa.
23. Zwelakhe Sisulu, keynote speech to the NECC conference, Durban, March 1986.
24. Ibid.
25. *Weekly Mail*, Johannesburg, 9 May 1986.
26. Ibid.
27. Ibid.
28. Ibid.
29. P. van Niekerk, 'Middle Ground Laid to Waste', in *New Statesman*, London, 7 August 1987.
30. A. Mashinini, 'Dual Power and the Creation of People's Committees', in *Sechaba* (Official organ of the ANC), London, May 1987.
31. Ibid.
32. Ibid.
33. *Focus on Political Repression No. 22*, International Defence and Aid Fund (IDAF), London, March 1987.
34. The Internal Security Act allows for indefinite detention without trial in solitary confinement and without recourse to legal representation. Those held under this section are in a much more difficult position than detainees held under State of Emergency regulations.
35. *Focus on Political Repression No. 64*, International Defence and Aid Fund, (IDAF), London, May–June 1986.

36. Nyaka, op.cit. note 18 above.
37. IDAF *Focus on political repression No. 64*, May–June 1986.
38. Nyaka, op.cit. note 18 above.
39. Ibid.
40. *New Nation*, Johannesburg, 2 April 1987.
41. *The Star*, Johannesburg, 5 June 1987.
42. Government Proclamation No. 38 of 1986. *Financial Mail*, Johannesburg, 11 April 1986.
43. *Daily Dispatch*, East London, 26–28 September 1985, *The Star*, 8 November 1985.
44. *Daily Dispatch*, 13 March 1987.
45. *New Nation*, Johannesburg, 15 May 1987.
46. *Daily Dispatch*, 20–21 May 1987.
47. *Cape Times*, Cape Town, 9 December 1985.
48. *Weekly Mail*, Johannesburg, 18 January 1986, *Cape Times*, Cape Town, 6 January 1986.
49. *Daily News*, Durban, 14 August 1986, *The Star*, Johannesburg, 14 August 1986.
50. See N. Haysom, *Apartheid's Private Army: The rise of right-wing vigilantes in South Africa* (London: Catholic Institute of International Relations, 1986).
51. Meredith, 'The Black Opposition', op.cit. note 13 above.
52. Ibid.
53. G. Leach, *South Africa: No Easy Path To Peace* (London: Methuen, 1986), pp. 207–9.
54. *Weekly Mail*, Johannesburg, 5 June 1986.
55. M. Murray, *South Africa: Time of Agony, Time of Destiny. The Upsurge of Popular Protest* (London: Verso, 1987), p. 423.
56. *Umsebenzi*, Publication of the South African Communist Party, vol. 3, no. 2, Second Quarter, 1987.
57. *Sunday Tribune*, Durban, 4 May 1986, *Weekly Mail*, Johannesburg, 2 May 1986.
58. *Work in Progress*, no. 43, August 1986, p. 12.
59. *City Press*, Johannesburg, 10 May 1987.
60. Ibid.
61. Ibid.
62. *New Nation*, Johannesburg, 4 June 1987.
63. Ibid.
64. Ibid.
65. Ibid.
66. *Sunday Star*, Johannesburg, 21 September 1986.
67. *Umsebenzi*, vol. 3, no. 2, Second Quarter, 1987.
68. Murphy Morobe, address to the second national conference of COSATU, Johannesburg, July 1987.
69. COSATU pamphlet, 'A Living Wage'.
70. *New Nation*, Johannesburg, 23 July 1987.
71. Ibid., 4 June 1987.
72. The Black Sash is a long-established group of white women, now broadly sympathetic to the UDF.

6 The Afrikaner Establishment

Stanley Uys

INTRODUCTION

The Afrikaner establishment is given cohesion through a set of interlocking institutions which have attempted to unify the Afrikaner *volk*, consolidate their religious and cultural identity, promote their economic advancement, and which, since 1948, have secured their political hegemony over South Africa. This network has integrated the leadership of Afrikaner institutions, provided a safety net so that 'a child born into an Afrikaans family could move from the cradle to the grave within the framework of Afrikaner organisations', facilitated the formulation of collective goals for these organisations and introduced a unity of purpose into corporate Afrikaner action, and imposed on the Afrikaner a system which had the power to ostracise him and to influence his career and general social acceptance.[1] This chapter examines the origins and functions of the establishment, the recent weakening of its cohesion, and the decline of its influence.

The key Afrikaner organisations have been the Dutch Reformed churches, the National(ist) Party (1914) and the Afrikaner Broederbond (1919), and the critical period was the 1930s and 1940s. The establishment's power source has been Afrikaner nationalism, which assumed recognisable form in the last decade of the nineteenth century. All nationalisms need enemies and the Afrikaners' enemies were British imperialism, 'foreign' capitalism, and indigenous blacks. Like other nationalists, Afrikaners were motivated by a sense of alienation in their own country, of hurt and humiliation, of cultural and economic inferiority, and of political subordination.

Carefully cultivated political myths were used to foster Afrikaner nationalism: that whites had settled an uninhabited land, where they were threatened by black hordes, and had introduced a god-ordained paramountcy and taken no more than was their due. The history of South Africa came to be written as the history of Afrikaners alone. World history was seen in terms of competing nationalisms, and poverty was the natural state of blacks who were incapable of development and whose cultural distance from whites could never be bridged.[2] These myths strengthened Afrikaner cohesion. The 'sacred period' of Afrikaner history, with its heroes and martyrs, was characterised as falling between the British occupation of the Cape in 1806 and the execution of the anti-'English' war rebel Jopie Fourie in 1914. It included the two 'cycles of suffering and death' – the Great Trek (mid-1830s) and the South African War (1899–1902), which have been celebrated in the Afrikaners' lyric poetry of struggle.[3]

The Afrikaners achieved power through their exclusivism: a separate people claiming a common history, traditions, language, religion and culture, and pursuing a separate destiny. Unable to identify with non-Afrikaner whites or with blacks they imposed their hegemony on both. Cultural mobilisation was followed by economic and political mobilisation and the *laager* was closed. Without political, and, as a corollary, increasing economic power, Afrikaner nationalism would have remained a cultural phenomenon; with it, it bent the country to its will. Being god-ordained, it was predestined to rule. The Afrikaner *volk* equalled the nation who equalled the state. The rest were second- and third-class citizens.

Since Union in 1910, political power had always been an attainable goal: the franchise was restricted to whites and Afrikaners were therefore in the majority. What was needed was ideological mobilisation towards hegemony, and this they pursued through the establishment. Out of Afrikaner nationalism, and earlier practices of segregation in South Africa, emerged the policy of apartheid. The step was made from Afrikaner exclusivism to the doctrine of the natural diversity of men – Afrikaner nationalism and apartheid between them destroyed the idea of a united South African nation.

In the late 1960s, but more particularly in the 1970s, when apartheid began to falter, the National Party applied the remedy of 'reform'. This, however, only opened schisms in Afrikaner ranks. Instead of modernising and renewing Afrikaner rule, reform destroyed the crucial ideology and played havoc with Afrikaner unity. The first defections from the National Party came in 1969 when four members of parliament formed the Herstigte Nasionale Party (HNP). But a more serious break was the formation of the Conservative Party in 1982, when seventeen MPs defected. This break was a direct response to the National Party's reform programme.

Reform might not have had such a devastating effect on Afrikaner unity if it had succeeded in its primary aim of conciliating blacks. But it simply raised the black struggle to higher levels. Blacks recognised that reform was a major retreat from the ideology painstakingly constructed since 1948, and an omen of an impending crisis in white rule. The establishment in 1984 of the tricameral parliament was a case in point. President Botha's addition of a (coloured) House of Representatives and an (Indian) House of Delegates to a hitherto whites-only parliament, instead of being accepted as democratisation of the legislature, dramatised the total absence of Africans and introduced a new and explosive issue into the black struggle.

From the start, reform was an illusion: the supposition that 'crude' and 'outdated' forms of discrimination could be replaced by modernised and more cost-effective ones, that ascendant economic interests could be freed from restrictive race practices without essential white controls being relinquished, that the black opposition and international opinion alike would be mollified, and that all this could take place within the framework of Afrikaner unity and National Party hegemony. In fact what happened was that the apartheid ball of wool started to unravel.

The more reform failed to reinvigorate white rule, the more schisms opened on both the National Party's left and right flanks. Hypnotised by the challenge from the fundamentalists of the far right – Afrikaners laying claim to the true legitimacy of their *volk* – Botha nevertheless knew there was no turning back. He could stall reform, but not reverse its direction. In any event, his credentials with the far right had been permanently destroyed. The strains in the establishment soon became evident, with almost every Afrikaner 'service' organisation, from the church and the Broederbond to the lowliest school committee, showing signs of disarray. The National Party remains the emotional home of the majority of Afrikaners – and the dispenser of vast state patronage to them – but it can no longer unify them. This was proved conclusively by the general elections of 6 May 1987.

THE NATIONAL PARTY

The South Africa Act of 1909, which united the Cape and Natal with the two defeated Boer republics of the Transvaal and the Orange Free State, achieved the primary aim of British policy makers, which was to establish a British dominion

> under a government which could fairly claim to represent both the white communities and which was led by men who were sincerely committed to a policy of Anglo-Afrikaner conciliation and

> co-operation with the other members of the British Empire . . . On the other hand . . . in attaining the primary goal of its South African policy, Britain had sacrificed the secondary goal . . . Great Britain left behind a caste-like society, dominated by a white minority. The price of unity and conciliation was the institutionalization of white supremacy.[4]

But even white unity was short-lived. General J.B.M. Hertzog was appointed (reluctantly) to the first Union cabinet by General Louis Botha. Within two years, he was making his famous De Wildt speech (12 December 1912) in which he said: 'The time has come when South Africa can no longer be ruled by non-Afrikaners.' Hertzog enunciated a 'two-stream' policy for South African whites which prepared the way for the establishment of the National Party in 1914. With this event,

> Afrikaner nationalism thus for the first time became a co-ordinated, country-wide movement and vehicle for the strivings and aspirations of a people who wanted to retain their separate identity and their independence . . . as Dr (Hendrik) Verwoerd was to assert . . . 'The National Party was never and is not an ordinary party. It is a nation on the move.' This identification was perhaps the chief magnet which finally drew and kept the overwhelming majority of Afrikaners together after generations of schisms and squabble.[5]

The National Party contested its first elections in 1915 and won twenty-seven seats in the 130-seat House of Assembly. The Botha-Smuts South African Party won fifty-four, and the Unionist Party and the Labour Party, both predominantly English-speaking, won thirty-nine and four seats respectively. There were six Independents. Racism – whether involving language or colour – has been a major factor in every South African general election since that time.

In the 1920 elections, the National Party increased its representation to forty-four in a 134-seat House of Assembly. Two years later white miners on the Witwatersrand gold mines went on strike in protest against a decision by the Chamber of Mines to increase the ratio of black to white miners as a cost-reducing measure. The strike developed into a full-scale rebellion and Smuts called out the troops. In several days of fighting, between 230 and 250 people were killed. A result of this rebellion was to bring the National and Labour parties together in agreement on a 'civilised labour' policy to protect unskilled but 'civilised' whites from competition with lower-paid blacks. The pact brought the two parties to power in the 1924 general elections, the Nationalists winning sixty-three seats and Labour eighteen.

The National Party won its first overall majority in parliament in 1929 – seventy-eight seats in a 148-seat Assembly. The depression had started, however, and Hertzog, facing an economic blizzard, was forced into a coalition with Smuts' SAP which in 1933 won 138 seats in a 150-seat Assembly. In response to fusion, the National Party's Cape leader, Dr D.F. Malan, broke away to form the Gesuiwerde Nasionale Party (Purified National Party), and in the 1935 parliamentary session they formed a nineteen-strong official opposition.

For four years after 1934, Nationalist Afrikanerdom was in the wilderness. The year 1938, however, was the centenary of the Great Trek and the Nationalists 'capitalised the occasion with endless ingenuity, astonishing vigour, and very comfortable success'.[6] Against this background of an Afrikaner revival, a deeply divided cabinet met on 2 September 1939 to discuss whether South Africa should enter the war or not. Hertzog's six followers favoured neutrality, Smuts' seven adherents demanded war. On 4 September, with 147 of 153 members present, the Assembly voted by 80 to 67 for war. Hertzog resigned immediately and crossed over to the Nationalist benches. Within days the Afrikaner breach had been formally healed.

The basic incompatibility between Hertzogism and Malanism, however, persisted. A unity conference in November 1939 broke down on the issue of republicanism, with the Malanites demanding a Boer republic and Hertzog pressing for a common South African nationhood. The disagreement was patched up, but Hertzog's hopes of imposing Hertzogism on the Nationalists was illusory. They had rejected it in 1933 and they were rejecting it again. By the end of 1940 Hertzog was a spent force in politics. He retired to his farm where he died two years later. The Nationalists were at a low ebb. In the 1938 general elections they had won only twenty-seven seats (out of 150). They fared somewhat better in the 1943 elections with forty-three seats under the new name Herenigde Nasionale Party (Reunited National Party). But the war was only an interregnum.

Hertzog's experience with Malanism was both painful and illuminating. Hertzog claimed that after Malan had joined the Broederbond he had discarded support for Afrikaner-English unity in favour of Afrikaner domination. In his famous denunciation of the Broederbond in 1935 Hertzog said that the organisation's aim by its own definition was 'to let Dutch-speaking Afrikanerdom gain domination in South Africa and to bring about that the Dutch-speaking Broederbond shall rule South Africa'.[7]

Hertzog's disciple N.C. Havenga had formed the Afrikaner Party to keep Hertzogism alive, but in 1947 he accepted an electoral pact with Malan, and the combination won the 1948 general elections, the Nationalists with seventy seats and the Afrikaner Party with nine, against the United Party's sixty-five, Labour's six and Native Representatives three – an overall Nationalist majority of five. The Afrikaner Party merged with the National Party in 1951 and that was the beginning of the end of Hertzogism. Throughout the past four decades of National Party rule, English speakers have had no more than token representation in the cabinet and in the National Party's parliamentary ranks. The National Party was a party of Afrikaners for Afrikaners.

Another important actor was the *Ossewabrandwag* (Ox-Wagon Sentinels (OB)), which was formed in 1938 as an offshoot of the Great Trek centenary celebrations. It was formed at a significant moment in Afrikaner history when 'divisions and political defeat had brought them to a state of deep depression'. At its peak, it claimed 250 000 members, including a paramilitary *Stormjaer* (storm troop) section which, during the war, committed numerous acts of sabotage. It threatened to usurp the National Party's leadership position and even published a draft republican constitution. Malan took up the challenge, argued the case for parliamentary democracy against the OB's authoritarianism, and won – even though some of his followers had never had much enthusiasm for the parliamentary system 'which they had derided, in the early days of the war, as being inspired by British-Jewish-Capitalist-Imperialist-Masonic influences'.

Some analysts have compared the OB with the present-day *Afrikaner Weerstandsbeweging* (Afrikaner Resistance Movement (AWB)), a paramilitary organisation which says it is holding itself in readiness to intervene if Botha's reformist rule collapses and whites need armed protection. There are similarities – the AWB parades with uniforms, its marshals have carried holstered pistols, it uses the rhetoric of violence, and it is brazenly authoritarian. Nevertheless, it is still puny and functions as no more than an adjunct for the far right. The Conservative Party uses it to provide political theatre. On its own, the AWB is unlikely to present a political challenge to the National Party. Its real menace lies in its white vigilanteism and the havoc this can play with race relations.

After 1948, the National Party steadily consolidated its parliamentary strength: ninety-four seats in 1953, 103 in 1958, 105 in 1961, 126 in

1966, 118 in 1970, 123 in 1974, 136 in 1977, 132 in 1981 and 123 in 1987 (these figures exclude nominated and proportionally elected MPs and the earlier white MPs who represented African and Coloured voters). The National Party reached its peak, therefore, in 1977 when it obtained 82 per cent of the seats with 66.1 per cent of the votes. A dominant element in the 1977 election was the National Party's campaign against 'foreign interference' from the Carter administration in the United States.

Features of South Africa's electoral pattern are worth noting. Only twice since Union in 1910, for example, has a government been voted out of office, and on each occasion the Nationalists achieved it. Second, the interruptions in the National Party's ascent to power were due to schisms in Afrikaner ranks. Third, the National Party's ascent set a pattern of politics which resulted in the elimination of the early predominantly English-speaking parties (Unionist and Dominion), and of the Labour Party, which could not match the National Party's appeal to white workers.

The revolt in the National Party against apartheid reform created an entirely new problem for the party leadership. Under its first three post-war prime ministers (Dr D.F. Malan 1948–54, Hans Strijdom 1954–58, and Dr H.F. Verwoerd 1958–66), the National Party had been in what might be called the ideological ascendancy. The Vorster premiership (1966–78) is seen by the far right HNP as the beginning of the ideology's dilution. The critical period, as fixed by the HNP, was the late 1960s when Vorster responded to the international sports boycott by allowing sport in South Africa to become multiracial. If Vorster had not done this, the HNP claims, 'the present mixed constitution would not have been possible'.[8]

The far right in South Africa, according to Adam[9], is not monolithic. He divides it into 'labour racists' (HNP), 'orthodox ideologues' (Conservative Party (CP)) and 'neo-fascists' (AWB). It is significant that the HNP, which polled 14.1 per cent of the votes cast in the 1981 election and won its first parliamentary seat in a by-election in 1985, lost this seat in the 1987 election and polled only 3.2 per cent of the votes. It was overtaken by the less extreme Conservative Party. The HNP's aggressive racism ruled out partition or an Afrikaner homeland, arguing that whites were entitled to rule the whole of South Africa, excluding the independent homelands, and that the emphasis should not be shifted from race to *volk*. 'Afrikaners', it said, 'must immerse themselves even more in the study of race, because it lies at the root of the present challenge'. Removal of the race issue as the distinguishing factor of the political debate 'is the most effective way to frustrate and eliminate nationalism'. A fundamental difference between the HNP and the Conservative Party was the HNP's insistence on Afrikaans as the only official language, a demand the Conservative Party feared would alienate right-wing English speakers.

The Conservative Party's less strident and less uncompromising brand of right-wing politics triumphed in the parliamentary elections on 6 May 1987. It took a gamble in rejecting an election pact with the HNP, and this paid off. Contesting its first parliamentary elections, the Conservative Party won twenty-two seats with 26.11 per cent of the votes. The HNP was virtually eliminated. An estimated 43 per cent of Afrikaners voted for the Conservative Party and the HNP, and 6 per cent of English speakers. Some 50 per cent of Afrikaners and 57 per cent of English speakers voted for the National Party. Parties to the left of the National Party, mainly the Progressive Federal Party and the New Republic Party, both English-speaking strongholds, gained only about 37 per cent of the English-speaking vote and 7 per cent of Afrikaner votes. This represented a seismic shift in voting patterns.[10] The following conclusions may be drawn from these election results.

National Party

The National Party is no longer the undisputed party of the Afrikaner. Even allowing for some distortions in the above calculations, Afrikanerdom is split almost down the middle. A massive bloc of Afrikaners have withdrawn their support from the National Party and transferred it to the far right. The influx of English speakers substantially changes the composition of the National Party, although for the present they are voting fodder with no voice in decision making. Control of the National party remains an Afrikaner monopoly. The Afrikaner establishment is similarly split and can no longer speak for unified Afrikanerdom. The voters who deserted the PFP-NRP in droves for the National Party and those who deserted the National Party in droves for the CP-HNP were motivated by a search for security: the English speakers sought security in the National Party *laager*, while the deserting Afrikaners put their faith in a return to traditional policies. The National Party emerged from the elections in a 'centrist' position, but the increase in its support (from 117 to 123 seats in an Assembly of 166 elected seats) cannot be interpreted otherwise than as a shift to the right by the electorate. A vote for security cannot be separated from a vote for whatever race policies are necessary to maintain that security – and the entire apartheid reform programme has been scaled down since the election and accompanied by security controls, censorship, etc., on a scale unprecedented in the past forty years of National Party rule.

Conservative Party

With twenty-two seats, the Conservative Party has displaced the PFP as the official opposition in the Assembly. It is now able, to some degree, to regulate the pace and nature of apartheid reform – though not to veto it. It has succeeded in making Afrikaner dissent respectable, and a line of continuity now stretches from the far right into the National Party's parliamentary caucus. The Conservative Party's rejection of a pact with the HNP was a shrewd tactical move, enabling it to play for much higher stakes. Its rejection of an HNP inspired attempt to split the Dutch Reformed churches points to its mainstream ambitions. Its strategy recognises that there are limits beyond which white extremism is not sustainable in South Africa.

Progressive Federal Party

The psychological setback suffered by the Progressive Federal Party in the elections was far more severe than the actual loss of seats (twenty-six reduced to nineteen). The PFP's strategy was based on a recognition that it could not aspire to being an alternative government and that 'bridge building' was its only realistic course: encouraging alliances not only with the NRP but also with *verligte* (enlightened) Afrikaner Nationalists. This strategy collapsed ignominiously. The NRP's English speakers flocked to the National Party, as did many of the PFP's, and there was no reciprocal influx from the National Party's Afrikaners who persisted in the stereotyped view that the PFP was anti-Afrikaans and pro-black. Even the newly formed Independent grouping (comprising Wynand Malan, Dr Esther Lategan and ex-South African ambassador Denis Worrall), which won only one parliamentary seat (Malan's) and that with PFP support, kept the PFP at arm's length. Effectively, therefore, the centre of gravity of 'progressivism', or whatever term can be used to describe this form of white enlightenment, shifted from the PFP to the Independents, meagre though their following was.

The 1987 elections, therefore, introduced an even greater degree of Afrikanerisation of white politics than had hitherto existed and established that the lines of division in future would be within this Afrikanerised framework and not between Afrikaners and non-Afrikaners. Any future enlightenment on race policies would be one approved by an Afrikaner majority among the enlightened. The PFP had finally fallen victim to the same dilemma which destroyed its predecessor, the United Party: how to secure the support of white voters while mounting a credible defence of black rights. Immediately after the elections, a debate opened in the PFP on the compatibility or otherwise of the party's parliamentary and extra-parliamentary roles. The election closed the post-1948 chapter of white parliamentary representation. Although the PFP still had nineteen MPs (and 14.26 per cent of the votes), it had lost its sense of direction. Some of its MPs concluded that the future would lie with the Independents; others were resigned to playing the largely symbolic role of championing civil liberties. Since the 6 May elections, three PFP Members of Parliament have defected – two to the National Democratic Movement founded by the only Independent who won his constituency, Wynand Malan. Other PFP MPs believe the PFP should form an alliance with Worrall, who was excluded from Malan's NDM.

Some commentators interpreted the PFP's decline as the disappearance, finally, of a separate political role for English speakers. *Business Day* editor Ken Owen wrote:

> The glue has gone, and the English have scattered in all directions, without common purpose . . . The election has confirmed the view that there is no future for a party whose leading members export their children, whose remaining children cheer Mrs [Winnie] Mandela and jeer Mrs [Helen] Suzman, and who expect a shattered English community to retain the habits of Europe.

The reference to the cheers for Mrs Mandela and the jeers for Mrs Suzman was a comment on the PFP's dilemma over parliamentary and extra-parliamentary activity. When Dr F. van Zyl Slabbert quit as PFP leader in January 1986, he gave as his reason the 'irrelevance' of parliamentary politics. The anti-apartheid United Democratic Front took up the cry, calling on whites to join them and boycott the 'election circus' (although this was qualified by some). Some who might have been expected to vote for the PFP, mostly students and counted in hundreds rather than thousands, responded to the boycott call and their abstention was possibly responsible for the loss of two or three PFP seats. In some of the more homogeneous, affluent PFP seats, however, the PFP vote remained firm and even increased. The election undoubtedly opened up a gap between the PFP and both black and white radicals, particularly at the 'liberal' universities of Cape Town and Witwatersrand which were blamed for helping to frighten English speakers into the National Party *laager*. The long-standing symbiotic relationship between the English-speaking PFP and the English-speaking universities was impaired.

THE AFRIKANER BROEDERBOND

In 1934 the Broederbond issued a notorious circular stating: 'Let us focus our attention on the fact that the primary consideration is whether Afrikanerdom will reach its ultimate destiny of *baasskap* [domination] in South Africa. Brothers, our solution for South Africa's ills is that the Afrikaner Broederbond shall rule South Africa.'[11] Today, almost the whole cabinet and more than 80 per cent of National Party members of parliament belong to the Broederbond.

The Broederbond became a secret society in 1922 in order to function more effectively. Membership was by invitation only and invitations were restricted to Afrikaans-speaking Protestant males, financially sound, of approved behaviour, and who were prepared to be active members. Many non-Broeder Afrikaners came to resent the Bond as an elitist organisation of 'super-Afrikaners'. The wartime Smuts government investigated the Bond as a suspected subversive organisation. In 1944 its membership consisted of one-third teachers and one-tenth civil servants, plus wealthy farmers, businessmen, clergymen, trade unionists, etc. Bond members helped fellow Afrikaners, but they also helped each other in a network of nepotism. In *Brotherhood of Power*, Serfontein published an extensive membership list, claiming that there were 11 000 Broeders grouped in 800 cells.[12]

At first the Bond was dedicated to the uplift of all Afrikaners, arousing their national self-consciousness, inspiring love of their language, religion, traditions, country and people, and furthering their every concern. In time, however, the Bond became fiercely partisan, siding for example with Malan when he left the National Party in 1934 to establish the Purified National Party. In his 1935 denunciation, General Hertzog, then Prime Minister, said that the Broederbond's real aim was 'to put their foot on the neck of English-speaking South Africans'.[13] It was the Bond which inspired and implemented the Afrikaner separatist movement in the early 1930s.

According to Serfontein, the Bond, under the guidance of its chairman, Dr P.J. Meyer, and executive members such as Dr Andries Treurnicht, turned against Vorster during his premiership for diluting apartheid policies. The turbulence which the National Party was experiencing on this issue extended into the Bond. In 1968, a year before the HNP breach, both *Die Burger*, the flagship of the Afrikaner press, and P.W. Botha, then Minister of Defence and Cape National Party leader, criticised the Bond, warning that both it and its junior version, the Rapportryers, were 'outside organisations' and not political bodies. By the time the HNP split occurred in 1969, Meyer and Treurnicht had abandoned support for the dissenters. When the 1982 split occurred, however, Conservative Party supporters tried unsuccessfully to capture control of the Bond. Treurnicht, then leader of the Conservative Party, was ousted as chairman of the Bond and replaced by Professor Piet de Lange, then principal of the Rand Afrikaans University.

According to de Lange, the 1982 turbulence in the Bond was over how Afrikaner interests could best be protected.[14]

> The exclusionist view was that such a small, vulnerable community should be aggressively protective of its language and culture, excluding the opposing other cultural elements. Against this the more self-confident 'inclusionist view' held that Afrikaners had established themselves sufficiently and that the best way to protect their culture was to allow others to be attracted to it.

The 'inclusionists' won, de Lange claims, but 'We lost about 10 per cent of our members. But once the decision had been taken, it enabled the Broederbond to look anew at its own task.'

The principle of interlocking organisations reached its peak in the Bond. At the top was an executive consisting of '12 Apostles', followed by a general council whose lines of communication extended into every walk of Afrikaner life, and particularly into cultural organisations, the public service, church, education, the economic front, agriculture, social welfare, charities, youth organisations, etc. With every schism in the National Party, the Bond was correspondingly weakened, while public exposure of its activities – and disputes – has resulted in its demystification. It is now more of a think-tank than a conspiracy. The issue of apartheid reform has undermined its cohesion and influence. The orthodox Bond position favours reform, but the Bond is not able to enforce this position on Afrikaners as a unified group.

In October 1986 an unsigned 'working document', marked 'strictly confidential', was circulated to Bond members (and leaked to the press). It took stock of the controversy over reform and defined the minimum conditions for the Afrikaner's survival 'as an Afrikaner'. These were: no race group must dominate another; residential segregation is desirable for the present, although racially mixed areas on a voluntary basis will not necessarily threaten Afrikaner survival; 'culturally-linked' mother-tongue education in Afrikaner schools is essential for 'meaningful survival'; the best way to protect human rights is for the government not to interfere; statutory discrimination must be abolished and freedom of association allowed; blacks must be included in the constitutional process up to the highest level, sharing either directly or indirectly in the election of the government and participating at all levels of decision making which affect their interests; all races must be able to serve in the highest legislative and executive positions and even become state president or prime minister, again provided no group dominates another; and no government, white or black, can be entrenched any longer.

The Bond denies that it is the National Party's mouthpiece; nevertheless in recent years President Botha and his ministers have supported almost every essential point contained in the working document. For all its vagueness of detail, therefore, the 'working document' is a significant event. Defensive in both content and tone, it concedes the failure of forty years of apartheid. There appears to be broad agreement between the Bond and the National Party that the document represents the Afrikaners' bottom line, but no sense of urgency is yet evident in its implementation. For the present it is a theoretical document, projecting a long-term rather than a short-term blueprint.

THE DUTCH REFORMED CHURCHES

About 95 per cent of all Afrikaners belong to the three Dutch Reformed churches and about 80 per cent of cabinet ministers and 70 per cent of National Party members of parliament belong to the biggest of the three churches, the Nederduits Gereformeerde Kerk (NGK). According to the NGK's Moderator, Dr Johan Heyns:

> This is a unique situation in which we have direct access . . . we have a church commission responsible for communications with the government. Commissioners can go to the offices of government members

and they can point out where they have problems with government policies. This is not all that well known.[15]

The Dutch Reformed (DR) churches are loosely descended from the Church of the Reformation in Holland, which some of the first white settlers brought to South Africa in 1652. The NGK, which held its first synod in 1824, has 970 000 followers; the Nederduitsch Hervormde Kerk (NHK, 1852) has 246 000; and the Gereformeerde Kerk (1859) has 128 000, one-third of them black. Calvinism divided humanity into the elect and the rest and the Calvinism which took root in South Africa during the nineteenth century affirmed the doctrine of a divinely ordained state whose rulers were responsible to God. Calvin, in his doctrine of predestination, embraced the Old Testament idea of an ethnic covenant between God and the chosen people. The NGK 'did not only perpetuate the inherent isolation of the Afrikaner people, but made a theological principle of it . . . Afrikaner isolationism not only hampered the Afrikaners' adaptability to twentieth century situations, but seriously complicated race relations and ecumenical issues in South Africa.'[16] Religion contributed powerfully to the Afrikaners' view of the world as an arrangement of subordination and superordination.

The three Calvinist churches bear a major responsibility for the Afrikaners' present race views. Until 1857 the NGK was one church. Then in the Transvaal it entered into a union with the NHK, one of the 'principles of union' being that 'The church allows no equality between whites and non-whites'. A further clause said that, 'The members of the mission congregation shall not make use of church buildings of the white members of the church.' The restrictive membership clause was never put in writing by the other provinces, but they adopted the Transvaal's practice of mission churches for non-whites.

In 1950 a specially convened conference of DR churches approved segregated residential areas for race groups and even called for total territorial apartheid – going further than Malan's government was prepared to go. In 1956, a report by the NGK's Federal Council offered theological justification for separate churches. These were 'in accordance with our understanding of the nature of the church of the Lord Jesus on earth', and in 1974 DR churchmen produced a notorious document, *Ras, Volk en Nasie* (*Race, People and Nation*) in which they offered biblical justification for apartheid. Heyns admits 'We did in the past give to apartheid a theological, ethical justification'.[17]

The 1972 report of the Spro-Cas Church Commission on *Apartheid and the Church* noted:

> The most recent and most extended justification of racial separation in the [Afrikaans] churches is the report on race relations adopted by the General Synod of the NGK and published in English under the title 'Human Relations in South Africa'. This uses what are the favourite texts today for supporting apartheid, namely Gen. 1,2,11, Deut. 32:8 and Acts 17:26f, to argue that the stories of the creation and the Tower of Babel show that God's will for mankind is diversity and pluriformity, not only on linguistic lines, but also 'somatic' (physical), cultural and racial. On this basis it argues: 'Mixing and integration . . . on a large scale . . . or . . . the obliteration of dividing lines' would result in this 'God-willed diversity . . . being levelled down to a colourless uniformity, the distinctiveness of *volke* (being) destroyed, and their particular culture bastardised.' 'Then the pure religion of Christianised *volke* would be threatened and the *volke* would, in short, not be able to fulfil their independent vocations and live according to their distinctive character.' Therefore 'such a development must be opposed in principle'. It is assumed here that God must will the preservation of all the *present* differences between races, nations and language groups as they are. For the above reason the Church should in no way contribute to such mixing and integration.[18]

Neither have the Dutch Reformed churches shown any enthusiasm for ecumenism. Since 1936 the Christian Council of South Africa, now the South African Council of Churches, has existed as an attempt to establish greater contact and co-operation between the various churches. 'It is a tragedy, however', says the Spro-Cas Report, 'that excepting the Transvaal NGK from 1936 to 1939, the Afrikaans Reformed Churches have never belonged to the Council.' The Afrikaans churches were woven into the pattern of Afrikaner nationalism.

Just as the National Party and the Broederbond have changed, however, so have the Afrikaner churches, and indeed the far right detect in these changes a conspiracy. But the changes are very recent. In 1982, Dr Heyns (before his election as NGK Moderator) and other dominees tried to persuade the NGK synod to accept desegregated worship, but they were told that the time was not ripe. Suddenly, in 1986, it became ripe. At its synod in that year, the NGK issued a policy document *Kerk en Samelewing* (Church and Society) which Heyns welcomed as a 'miracle'. It declared apartheid an unscriptural error, urged NGK members to 'confess their participation in apartheid with humility and sorrow', resolved to come to terms with its 'mission' or 'sister' (non-white) churches and with reformed churches abroad, and agreed that there should be only one church and that structures should be established to express this unity. The document admitted that the NGK was 'completely isolated'.

The synod's decisions, according to Heyns, meant that all future attempts by the NGK to establish theological justification for apartheid had been 'completely abolished . . . there is no such thing as white superiority . . . there may not be under any circumstances a political policy based on oppression, discrimination and exploitation'.[19] Heyns added (in a BBC television interview) that 'if the government applies apartheid, we will have to contradict them and reject it'. Heyns said that he did not see himself as a liberal. 'As a reformist, yes. I would like to reform my church. We can't go on like this.'

Some NGK dominees claim that the synod's decision to abolish segregation is qualified. If a member of a 'sister' (non-white) church applies for membership of the NGK and attends its services, he may be admitted, but the 'sister' churches will maintain their separate existence. 'It means it is still an apartheid church', concluded a 'sister' church dominee, Johan Retief.

The NGK's *Church and Society* document created controversy in church ranks, with the HNP leading the protest. A Continuation Committee of Dissatisfied Members (CCDM) sent a delegation to address the thirty-member General Synodal Commission of the NGK. The CCDM rejected both open membership and acceptance of racially mixed marriages (in 1986 the government introduced amending legislation to abolish the Mixed Marriages and Immorality Acts, which prohibited marriage and sexual relations between the races). The CCDM presented their protest in a twenty-eight-page booklet *Geloof en Protes* (*Faith and Protest*). The meeting between the CCDM and the Commission failed to reach agreement, and a breakaway church was formed, the Afrikaans Protestant Church. The Conservative Party opposed the breakaway. The HNP's weekly newspaper *Die Afrikaner* published the synod's document alongside the African National Congress's Freedom Charter, claiming (incorrectly) that the Freedom Charter had been drawn up by the South African Communist Party and approved by the Africa Institute in Moscow.

THE ECONOMIC FRONT

From the closing years of the nineteenth century, economic circumstance began forcing Afrikaners off the land, a process which was accelerated by the South African War. In 1900 fewer than 10 per cent of Afrikaners lived in towns and cities; by 1926 it had risen to 41 per cent. During the 1930s depression, under the 'civilised labour policy', Hertzog's government gave public sector preference to poor-white job-seekers. Afrikaner poverty was a highly-charged issue, 'allowing ethnic mobilisers to hold British imperialism responsible for the condition of their people rather than accepting it as part of the generally painful process of industrialisation and of the breakdown of the Western economic order'.[20] By 1939, close on 300 000 whites were still living in 'terrible poverty' (see Chapter 1).

Ethnic mobilisation of Afrikaners to improve their economic lot began seriously in the 1930s under Broederbond direction. The strategy was two-pronged: to secure an increasing share for Afrikaners in the country's economy, and to prevent the recruitment and 'denationalisation' of Afrikaners by multiracial trade unions. A National Council of Trustees, established in 1936, began to fund 'Christian-National' trade unions, pre-eminently the white Mineworkers Union, and a *Blankewerkers Beskermingbond* (White Workers' Protection Society) campaigned for race separation in employment, job reservation for whites, and severance of all contact with the multiracial unions. The fear that haunted less educated and skilled Afrikaners, and still persists among white miners today, is that non-Afrikaner employers would replace them with cheap black labour.

In 1933 the Broederbond had convened a congress on 'Nationalisation of Finance and Planned Co-ordination of Economic Policy', and five years later, in 1938, the *Reddingsdaadbond* ('rescue' association (RDB)) was formed – 'a great ethnic organisation, Christian-National in principle, whose aim was to knit together all Afrikaners to further their cultural and, above all, their economic interests'.[21] Financed by subscriptions, the RDB had 65 000 members by 1946, and it was providing small Afrikaner businessmen with loans and encouraging them to venture into trade and industry. Ninety per cent of the RDB's funds were invested in Afrikaner businesses, and particularly in Federale Volksbeleggings, an investment house. Steadily, Afrikaner businesses began to increase, and the long-term challenge to the dominance of non-Afrikaners in the economy was launched. Afrikaner sentiment was skilfully exploited to promote the growth of Afrikaner co-operatives, insurance companies, building societies, etc.

In 1938 the first People's Economic Congress took place – 'the greatest single catalyst in the economic independence process of the Afrikaner'.[22] Out of this congress was born, a year later, the Economic Institute, one of whose aims was to promote *volkskapitalisme* (people's capitalism), by mobilising Afrikaner capital and purchasing power behind Afrikaner enterprises and bringing liberal capitalism under Afrikaner control. Since non-Afrikaner capitalism was so strong, state capitalism was encouraged, and the economy became increasingly cluttered with parastatals and control boards. In *Assault on Private Enterprise*, written in 1977 by one of the Afrikaner economic movement's leading personalities, Dr A.D. Wassenaar, South Africa's 'real enemy' was identified not as communism, but nationalisation.

In 1938–39 Afrikaner controlled enterprises contributed just 8 per cent of total turnover in commerce, 3 per cent of industrial output, 10 per cent of mining and 5 per cent of finance.[23] By 1980, of 3000 South Africans of all races who earned more than R100 000 a year, 2212 gave their home language as Afrikaans.[24] Between 1948 and 1973 the public sector of the economy doubled. The more Afrikaners advanced economically, the more they were caught in a dilemma. They depended largely on Afrikaner sentiment and government patronage for their new prosperity – both of which could be withdrawn if they overstepped the mark – and yet increasingly they perceived a common interest with non-Afrikaner businessmen who were advocating apartheid reforms. Repeatedly, if erratically, and particularly since the Sharpeville killings in 1960, Afrikaner businessmen and their organisations have entreated the government to reform apartheid policies. The government responded by giving statutory recognition to black trade unions, abolishing job reservations for whites, etc., but in other sectors political considerations came first. Mr Tony Bloom, liberal chairman of the Premier Group, claims that the opinions of non-Afrikaner businessmen 'bounce off the government like ping-pong balls', and that only about eight Afrikaner businessmen carry weight with the politicians in Pretoria.

On the whole, Afrikaner businessmen are inclined to make their representations to the government not as businessmen but as fellow-Afrikaner nationalists, raising their problems in private. Ten years ago, Dr Wassenaar warned that this approach was futile.

> Everybody in Afrikanerdom said to everybody else: 'Don't criticise the government in public . . . go to the ministers in private and

discuss matters with them. Their doors are open to you. Go and speak to them privately, you will get more done that way.' This policy has not been successful. It's my opinion that it cannot be successful unless there is a complete change in the governmental approach to the private sector.[25]

This is the approach employed by both the Broederbond and the Dutch Reformed churches.

CULTURE AND EDUCATION

On the Broederbond's initiative, the Federasie van Afrikaanse Kultuurvereenigings (Federation of Afrikaans Cultural Associations (FAK)) was formed in 1929, sharing for some time the same executive officials as the Bond. Its aims were to promote the Afrikaner's cultural identity and ensure that the Afrikaans language permeated all spheres of Afrikaner life. By 1937 more than 300 organisations were affiliated to the FAK, one-third of them language and cultural bodies and two-thirds church groups, charities, student and youth societies, scientific study circles and various educational organisations, representing schools, teacher training colleges, universities, etc. In 1939 the FAK convened a conference on 'Christian National education' which called for separate Afrikaans schools. The FAK's fundamentalist approach to education endorsed predestination and excluded the teaching of evolution. The FAK helped to organise the 1938 Ox-Wagon Trek, commemorating the centenary of the Great Trek. About 100 000 Afrikaners, one-tenth of Afrikanerdom, assembled outside Pretoria on the site of the present Voortrekker Monument.

Education has been critically important in the rise of Afrikaner nationalism. From the Cape settlement in 1652 and for the next 200 years, education was the church's special responsibility. After the South African war, the Dutch Reformed churches supported private schools, and some 200 Christian National Education schools were established in the Transvaal and Orange River Colony with funds raised from Afrikaners determined to resist Lord Milner's anglicisation policy. A teachers' union provided the institutional base after 1919 from which Afrikaner teachers could be mobilised, and their strong ties with the Broederbond furthered the teaching of the ethnic concept of culture in the classrooms, while school textbooks peddled a race concept of history. In 1939 the Institute for Christian National Education was founded.

A Potchefstroom University study identifies twelve 'master symbols' in education, the first four being: acceptance of authority, superiority of whites and inferiority of blacks, the Afrikaner's special relationship with God, and the proposition that South Africa rightfully belongs to the Afrikaner.[26] In the 1930s young Afrikaner intellectuals returned from doctoral study in Europe 'inspired with the ideals of neo-Fichtean nationalism'.[27] Among them were Dr Nico Diederichs (post-1948 Minister of Finance), Dr Hendrik Verwoerd (Prime Minister), Dr Albert Hertzog (Hertzog's son, Cabinet Minister and first leader of the HNP), and Dr Piet Meyer (Broederbond chairman and head of the South African Broadcasting Corporation). While DR church theologians sought scriptural justification for ethnic separation, the Afrikaner professors and lecturers provided the academic gloss, particularly in the South African Bureau for Racial Affairs (SABRA), the Afrikaner counter to the liberal South African Institute of Race Relations. Presently, SABRA is under the control of the far right.

In both the cultural and educational fields, Afrikaner nationalism is now in confusion. At its August 1987 congress, the FAK, after prodding by the Cape Town Nationalist newspaper *Die Burger*, raised the question of opening its membership to all races. But when Dr Leon de Stadtler proposed that the matter should be given serious consideration, he was heard in 'great silence'. The chairman, Mr Hendrik Sloet, on the other hand, was applauded when he said that the FAK had always been 'an organisation of white Afrikaners'. *Die Burger*'s sister newspaper, *Beeld*, thereupon called for action to ensure that this 'leap into the future' was made at the FAK's next general meeting. The thought gnawing at the two newspapers, as it is at Dr Heyns, is that the situation has changed so much that a small *volk* like the Afrikaners (65 per cent of the 4 800 000 whites) can survive only if it opens its ranks to non-Afrikaners, which means the end of Afrikaner exclusivism.

As for indoctrination in the classroom, this has boomeranged. The far right, according to Heyns, are ceaselessly active in the schools and cultural organisations.

> True Afrikaners are called on to penetrate existing cultural organisations to gain control of them and to influence their members. The control of schools and parents' organisations is particularly important to ensure that the children are educated in the right political climate and opinion. In every town and every region spiritual forces will have to be united, while there must be a clear realisation that the Afrikaner economy must not be controlled by alien groups or

> constructed on foreign labour. Clearly this section of the Afrikaner right-wing will not disappear . . . [it will] perpetuate restlessness, tension and internecine conflict among Afrikaners.[28]

Two cabinet ministers have also voiced their concern over 'the lack of political literacy' of white pupils and over bringing politics into the classroom – the very situation the National Party helped to create.

The cohesion among Afrikaner academics was already wearing thin in the first decade of post-1948 rule. In 1956, thirteen Afrikaner professors declared their opposition to the removal of coloureds from the common voters' roll. They were hounded and ostracised by the Afrikaner establishment and this inhibited much further dissent. Much later, an Afrikaner historian was tarred and feathered by the far right. Yet over the years the alienation of Afrikaner intellectuals from apartheid policies proceeded apace until, in March 1987, a delegation from a thirty-five-member discussion group at Stellenbosch University (the mother Afrikaner university) was granted a meeting with President Botha to discuss apartheid reforms; this meeting ended in 'fiasco'. Defections from the National Party followed swiftly, with 300 of the university's academics – half the academic staff – declaring their support for the Independents who were contesting the 6 May parliamentary elections. Immediately afterwards, forty-six academics at Potchefstroom University, formerly an Afrikaner nationalist stronghold, announced that they would boycott the elections.

A climate has been created at Stellenbosch University now in which dissent is possible without the dissenter being expelled from Afrikanerdom, although the rebellion remains one of quality rather than quantity. Professor David Welsh of Cape Town University argues:

> Afrikaner society has transformed itself and diversified. Ninety percent are urban – perhaps more than 50% are middle class – and more than 30% proceed from school to university or technikon. In short, the process of embourgeoisement ('bourgeoisification') is far advanced. Inherently such a group is more difficult to control or unify, and is incapable of having its activities 'co-ordinated' – which was supposed to be the Broederbond's major task. Today hardly any intellectuals of stature support either apartheid or even the National Party, except with the gravest of reservations.[29]

The experience of Professor Sampie Terreblanche (Economics, Stellenbosch University) confirms Dr Welsh's assessment. For some years Professor Terreblanche was a member of the government's think-tank and vice-chairman of the South African Broadcasting Corporation. Then, declaring that Afrikaners at the university were 'in a kind of moral crisis', he switched his support to the Independents to become their leading theoretician. The government promptly dismissed him from his SABC post. Another Afrikaner academic, Professor Marius Wiechers of the University of South Africa, interprets academic dissent as the beginning of the National Party's disintegration.

THE YOUTH

Mobilisation of the Afrikaner youth began in the classroom mainly by teachers belonging to the Broederbond. It extended outside the classroom too: in 1929, for example, Afrikaner youth were prised away from the Boy Scouts which refused to drop 'God Save the King' and the Union Jack from its Afrikaans sections. It was particularly intense in the higher educational institutions, such as teachers' training colleges and the universities. In 1933 the Afrikaner Nasionale Studentebond (Afrikaans National Students' Association (ASB)) was established after student governments at the Afrikaans universities had broken away from the predominantly English-speaking National Union of South African Students (NUSAS), following disagreement over the admission of black students. By 1935 ASB branches had been formed at all the Afrikaans universities, enrolling students in the cause of a separate Afrikaans nation.

For fifty years the ASB was a monolithic Afrikaner nationalist organisation and training ground for future National Party politicians in spite of the claim in its constitution to be non-political and based on 'the Christian-National life and world outlook, founded on the bible as the infallible word of God'.[30] Stellenbosch was the exception to the rule, disaffiliating from the ASB in 1976. The ASB's unity, however, was not seriously challenged until schisms opened in the Afrikaner political establishment in the early 1980s. By 1986 these schisms had been formalised in the ASB whose unity was finally shattered. At the ASB's annual congress in 1986, *verligte* candidates for the national executive withdrew their candidatures and walked out, leaving conservative students to be elected unopposed.

Afrikaans students then split into three broad camps: those seeking to maintain the 'non-political', traditionalist stance of the ASB; those insisting on the need for young *verligte* Afrikaners to involve themselves directly in parliamentary politics; and a tiny minority convinced of the need for contact with black extra-parliamentary groups like the United Democratic Front. The ASB went into rapid decline, becoming no more than 'a ghost ship without a crew' (as the Afrikaans newspaper *Beeld* described it). The self-styled 'moderates' coalesced in 'Jeugkrag' ('Youth Power' but translated as 'Youth for South Africa') and launched a series of aggressive, reformist inclined campaigns, including highly publicised joint meetings with Chief Mangosuthu Buthelezi's Inkatha Youth Brigade. Jeugkrag claimed to be non-party political in character, but it clearly located itself with the Independents and within the *verligte* section of the National Party. Since the ASB's decline, students supporting the far right have turned increasingly to the Afrikaanse Studente Federasie (Afrikaans Student's Federation), which is unapologetically white supremacist. Differences between these various student groups have, on occasions, led to blows being exchanged.

This fission in the Afrikaner student movement has produced two centres of activism – on the far right and among the 'moderates' – but apparent stasis among those who might be expected to restock the ranks of the traditionalist National Party as represented by President Botha. Jeugkrag's president, Marthinus van Schalkwyk, himself a former ASB president, identified the shift in attitude among Afrikaner youth:

> We felt we were not there where the future was being built in the political arena. There was a restlessness among Afrikaner youth, but no political organisation for us to have a voice in the building of a new South Africa. To the right we cut off people belonging to the right-wing, and to the left we cut off people believing in violent change and socialism . . . We are pulling to ourselves the broad middle group of people, the moderates . . . The situation on the Afrikaans campuses has changed a lot in the past two or three years. People are willing to compromise a lot more on political issues. They know we are moving towards a new future where whites won't have all the privileges they are used to. They are willing to accept that. The youth . . . want security about where they are going in the future. They are willing to push for faster reform; they are willing to accept things that the older generation of Afrikaners . . . did not accept. We are going to be a voice to be listened to in white politics.

But, van Schalkwyk added:

> I don't want to be too pessimistic, but I think there will be a fight in

> this country in the end, and there will be an escalation of violence in the next few years. The question is who is going to fight whom in South Africa? Is there going to be a race war or a war between ideologies? I will do everything in my power to prevent the first, and that is where Jeugkrag comes in.[31]

Beyond the confines of the ASB and Jeugkrag, a small but vociferous group of young Afrikaners, largely centred in Stellenbosch, has established contact for the first time with black extra-parliamentary groups. They formed the Stellenbosch Student Council which caused the government acute embarrassment late in 1985 when it attempted to send a delegation to Lusaka to meet the ANC – the university witnessed the unprecedented intervention of government officials on the campus to seize passports. The young dissenters, led by former Students' Representative Council president Phillip Verster, responded by issuing a public call for the release of Nelson Mandela and the unbanning of the ANC.

Verster said there was a new mood among Afrikaner students who felt they had to get involved in the country's crisis.

> There is a real uncertainty among Afrikaner students. They are forced into the mould of thinking that all there is in South Africa is *lekker* [nice] rugby, chatting up girls, and *alles is reg in die land* [all is well in the country]. But now they see Casspirs [armoured police vehicles] on their way to the airport. They can't go to the beach in summer because they've got an army call-up for township duty . . . The complacent attitude goes way back, even as far as the Afrikaner is educated at home – respect for your government, respect for parents, for your leaders, etc. But many youngsters – maybe only [youth] leaders, but still – are waking up, informing themselves, and saying: 'This is what is going on and I don't find it acceptable.'[32]

Verster's group rejected both the ASB and Jeugkrag, describing the latter as a National Party front. 'We cannot just talk about reform', Verster said. 'We must confront real change, informed by the concept of one-man one-vote – inevitably.' Jeugkrag did not go nearly as far. While it called for the abolition of Group Areas and segregated schools, for example, it drew the line clearly at one-man one-vote, supporting instead the official National Party policy of group representation for all races. During 1987 the Verster dissenters, having been replaced on the Students' Council by a more conservative group, formed a 'United Stellenbosch Front' as a channel for their views. The

USF went so far as to refer sympathetically to the ANC's 1955 Freedom Charter. Although numerically insignificant, the dissenters are mould breakers in the sense that they have confronted the bedrock issue of Afrikaner recognition of black extra-parliamentary resistance. Verster himself set a symbolic seal on this by travelling with the group of mainly Afrikaner South Africans who, under Dr F. van Zyl Slabbert, the former leader of the PFP, held three days of talks with the ANC in the Senegalese capital, Dakar, in July 1987.

As in all other sectors of Afrikanerdom, the threat to white hegemony has created an unprecedented political fluidity among the Afrikaner youth, manifested most clearly in the '*klein broedertwis*' (battle among little brothers) between student organisations. A survey conducted at the Rand Afrikaans University and published in March 1986 showed that the Afrikaner youth had a high degree of political awareness, but a low level of political participation. Most of the students had 'a protective screen of ignorance and blind faith in government leaders who know best. They do not perceive any real need to involve themselves in politics, because they experience their needs as being looked after by the current regime'. Ninety-four per cent 'hardly ever discussed politics with black people', and the survey suggested that 'those youths with the least political participation and exposure are inclined to have the most right-wing political inclinations'. The survey concluded: 'Political processes in South Africa would have to become much more severe before the Afrikaner youth will realise the need for political change.' The survey was conducted during a State of Emergency, with tear gas in the townships and bombs at bus-stops, and with the threat of international sanctions being imposed against the country.

THE AFRIKAANS MEDIA

None of the Afrikaans Nationalist newspapers was founded as a commercial enterprise or even primarily as a news medium. 'Their task was to spread the gospel of Afrikaner nationalism and Afrikaner culture.'[33] They made a critical contribution to mobilising Afrikaners, sustaining their language and consolidating their political strength.

Pioneering work in this field was done by a succession of political editors. Dr D.F. Malan stepped down from the pulpit of the NGK to become *Die Burger*'s first editor – the newspaper was founded in Cape Town in 1915, one year after the National Party's formation. Malan turned it into the National Party's flagship and an important innovator of party principles and policies; in 1948 he became Prime Minister. General Hertzog established *Die Vaderland* (formerly *Ons Vaderland*) in Pretoria in 1936 as his personal mouthpiece when he was Prime Minister. Dr H.F. Verwoerd, a sociology professor at Stellenbosch University, was the first editor of *Die Transvaler* in Johannesburg in 1937; Verwoerd was Prime Minister from 1958–66. Dr Andries Treurnicht, now leader of the Conservative Party and before that a Cabinet Minister in the National Party government, edited *Hoofstad* in Pretoria.

Historically, the South African newspapers, with few exceptions, have been divided between Afrikaans newspapers supporting Afrikaner nationalism and English-language newspapers supporting the opposition to Afrikaner nationalism. From their inception, the Afrikaans newspapers were no more than party organs – the *Transvaler* proudly proclaimed itself as such, and in the 1950s the *Burger*'s editor, Dr A.L. Geyer, regularly attended the closed meetings of the National Party's parliamentary caucus. It was also the practice for cabinet ministers to serve on the boards of directors of the Afrikaans newspapers. P.W. Botha discontinued the practice in the late 1970s.

McClurg dates the emergence of independent Afrikaner journalism to criticism by the *Burger*'s editor Piet Cellie in 1959 of a government ban on blacks attending a performance of the Messiah in Pietermaritzburg, Natal.[34] Other voices began to be heard. The *Vaderland* made itself unpopular in party circles for urging the removal of 'irritating' aspects of apartheid – now official policy. After Sharpeville in 1960 some Nationalist newspapers waged a 'guerrilla war' against the harsher forms of apartheid, suggesting that some 'fixed concepts' should be changed. Tensions built up between the party and its press, and in 1967 a cabinet minister felt impelled to explain to the party faithful that the party did not control the newspapers and had minimal shareholdings in them. Once during his premiership Verwoerd publicly asked Afrikaans editors to discipline themselves and not to 'exploit the turbulence and tensions in Nationalist ranks', although he conceded that the editors had a right 'constructively to criticise and to differ on the practical applications of policy'.

As the apartheid reform programme progressed, erratically, Afrikaans editors had more scope to flex their muscles. The more the apartheid ideology disintegrated, the less cohesive the National Party became, and the less it was able to enforce discipline on the Afrikaans editors. The rift widened, and by 1974 Vorster (then Prime Minister) was accusing the *Vaderland* and the Sunday newspaper *Rapport* of 'meddling in internal party affairs'. But in March 1987 Dr Willem de Klerk, who had earned a reputation for himself as a *verligte* Afrikaner (he coined the terms *verlig* and *verkramp*, the latter meaning reactionary, to describe the schism in Afrikanerdom), resigned as editor of *Rapport* in protest against the unacceptable pressures that were being put on him to toe the party line during the run-up to the 6 May elections. Earlier, the *Vaderland* had sacked its equally *verlig* editor Harald Pakendorf. Another resignation in 1987 was that of Dene Smuts as editor of *Fair Lady*, a journal owned by the *Burger*'s publishing group. She was prevented from publishing a profile of Denis Worrall who was standing as an Independent candidate in the Helderberg constituency against the National Party's Cape leader, Chris Heunis, Minister of Constitutional Development. (Worrall came within thirty-nine votes of unseating Heunis, probably gravely impairing Heunis' future career.)

The resignations and dismissal demonstrated that, at critical junctures such as parliamentary elections and states of emergency, the National Party was still capable of forcing its editors to toe the party line. After the elections, in which the National Party raised its total of seats from 117 to 123, President Botha expressed his gratitude. The four newspapers of the *Burger*'s publishing group, and other national newspapers, he said, were not slaves of the party, but they had rallied to the occasion.

> My view, in the best traditions of the Cape party, is that the party should not see itself as being in a controlling position over . . . newspapers. My view has always been that the newspapers and the party were fellow fighters from the earliest times. It is known that I have a very high regard for the contribution which has been given by the Nasionale [*Burger*] newspapers . . . I would like to thank them for the voluntary contribution . . . They deserve thanks for their patriotic co-operation.[35]

BUREAUCRACY

An estimated 43 per cent of economically active Afrikaners are employed in the public sector. As administrators of the apartheid system, they are its principal beneficiaries. Highly politicised, sheltered from buffeting economic winds, they are a Verwoerdian stronghold not easily breached by reformist politicians. Cabinet ministers have admitted that the bureaucrats have undermined official policy at certain levels. High-ranking officials generally are thought to be supportive of reform, but not those in the lower echelons.

The 'civilised labour policy' of the 1920s ensured public sector employment for less skilled Afrikaners. The public service became almost an Afrikaner preserve, and particularly since 1948 Afrikaners have dominated the senior positions. The Broederbond was the instrument through which most of this Afrikaner advancement in the public sector was achieved. Now, if there is to be power-sharing with blacks, Africanisation of the public service would be unavoidable.

Professor Wiechers notes:

> However optimistic or pessimistic you are about the willingness of politicians to change in South Africa, it is virtually impossible for them to break through the bureaucratic barrier. We have created a vast 'plural administration' to prove the fact that we are a plural society. In the long run this administration, which should be the servant of society, has become its master.[36]

Others take a more hopeful view, insisting that the bureaucracy is not monolithic, and that faced with a strong civil authority it would obey orders. The prospects of establishing a strong civil authority in an increasingly fragmented society, though, cannot be rated as very high.

THE MILITARY POLICE FACTOR

This subject is discussed in Chapters 7 and 8, but the point to be made here is that, like the public service generally, the military and the police have been Afrikanerised and now occupy a special position in decision making. Under P.W. Botha, first as Minister of Defence (1966–78) and then as Prime Minister and State President, the military have been drawn ever deeper into the civil administration, until the intermesh has blurred the boundaries between the two. This is not a situation likely to lead to a military coup, at least not yet, because there is no conflict between the military and the civil authority, as represented by President Botha, who is autocratically in control of his generals. There is the further factor that many senior officers perceive themselves as reformists and intend their contribution to the implementation of President Botha's post-election policies to be a significant one. The nationwide Joint Management Committees, on which the military and police presence is dominant, gives the military just the instrument they need to influence civil decision making.

In various ways, therefore, both internally in South Africa and externally in the southern Africa region, the military, under President Botha's tutelage, have been initiated into politicised intervention. The question is: what will happen when Botha retires? Almost certainly Botha is the last of the strong Afrikaner Nationalist leaders – if Afrikaner Nationalism itself is losing its strength, it cannot produce strong leaders. Botha would probably leave a vacuum which the military would be well placed at least partially to fill. The military's influence over the next National Party leader is likely to be substantial, although how cohesive the military itself would be by then is another question that needs to be asked. In a crisis management situation, the military would test civil decisions against security considerations, but South Africa cannot live forever under crisis management. Where would the military stand then?

The South African police are a different proposition. They have no reformist pretensions or any inclination to 'build bridges' to the black community. Many of their members are said to be sympathetic to the far right and even to the AWB, whose vigilanteism they are expected to monitor and control. It will need a strong civil authority to keep them under disciplined command.

RE-THINKING THE FUTURE

Circulation in October 1986 of the Broederbond's 'Working Paper' and of the NGK's *Church and Society* document signalled that these two key establishment organisations shared with the National Party the aim of reunifying Afrikaners and redefining the reform programme. Heyns expressed this aim succinctly: 'if survival means recasting basic political ideology, he [the Afrikaner] will do so. He is not a slave to his policy . . . We are now witnessing the most exciting event in the history of the Afrikaner: the birth of the new Afrikaner. The new Afrikaner is engaged in conquering his exclusivism.'[37] The import of Heyns' statement is that Afrikaners are prepared to accept the National Party not as the custodian of an inflexible ideology but as a vehicle for change, in the same way that English speakers voted for it on 6 May. In those elections, the English speakers were certainly not voting for an ideology, but for their physical security. Voters with these motivations are not constrained by the same in-house disciplines as traditional Afrikaner nationalists have been over the years. Their emergence in the National

Party suggests that the seeds of future instability have been sown in the party.

President Botha emerged from the 6 May elections consoled by the fact that less than 18 per cent of voters had supported left-of-National Party parties and that this, at least for the time being, staunched the threatening haemorrhage of *verligtes* from the party. Arresting the more serious haemorrhage to the far right was Botha's immediate problem and here his tactic was to remove ambiguities from the reform programme. In preceding years, the unrestrained rhetoric of reform ('apartheid is out of date', etc.) had persuaded many Afrikaners that reform was out of control, and the advice which party analysts tendered to Botha was that the 'uncertainties' over reform should be eliminated to correct this impression. Fear of the unknown would then diminish as an electoral factor.

Reversing the direction of reform was a closed option for Botha. His credentials with the far right had been permanently destroyed anyway. He had gone too far along the road of reform to turn back. F.W. de Klerk, Minister of National Education and leader of the Transvaal National Party and generally reckoned to be conservatively inclined, told a pre-election meeting of his 'earnest acknowledgement that the old system that had served well over decades no longer worked'. Decisive changes were needed if 'big trouble' was to be avoided. 'We dare not drag our feet on this issue.' It was no longer tenable for a white minority to rule over a black majority. A more conservative government might

> possibly keep the lid on the pot for another five years. But after that the pot will explode and blow us and our future into the air . . . After 14 years in parliament, nine of these years as a minister, I can tell you we tried hard to make this work. But we have now come to the realization that it cannot work. Our theory is on the rocks. People want a vote where they live.[38]

This was Botha's post-election dilemma: how to reconcile the imperative of reform with the powerful resistance of many Afrikaners to reform. His immediate response was to narrow the concept of reform until it focused on the constitutional aspect, the establishment of a statutory National Council on which all four major race groups would be represented and which would advise the government on the re-writing of the constitution for what Deputy Minister Stoffel van der Merwe called 'a whole new South Africa'. The rhetoric of reform was toned down and the random speculation as to which apartheid measure would be the next to bite the dust was curbed.

The lesson that there were strict limits to reform was driven home both to conservative Afrikaners and black activists. The latter were told to lower their expectations substantially and the repressive apparatus of the state was invoked to make sure they did so. The nationwide State of Emergency introduced on 12 June 1986 had replaced the earlier partial Emergency and was entirely different in form and ferocity. Botha made it clear that he alone would determine the nature and timetable of reform. No extra-parliamentary activity or pressure groups would be allowed to accelerate the timetable. His ministers made it clear that the state's coercive powers would be used to the full if necessary. Van der Merwe warned:

> The actions of the government over the past year demonstrate that it has no intention of capitulating and submitting to black majority rule. There is no way anyone can take over the country without reckoning with us. This perception is getting through and is conducive to negotiation. The election has also cleared the air and shown more clearly where we want to go.[39]

Botha's rule became ever more autocratic. Professor Andre du Toit compared him with Sir Harry Smith, governor of the Cape from 1847–52.

> Smith, like Botha, came to political power . . . as someone who prided himself on his intimate knowledge of local conditions which he had essentially gained in command of the military. He deliberately adopted a histrionic public style, lecturing all and sundry at great length . . . and exploiting simulated rages to cow his opponents.[40]

Botha's autocratic style was not wholly idiosyncratic though. He was filling the vacuum left by the weakening of the Afrikaner establishment. The more reform exacted its price in Afrikaner disunity, the more Botha came to the fore with his domineering personality.

Another imperative of reform is that repression has its limits: if ruthless, it defeats its purpose in an integrated, interdependent, industrialised economy like South Africa's.[41] Repression creates instability instead of stability when the strain on white cohesion becomes too great. Interest groups then are too diverse to be unified by repression.

Can the National Party become an effective instrument of reform? Professor Terreblanche believes not, because of its 'outdated thought-processes, its frozen perceptions and its conceptual blockages'.[42] Worrall, on the other hand, stresses that the National Party is 'the major white political party in South Africa and will continue to be the main expression of the Afrikaner community, which is the dominant community within white South Africa'. If Worrall is correct, then the PFP and the Independents alike can be no more than adjuncts, or at best catalysts, in a pending party political realignment, and no reform programme can be viable unless it is acceptable to a substantial number of Afrikaner nationalists, who hopefully will shift in a *verligte* direction. The Afrikaner seal of legitimacy, therefore, remains the critical one.

The spectre haunting the National Party is of increasing numbers of its supporters crossing over to the far right, where the Conservative Party, recalling 1934, conjures up images of a Second Purification. Some analysts suggest this cannot happen: that there is a demographic ceiling on the Conservative Party's growth. The party's support, it is argued, is limited to rural dwellers, white miners and other blue-collar workers, mainly on the lower levels of industrial skills. This analysis glosses over the Conservative Party's phenomenal growth, its 'respect-abilising' of Afrikaner dissent, and the lines of communication and continuity which it has preserved with the National Party. It is no great wrench these days for an Afrikaner nationalist to cross sides.

There is compelling evidence that the National Party's existence as a traditionalist, exclusive party of Afrikaners for Afrikaners is drawing to a close; and further (as Professor Terreblanche claims), that it does not have the capacity to transform itself into a viable, effective vehicle of reform. The haemorrhaging of its intelligentsia to the left is one omen. The pattern of change among the Afrikaner youth is another – the centres of activism are located now only on the far right and the *verligte* left, leaving the orthodox 'centre' inert. There is also the evidence from the Afrikaner working-class: many of them feel bereft and betrayed now that the National Party no longer fulfils its protective role as an all-powerful white trade union. To them, the National Party 'has lost its raw, working class appeal and has become gentrified, prosperous and reform-minded . . . increasingly the NP are regarded as a bunch of rich careerists who, at the behest of the international community, are preparing to sell out the white working man to the blacks.'[43]

The new lines of cleavage point to a gathering of forces on the far right and, on the *verligte* left, a coalition of convenience embracing the National Party, the PFP and the Independents. Such a realignment is no doubt unlikely under the Botha presidency – Botha's powerful, autocratic style of government obscures the new cleavage. But Botha in 1988 is 72 years old, and unless he can produce rabbits out of the reform hat, he may well soon tire of attempting the impossible. His successor would inherit an increasingly unstable party. The scene then would be set for a *verligte* coalition of convenience, although the possibility cannot be discounted that the military, confronted by fractious and floundering politicians, would see their role as interventionist and stabilising.

The flaw in this drawn-out scenario is the time span, which assumes that black opposition can be controlled and regulated while 'white politics' pass through their elaborate manoeuvres and convolutions at their own ox-wagon pace. This is where the conflict is likely to lie: that the dynamics of 'white politics' are out of phase with the dynamics of black liberation.

NOTES

1. F. van Zyl Slabbert, in L. Thompson and J. Butler (eds), *Change in Contemporary Africa* (Berkeley: University of California Press, 1975).
2. L. Thompson, *The Political Myths of Apartheid* (New Haven: Yale University Press, 1985).
3. T Dunbar Moodie, *The Rise of Afrikanerdom* (Berkeley: University of California Press, 1975).
4. L. Thompson, 'The Compromise of Union', *Oxford History of South Africa, Vol. 11* (Oxford: Oxford University Press, 1971).
5. R. de Villiers, 'Afrikaner Nationalism', *Oxford History of South Africa, Vol. 11* (Oxford: Oxford University Press, 1971).
6. M. Roberts and A.E.G. Trollip, *The South African Opposition* (London: Longmans, Green, 1947).
7. J.H.P. Serfontein, *Brotherhood of Power* (London: Rex Collings, 1979).
8. *Die Afrikaner*, Pretoria, 26 November 1986.
9. H. Adam and K. Moodley, *South Africa Without Apartheid* (Berkeley: University of California Press, 1971).
10. Total votes cast on 6 May were 2 062 000 (69.97 per cent poll). The Afrikaans:English population ratio is approximately 65:35. Opinion polls in the Afrikaans Sunday newspaper *Rapport* indicated 7 per cent Afrikaner support for left-of-National Party parties and 6 per cent English-speaking support for right-of-National Party parties. The above calculations are based on these figures. Of the total votes cast, 52.28 per cent went to the National Party, 29.3 per cent (26.11 + 3.20 per cent) to the Conservative Party and the HNP, and 17.47 per cent to the left-of-

National Party parties (PFP 14.26 per cent, NRP 1.96 per cent, Independents 1.31 per cent). Thus, 81.59 per cent of the votes were cast for the NP, CP and HNP.

11. de Villiers, op. cit. note 5 above.
12. Serfontein, op. cit. note 7 above.
13. de Villiers, op. cit. note 5 above.
14. A. Sparks, *The Observer*, London, 15 March 1987.
15. J. Heyns, *Leadership*, Cape Town, vol. 5, no. 5., 1986.
16. P.G.J. Meiring, *Church and Nationalism in South Africa* (Johannesburg: Ravan Press, 1975).
17. Heyns, op. cit. note 15 above.
18. *Apartheid and the Church*, Report of the Spro-Cas Church Commission, (Johannesburg: Christian Institute, 1972).
19. Heyns, op. cit. note 15 above.
20. H. Giliomee, in H. Adam and H. Giliomee, *Ethnic Power Mobilised* (New Haven and London: Yale University Press, 1979).
21. Dunbar Moodie, op. cit. note 3 above.
22. de Villiers, op. cit. note 5 above.
23. D. Walsh, 'Political Economy of Afrikaner Nationalism', in A. Leftwich (ed.), *South Africa : Economic Growth and Political Change* (London: Allison & Busby, 1974) pp. 262–3.
24. *South African Digest*, Pretoria, 17 May 1985.
25. A.D. Wassenaar, *Assault on Private Enterprise* (Cape Town: Tafelberg, 1977).
26. H. Giliomee, *Business Day*, Johannesburg, 29 March 1987.
27. Dunbar Moodie, op. cit. note 3 above.
28. Heyns, op. cit. note 14 above.
29. D. Welsh, *Sunday Times*, Johannesburg, 29 March 1987.
30. Constitution of the Afrikaanse Studentebond.
31. See S. Johnson 'The klein broedertwis', *Weekly Mail*, Johannesburg 13 September 1986, and 'The youngster who turned Stellenbosch upside down', ibid. 31 October 1986; and unpublished interviews.
32. Ibid.
33. J. McClurg, *Leadership*, Cape Town, vol. 5, no. 6, 1986.
34. Ibid.
35. *Business Day*, 9 May 1987.
36. M. Wiechers. Cited by Ivor Wilkens in 'A Nation of Bureaucrats', *Sunday Times*, Johannesburg, 16 July 1978.
37. Heyns, op. cit. note 14 above.
38. *The Times*, London, 11 March 1987.
39. S. van der Merwe, *Financial Mail*, Johannesburg, 26 June 1987.
40. A. du Toit, *Cape Times*, Cape Town, 1 September 1987.
41. H. Adam, 'Ethnic Politics, Violence and Crisis', paper presented at symposium of the European Consortium of Political Research on 'Violence and Conflict Management in Divided Societies', held at Freiburg, Federal Republic of Germany, from 20–26 March 1983.
42. S. Terreblanche, *Leadership*, vol. 6, no. 2., 1987.
43. A.R. Kenny, *Spectator*, London, 5 September 1987.

7 The Military in South African Politics

J. E. Spence

'He do the Police in different voices'

T. S. Eliot

THE SOLDIER AS TECHNOCRAT

In the early 1970s it was fashionable, following Heribert Adam's seminal analysis, to define South Africa's ruling elites – whether in business, the parastatal corporations, the senior echelons of the civil service, or the military – as a modernising technocracy, 'an increasingly unshakeable oligarchy' capable of internal liberalisation through a process of 'gradual deracialisation and economic concessions'.[1] Their capacity to manage change without provoking a crisis of expectations was regarded as falsifying the widely-held assumption that 'mounting internal tension will make a violent revolutionary change inevitable'.[2]

This Platonic view of the Republic's guardians was understandably attractive after a decade of rapid economic growth, a seemingly inert black opposition, and an explicit external acceptance, via the rubric of the Nixon Doctrine, of South Africa's hegemonial role in the region. It is true that in the early 1970s the military had yet to emerge as fully-fledged technocrats: their role was still defined in rather traditional terms as a weapon of last resort in the event of insurgency and as a deterrent against external attack. Its importance in this context – in the absence of any significant internal threat – was political and symbolic rather than strategic, in effect to demonstrate to friend and foe alike that the Republic was no pushover in conventional terms. More positively, it aspired to provide a well-endowed 'strategic bastion' in the global struggle against communism. The soldier still perceived himself to be the servant of his political masters and the structure of civil-military relations retained in tone and substance the demarcation prescribed by a Western political tradition.

Nevertheless, from the mid-1960s onwards a gradual transformation of the role and purpose of the South African Defence Force (SADF) began under the guidance of P.W. Botha, appointed Minister of

Defence in 1966 and destined to spend the next twelve years modernising and expanding force capabilities as well as streamlining the system of command and control. Thus began the technocratic revolution in the status and function of South Africa's armed forces, although the changes Botha initiated went largely unnoticed by most commentators, principally because, until 1974, the Republic's military kept a low political profile and – apart from in Namibia – had virtually no operational experience to boost their symbolic importance. There is evidence of covert military aid to both the Portuguese and Rhodesian governments in their counter-insurgencies against liberation movements, but political constraints weighed against large-scale intervention in these territories, though occasional *civilian* voices were raised suggesting this course of action. Regional policy remained firmly in the hands of the Department of Foreign Affairs (DFA) whose spokesman, echoing Dr Hilgard Muller, the Foreign Minister, made much of the role the Republic could play in establishing a Southern African Economic Community and thus enhance its standing in the West.

But with the sudden collapse of Portuguese rule in Angola and Mozambique in 1974, the military came into its own. The story of the 1975 intervention in Angola is a tangled one, but it is reasonably clear that the DFA was outmanoeuvred by the Defence Ministry. P.W. Botha and his advisers rejected the traditional principle of non-interference in neighbouring states on the grounds that the civil war in Angola would create 'opportunities for communist involvement and for a SWAPO presence on Namibia's northern border'.[3] The fact that South Africa's objectives were not achieved, that the military were compelled to pull back to Namibia, paradoxically did not weaken their position in the ensuing debate about the future direction of South Africa's regional strategy and the role the military might play. If anything, the arrival of some 20 000 Cubans in Angola strengthened it to the extent that additional resources were found to modernise and re-equip conventional forces with a view to providing a capability for the conduct of 'large-scale preemptive and punitive raids against guerrilla bases in neighbouring countries'[4], as well as the means to cope with any conventional retaliation. In effect, the army was to have two roles: counter-insurgency at home and the projection – if need be – of conventional power abroad.

Politically, P.W. Botha found himself in a stronger position after 1974: in the bureaucratic in-fighting over resources he could cite his Prime Minister, B. J. Vorster's, contention that 'when it comes to the worst, South Africa stands alone'.[5] If so, military force, and the will to use it, became even more important in the absence of any support from London or Washington. The collapse of the '*détente*' initiative, designed to promote a settlement of the Rhodesian crisis in 1975 was a body blow to the DFA whose senior officials had placed their faith in diplomatic and economic strategies designed to win acceptance of South Africa's position as an African power from the leaders of neighbouring states. Moreover, by the late 1970s P. W. Botha had a powerful constituency in the senior ranks of the military, many of whom he had promoted and whose needs and aspirations he understood from long experience of mutual co-operation in the task of modernisation. The Muldergate scandal revelations of a sorry tale of civilian incompetence and corruption left him virtually unscathed and well placed to defeat potentially stronger rivals for the premiership.

Once in office, P. W. Botha instigated a managerial revolution in the structure and process of government modelled on the reforms he had initiated in the military bureaucracy during the previous decade. He had been greatly impressed by the ambience of the military machine (which he himself had largely created); by the capacity of a military bureaucracy to issue clear directions and ensure that they were carried out; and by the seemingly efficient manner in which priorities were defined and action taken to achieve them. Like many civilians, he admired the soldier's ability to define reality in terms of stark opposites – presumably a welcome change from the muddle of orthodox politics with its emphasis on short-term gain at the expense of long-term objectives and characterised by ideological confusion and the search for political advantage to the detriment of the national interest.

Moreover, as Minister of Defence, P.W. Botha had pushed the careers of a generation of younger officers such as Magnus Malan (Chief of the General Staff and Botha's successor in the Ministry), all of whom had undergone an intensive education in the literature of counter-insurgency so beloved of their French and US counterparts in the staff colleges of the West. The writings of French soldier-scholars, such as Roger Trinquer and André Beaufre, were especially influential with their emphasis on the political dimension of revolutionary and counter-revolutionary war, all of which was regarded as highly relevant following the revival of black opposition and, in particular, the fortunes of the ANC in the post-Soweto phase of South African politics.

THE STATE SECURITY COUNCIL: TOTAL ONSLAUGHT AND TOTAL STRATEGY

The emergence of this military elite into the arena of public debate about the Republic's future had structural as well as ideological implications. On assuming the premiership in 1978, P.W. Botha revived the State Security Council, which had been established in 1972 but had lain dormant in the bureaucratic maze of committees created by his predecessor. What was required, in Botha's view, was a body which would give both tone and substance in day-to-day political terms to the notion of a 'total strategy' required to cope with a 'total onslaught'. These concepts – part cause and part effect of P. W. Botha's determination to give the senior military a political role commensurate with their political skills – first surfaced in the 1977 Defence White Paper and were designed to provide a comprehensive ideological framework in which the threat to South Africa could be assessed and a policy devised to counter it.

How far these related notions were 'internalised' by those who enunciated them is a matter of debate, as is the extent to which they still govern policy making, and this will be examined below. Certainly, their exposition on the syllabuses of military colleges and the absence of any alternative critique by more sceptical defence and civilian intellectuals must surely have contributed to the creation of a *weltanschauung* which encouraged the soldier in a beleaguered society to define reality in simple-minded, black and white terms. Hence, however self-consciously instrumental as a mechanism for white mobilisation the concept of 'total onslaught' may have been perceived by the generals of the 1970s, it is probable that a later generation of colonels and majors have imbibed the doctrine uncritically, and in this respect they constitute a cadre of true believers.

There is no shortage of ministerial statements outlining the nature and scope of the 'total onslaught'; perhaps the clearest definition was that provided by P. W. Botha himself in 1978:

> The ultimate aim of the Soviet Union and its allies is to overthrow the present body politic in the Republic of South Africa and to replace it with a Marxist-oriented form of government to further the objectives of the USSR. Therefore all possible methods and means are used to attain this objective. This includes instigating social and labour unrest, civilian resistance, terrorist attacks against the infrastructure of South Africa, and the intimidation of black leaders and

> members of the security forces. This onslaught is supported by a world-wide propaganda campaign and the involvement of various front organisations, such as the trade unions and even certain church organisations and leaders.[6]

This proposition, with its stress on a single, omnipotent source of evil intent, is a good example of what Hans Morgenthau calls the 'devil theory' of international relations. The Soviet Union is credited with an infinite capacity to manipulate and infiltrate at will; with a long-term ideological motivation; and, more important, both the will and the means to ignore the constraints and short-term expedients to which all states – even superpowers – are normally subject. Its leadership is perceived as omnipotent, giving the Republic the status of a primary target in the struggle to advance the aims of world communism. Furthermore, the parlous state of Russian studies in South African universities (the sheer difficulty of getting hold of the key texts and subjecting them to critical scrutiny should be noted),[7] together with the absence of official cosmopolitan ties with military and political counterparts abroad (apart from Israel), make for a limited and highly tendentious world view, and one lacking first-hand knowledge of the complexities of modern strategic doctrine. That the Soviet Union has profound domestic problems and regards relations with the West and its interests in the Middle East and Asia as greatly more significant than any key advantage to be gained from actively promoting revolution in South Africa, are things 'not dreamt of' in South Africa's military philosophy.

Yet the strategy has advantages for the Republic's rulers. As Joseph Hanlon argues:

> The concept of total onslaught equates the 'red peril' with the 'black peril', and defence of apartheid with defence of Western Christian values. This formulation of the problem has two important advantages for white South Africa. On the one hand, all criticisms of apartheid can be dismissed as communist-inspired. On the other hand, it allows South Africa to demand that the West support it as a bastion against communism, despite any distaste for apartheid; when the West attacks apartheid it only aids Moscow.[8]

Structurally, the 'total strategy' is the abiding concern of the State Security Council. Its membership provides a roll-call of the top decision makers in South Africa and includes the State President as chairman; the Ministers of Defence, Foreign Affairs, Justice, Law and Order; the

Director of the National Intelligence Service; the Chief of the Defence Force; the Director General of Foreign Affairs; the Director General of Justice; and the Commissioner of Police. On the face of it, civilians appear to outnumber the military, but this is to ignore the Council's terms of reference which are exclusively concerned with *security*, defined as the preservation of the State against threat from whatever source and, therefore, very different from, say, the National Security Council of the United States which has responsibility for advising the President on foreign policy only. This objective requires that 'total strategy' be co-ordinated by a 'national security management system', and the consequence is a remit 'broad enough to embrace virtually every area of government action both at home and abroad'.[9] Thus, unlike its equivalents abroad (in so far as they exist), the State Security Council's mandate is to scrutinise *all* aspects of foreign policy for security implications; as Grundy remarks 'regional policy, economic policy, manpower planning, constitutional planning – the whole gamut is influenced by security and internal stability considerations'.[10] Furthermore, the secretariat is well placed to fulfil a 'gate-keeper' role not only for the Council but for the Cabinet as well: in effect, it prepares agendas and ensures the flow of paper and intelligence briefings in particular.

The secretariat is staffed by military bureaucrats (65 per cent), officials of the National Intelligence Service (25 per cent) and Department of Foreign Affairs (10 per cent) and has four functions:

(1) the provision of strategic options;
(2) the interpretation of intelligence provided by the Department of Military Intelligence (DMI), the National Intelligence Service (NIS), the security police, and the Department of Foreign Affairs (DFA);
(3) a propaganda function, i.e. 'combating the war of words';
(4) administration.

As the only Cabinet committee established by statute and chaired by the State President, the State Security Council (SSC) is in an unassailable position in so far as it determines in advance what matters are relevant for wider Cabinet discussion. It is underpinned by a Work Committee which discusses proposals in advance of their appearance on the Council's agenda; it makes recommendations 'regarding the advice the SSC should give to the Cabinet. It also reports on the implications of policy mandates given by previous SSC meetings'.[11]

Most governments risk being swamped by information; 'overload' is a common complaint of ministers the world over. To this extent, it could be argued, the SSC has an important selective function, but it is all the more powerful for that reason. And it is significant that the Secretary of the Council is a senior military intelligence officer (General P. W. van der Westhuizen is the current office-holder and lately responsible for regional military operations), backed up by a dominantly military bureaucracy servicing the needs of the Council.

Grundy has warned against endowing the military with a *decisive* influence over government policy; the garrison state, he claims, is not yet with us – rather 'the military voice is clear and . . . well placed, but in the end it, too, must come to accept this is an elected government answerable to an exclusive electorate, but nonetheless answerable'.[12] Nevertheless, the crisis that erupted in September 1984 and its continuation (unlike its counterparts in 1976 and 1960) has inevitably elevated internal security issues to a commanding position on the government's agenda. As Annette Seegers remarks, summarising the Grundy thesis: 'If you think you're at war, instruments of war will be your first choice of policy making'.[13] Indeed, the constitutional restructuring which took effect in 1987 strengthened the executive (and by implication its servicing institutions such as the SSC) at the expense of a tricameral legislature, the component parts of which have been unable to interact profitably as a significant check on executive action. As the author has argued elsewhere:

> Thus a commitment to limited reform of the kind enshrined in the new constitution – to win the 'hearts and minds' of the Coloured and Indian minorities – is not inconsistent with an enhanced role for the military both as social engineers concerned with filtering economic and social policy through a security lens and as an increasingly visible presence to deter and defend against the threat of black violence. Thus, when ministers justify military action in the black townships (as in October 1984 and during much of 1985) or destabilizing raids against South Africa's neighbours, they invariably talk of rooting out 'revolutionary elements' – a conception which it is easy to square with the assumption that South Africa is threatened by 'total onslaught'.[14]

Further, a theory of political change which emphasises the need to veer between the twin poles of reform and repression, maintaining at all times a balance between the two, is one with a particular appeal to the military mind, if only because of the decisive role assigned to the armed forces in putting the second half of the equation into practice. This technocratic vision is well-expressed by General Jannie Geldenhuys, currently Chief of the Defence Staff: 'In the management sciences they say the key to this is you must scientifically manage change and keep it as subtle as possible.'[15]

The reform/repression thesis, designed to manage change and keep political expectations within acceptable limits, is regarded as a pertinent application of counter-insurgency theory which – as remarked earlier – has been the staple intellectual diet of several generations of South African soldiers. After all, Namibia has long provided a test bed for its implementation in the wider South African theatre. WHAM ('winning hearts and minds' via the orthodox 80:20 ratio of political and military action) has meant a civic action programme in which servicemen take on civilian roles as doctors, teachers, engineers and administrators in both Namibia and the black areas of the Republic. To this extent, then, the military have had a crucial role in the reform programme and, by definition, an inevitable influence on its scope and substance.

Whatever qualms the DFA may have felt in the past, for example, about coercive regional policies have been quelled by the capacity of the military to impose their definition of reality on civilian policy makers – witness Foreign Minister Pik Botha's sabre-rattling about the alleged threat of ANC disruption of the May 1987 election campaign. This is where the influence of the military has been truly felt; whether by default rather than design is beside the point, although no doubt the more ambitious have seized the opportunity provided by a deteriorating security situation to advance influence and prestige.

Some scholars have called into question the continuing utility of the 'total onslaught' strategy for the South African state. On the basis of evidence gained from interviews in 1983, John Seiler, for example, detected a note of scepticism on the part of senior military and police officers who claimed that the concept was 'an exaggerated and counter-productive rubric for strategic planning'; that Magnus Malan and colleagues have emphasised its value primarily as a device 'to justify military expenditure' on conventional forces despite the fact that the Front Line States presented no more than a 'paper threat'. Yet, Seiler acknowledges that these very same senior officers 'assume Moscow *control* of ANC and SWAPO rather than *influence* over them, and . . . remain unfathomably apprehensive of all Soviet regional presences, unable yet to make analytical judgements about varying threats in different regional situations'.[16]

It is, therefore, reasonable to conclude that however much the notion of 'total onslaught' was played down in the early 1980s, its instrumental resurgence as blacks mobilised in opposition was hardly surprising; after all, the United Democratic Front – the most dramatic manifestation of this opposition – provided a tempting target, if only because of its success in helping to articulate the aims and aspirations of the banned and exiled African National Congress – an organisation which, in the eyes of the state, was Moscow's most provocative tool. These developments, together with the increase in ANC military activity (after a short-lived decline following the Nkomati Accord of March 1984) and the organisation's success in establishing itself as a legitimate political actor in the eyes of businessmen and some other whites at home and in political circles abroad helped to swing the balance decisively from reform to repression and required ultimately the despatch of the army to the townships. Thus, the military perspective was vindicated at the expense of *verligtes* in the DFA and on the backbenches of the Nationalist government – to the extent that some supporters felt obliged to defect, not least a major architect and defender of the reform programme, Denis Worrall, the Ambassador to the Court of St James!

THE ARMY ENTERS THE TOWNSHIPS

Political and security considerations blended together to produce the declaration of a second nationwide, State of Emergency in June 1986. Intelligence sources had indicated what was described as a 'misperception of the state's will and power' to bring unrest to an end shared by both the left and the right of the political spectrum. The mood of the townships – on this reading of the evidence – was overly optimistic about the likelihood of sudden and convulsive change as internal and external pressures mounted. By contrast, the white right-wing accused the government of lacking the will to enforce its authority. Both these misperceptions – so government spokesmen argued – required correction, hence the clampdown on individuals, organisations and the media.

During the current crisis, the SADF first became involved in internal security operations in October 1984 with the deployment via Operation Palmiet of some 7000 troops in a 'seal-and-search' operation in Sebokeng township. In the course of 1985 some 35 000 troops were on duty in the townships, and it is reasonable to conclude that the WHAM strategy has given way to the implementation of straightforward military measures regardless of their political consequences. Those in the military who still cling to a Clausewitzian notion of counter-insurgency emphasising the subordination of military means to political goals find themselves supporting the operations of the South African police, many of whose senior officers are alleged to be supporters of the conservative right and therefore unimpressed with the political orthodoxies of counter-insurgency theory. Indeed, those ultimately responsible for police operations, for example, Louis le Grange (former Minister of Law and Order), General Hennie de Witt (Police Commissioner) and Major-General Johann van der Merwe (Chief of the Security Police) are identified with the right-wing of the Nationalist Party. Thus, the soldiers involved in police support – whatever their private and public reservations about playing a 'police' role in the townships – have little alternative but to accept a 'law and order' approach rather than a commitment to maintain a balance between reform and repression of the kind that was popular in the military in the early 1980s. In any case, the latter thesis was badly punctured in the 1982/4 period as black opposition refused to accept its assigned, relatively passive, role in the official scenario of change.

WHAM has therefore been substantially modified to a simple-minded commitment to restore law and order first, and only then to get on with the business of politics, the assumption being, in the revealing words of Adriaan Vlok, le Grange's successor as Minister of Law and Order, that

> we have evidence to show that whenever we re-established law and order, people began feeling more secure, children started going back to schools, and life began to return to normal. Only then can you move to the second stage and this is the addressing of grievances . . . This is a fact and the government very well realises this. It is because of this knowledge and our determination, that we are going to win this war.[17]

What is especially interesting here is the frank acknowledgement that the government is involved in a *war*, and the confirmation that a little book-learning can be a dangerous thing, especially if it involves the wholesale and relatively uncritical application in South Africa of military theories based on Western experience in Malaya, Vietnam, Algeria and the Portuguese colonies, where, incidentally, failures out-numbered successes.

Of course, the staff college instructor at Voortrekkerhoogte would no doubt retort that the Republic is a special case; that it has massive military and bureaucratic capabilities; that orthodox revolution is unlikely to succeed; that unlike Iran, the Philippines, and Haiti, the loyalty of the security forces and the civil service is absolute and therefore unlikely to act as the spearhead of black revolution against the state.

Yet something significant has happened over the last three years to challenge the conventional interpretation: in the past – between 1961 and 1974 – the maintenance of internal security was largely achieved by the legislative elaboration of techniques of social control which provided the state with a counter-insurgency capability in advance of any threat to its security rather than being compelled to improvise after the event – like the British in Malaya and the French in Algeria. But government policy in, for example, relaxing trade union restrictions and influx control, in generating and raising black political expectations by paradoxically denying them, has weakened the deterrent effect of these bureaucratic structures. The result is that the state has been forced into a posture of defence in a self-styled 'revolutionary war' – hence the deployment of a massive military presence in the townships and the establishment of Joint Management Committees (JMCs) at regional and local levels with a combined membership of soldiers and civilians.

These committees are part of the National Security Management System (NSMS): the twelve largest ones correspond to the area commands of the SADF which will – in time – reduce to nine to correspond with the demarcation of economic development areas. Lower down the hierarchy of the systems there are sixty JMCs which operate at the level of the recently established Regional Services Councils; and finally, 448 committees to cover local authority areas. Their function is to gather intelligence on issues which might lead to black mobilisation – poor housing, rent and rate increases, etc. – and take the necessary action to prevent confrontation either by attempting to defuse a local grievance or, alternatively, detaining those likely to cause trouble in the event of failure. (An interesting example of the work of a local JMC is the recent decision to redevelop and upgrade Alexandra township on the outskirts of Johannesburg; R95 000 000 has been promised to improve roads, rebuild houses and install better drainage facilities. There is, however, evidence of strong local scepticism and indeed opposition to the programme.)

This new structure is alleged to be capable of speedily bypassing more orthodox and cumbersome bureaucratic procedures for redressing grievances; its great disadvantage – according to critics of the NSMS – is that its officials are not accountable to elected authorities, either at a local or a national level. Thus, Helen Suzman, a leading Progressive Federal Party MP, has, for example, described the NSMS process as tantamount to a 'creeping *coup d'état* by consent in which accountable politicians have abrogated their power to non-accountable members of the security forces'.[18]

James Selfe claims that: 'The JMCs don't worry about intelligence for the whole country [only] about their particular areas. They will worry so many stones have been thrown this morning, there is a shortage of water here, electricity lines have been blown down by strong winds there.' Allister Sparks cogently remarks that the system

> abandons the democratic ideal of a politically neutral defence and police force; political decisions are becoming too heavily influenced by security considerations; the increased political power of the police and defence force will give them a big stake in the status quo and make them resistant to reform; and, worst of all, the whole structure from top to bottom is swathed in secrecy.[19]

This is the stuff of classic counter-insurgency, but it appears to operate in a political vacuum; for in the absence of an alternative vision of society (an essential prerequisite for any government attempting to compete for popular support against its opponents), short-term military tactics become long-term strategy, demonstrating all too clearly the intellectual poverty and political emptiness of what passes for reform in the minds of soldier and politician alike. What this analysis suggests, then, is that the Nationalist government appears to have nothing to offer its constituents except a strategy of punishment for those who challenge it on the improbable assumption that once law and order is restored, suitable candidates for negotiation and hence co-option will step forward.

Perhaps the greatest error consistently running through the variations that time and changing circumstance have forced upon WHAM doctrine is the implicit belief that economic and social amelioration would be an effective substitute for political incorporation. The consequence is that the state and the opposition are locked in stalemate; white security can, and no doubt will, be maintained by increasingly draconian measures, but 'winning hearts and minds' to a refurbished, co-optative style of apartheid is a political goal lacking ideological legitimacy and therefore the gravest shortcoming in the South African version of counter-revolutionary war. Technocracy, like patriotism, is rarely enough.

RELATIONS BETWEEN THE POLICE AND THE ARMY

Political differences cause real and immediate problems for the government in the area of policing. It is symptomatic of the reform process in South Africa that its pace and content owes more to what the right will accept than what blacks need, and this affects policing. Reformist elements in the government are aware of the domestic and international repercussions of police atrocities, and even the State President is alleged to be concerned that the police are out of control. His difficulties in restoring control stem from many sources. Right-wing sentiments are alleged to be widespread within the South African Police (SAP)[20]: P. W. Botha has been reported as believing that nearly two-thirds of white members of the SAP support the Conservative Party against his reform policy. The local autonomy embedded in the organisational structure of the SAP adds to the difficulties of the more technocratically-minded police hierarchy enforcing authority on local commanders.[21] The *verligtes* in the government are also in a weak position as a result of the political revitalisation of the Afrikaans right-wing. The government's inability to implement effective monitoring procedures of police conduct and their reluctance to prosecute offenders arise out of a fear of appearing to the right as soft on security. For years Botha was burdened with a conservative Minister of Law and Order, Louis le Grange, who Botha believed to be opposed to the reform policy but who could not be removed, despite serious illness, because of support for him among the conservative sections of the party. His successor, Adriaan Vlok, is reported to have little influence among the police, and in this regard the decision to deploy the SADF in civil unrest can be seen as an attempt to reassert control over the police because the SADF is said to be more in favour of reform and therefore more pro-government.[22] It was for this reason that Adriaan Vlok was moved in as le Grange's deputy while retaining his position as Deputy Minister of Defence. This argument fits the familiar portrayal of the SADF leadership and the Ministry of Defence as enthusiastic reformers and suggests that the military view the police as inept. On the other hand, some members of the SADF have been as zealous in their misconduct as policemen. In February 1987, the Minister of Defence revealed in parliament that 'about twenty-four' members of the SADF had been tried and seventeen convicted in 1986 for exceeding the bounds of their duty while serving in the black townships. Complaints against the SADF made by members of the public during 1986 included allegations of murder, assault and rape: in all, twenty-six complaints were made and 163 civil actions begun during that year. This suggests that the technocratic leadership within the military face some of the same problems in controlling subordinates as the SAP and that the lower echelons of the SADF on the ground have a more favourable view of the police.

THE MILITARY AND DESTABILIZATION

The record of South Africa's destabilisation of its neighbours is dealt with in Chapter 11; the emphasis in this section is on the assumptions underpinning that strategy of destabilisation.

The Republic's leaders often maintain that their strategy in the southern African region is one of deterrence. However, Thomas Schelling's term 'compellance' provides a better description, in so far as the Republic's military intervention in neighbouring states has involved 'initiating an action . . . that can cease or become harmless only if the opponent responds'.[23]

A variety of political objectives have been ascribed to the destabilisation strategy:

1. to demonstrate to neighbouring states the Republic's determination to resist external attack on its domestic order;
2. to demonstrate in forceful terms Republican hegemony and undermine the efforts of alternative 'constellations' such as the Southern African Development and Co-ordination Conference (SADCC) to escape Pretoria's economic domination. In the process, neighbouring states are compelled to pay a price in terms of resources devoted to coping with the danger caused by destabilisation which would otherwise be available for positive economic development;
3. to 'actively turn back the tide of foreign or Marxist influence in the subcontinent'.[24]

Finally, in a climate of mounting pressure for comprehensive sanctions against the Republic, continued support for proxies, for example

UNITA and the MNR, is a major imperative, on the grounds that the latter's disruption of the East-West transport routes will:

1. tie the Front Line States still closer to the South African rail and road network; and
2. so absorb the defensive energies and resources of these states that the resulting impact on their economies will significantly reduce their commitment to take measures against the Republic.

In this context, too, the military perspective dominates decision making at the expense of the more *verligte* economic strategies preferred by the DFA and the low-key 'transport diplomacy' of technocrats such as Kobus Loubscher. This division or opinion emerged very clearly in the closing stages of the Eminent Persons Group (EPG) mission to Pretoria in May 1986 when military raids on three neighbouring Commonwealth states effectively ended any prospect of a positive outcome. What was striking was the extent to which Pik Botha, the *verligte* Foreign Minister, was outmanoeuvred (and not for the first time) by his right-wing colleagues once he had publicly suggested the possibility of a diplomatic breakthrough. Indeed, controversy still lingers on how far the SSC was involved in the decision to deploy military force; some commentators have suggested that it was unilateral action by the military (as appeared to be the case with respect to support for the Mozambique National Resistance (MNR) after the signing of the Nkomati Accord) without reference to the SSC or to the Cabinet. Whatever the truth of the matter, both developments indicate very clearly the confidence and the capacity of senior military advisers to press for and succeed in getting tough military action if politicians appear to waver in their commitment to the 'total strategy'.

There has been some discussion in the literature over the extent to which Pretoria's regional strategy demonstrates a 'coherent inner logic'[25] rather than pragmatic short-term commitment to the principle of 'let us destabilise them, lest they really succeed in destabilising us'.[26] This debate has centred on the role the South African government ascribes to the constellation of states thesis and its capacity to incorporate the neighbouring countries. The aspiration to build a constellation may still survive among some members of the Nationalist elite, but accepting this is very different from postulating a long-term goal against which every strategy – military, political and economic – is tested for relevance and conformity. As politicians everywhere know to their cost, the press of events, the world of 'telegrams and anger', inevitably absorbs their time and energy, smothering efforts to conduct foreign policy on the basis of long-term planning and goal setting.

South Africa's policy makers have, over the last two decades, demonstrated a ruthless pragmatism in their conduct of regional relations – an attitude which does not square easily with an unchanging commitment to grandiose external visions of the future. The military, in particular I suspect, show little enthusiasm for a Pax Afrikaner which goes beyond the maintenance of regional security by means other than the threat or use of force when neighbouring states prove hostile. If they are concerned with non-military, that is economic and political, techniques for enhancing the Republic's security, it is primarily as an aspect of that counter-insurgency strategy which the more perceptive amongst their ranks have always acknowledged as crucial to maintaining white rule within the Republic.[27]

THE FUTURE: PROSPECTS FOR A COUP?

A military coup in South Africa would seem unlikely for the following reasons:

1. despite technocratic pretensions, South Africa's military elite is not a caste in the Latin American sense; the civic culture of white South Africa has deep historical roots and its political beneficiaries are committed to its preservation. Nor is there anything like the vacillation, indecisiveness and, indeed, corruption which have prompted puritanically-minded soldiers to take over in societies where political institutions are frail and exposed;
2. South Africa is an advanced and industrial society and the relatively small officer class – however technocratic in outlook – is ill-equipped (and it knows it) to cope with the problems of economic and political management on the grand scale;
3. finally, as Heribert Adam and Kogila Moodley argue, the close working relationship between the military and the ruling National Party that consolidated with the ascendancy of former Defence Minister P.W. Botha has made the military an integral part of government decision making, so that there is no need to take it over formally.[28]

Of course, P.W. Botha's departure may usher in a new phase of civil-military relations, but it is unlikely that his successor will wish or indeed be able to restructure fundamentally a system which has such obvious short-term utility in a period of domestic crisis. Moreover, we must avoid ascribing monolithic unity of outlook to the senior military. There is division within the armed services: between those who have imbibed the orthodoxies of counter-insurgency theory ('winning hearts and minds') and define their role as providing a stable and secure context in which social and economic reform can take root, and those who regard themselves simply as the guardians of law and order and who are not inclined to philosophise about the long-term political significance of what they do.

The latter are in the ascendancy, but then so are the politicians who share their view. Moreover, it is not insignificant that no military general or colonel has so far joined the ranks of those who have recently defected to the Independent cause from the Nationalist Party.

Like the politicians, the military divide into hawks and doves on most issues of crucial national interest; but both groups will continue to support a government which clearly esteems their advice and makes resources readily available and, perhaps most important, provides ample opportunity for their use – whether in the region, in Namibia, or in the townships at home.

NOTES

1. H. Adam, *Modernizing Racial Domination* (Berkeley and Los Angeles: University of California Press, 1971), pp. 181–2.
2. Ibid. p. 181.
3. D. Geldenhuys, *The Diplomacy of Isolation: South African Foreign Policy Making* (Johannesburg: Macmillan for the South African Institute of International Affairs, 1984), p. 79.
4. R. S. Jaster, *Southern Africa's Narrowing Security Options* (London: International Institute for Strategic Studies, Adelphi Paper 159, 1980), pp. 27–8.
5. Geldenhuys, op. cit. note 3 above, p. 81.
6. J. Hanlon, *Beggar Your Neighbours – Apartheid Power in Southern Africa* (London: James Currey for the Catholic Institute of International Relations, 1986), p. 8.
7. An honourable exception in this context is the Institute for the Study of Marxism at the University of Stellenbosch under the directorship of Dr Philip Nel.
8. Hanlon, op. cit., note 6 above, p. 8.

9. Geldenhuys, op. cit. note 3 above, p. 92.
10. K. Grundy, *The Rise of the South African Security Establishment: An Essay on the Changing Locus of State Power* (Johannesburg: South African Institute of International Affairs, 1983), p. 35. (Quotation from statement by Harry Schwarz in *Financial Mail*, vol. 86, no. 2 (1982), p. 144).
11. *Africa Confidential*, vol. 28, no. 14, 1987, p. 2.
12. Grundy, op. cit., note 10 above, p. 34.
13. A. Seegers, 'The Military in South Africa – A Comparison and Critique', *South African International*, vol. 16, no. 4, 1986, p. 194. See also Grundy's revised analysis in *The Militarization of South African Politics* (London: Tauris, 1986) in which recent developments are perceptively discussed.
14. J. E. Spence, 'South Africa's Military Relations', in Simon Baynham (ed.), *Military Power and Politics in Black Africa* (London: Croom Helm, 1986), p. 302.
15. *Weekly Mail*, 14–20 November, 1986.
16. J. Seiler, 'The South African State Security System: Rationalization to What Ends?', unpublished paper, 1984.
17. Interview in *Leadership*, vol. 6, no. 1, 1987, p. 30.
18. '*Johannesburg' Star*, 5 June, 1987.
19. Allister Sparks, citing James Seife in 'Botha's Secret Army', *The Observer*, 28 December 1986.
20. H. Adam and K. Moodley, *South Africa Without Apartheid* (Berkeley, University of California Press, 1986) p. 67.
21. On the organisational structure of the South African Police and the question of police autonomy, see the chapter on the South African Police in J. Brewer *et al*, *Police, Public Order and the State* (London: Macmillan, forthcoming).
22. This claim was made by a leading Afrikaans social scientist in a private conversation.
23. T. C. Schelling, *Arms and Influence* (New Haven and London: Yale University Press, 1966), p. 72.
24. J. Barratt, 'The Outlook for Namibian Independence: Some Domestic Constraints', *International Affairs Bulletin*, vol. 71, no. 1, 1983, p. 23.
25. R. M. Price, 'Pretoria's Southern African Strategy', *African Affairs*, vol. 83, no. 330, 1984, pp. 11–32.
26. Geldenhuys, op. cit. note 3 above, p. 145.
27. See Spence, op. cit. note 14 above, pp. 303–13, for an extended discussion of Price's thesis.
28. Adam and Moodley, op. cit. note 20 above, pp. 66–7.

8 The Police in South African Politics

John Brewer

POLICING IN SOUTH AFRICA

There are a number of police bodies in South Africa functioning at regional and national levels (see Table 8.1) and it is necessary to distinguish these briefly before any consideration can be given to their role in politics.

Table 8.1 Police Forces in South Africa

National
South African Police (incorporating the former South African Railways and Harbour Police)
Police Reserve (ex-members of the regular force, part-time)
Reserve Police Force (part-time volunteers)
South African Police Wachthuis (part-time volunteer radio operators)

Regional/local
Provincial Traffic Police
Municipal Traffic Police
Area Defence Units (voluntary part-time rural militia)

African areas
'Independent' homeland police
'Non-independent' homeland police and paramilitary forces
Township Municipal Law Enforcement Officers
Township 'Kitskonstabels'

The South African Police (SAP) was formed in 1913 and has gradually absorbed a number of autonomous police forces, although the provinces and larger municipal authorities have retained their own traffic police. The force suffers from severe manpower shortage. This first became apparent in 1976 when the SAP was tested by the township disturbances, and between 1976 and 1984 regular manpower levels rose by 29.7 per cent, to total 44 696 officers (see statistical appendix). The intensification of black unrest since 1984 has seen manpower levels in the force rise sharply beyond this. In reply to a parliamentary question, the Minister of Law and Order said in August 1986 that South Africa had 55 000 policemen and women, representing 1.7 per 1000 of the population, which compares favourably with liberal democracies. The ratio has oscillated around this proportion since the inception of the SAP: at the height of the Soweto disturbances in 1976 the ratio was 1.3, the same as in 1931. One index of manpower shortage is provided by the low number of officers who are dismissed from the force after being found guilty of criminal offences. For 1969–70 the figure was 5.2 per cent, while for the period between 1980 and 1985 it was still only 7.9 per cent. In 1986 only one police officer was dismissed from the force as result of 'unrest activities'.

The ratio of police to population in South Africa is misleading because of the amount of social control generated by the structure and institutions of apartheid itself. Manpower is also supplemented by the resources of functionally compatible forces, such as the guards employed by mining companies, and numerous security personnel working for private companies, who under some statutes are given the same powers as the civil police. These forces are particularly important in policing key installations and sites. Part-time forces are also widely used. The SAP is assisted by a volunteer Reserve Police Force, intended primarily to attract schoolchildren, and the Police Reserve, consisting of ex-members of the SAP who may be called to do duty for thirty days a year up to five years after leaving the force. In 1984 these two part-time forces had a manpower of 37 477. White civilian volunteers are also integrated into police roles through the South African Police Wachthuis, a force of amateur radio operators who act as a communications link, and Area Defence Units, which form a rural militia designed to monitor infiltration by guerrillas. Since 1975 young national servicemen have been able to undertake their tour of duty in the SAP, and the South African Defence Force (SADF) has become increasingly involved in policing the townships. However, so intense has township protest become that, despite being able to draw on extra manpower resources, the size of the regular force is set to rise sharply. The projected manpower for the SAP in 1987 is 94 000, giving an estimated ratio of 3.4 per 1000 of the population, which would increase still further with the projections of manpower up to 1995, when the force is expected to have doubled again.

Expenditure on the SAP has increased in parallel (see statistical appendix). From 1960 there has been an average annual percentage increase in expenditure on the regular force of 13.9 per cent in nominal terms, while expenditure rose by 69 per cent between the financial years 1983–84 and 1985–86, compared with a 21.4 per cent increase in expenditure on the SADF. Since 1986 the SAP also has its own secret expenditure account, monitored only by the Minister of Law and Order, similar to the special accounts for foreign affairs, national intelligence, and defence. There is little doubt that expenditure of this sort can be sustained, for in relative terms its magnitude is not excessive. In the 1985–86 financial year expenditure on the regular force represented 2.98 per cent of total government expenditure, a proportion which fell below that which existed throughout the 1960s. This proportion has oscillated but overall shows a downward trend from the financial year 1960–61 until 1980–81, since when it has risen by almost a third.

The SAP is also aided by the intelligence services. The SAP's Security Branch is independent from the National Intelligence Service (NIS) and the Military Intelligence Branch, although it works in close concert with them. The NIS co-ordinates the various security services outside the SAP, although there is said to be rivalry between them, with the NIS feeling that there is a need for only one security force independent of the SAP.[1] The intelligence services are very important but very little is known about them. Expenditure comes from a secret account, although the government does reveal expenditure on what it calls 'secret services'. In the 1985–86 financial year this amounted to R95 million, representing a 13.1 per cent increase over the previous year, which itself had shown a 25 per cent increase over 1983–84. However, this figure does not include total expenditure on the intelligence services. Nor are manpower levels divulged, but from what is revealed in court about the conduct of the various intelligence agencies, they operate an extensive network of informers, most of whom seem to be black, allowing them successfully to penetrate black organisations and take pre-emptive action against whomsoever they wish.

One of the forerunners of the NIS was the Bureau of State Security (BOSS), which had a much higher profile than the NIS currently has. This profile was the result of the regular public revelations concerning the conduct of BOSS, and its political prominence, itself partly the product of the close personal relationship between the then Prime Minister, John Vorster, and the head of BOSS, General Hendrik van den Bergh. One's impression is that the NIS is as heavily involved in policy issues as BOSS was, but in a much more low-key manner, with its role being concealed within the bureaucratic structure of the State Security Council (SSC).

A range of black forces also supplement the resources of the SAP. Homeland governments place considerable prestige on having their own police force and recognise the localised power this affords, although senior officers are occasionally seconded from the SAP. All the 'independent' homelands have developed their own police force under their control and some of the non-independent homelands have police and more *ad hoc* paramilitary forces under the direct responsibility of the local Chief Minister. The *Weekly Mail* wrote in September 1986 that a sixth non-independent homeland was about to form its own police force, estimating there to be between 18–20 000 policemen and women in the homelands, which excludes the 'independent' homelands. In KwaZulu the police have their own paramilitary section and Chief Mangosuthu Buthelezi doubles as his own Minister of Police. In 1987 the KwaZulu government was granted control over police stations in the homeland, along with which came the power to issue firearm certificates, which is a worrying development in view of the violence for which Buthelezi's supporters are often responsible. In ways such as these, Buthelezi shows how important the police are to him in KwaZulu. The KwaZulu government spent R5.4 million on policing in the 1983–84 financial year, representing 1 per cent of its total expenditure, but the South African government spent a further R20.62 million from central government funds. In the same financial year the central government gave R0.28 million from its funds to 'community development' in KwaZulu, thus spending nearly seventy-five times more on policing. After 'independence', Venda established its own force based on the shadowy paramilitary group known as the Venda National Force and during 1987 it became known that even the Bophuthatswana police have their own secret account. The Ciskei police have become notorious for their brutality in suppressing unrest in the homeland. Such forces are playing an increasingly prominent role. The 1984 Annual Report of the Commissioner of the SAP revealed that thirty-three policemen from Transkei, forty-one from KwaZulu and thirty-eight from Ciskei had undergone training with the SAP in counter insurgency and riot control. This is not only an attempt to prevent infiltration by guerrillas but reflects how unrest is beginning to occur in rural areas. Homeland police are therefore becoming more important both in the context of fighting local crime and in releasing the SAP to concentrate on urban areas.

In terms of non-political crime, the urban townships have always been under-policed. In 1984, for example, Mamelodi had one police station for an official population of 106 704, and the *Makgotla* (parliament) decided to give themselves a policing role, complaining of the SAP's inability to pursue ordinary crime. It is for this reason that residents in some townships have set up their own neighbourhood groups to defend law and order, as have some religious sects. Others also do so because they reject the civil police. The power to have their own police force was granted to thirty-two township authorities in December 1984. The Department of Information revealed that by October 1986, 1259 Municipal Law Enforcement Officers, as they are called, had graduated from the Lenz military base, where they are trained separately from the SAP. These numbers came nowhere near the expected 5000 which the government proudly boasted would be in service within the first six months of 1985. Statistics on manpower levels are, however, unreliable; the *Weekly Mail* reported in September 1986 that 6000 municipal officers were deployed around the country, with another 10 000 to be trained. The financing of this force is the responsibility of the local authority, although the government gave a grant of R24.6 million in 1985 to help. Soweto Council, the largest African authority, had 270 officers by 1985 and spent R1.7 million on security, which only partly included policing. The *Weekly Mail* mentioned a figure of 900 municipal officers in Soweto by September 1986. Lekoa Council, in the Vaal Triangle, currently spends R2.7 million per annum on security. Indeed, in order to attract police officers, Dobsonville and Alexandra councils offer salaries which are higher than those pertaining in the SAP.

The role of Municipal Law Enforcement Officers is an auxiliary one to the SAP. They are charged with protecting the lives of African councillors and guarding municipal installations and government buildings, thus freeing the SAP to concentrate on policing township unrest. But the forces are also required to support the SAP in maintaining law and order and preventing crime in the townships, and to assist the SAP in 'riotous conditions'. They also have the role of ensuring 'the implementation of council decisions', which can range from tracing outstanding library books and distributing council notices to pursuing residents for non-payment of township service charges. Duties of this sort encourage the portrayal of the force as a community service, as the Divisional Commissioner for Police in Soweto tried to suggest at the passing out parade of new recruits in October 1986, but the officers have become embroiled in the suppression of unrest as township protests have intensified. When objections from employers' federations led to the withdrawal of a proposal that employers should deduct township service charges from wages in order to counter the service charge boycott, Soweto's Municipal Law Enforcement Officers took to cutting off the electricity supply of residents participating in the boycott, resulting in the deaths of six people. In January 1987, Municipal Officers were also responsible for the deaths of three supporters of the United Democratic Front (UDF) in Tembisa. These incidents seem to confirm the allegations, made by international aid and monitoring organisations, that the municipal police have been as heavily involved in township violence as black members of the regular force.

In September 1986 the government announced the formation of yet another force to police the townships. This was partly out of a desire to enhance the public image of Municipal Officers by restricting their role to policing ordinary crime, as well as a recognition that the municipal forces have not expanded rapidly enough to enable them to do this, itself a product of their lack of legitimacy. Indeed, some municipal forces lost manpower as members resigned under fear for their lives as a result of attacks by radical opponents. The government does not provide statistics on the number of resignations from the municipal forces, but it is reputed to be high. However, one index of the pressure they are under is provided by the number of attacks they have been subject to. The State President revealed in Parliament that between 1984 and 1986, thirty-eight black policemen had been killed in the unrest, 600 injured and the homes and property of 910 destroyed.

In this context the government resurrected 'black special constables', who had first been deployed in 1976.[2] The later variety are colloquially known as *kitskonstabels* (instant constables) because they have only six weeks training, although they can be on the streets after three. They wear a distinctive blue overall rather than a uniform, which further reinforces their temporary and marginal image. The first cohort of 320 graduated from Koeberg training centre in October 1986, and many more are expected: the centre has capacity for 1000 trainees at a time. In March 1987 the Minister of Law and Order said in a parliamentary reply that 1750 *kitskonstabels* had been deployed and the target was 6000. Perhaps indicative of their intended role, the passing out parade of the first recruits was taken by the head of South Africa's Counter Insurgency Unit, Major General Wandrag, who explained that they would 'go on foot patrols to combat crime [and] violence perpetrated by leftist and radical elements'. Stretched in numbers as they are, the regular police find *kitskonstabels* useful reinforcements, although their inexperience makes them catalysts for further violence. In February 1987 three *kitskonstabels* appeared in court for killing four residents in an Eastern Cape township; they had been guarding a local school and shot wildly into surrounding houses when confronted by a crowd. The speed with which they were brought before magistrates suggests that *kitskonstabels*, like black members of the regular SAP generally, will not receive organisational support and loyalty in cases of misconduct, but will be used politically as a means of managing public disquiet over police methods.

THE ROLE OF THE POLICE IN POLITICS

It can be argued that all policing is political in that police forces are deployed by the state to facilitate stability and inhibit change.[3] In these terms, even when they are seen as neutrally upholding the constitutional order, police forces are entering politics. In South Africa's case, the constitutional order is so closely identified with the policies of a particular party that it is more difficult for the police to be seen as politically neutral. Even so, however, the conduct of the police does seem to show political partisanship, both in upholding the policies of the government and in resisting opposition thereto. There are three dimensions along which one can begin to assess this.

States typically deploy a combination of three strategies for order maintenance: accommodation, criminalisation and suppression.[4] The strategy of accommodation attempts, in some form or other, to meet the grievances of the group from which disorder emanates. On one level criminalisation involves the police treating public disorder as ordinary breaches of the law without regard to the political context in which the offences occur, but it can also be a much more ambitious strategy by extending the scope of criminal law to cover actions previously regarded as innocent of criminal intent. By this strategy the state avoids the necessity for using bannings and detentions. The hallmark of suppression is the state's recognition of the political character of the disorder, but it confronts this challenge to its authority by such means as repressive legislation and harsh tactics in quelling unrest. The police play a vital role in implementing such strategies and it is possible to explore the political role of the police along these three dimensions. In practice, the particular mix of these strategies varies both among states and within the same state over time, giving the police a variety of different political roles simultaneously. For example, as a result of the hesitant reform process, the use of all three strategies is now apparent in South Africa, extending the political role of the police.

The South African state is attempting to go part of the way in meeting some of the demands of black South Africans, although the form of accommodation it deploys rejects equality and integration in favour of policies of cultural pluralism designed to sponsor unequally what are assumed to be the separate special needs and interests of the respective racial and ethnic groups. The police can be passive actors in implementing or upholding this form of accommodation, such as when they facilitate the election of black local government and parliamentary candidates by protecting them from their critics, or enforce some of the 'deracialisation' measures, from the tearing down of notices unlawfully reimposing segregated park benches to policing multiracial facilities and events. However, the police can themselves be used by the state as a means of achieving accommodation, and it is in this respect that the police in South Africa play their greatest political role in the strategy of accommodation. For example, some attempts have been made to monitor the police's operation of some of South Africa's security laws in order to assuage the contempt black South Africans feel for the legislation, and for the same purpose guidelines have been adopted to govern the treatment of detainees by the police. But the controls are weak because they are not independent of the political bureaucracy, nor do they apply to all security laws and detainees and they can be suspended when a State of Emergency is promulgated. Far more effective moves towards accommodation have been made via police recruitment. In divided societies it matters a great deal who the police are, and the composition of the force is an important variable in the state's capacity to contain and regulate conflict. In South Africa in recent years the composition of the various forces has been used in a political manner to achieve a measure of accommodation. Consequently, while the police could make a positive contribution to the strategy of accommodation by the manner in which they conduct themselves, the role they actually play ends by being more negative.

The government now tries to ensure that blacks police their 'own' areas in an attempt to produce better compliance with and enforcement of the domestic laws of the country. This policy also reflects a recognition of the shortage of white manpower and the unfavourable publicity attracted by white officers brutalising black citizens. In this regard, black policemen play an important political role, for they allow part of the policing of apartheid to be carried out by the victims themselves and so counteract some of the criticisms of police methods. Hence the development of the separate homeland and township forces and the expansion in black membership of the regular SAP. In 1912 the ratio of black to white policemen and women was 1:3, but by 1984 there were many more blacks, with a ratio in the SAP of 1:1.07. This has also allowed black members of the SAP to be deployed in policing their 'own' areas. In 1984, forty-two SAP stations were staffed exclusively by Africans, eleven by coloureds, with another twelve planned, and two by Asians, with a further four planned.

The accompaniment of this has been an improvement in the promotion prospects of blacks in the SAP. For many years the SAP operated its own apartheid, but gradually this has been overcome to the extent that the SAP, like the SADF, is now presented as evidence of the state's commitment to 'deracialisation', providing another example of a political role for the police in the strategy of accommodation. The first black major was appointed in 1978, the first lieutenant colonel in 1980 and the first station commander in the same year. By 1983 there were 5198 black policemen at the level of sergeant or above, representing 25 per cent of all blacks in the force. There is still considerable inequality because the corresponding figure for whites was 57 per cent. But moves have been made in other areas of SAP organisation. In 1976, black officers were allowed to wear the same uniform as white officers, although black constables within the SAP did not obtain this dispensation until 1984. Blacks were allowed to join the SAP's Staff Association in 1979 and in 1980 black officers were given authority over lower ranking white policemen and women. Although recruits from the various population groups are still trained separately, all forms of discrimination in salary, pension rights and housing benefits were abolished in 1984.

At first sight it seems surprising that police forces are able to attract sufficient numbers of black South Africans who allow themselves to be used by the state in this political manner. The SAP has had little difficulty in finding black recruits (Mandela's brother-in-law is a policeman in the Transkei) and they are always able to reject a proportion of the applications they receive; in 1984 this was 21 per cent, more than one would expect. The volunteer Reserve Police Force cannot match this, with 18 per cent of its members in 1984 being black, which suggests that it is not public service which attracts blacks to the police. Black members of the regular force are relatively well paid and Frankel notes that as long as black unemployment remains high, the police will continue to be seen as a channel for mobility.[5] Unfortunately, the Annual Report of the Commissioner of the SAP does not provide an ethnic breakdown of black members of the force, although Frankel argued that because of the hostility of many black South Africans towards the police, their recruitment depends heavily on conservative rural Africans or insecure migrant workers rather than the more politically aware urban blacks.[6] In relation to *kitskonstabels*, Heribert Adam has noted a similar process, although with black unemployment being so affected by South Africa's current economic downturn he argued that *kitskonstabels* were also being recruited from the ranks of former comrades in the townships.[7]

Motivations which owe more to pay than public service or political ideology leave most black policemen and women with a more conditional loyalty to the police than their actions in quelling unrest suggest, and it is difficult to estimate how many could be relied on by the state in the midst of any revolutionary change. This seems especially the case with those blacks employed in forces outside the regular SAP, who lack the latter's more strict organisational and disciplinary ethos; in the first eighteen months of their operation there were three strikes within the ranks of Municipal Law Enforcement Officers. Even so, there are cases of former members of the SAP joining the African National Congress (ANC) to become guerrillas, and there are a few instances of serving policemen being accused of aiding the ANC, most notable being the case of two security policemen in 1986 who would have had access to sensitive information of value to the ANC. This is the corollary to the expansion of black recruits in the various police forces, for there are increased possibilities of informers working for black opposition groups.

A characteristic of the strategy of accommodation is that the political roles it grants the police are largely passive. There is a suspicion that the police have been more actively political in their policy of allowing blacks to police themselves by deploying them in such a way that tribal and ethnic tensions are deliberately manipulated to help control the urban areas.[8] However, in the other strategies there is firmer evidence to show that the police have more overt political roles. This is why Grundy claims that the various police forces are designed to destroy black opposition as much as to fight crime.[9] Some believe this to be the primary function of the SAP.[10] However, the police forces achieve this as much by a process of criminalisation as by a strategy of suppression.

Criminalisation is the process whereby legal and peaceful acts are criminalised in order for them to become the object of police action. This has a number of features. The first is extending the scope of the criminal law beyond direct manifestations of opposition to cover actions previously regarded as innocent of criminal intent. Clear examples of this are the 1982 Intimidation Act, which now makes it an offence to encourage someone to participate in collective action or industrial disputes, and the Demonstrations In Or Near Court Buildings Prohibition Act, which bans any form of activity in support of prisoners which occurs near court buildings. The 1985 State of Emergency promulgated a number of new offences punishable by a prison sentence of up to ten years. They include such innocuous acts as: verbally threatening harm to another person; preparing, printing, publishing or possessing a threatening document; hindering officers in the course of their duty; destroying or defacing any notice of the emergency regulations; disclosing the name or identity of anybody arrested under the regulations before their name has been officially confirmed; causing fear, panic and alarm or weakening public confidence; and advising people to stay away from work or to dislocate industry. While in detention, people were forbidden to sing or whistle, make unnecessary noise, cause unnecessary trouble or be a nuisance. Anybody committing these offences could be placed in solitary confinement, deprived of meals, and given six strokes if they were under 14 years of age. However, the most flagrant example of this feature of criminalisation is provided by the definitions of 'terrorism' and 'sabotage' in the 1982 Internal Security Act. These are so broad that under this guise the police can act against workers in industrial disputes, schoolchildren boycotting classes and participants in peaceful demonstrations.

Another form of criminalisation is affixing the label 'political' to action that is lawful in terms of the ordinary criminal law, in order for it to be portrayed as falling outside the realm of legitimate behaviour as the police see it. Describing a lawful act as being politically motivated gives the police the discretion of operating with a wider definition of illegitimate behaviour than the ordinary criminal law allows. Hence a number of acts have been criminalised in the sense that while they are still legal under ordinary criminal law, their political intent allows them either to be made the object of police action or to come within the ambit of emergency powers which suspend ordinary criminal law. This has affected such things as funeral processions, church services, carol singing, motorcades, the wearing of certain t-shirts and the formation of 'people's education' classes in the townships. In order to discover political intent, the police have infiltrated many lawful organisations. The Special Branch of the SAP and other intelligence organisations have in the past infiltrated the International University Exchange Fund (IUEF), the National Union of South African Students (NUSAS), and Inkatha. Some policemen have been murdered by crowds when their covert presence became known at funeral processions. A number of revelations in recent years have shown that security police have intercepted the mail of legitimate party politicians, ranging from Helen Suzman to members of the Herstigte Nationale Party (HNP), and have bugged the telephones of the HNP and its newspaper *Die Afrikaner*, and that of UDF patron Allan Boesak. It became known in 1986 that security police planned to infiltrate the South African Allied Workers' Union (SAAWU). It is criminalisation of this sort which also explains the 'dirty tricks' campaigns which the police have undertaken against prominent opponents of the regime who act legally in terms of the ordinary criminal law. Two colonels admitted in the Johannesburg *Star* in 1986 to running such campaigns, whereupon the Minister of Law and Order reported the paper to the Media Council, but the Council ruled in favour of the newspaper when the colonels repeated their admission that they had distributed misleading pamphlets and tape recordings about Allan Boesak.

Criminalisation can also involve an opposite process to the above, by treating political acts as simple breaches of law without regard to the political context in which the offences occur or their political content. This represents an attempt to delegitimise behaviour by preventing the perpetrators from claiming that political motivation makes otherwise illegal acts legitimate. A subtle form of this is the treatment of intra-black violence by the police as a form of 'mindless anarchy' rather than a struggle that is a function of a larger political conflict. A more obvious illustration is the frequent denial of political intent behind guerrilla attacks. The description of guerrillas as criminal elements becomes reinforced when the police are made primarily responsible for pursuing them. Initially it was the SAP who policed the border, and tours of duty in the operational areas were once the rule for all policemen under fifty years of age. The training of the SAP reflects this, for basic skills cover weapons knowledge, including instruction and familiarisation in the use of mortars and machine guns, and aspects of anti-vehicle and anti-personnel mine warfare. The police were given special powers within the border areas. The Police Amendment Act No. 70 of 1965 empowered any policeman or woman, at any place within a mile of the South African border, to search without warrant any person, premises, vehicle, aircraft or 'receptacle of any nature' and to seize anything found. Such has been the growth in the spread and intensity of political opposition that this power was extended to the whole country in 1983, and in 1985 the SAP was withdrawn from border duty to allow it to concentrate on the urban areas. This has not affected the treatment of ANC activists by the police; they are treated as mere criminals, thus maintaining the police's political contribution to the strategy of criminalisation.

The political role for which the police in South Africa are most notorious is that of suppression, where some forms of opposition to the state are crushed by the police with a forcefulness which is intended to deter further protest. There are two aspects to this role: the repressive powers granted to the police in legislation, and the harsh tactics they use. As noted above, the SAP has powers of arrest and search without warrant anywhere in the Republic. Section 49(2) of the 1977 Criminal Procedures Act allows the SAP (and others, including mines police and private company security guards) to use such force 'as may in the circumstances be necessary' to overcome resistance or stop a fleeing person. The killing of a person who cannot be arrested or stopped in flight by other means is deemed to be justifiable homicide. In 1984, ninety-eight people were killed in terms of this provision. The 1982 Internal Security Act gives officers in the SAP of the rank of lieutenant colonel or above the power to order preventive detention, detention of witnesses and for interrogation. Under the 1977 Criminal Procedures Act, the SAP has the power of short-term detention, being able to arrest and detain 'in specific situations of unrest', without good cause being shown, for a period of forty-eight hours. The new protections for detainees established in the Internal Security Act do not apply to the Criminal Procedures Act, whereas most detentions come within the terms of this act.

In a State of Emergency, the police are given further repressive powers. Under the regulations, any police officer, soldier or prison officer of any rank can arrest and detain without warrant. In the first State of Emergency during 1985 such detentions were restricted to fourteen days, unless extended further by the Minister of Law and Order, but this was lengthened to 180 days in the second State of Emergency. Police officers can use force 'resulting in death' if people refuse to heed instructions given in 'a loud voice'. The Commissioner of the SAP has the power to ban gatherings, close premises, control traffic, essential services and the dissemination and reporting of information, to seal off areas, remove people from particular places and impose curfews. Should these powers prove insufficient, the regulations allow the commissioner command over 'any other matter which, in the commissioner's opinion, affects the safety of members of the public or the maintenance of law and order'. These orders give the police powers to control every facet of resistance and organisational activity, even down to the issuing of statements and the placing of newspaper advertisements. All gatherings come within the terms of the regulations irrespective of their nature, venue or purpose. During the second State of Emergency, when the courts agreed that divisional police commissioners had unlawfully given unto themselves the same powers, the government redrew and back-dated the regulations to extend the definition of 'Commissioner of the SAP' to include divisional commissioners, even those deployed in 'independent' homelands.

Brutal police tactics are partly the result of the stereotypes of blacks which pervade the occupational culture of the SAP, presenting black South Africans as criminals and threats to the state.[11] However, they are also the product of legislative limits on the disclosure of police misconduct. The 1958 Police Act prevents the publication of 'untrue material' relating to police misconduct, with the onus of proof of the veracity of the material resting with the publisher. The Police Amendment Act No. 82 lays down that no person is allowed to publish information relating to the constitution, conditions, methods of deployment or movement of any force concerned with the prevention of terrorism, including the SAP. There are also statutes which prevent the publication of photographs or sketches of people in police custody, and which limit civil prosecutions arising from police misconduct. The State of Emergency suspended the few controls on police conduct provided by the Internal Security Act and the 1960 Childrens Act, which protects the rights of children under 16 years of age. This latter suspension was important because 22 per cent of the 18 966 people detained for 'unrest offences' in 1985 were under sixteen years of age (72 per cent were under twenty-one years of age and hence were juveniles in terms of the 1959 Prisons Act). There was widespread mistreatment and torture of minors, among others. Moreover, the State of Emergency gives all members of the police force, security force and prisons service indemnity from civil and criminal prosecutions, so long as they 'act in good faith'. They are deemed to be acting so when under the 'orders, direction, command and instructions' of superior officers. The SAP has a reputation for violence and brutality even without indemnity. For example, between 1976 and 1985 the SAP alone killed or wounded 9771 people in the course of their duty and paid compensation of R8.25 million for assault, wrongful arrest and injury. But along with indemnity came an increase in the number of deaths and injuries: 32 per cent of the deaths and woundings in this nine-year period occurred in 1985 when the first State of Emergency operated for part of the year. The first month of the 1985 State of Emergency saw a death toll double that of the previous month, most of the increase resulting from action by the security forces, and the South African Institute of Race Relations (SAIRR) estimated that 50 per cent of the 879 deaths due to unrest in 1985 were the responsibility of the security forces.

This suppression has to be seen in the context of the arms policemen and women carry. All members of the SAP, irrespective of race and gender, carry a side arm and are issued with a R1 semi-automatic rifle. The rifle is kept in a strongroom at the station and never taken home, although the side arm can be, with permission. In 'riotous circumstances' they can also be issued with submachine guns and shotguns. Live bullets seem to be an essential part of the riot control equipment which the police are empowered to use, but they also deploy birdshot, water cannon, rubber bullets, sneeze machines and, since 1986, four helicopters, from which firing has been reported. During 1985, an extra R42.7 million was given to the SAP to replenish 'stores and equipment' depleted by the unrest; the SADF got an extra R288 million, which is indicative of how involved they became in policing the townships.

The frequent government statements which defend officers against criticism of their misconduct, despite instructions to them to use minimum force, add up to a situation where harsh police tactics seem to be politically endorsed by the state. The unwillingness of government commissions and courts of enquiry into specific incidents to apportion blame to the police, despite the criticisms sometimes made, further reinforces this. A good example of this endorsement is provided by the case of the missing identification tags. To evade the complaints procedure which members of the public can initiate against the security forces, an increasing number of security personnel patrol the townships without identification. In response to a parliamentary question, the Minister of Law and Order estimated this to be 20 per cent of all security force personnel in March 1986. But, after a lengthy departmental enquiry, he claimed it to be simply the result of the failure of suppliers to provide enough identification tags. This was after a judge had described those who patrolled in this way as inept, hamfisted and threatening.

Another tactic the police use to evade the complaints procedure is to employ surrogates, such as vigilantes, who have even less hesitation in using brutal tactics to suppress political opposition. Vigilante groups are not a new feature of South African politics. Zulu migrant workers were deployed by the police to attack students in 1976 and vigilantes were used by rival political organisations against one another in the 1950s, as well as being deployed by the police. But current groups, such as 'The A-Team', 'Phakathis' and 'Ama Africa Poqo', sometimes wearing white armbands to distinguish colleagues in the *melee*, have become more prominent as the level of political violence for which some of them are responsible has escalated. However, because of the emergency regulations, it is extremely difficult to assess the upsurge of vigilante violence and the relationship between vigilantes and the police. As far as it is possible to tell, there are six types of vigilante: those created by communities as alternative sources of law and order because they reject, or fail to get sufficient protection from, the police; Asian and coloured vigilantes who protect their communities from attacks by Africans; those established by the African local councils to act as their personal forces; those connected with homeland governments; groups dominated by political organisations, such as Inkatha and the Afrikaner Weerstandsbeweging (AWB); and, finally, those directly sponsored by the security forces.

Not all types of vigilante engage in violence or work with the police, but the police appear to play three roles. First, many policemen and women from the township and homeland forces are active members of vigilante groups. *Kitskonstabels* and Municipal Officers are suspected of heavy involvement in the vigilante groups established by the local councils. One group in Tumahole, which was responsible for whipping people found on the streets after the 9.00 pm curfew and for beating children who were late for school, is reputed to have at its core a black policewoman and her family and friends. Second, some police forces have supported vigilante groups in their attacks on opponents of the state. In May 1986 conservative vigilantes known as 'the fathers' launched an attack on the satellite settlements that comprise Crossroads to drive out radical black youths who opposed the move to Khayelitsha. It was widely alleged that the police had assisted the vigilantes, although this was denied by the authorities. Another group calling itself the *witdoeke* is alleged to have aided the police and army in removing the squatters once resistance had been overcome. In December 1986, members of the radical Congress of South African Trade Unions (COSATU) were set upon by vigilante groups associated with Inkatha and by members of the KwaZulu police, leaving thirty-nine people dead in a week of violence. Vigilantes connected with Inkatha have been seen being driven to townships in police transporters. The third role of the police is allegedly, in conjunction with other security forces, directly to sponsor and establish vigilante groups to work on their behalf, particularly to attack the neighbourhood and street committees lawfully established by radical resistance organisations as an alternative local government. Some of the vigilante groups have set up grassroot political structures to rival those they attack, and the International Defence and Aid Fund has alleged that some *kitskonstabels* are taking a leading role on these more conservative committees.

THE POLITICISATION OF POLICING

The multifarious political roles played by the police are becoming increasingly important to the state as the challenge to its authority intensifies. A related consideration is the growing politicisation of policing in South Africa. This has two features. First, the state is beginning to give the SAP a direct input into political decision making, and, second, policing is becoming a prominent issue in political debate.

The SAP's input into political decision making has come with the emergence of what Grundy[12] calls the 'security establishment', where decision making is centralised around a managerial committee system which has co-opted, among others, top military and security personnel, including the SAP. At the centre is the State Security Council (SSC). It is supposed to oversee security matters and to this end the heads of the SADF, SAP, NIS, Prisons Service and 'other military and police personnel' sit on the committee. A variety of government ministers have been co-opted, illustrating the ministries which are felt to touch security matters. These include the ministers of Law and Order, Defence, Foreign Affairs, Justice, Constitutional Development and Planning, and Co-operation and Development, the latter two dealing with urban black affairs. The SSC is serviced by a secretariat, which is also dominated by military and police personnel. In March 1986 there were thirteen interdepartmental working committees to assist the SSC, consisting mainly of politicians, civil servants and representatives of the military and security forces.

The SSC has become one of the major decision-making forums within the government, with some commentators claiming it to be more important than the cabinet. It increasingly involves itself in a wide spectrum of issues beyond security, including foreign policy, economic matters and constitutional change.[13] The interdepartmental committees give advice to the SSC on such questions as security force manpower, cultural matters, civil defence, transport, national supplies and resources, telecommunications, community services, the economy and political affairs.

Allegations have been made that the SSC has involved itself in specific political issues, ranging from particular industrial disputes to land redistribution between KwaZulu and Swaziland. The States of Emergency were said to have been imposed on the recommendation of the committee against the advice of some leading members of the cabinet. Therefore, in as much as the SSC has a decision-making role and the SAP is a member of that committee, the SAP has a direct input into decision making. In this context, it is significant that upon retiring as Commissioner of the SAP in 1987, General P.J. Coetzee was given a post in the Department of Foreign Affairs, to oversee difficulties in relations between Transkei and Ciskei.

Another component of the 'security establishment' is the system of Joint Management Committees (JMCs), which co-ordinate security at local and regional levels. They are also assuming a political role, giving the local representatives of the military and police who sit on them an input into community politics. These committees work under the overall direction of the SSC, which also funds them. By March 1986 the SSC had established twelve JMCs covering the large conurbations, another sixty working in smaller towns and a further number operating at the level of local authorities. The names of 348 of these were listed in the South African press in October 1986. They have no executive power, but are primarily deployed to ensure the co-ordination of government security policy at local and regional levels and to act as an early warning system to identify areas of unrest. They report on these matters to the secretariat of the SSC. Membership comprises local representatives of the military and SAP, as well as civil servants and members of the business community. Each JMC has its own chairperson, which in every case happens to be a member of the SAP or SADF, but little else is publicly revealed, so that it is difficult to identify membership or assess the relative weighting of the police and army on the committees.

The JMCs have been especially involved in overseeing the co-operation of the SADF and police in instances of joint action. Since 1984, the SADF have become heavily involved in policing the townships, with 35 372 army personnel acting in support of the police in civil matters during 1985. The 1957 Defence Act was even amended to enshrine the SADF's role in civil unrest, giving it conventional policing duties of promoting internal security, maintaining law and order and preventing crime. The SADF has the same powers under the State of Emergency as the civil police, including indemnity. To accomplish these duties, army personnel are given 'between three and four days training' in patrolling townships, covering riot control techniques, roadblocks, vehicle and foot patrol, 'immediate action drill', and searches. Co-operation between the SADF and SAP was departmentally institutionalised in 1985 when the deputy Minister of Defence also became the deputy in the Ministry of Law and Order, subsequently going on to become Minister of Law and Order. Although the army and police maintain their separate command structures while on joint operations, security policy itself is co-ordinated by the JMCs. Some JMCs, however, have taken political decisions regarding local unrest, such as the decision by the Cape Town JMC to initiate a strategy to counter the influence of a residents' association in the Atlantis township. In August 1986, the press in South Africa published a document which showed that the JMC in Johannesburg had decided to break the service charge boycott in the townships of the Vaal Triangle. The plans included the formation of local 'collective action groups', composed of police and government officials, which would enforce the collection of rents and the eviction of non-paying tenants. It was also seeking employers who would be prepared to deduct service charges directly from the wages of employees, an idea subsequently withdrawn by the government and then reintroduced. The JMC also took the decision to institute a system of weekend camps in an attempt to win 'the hearts and minds' of the young and to recruit them to persuade their parents to abandon the boycott. Documents were leaked to the press which also showed that some local JMCs had instructed black township authorities not to negotiate an end to the boycott with 'radical organisations'. As a result of actions like this, the SAP, through its membership of the JMCs, is having an input into political decision making at the community level.

Along with the heightening of the political profile of the police, the issue of policing has become a prominent feature of political debate. Given that political discourse is dominated by the varying attitudes towards reform and change, the issue of policing is naturally placed in this context and has become one of several important litmus tests of the state's commitment to reform. Liberal Afrikaans and English language newspapers comment critically on policing when it threatens the reformist policies of the state. Most black South Africans infer from the way in which the police conduct themselves that the state is not seriously committed to change, so that policing affects black attitudes to the whole process of reform. Paradoxically, the Afrikaans right wing applies the same test, but the inference it draws is that the government is giving too much too rapidly and is, in the process, hindering the police in the maintenance of law and order. Traditionally, the mode of political representation for the police has been through the National Party, but the formation of the more reactionary Conservative Party has intensified the political competition to speak for the police, pushing policing further into the political arena. The Conservative Party tends to feel that police conduct is justifiable given the threat to law and order which black unrest poses. It defends the police against criticism from wherever it emanates, even endorsing the mistreatment of minors on the grounds that no police force should tolerate being humiliated and goaded by children. Casper Uys told the white Parliament in March 1985 that South Africa owed a debt of gratitude to the police, who were simultaneously being pilloried in the eyes of the world and undermined by *verligte* corners of the government. In by-elections in October 1985, a National Party poster ran 'Don't shoot. Think'; the Herstigte Nasionale Party reversed this to 'Shoot. Don't think', while the leader of the Conservative Party argued that the security forces should be 'unleashed', portraying government security policy as the cause of continued unrest. By intensifying the political debate on policing in this way, the Afrikaans right wing has created a situation in which, for the first time, the political loyalty of the police to the National Party cannot be guaranteed, although their commitment to a system of white political supremacy remains unshaken.

With the Afrikanerisation of the SAP that occurred with the National Party's electoral victory in 1948, white policemen and women in the regular force are almost entirely Afrikaans. The police have low status and reward, so much so that they attract mainly working-class Afrikaners, many with an insular rural background.[14] By nature, therefore, most white members of the SAP tend to be loyal to Afrikaner hegemony, of which support for Afrikaans political parties is a component. Since the government made it possible for members of the English-speaking community to serve three years with the SAP instead of two years national service on the border, their numbers in the force have increased, but Leach reports that they tend to get sent to the larger cities, leaving the poorly educated Afrikaners to police the townships and rural areas like the Eastern Cape.[15] If this is correct, those white officers who police unrest tend to be loyal to the political interests of Afrikaners. However, there is now a strong suspicion that many have narrowed their loyalties to the Conservative Party. Helen Suzman has made this allegation in Parliament and the Conservative Party believes it to be the case, although the Minister of Law and Order has issued strong denials. However, Adam[16] argues that right wing sentiments are widespread within the police, and P.W. Botha has been reported as believing that nearly two-thirds of white members of the SAP support the Conservative Party against his reform policy. The evidence for this is circumstantial but it does build up to a convincing case. First, lower echelons of the SAP tend to come from that part of the Afrikaans social structure most threatened by the reforms implemented by the National Party and from which the Conservative Party draws its electoral support. This explains why some former policemen came out of retirement to stand as candidates for the Conservative Party in the 1987 general election. Second, if the experience of Northern Ireland is applicable, the contradictory position in which the police have been left as a result of government reforms will create a sense of alienation among some ordinary members of the SAP, feeling that they can no longer call upon the same unthinking loyalty from the state as before or act with the same lack of restraint. If this alienation exists, it is likely to increase police support for the more right-wing parties, such as the Conservative Party, who urge stronger support for and greater understanding of the problems of the SAP. However, the State of Emergency has probably allayed this feeling of alienation, but, likewise, considerations of this sort act as a powerful constraint against its abandonment.

Finally, there are incidents which show that the police have failed to act against right-wing extremists or have done so only after considerable delay. In April 1985, around one thousand members of the AWB marched on Pretoria Central Police Station to deliver 'a message of gratitude' to the police for their efforts in maintaining law and order. The march was illegal and could have led to prosecutions under the Internal Security Act, but the police failed to take any action, yet similar occurrences are dealt with severely if they involve blacks. A meeting in May 1986 which would have been addressed by Pik Botha was broken up by AWB members. Amidst wild chanting and considerable fighting, the AWB took over the meeting, whereupon its leader, Eugene Terre'Blanche, who is himself an ex-policeman, delivered a speech attacking the government's reform policies. The local police refused to protect the meeting and a special squad from outside had to be brought in, using teargas to clear the hall. Nor did the police prevent the AWB from holding an illegal gathering in a nearby rugby stadium to continue the speeches attacking the government. The pro-government Afrikaans-language newspaper *Rapport* was shocked at the conduct of the police, asking the police authorities 'to ensure that the actions of its men do not in the least create the impression of partiality', and a cabinet colleague of Pik Botha publicly criticised the local police division. Shortly after this incident, the deputy Minister for Law and Order confirmed in Parliament that members of police forces and reservists could belong to any political organisation as long as it was not radical, specifically identifying that this precluded membership of the AWB, although many AWB members serve in auxiliary commando units and therefore liaise with the police. It is symptomatic of the political divisions within the SAP that some attempts by AWB members to break up National Party meetings are met with a vigorous police response and court appearances. However, such are the political differences among Afrikaners, that some AWB members have faced magistrates who treated their offences quite leniently.

In this way, the politicisation of policing in white politics is likely to intensify as divisions between Afrikaans political parties increase, although it will be in an entirely different direction to the politicisation resulting from black opposition to apartheid. The right and left of South Africa's political spectrum place policing in the context of a wider debate about reform, and the politicisation that occurs is determined by their differing opinions of the changes being introduced by the government.

CONCLUSION

In his 1985 Annual Report, the Commissioner of the SAP felt the need to remind the public that the creed of the SAP was 'we protect, we serve'. The preceding arguments have attempted to demonstrate the complex variety of ways in which the police are politically partisan, and to show that they are so to such an extent that they neither protect nor serve those three-quarters of South Africa's citizens who are black.

STATISTICAL APPENDIX

Table 8.2 Expenditure on SAP 1960–86

Financial year	*Expenditure on regular SAP (Rm)*	*% of total state expenditure*
1960–61	36,854	4.03
1961–62	38,396	3.91
1962–63	40,800	3.75
1963–64	45,478	3.76
1964–65	49,192	3.24
1965–66	56,358	3.42
1966–67	58,697	3.17
1967–68	66,950	3.22
1968–69	72,130	3.18
1969–70	85,590	3.16
1970–71	94,288	2.74
1971–72	104,422	2.78
1972–73	111,993	2.74
1973–74	118,980	2.87
1974–75	153,127	2.81
1975–76	168,027	2.36
1976–77	176,900	2.13
1977–78	204,000	2.33
1978–79	220,450	2.19
1979–80	245,247	2.07
1980–81	309,765	2.33
1981–82	—	—
1982–83	—	—
1983–84	564,282	2.47
1984–85	795,640	3.00
1985–86	954,700	2.98

Notes: Figures for SAP expenditure are taken from the Auditor General's Annual Statement of Accounts. Statistics on total government expenditure can be found in *International Financial Statistics*.

Table 8.3 Regular SAP manpower 1960–86

Year	*Regular SAP manpower*
1960	25,724
1961	–
1962	26,631
1963	27,443
1964	28,340
1965	28,758
1966	29,493
1967	31,126
1968	31,753
1969	31,908
1970	31,877
1971	32,099
1972	32,281
1973	31,588
1974	32,575
1975	33,082
1976	34,437
1977	35,019
1978	34,965
1979	34,076
1980	34,214
1981	34,271
1982	42,426
1983	42,740
1984	44,696
1985	–
1986	55,000

Source: Taken from the Annual Reports of the Commissioner of the South African Police, with the exception of 1986 which is from a parliamentary reply given by the Minister of Law and Order.

NOTES

1. P. Frankel, 'South Africa: the Politics of Police Control', *Comparative Politics*, vol. 12, no. 4, 1979, pp. 486–7.
2. K. Grundy, *Soldiers Without Politics: Blacks in the South African Armed Forces* (Berkeley: University of California Press), 1983, pp. 147–8.
3. See D. Bayley, 'The Police and Political Change in Comparative Perspective' *Law and Society Review*, vol. 6 (August), 1971, and A. Turk, 'Policing in Political Context' in R. Donelan, *The Maintenance of Order in Society* (Ottawa: Canadian Police College, 1982).
4. J. Brewer, A. Guelke, I. Hume, E. Moxon-Browne and R. Wilford, *Police, Public Order and the State* (London: Macmillan, 1988).
5. P. Frankel, op. cit. note 1 above, p. 489. See also K. Grundy, op. cit. note 2 above, p. 143.
6. P. Frankel, op. cit. note 1 above, p. 489.
7. H. Adam, personal communication, 1987.
8. P. Frankel, op. cit. note 1 above, pp. 485–6.
9. K. Grundy, op. cit. note 2 above, p. 147.
10. P. Frankel, op. cit. note 1 above, p. 490.
11. See P. Frankel, op. cit. note 1 above, pp. 486 and 492, and K. Grundy, op. cit. note 2 above, p. 143.
12. K. Grundy, 'The Rise of the South African Security Establishment', Bradlow Paper No. 1, South African Institute of International Affairs.
13. Ibid., p. 14.
14. See P. Frankel, op. cit. note 1 above, p. 486, and K. Grundy, *Soldiers Without Politics*, op. cit. note 2 above, p. 143.
15. G. Leach, *South Africa* (London: Methuen, 1986), p. 177.
16. H. Adam, 'The ultra right in South Africa', *Optima*, vol. 35, no. 1, 1987.

9 Disinvestment and the South African 'Siege Economy': A Business Perspective

Christopher Coker

INTRODUCTION

Most exercises in prediction or futurology, however much grounded on economic fact, nearly always fall short of reality. As Italo Calvino remarked in one of his lesser known novels, 'The art of writing tales', which is what scenario building is about, 'consists in an ability to draw the rest of life from the little one has understood of it.' Most political scientists as a result are seen by many of those they write about – the business community for one – as an enclosed order, an obsessive caste, whose pre-occupations are peculiarly their own; a caste which either avoids contact with the outside world, or which cannot understand it; a group, in short, which has little capacity to observe the society it is meant to serve.

In this chapter I intend to restrict my perspective to the immediate future, to the mid-1990s and not beyond that. I do not intend to address the possibility of sanctions against the South African government on the scale of a total trade embargo, particularly of oil, with all this would entail in terms of unemployment, economic dislocation and political chaos. My departure point will be the 'siege psychosis' of white South Africa which created, in the past ten years, the conditions for disinvestment long before foreign companies were forced to consider the political implications of their presence.

The 'siege economy' I will look at will be an economy starved of foreign capital and inter-bank loans, not one besieged by sanctions. It will be an economy which will need to dismantle the large public sector corporations which were established in the 1960s to protect the Republic from possible international pressure; as well as the post-1978 programme of 'reforms' which was a belated attempt to defuse the threat of internal 'sanctions' (Johan Galtung's description for civil disobedience, industrial unrest and all the other measures which non-state actors can use against a state).

THE SOUTH AFRICAN ECONOMY

Economically, South Africa has suffered two severe blows since 1984, the first concerning international perceptions of its strategic importance, and the second concerning the day-to-day risk assessments of companies that have played a major part in the phenomenon of disinvestment.

The South African economy is heavily reliant on the sale of gold, platinum and diamonds, which at present pay for all but R4 billion of its imports (up to 70 per cent). It is also a major mineral producer. South Africa ranks about eighth in terms of world production of iron-ore. With regard to iron and steel products, in 1985 it exported one-third of its local production. Were sanctions to be applied world-wide, at least three major development regions (Sishen, Witbank/Middelburg and Newcastle) would be adversely affected. In addition, desperate measures are being taken to protect the vital Japanese market for coal if Europe should be lost. South Africa's major oil companies distribute at least 40 per cent of its coal exports. Plans for new mines are being shelved as anxiety about the future grows.

It is nevertheless important to see the South African economy in an international perspective. Perhaps the only legacy of the Reagan administration's ill-fated policy of 'constructive engagement' has been the strategic downgrading of the South African economy in US thinking. In an attempt to 'sell' constructive engagement on its own merits, the administration refused to over-emphasise or exaggerate the West's dependence on South African minerals. In so doing, it challenged the illusions of a whole generation of scholars who had taken for granted the fact that the West was highly vulnerable to a minerals embargo. It reminded us that we live in a world where vulnerability is a comparative term determined not by availability or easy access, but by cost-effectiveness. Such thinking was reflected in the report of the President's Foreign Policy Advisory Committee on South Africa; a report little noticed in Europe, which, while recognising the importance of specific mineral imports from South Africa, refused to accept that the difficulties resulting from counter-sanctions or a breakdown in the South African economy should influence, let alone determine, US policy.

Indeed, the only recent report to have reached an opposing conclusion was produced in July 1985 by an inter-agency task force representing the departments of Commerce and Defense. Even then, this report took on a different light when its recommendations were considered as a whole: they comprised a clear exhortation to the private sector to change its demands, and on the government to press ahead with recycling, substitution and stockpiling to reduce the United States' vulnerability by the mid-1990s, if not before.

The Congressional Office of Technology Assessment (OTA) published a study in the same year suggesting that the term 'strategic' had frequently been misused, and that at best it applied to specific industries or programmes (such as the space shuttle), and not necessarily to the economy as a whole. The OTA concluded that the West should develop new resources outside southern Africa, decrease industrial demand by improving manufacturing processes and identify substitute materials where the content of product manufacturing permitted. The idea that new technologies of the future will be less 'material intensive' has largely informed the President's proposal to trim the national raw material stockpile by $10 billion.

These developments suggest that, as the South African Chamber of Mines commented in 1986, South Africa itself is much more vulnerable to an embargo of mineral exports than the West is to counter-sanctions. The concept of vulnerability – in a word – no longer seems able to bear the weight that South Africa has traditionally assigned to it.

Economically, South Africa has been under 'siege' for fifteen years, perhaps longer, as a consequence of the government's own actions. The fiscal and monetary solutions which sustained economic growth in earlier years proved unable, after the mid-1970s, to arrest the country's long-term economic decline, or to satisfy even the basic expectations of black workers. In that sense, the political struggle has involved minor, if important, semantic skirmishes: is the reform programme significant or not; is it an example of twelfth-hour action; is it too little too late? For many businessmen these questions should have been thrust aside by the economic crisis through which the country has passed in the last ten years, and to which the reform programme has offered no solution.

Between 1973 and 1984 the South African economy grew at a real rate of only 0.5 per cent a year, a strikingly depressing performance compared with neighbouring countries such as Botswana (5 per cent), Lesotho (4 per cent), or even Malawi (1 per cent), though these countries started from a much lower point. Only once since 1980 has the Republic's GDP grown by more than 5 per cent (the minimum required to keep a ceiling on its dismally high unemployment figures – to absorb the 300 000 new workers coming on to the labour market every year). Because of the recession, rationalisation measures and alleged government mismanagement of the economy, 200 000 workers in the manufacturing sector have lost their jobs since 1983. Jobs in the steel and engineering sector have shrunk by 100 000 since the early 1980s. A further 40 000 workers in the motor manufacturing plants lost their jobs in 1986.

For the last seven years in succession, manufacturing output has grown by only 2 per cent a year. Inflation has been in double digit figures since 1973 and shows no immediate signs of coming down in line with the low inflation rates of the rest of the industrial world.

South Africa has been a classic example of a system that cannot 'deliver', that cannot generate wealth quickly enough to meet the basic expectations of its workforce. It is a better than classic example, perhaps, since it is an economic anachronism. With every major increase in unemployment, the Republic seems to explode into political violence. It did so in 1960 and again in 1976. With 40 per cent of the black population permanently unemployed it is hardly surprising that history should have repeated itself, this time more forcefully, in the unrest in the townships which broke out in September 1984. There, increases in rents and services could not have come at a worse moment: in real terms, the wages of non-agricultural labour had fallen by 4.4 per cent.

The lack of growth in employment has been potentially the most disappointing factor of all, as well as the most significant politically. The annual increase in wage earning employment has averaged only 0.6 per cent since 1980, compared with an averge growth in the population of 2.5 per cent. Indeed, as the annual increase in employment has lagged behind that of the population for the past thirty-five years, the percentage of blacks in wage-earning employment has actually declined. In five of the most important production sectors, the number of paid employees was lower in 1985 than in 1980, a fact which had nothing to do with mechanisation, or increased productivity, but which was a result of the market's failure to train labour. Even in the 1960–70 period, which experienced a high growth rate of 5.9 per cent a year, the relative position of blacks in wage-earning employment deteriorated considerably when compared with the other population groups.

There is no apparent end to this problem; indeed it is likely to get far worse. At present the shortage of skilled labour stands at 21 per cent with projected estimates suggesting that there will be shortages of almost 1.5 million white collar workers in addition to approximately three quarters of a million more in skilled and semi-skilled jobs by 1995.

In short, even without the 1984–86 'insurrectionary' crisis, the banking community would eventually have come around to qualifying its commitment to the country. Citibank imposed a credit ceiling in 1976. Barclays reduced its holding in its South African subsidiary in 1975 even after the Franzen Commission had been persuaded to drop its recommendation to reduce foreign holdings in the banking sector to 10 per cent.

Nor were the banks especially impressed by P.W. Botha's package of reforms. For one thing, they never believed that South Africa could afford them. Over the years they have increasingly lost faith – not only in the government's ability to 'reform' South Africa out of a revolution, but also in its capacity to handle the economy. Not only did Pretoria fail to lead the country out of a recession, it even failed to sustain its recovery. This was particularly true during the 'mini-boom' of 1983–84. Then, instead of boosting investor confidence, the government borrowed on a massive scale to finance its reform package – its ultimate guarantee against retreating into the *laager* at home; and to develop the public sector – its ultimate defence against sanctions. All it succeeded in doing, however, was to stimulate inflation, with the result that investment failed to rise as predicted. Scepticism about future profitability made the business community excessively cautious – willing at most to bring under-utilised capacity back on stream.

The subsequent rise in imports was not stimulated, as in earlier booms, by new investment in machinery and equipment, but by higher imports of consumer durables. By lending to the government without any thought to the future, the banks actually contributed to this period of wasted opportunities. The experience has convinced them that the government can no longer sustain cyclical upswings, as in the past, by remedial monetarist measures.

The 'reform' programme was unpopular with many bankers, not because it offered too little too late, but because it offered too much too quickly: because the government was forced to combine a tough fiscal policy, which added to the relative deprivation of the black community (in the form of increased service charges and rents), with high government spending (at one time as high as 27 per cent of GDP).

Both measures were highly inflationary. As if this were not enough, Pretoria chose to fund its budget deficit not by printing more money but by increasing interest rates, over-borrowing abroad and increasing company tax by an effective rate of 15 per cent.

If the government cannot *afford* the reforms, there seems little point in investing much time in arguing in support of, or in opposition to, the programme. Before arguing what the government should be doing, it would seem more important to ask what purpose, if any, is likely to be served by what it is doing already.

This is the background against which the country's present drift towards a siege economy must be seen. It is a drift from a very weak economic performance, not a strong one, which suggests that the transition may be less traumatic for the business community (if not for the population at large) than some observers predict. In some specific respects it may even be salutary, at least in the short-term, injecting an element of efficiency and sound management of which the economy has long been in need.

STRUCTURAL DISINVESTMENT

Compared with the very serious problems of limited capital, disinvestment has not been the disaster for the South African government which the anti-apartheid movement hoped for. Most companies have not been able simply to pull out overnight. In many cases they have chosen to sell their holdings, frequently to their previous managers, for a fraction of the market value. In some cases, as with General Motors, even US managers have joined in.

On other occasions disinvestment has prevented a net capital drain. In November 1986 Anglo American purchased (albeit reluctantly) South Africa's largest bank, Barclays National, from its British parent, thus saving South Africa $14 million in foreign dividend payments a year. Over the years, disinvestment has been a vital factor in encouraging the growth of an indigenous industrial base, notably in electronics. ITT's decision to sell out in 1976 enabled local businessmen to build up the $650 million Allied Electronics Corporation (Altron), the first major South African-owned electronics company.

Free from restraints imposed by IBM, its former parent, the new Information Management Services (IMS) still markets IBM mainframe computers, and will doubtless continue to do so until its debt to IBM has been repaid. Disinvestment has not prevented IBM or Honeywell from operating a profitable sales and service operation, which makes their much publicised decision to disinvest seem little more than sleight of hand.

Disinvestment has also proved useful to the South African state in a more profound sense, forcing a top-heavy economy to rationalise its procedures. 'Structural disinvestment' has been largely economically motivated. It has benefited both the South African economy and foreign business. Long before the entrenchment of the present political crisis, Pretoria found itself on the horns of a dilemma. It could have attempted to reduce its balance of payments deficit either by export led growth, or by reducing imports at the risk of pushing the economy even further into recession. That the deficit had to be cut was the only point on which the government was in full agreement; internationally, the country was spending far more than it earned by over-borrowing from the banks at unusually high rates of interest.

Export-led recovery would not have overcome two basic obstacles. It would have been massively inflationary, drastically increasing import costs even if a falling rand had succeeded in stimulating exports. It might also have been short-lived, possibly both, with increases in productivity falling well behind the rate of inflation. Export led growth would not have reduced interest rates substantially. High interest rates did at least keep foreign capital in the country. If they had fallen too quickly, some multinationals might have moved elsewhere.

In the end, therefore, it was perhaps not surprising that the government chose to reduce the balance-of-payments deficit by pushing the economy into a recession. The effect was not great enough to change the economy's adverse debt profile, but it was sufficient to reduce the profitability of the market for many foreign corporations in a number of sectors, of which the car industry was perhaps more adversely affected than most.

The government's measures boosted interest rates which in turn reduced consumer spending, an economically necessary and even possibly overdue course of action given the fact that private consumers had been over-borrowing for years to finance high rates of consumption. In applying a ceiling to available credit, however, the state forced many companies to reduce production, especially on the large capital expansion programmes of which the motor industry was in urgent need. Foreign automobile companies were hit especially severely since they found themselves in a highly competitive market.

The combination of lower sales, higher foreign exchange losses, lower operating profits and higher interest rates had already taken its toll. In January 1985 Ford was forced to merge its operations with South Africa's third largest domestic producer, a subsidiary of Anglo American, simply in the expectation of retaining its existing market share (25 per cent). This still left eleven motor manufacturers and seventeen truck producers (including such giants as General Motors, which was shortly to disinvest, Toyota, Nissan and BMW) which had all incurred a loss in a market which was marginal to their international operations.

Chrysler took little persuading to sell out in 1983. General Motors stood out as long as it could but the writing was clearly on the wall when it was forced to send all its employees on a seven-week 'vacation' in 1985. For three consecutive years, 50 per cent of all the motor industry's production capacity lay idle.

The structural disinvestment which has taken place helped turn the situation around to the point where, in 1987, the car industry attained significant profitability. Disinvestment enabled the companies that chose to remain to adjust to the reality of far lower production rates than hoped for some years ago, with a vehicle market in which production was 37 per cent down on the peak year of 1982. Toyota benefited most of all, with profit margins which rose by 75 per cent. Although price increases have played a part, the fact that margins widened so significantly in a year in which the rand slumped against both the yen and the dollar would seem to indicate much greater efficiency than hitherto.

CAN THE SOUTH AFRICAN ECONOMY FUND ITSELF?

Although South Africa has repaid \$2.3 billion, it has barely dented its foreign debt burden. At the exchange rate of Summer 1986 the total debt stood at \$23.2 billion, almost as much as the \$23.7 billion debt which was identified when the debt moratorium was first declared. The principal has remained largely the same.

South Africa will therefore continue to face a serious debt problem for many years to come, a fact which is unlikely to be influenced by any move towards a siege economy. Indeed, in a study produced by the Federated Chamber of Industries (FCI) in 1986, it was claimed that even if a full sanctions package were to be implemented over a period of five years, South Africa would merely reschedule its debt, not renege on it entirely. This is particularly likely to be the case now that it is clear that the extent of the country's non-dollar denominated currencies was originally seriously under-estimated. The unilateral cancellation of debt would be politically disastrous. It can safely be assumed that a major part is in deutschmarks, yen or sterling. Even if most of the major US companies will have disinvested by the end of 1989, most European and Japanese companies will probably remain well into the 1990s.

In addition, there is little chance of South Africa unilaterally rescheduling its debt in the manner of Peru or Brazil. It has never wished to present an image of itself as a Third World country (chronically indebted), as the US Department of Commerce described it in 1986. Any selective decision to discriminate against US banks is unlikely, given that the US market is so crucial to the European and Japanese banks as well.

There is one scenario, however, which should not be ruled out entirely, namely South Africa's 'obligation' to export capital to neighbouring countries. Like Brazil, South Africa is a net creditor. The South African government could argue that it is – in its own right – a substantial supplier of credit to the rest of Africa; credit which, provided by both the public and private sectors, amounted in June 1987 to R1.6 billion (excluding the homelands). Recently the Development Bank of Southern Africa, in addition to providing funds to the Republic's nine 'development regions', began lending money to neighbouring states including Lesotho. Moreover, its decision to fund black investment in urban areas (with a recent agreement to provide R6.2 million in Natal), suggests that the need to find new funds in the future will place increasing strain on the availability of existing capital.

South Africa's debt burden is, however, likely to have a significant impact on the capital available to fund a siege economy. Much will depend in the first instance on how large the foreign debt is as a proportion of GDP. From 48.3 per cent in 1986 it dropped to 43.9 per cent in the first half of 1987. Interest payments were only 10.5 per cent of exports (including gold and services) in the first half of 1986 (annualised), compared with 10.8 per cent the previous year. By African standards this is a 'reasonable' debt burden, especially if economic growth rises to 2 per cent in 1987–88 and beyond, as some banks predict.

Of the revised $23.2 billion debt, $4.4 billion matures in 1987 and only $1.9 billion in 1988. These are much higher figures than those projected by the government at the end of 1985, but as long as there is a continuing high current account surplus, prospects for more comfortable debt management seem quite good.

The South African government will, however, need more than this to fund its capital programmes in the 1990s. It will need a renewal of inter-bank lending. The most dramatic surge came in 1980–84, a period which saw no less than a 700 per cent increase, prompted in part by the extent to which the government came to rely on the banking sector to fund programmes such as SASOL 3. From mid-1982 until the end of 1984 – when the present cycle of political unrest first began – South African banks lent $1.3 billion to South African borrowers, including the government, which made them the third, as opposed to the twelfth, largest source of government borrowing.

The problem is that inter-bank lending is unlikely to pick up either in the immediate or the distant future. It is true that some banks – notably Toronto Dominion – have continued to lend to the South African sector, even to public sector corporations. The banks' contradictory attitude – calling in loans and at the same time extending credit limits – can be explained by their overwhelming interest in securing their own money. For the most part, however, once the loans have been repaid, funds are no longer going to be readily available to local companies, let alone government controlled corporations, as they were in the past.

The Reserve Bank is sanguine about rolling over trade credits which have already resumed in the case of some European banks, as well as Japan. Two Japanese banks, the Bank of Tokyo and Sumitomo, are believed to have at least $3 billion exposure in South Africa, much of it contracted in the last twenty-four months. Although most types of lending, including the holding of deposits in South African banks, have been banned since 1975, trade related credits have continued to flow. Trade related loans since 1983 include deferred payments on exports of equipment to ESCOM (the electricity supply commission) and ISCOR (the iron and steel corporation) – an estimated $112 million and $10.4 million respectively.

While bank credit, syndicated loans, public bond issues and other money market instruments are no longer available to South African borrowers, export credits are. As long as ESCOM places orders overseas using credit lines with overseas institutions, it can still fund at least 85 per cent of its import requirements. There has been no indication that this sort of finance would be withdrawn and such measures are not expected in the future. Although some export financing agencies have talked of increasing the 'risk premium' on South African debt, there has been no increase in ESCOM's cost of borrowing. Individual investors, moreover, have found they can get excellent returns by dealing directly through the financial rand or by buying ESCOM's dollar-, sterling- or deutschmark-denominated bonds and note issues on the secondary market overseas; instruments which fall outside the debt standstill.

Trade credits notwithstanding, a number of local banks seem to be critically under-funded for the financing or re-financing of many of their own clients. In 1986 Bankorp had to raise R120 million through a rights issue to re-finance its merchant and investment banking subsidiary, Mercabank. At the end of March 1986 the market value of the gilt portfolio of Nedbank, the Republic's third largest bank group, was R142 million less than its book value. Ultimately, the insurance company Old Mutual came to the rescue when it agreed to underwrite plans for the bank to raise a record R345 million from the investment community. Never before had a leading South African bank been forced to 'go public' in search of funds on such a scale.

In addition, Old Mutual had to obtain a waiver of existing financial regulations to enable it to increase its shareholding in Nedbank above 30 per cent. In normal circumstances the bank would have borrowed from the international money markets, especially those of London and New York. The current enquiry by the Bank of England into such re-financing operations suggests that South African banks will increasingly have to look to domestic sources of funding in the foreseeable future.

It should be noted that Nedbank's performance in 1986 was unusual and that Mercabank was a small merchant bank which has since disappeared. Domestically, the Johannesburg Stock Exchange (JSE) is booming. In March and April 1987 European fund managers recommended South African shares for the first time in months (although only as a portfolio investment).

The general problem of liquidity, however, has forced the Reserve Bank to inject R181 million into the banking system to increase lending and to give added stimulus to a depressed domestic economy by cutting the commercial banks' cash reserve requirements against their short-term liabilities – from 8 per cent to 5 per cent. Liquid asset requirements, including cash reserves, have been reduced against short-, medium- and long-term liabilities; first to relieve banks of the obligation to rebuild non-interest earning cash reserves, and second, to enable them to switch some additional cash into interest earning liquid assets, thereby helping them to maintain a margin between deposit and lending rates. Whether these measures will enable the banking community to finance any further public sector projects on the scale of those of the 1970s without recourse to foreign borrowing is another question entirely.

The problem of drastically low local demand remains. Interest rates, which have been kept low because the Reserve Bank wishes to guarantee its loans, have forced many banks to move into the mortgage market – which at 12.5 per cent can offer better terms than short-dated bonds at 9 per cent. Mindful of the stock exchange crash in 1969/70, which was caused by over-borrowing by local customers, the banks have been advancing money mostly for speculative investments. SanLam and Mutual may between them provide a cash flow of R500 million a day but they have kept their money mostly liquid because returns are still low. Of R18 billion which will be available between 1987–88, 40 per cent will be invested in building societies rather than going into gilts.

Of the five major commercial banks, such as Trust, First National and Volksas, none has capital available for investment in the venture capital market, given five years of drought and an increase of debt by the farming community of 375 per cent in ten years. Given also the degree of bank involvement in such capital investment programmes as Mossel Bay, there may be remarkably little surplus capital available for real investment and the creation of real jobs.

It is generally accepted that South Africa can finance up to 90 per cent of investment from its own resources, but that the additional 10 per cent of foreign capital makes all the difference between two or five per cent growth a year. This seems to be well illustrated by a comparison of the period 1964–74 and the decade that followed. In the first period, when foreign investment amounted to ten per cent, the GDP growth rate was 5.1 per cent. From 1974–84 there was an average foreign capital outflow of 0.5 per cent, forcing the government to draw on reserves to meet the shortfall at a time when the economy's annual growth rate was only 2.6 per cent. These figures should correct any impression that the 1970s constituted, on the whole, a period of economic expansion. On balance, it may not have been a particularly bad period, but it was one in which the economy was very much in a state of flux.

Not that there is any shortage of money on the JSE; far from it. The only problem is that four large corporations already trade in 80 per cent of its shares, with Anglo American trading in half. One of the most worrying developments of the recession for the government has been the phenomenon of 'cartelisation': in 1984 there were twenty-one major takeovers involving assets of R1 billion, a great many of them engineered by companies controlled by English speakers. That is the threat. All that has happened is that the latter have further increased their control over the commanding heights of the economy, while at the same time reducing the role of foreign capital. It is conceivable that, if the trend continues within the siege economy, local (English-speaking) business may at last achieve the goal which has eluded it for forty years: that of securing political influence deliberately and consistently denied to it by the National Party, apart from a spurious offer of partnership at the Carlton House conference in 1979.

It is this challenge which is likely to dissuade the government from raising capital itself through the extended privatisation of parastatals. The sale of South African Transport Services (SATS) in 1986, for example, might have notched up a market value of R10 billion, making it the biggest listing on the Johannesburg stock exchange, worth more than Anglo American and SASOL combined. With a net operating profit of R2 billion in 1984 on a turnover of R6.5 billion there would have been no shortage of interested parties.

Although the business community tends to see privatisation as a more effective form of management of resources: a way of borrowing; of substituting for capital market issues; and of reducing an already over-large public sector; privatisation has not gone ahead as planned. In the end the government has been reluctant to reduce its control over the economy, which has been painfully carved out over half a century of National Party rule. The scandal over the sale of Samancor some years ago (which the government ensured would not be bought by Anglo American), was illustrative of Pretoria's determination that corporations owned by English speakers should not increase their political influence any further by buying into the public sector.

Twelve years ago the Franzen Commission warned that it could not 'allow foreign capital to be invested in a manner or in such amounts as will enable foreign control to be exercised over the whole economy or over certain strategic sectors'. In the event, South Africa never had to worry about foreign multinational corporations (MNCs). On the contrary, it was persuaded not to implement some of the Commission's own recommendations, so as to create a more favourable business climate. The government is clearly concerned, however, about the degree of influence which the English-speaking community might establish if its commercial outlets are allowed to grow much larger.

In part, the South African government cannot block the increasing inroads made by English-speaking business such as Anglo American, Barlow-Rand, Rembrandt and Southern Liberty, because of the relatively small scale on which the South African economy operates. If firms are to exist in industry on as large a scale as necessary then the existence of large companies is unavoidable. Disinvestment has also resulted in the inevitable acquisition of foreign operations by local corporations, thus increasing concentration both within the market sector concerned and at an aggregate economic level. In addition, exchange control regulations long predating the present crisis have precluded the major expansion of South African companies overseas so that they have been forced to expand within the country and thereby raise existing levels of market dominance.

Simplistic attacks on the existing structure of business – notably compulsory assets divestiture which is occasionally discussed – might well deconcentrate and help the government regain political control. But the ultimate aim of its economic policy is not deconcentration, but rather wealth creation at a time when the economy needs to expand by at least three per cent a year. Even if the current trend is towards subcontracting the services of companies such as ESCOM to the private sector, rather than selling them off *in toto*, the government is likely to lose the degree of control that it established in the 1960s. If it ever succeeds in creating a siege economy it may not find itself in control of it for very long.

SOCIAL AND POLITICAL CONSEQUENCES OF DISINVESTMENT

Nor is the situation especially encouraging for the South African government on the social and political front. Although it is difficult to measure precisely the impact that disinvestment has had on South Africa's economic development, there are three areas in which any significant pullout might have serious consequences, not, I believe, for the public sector but for the programme of reform.

(i) Multinational companies at present employ between 200 000 and 315 000 black workers, or between 2.6 and 4.6 per cent of the total black workforce. If the higher figure is correct it represents about a fifth of black labour in mining, manufacturing, construction, the wholesale and retail trade, as well as banking. The involvement of foreign capital may be minimal in some branches of mining and construction, but in some sub-sectors of manufacturing the role of MNCs may be crucial. The influence which they are able to bring to bear on labour practices in general – and those relating to black workers in particular – should not, therefore, be undervalued or ignored, especially when we consider that over 40 per cent of the labour force remains outside the formal economy.

For many years the real average increase in wages paid by the signatories of the Sullivan Code (a third of all US companies operating in the Republic) has been considerably higher than the national average for manufacturing: 5.8 per cent a year between 1978 and 1984 as against a national average of 3.2 per cent. Similarly, the rate of increase in the wages of coloureds and Indians was appreciably greater, with the wages of white employees rising more slowly (1.8 per cent compared with 2.0 per cent). There may be several reasons for the relatively sharp increase in salaries and wages of 'non-white' labour, including a determined, if somewhat belated, effort to improve the remuneration of disadvantaged workers. Clearly, however, if most of the Sullivan signatories were to pull out over the next three years (as many predict, with sixty-five leaving in 1987 alone), higher paid workers would suffer most directly – the very class, of course, which has benefited most from the government's recent reforms.

(ii) In addition to the crude factor of unemployment, the most skilled section of the black population would also suffer most. The fact that the average expenditure of MNCs in 1984 was far higher than that of most local companies was attributable, in part, to the greater need for training in the highly technical sectors in which they operated. German and US companies, according to their reports under the EEC and Sullivan Codes of Practice, provided training for 76 per cent of their workforce in 1982. Two years later this figure had risen to 79 per cent.

A survey conducted by the South Africa Foundation found that the figure for black workers occupying supervisory and managerial roles was slightly higher for MNCs (3.3 per cent) than for South African companies (2.8 per cent). This seems to have been particularly true for foreign banks which employed large numbers of clerical workers. Across the nation as a whole the percentage of blacks employed in clerical occupations doubled between 1965 and 1981.

Available data reveals that job-specific loss rates tend to differ appreciably. The rate among computer personnel between 1981–82 was especially high (25 per cent); significant enough to increase the labour related costs of some organisations. Most MNCs, unlike many local firms, were cushioned against the immediate effect by technical and apprenticeship programmes funded from the annual 'corporate responsibility' projects on which the parent companies budgeted every year. If disinvestment were to speed up appreciably in the high technology sector, black employees would probably suffer more critically than most, with obvious attendant implications for the further consolidation of a capitalist entrepreneurial class.

(iii) The same group would also suffer from any substantial reduction in housing programmes. Quite apart from the national housing problem (the present backlog is estimated at 400 000 units nationwide), building societies still cater almost exclusively for conventional housing, which represents a minute proportion of the housing which can be afforded by many clerical-grade and other employees.

Foreign companies' expenditure on housing-per-worker has risen at a substantially faster rate than that of local companies – by almost 10 per cent a year. In 1984, 61 per cent of all British companies assisted their workers in buying their own homes. Employee assistance by the Sullivan signatories was also above average. In 1984 their total employment figure stood at only one per cent of the economically active labour force, yet in the previous year their employees held 15 per cent of the existing ninety-nine-year leases whereby blacks are entitled to home ownership in urban townships.

Of course, it may well be objected that if the differences between foreign-owned and locally-owned corporations lie in their actions, rather than in their aspirations, even in seeking to foster the growth of a black middle class both probably aspire to too much. In the sphere of housing in particular, the government has passed the responsibility to the private sector, and the private sector has passed it back. The upshot has been paralysis.

It can also be objected that the $600 million in corporate funds which has been spent since 1982 on projects to help employees and their immediate communities represents nothing more than an ameliorative exercise which is unlikely to advance fundamental political change. These are matters on which observers will continue to disagree long after the corporations themselves may have passed from the scene. What had become clear by the end of 1986 was that US corporate disinvestment had dramatically reduced the amount of money spent on 'social responsibility' programmes, especially in education and housing.

General Electric, which sold out its subsidiary to nine local managers in April 1986, left, as part of the transaction, a R1 million endowment specifically to allow its Corporate Social Responsibility programmes to continue. Such action, alas, tends to be the exception rather than the rule. In any event, the funds are usually administered with less enthusiasm by a local company which, unlike its former parent, is not subject to evaluation on the actual results of the spending. Here, too, the role of foreign corporations is unique.

CONCLUSION

I have attempted to suggest that in the state of 'siege' in which South Africa already finds itself, either very little has changed (or, as far as the state is concerned, in the case of structural disinvestment it has changed for the better), or that the only real casualty has been the 'reform' programme as originally conceived in the heady days of 1978–79. This was, however, arguably a programme which the country could not afford in terms of high interest rates, and even higher borrowing; and one which probably never had much of a future in terms in which the government saw it: the growth of an affluent black middle class.

If South Africa moves any further into a state of siege, however, there is no reason to expect that the budget deficit would be reduced; quite the contrary. The government has already incurred a deficit of R8 billion (3 per cent of GDP) by creating huge development projects such as SASOL to resist sanctions; also to fund reforms which, in its view, will be as urgently needed as ever. Over the next ten years the budget for black schooling is set to increase by 20 per cent annually. In 1986 the black housing bill increased by a further R600 million – a quite inadequate sum given the fact that four million new housing units will be needed within the next fifteen years, requiring the construction of 600 units per working day. If present trends continue, spending as a percentage of GDP could rise to 30 per cent or more by the mid-1990s, a level so high that it would put an abrupt end to any further economic growth. Stagflation would be the inevitable outcome.

Clearly, if the infrastructure of apartheid were to be dismantled, enormous savings could be made. The country could reduce its 900 000 civil servants, 150 cabinet bureaux, 1900 MPs and their staffs. Direct spending on apartheid accounts for up to 14 per cent of the budget.

Unfortunately, this is not the entire picture. While much of this money is spent on keeping blacks out of the cities, or bringing them into work, or trying to encourage local industries to move to decentralised areas, much of it is being spent on essential services – many of which will have to be expanded, not merely maintained. With the expectation that decentralisation programmes will become even more expensive (as the demand for labour in the cities increases), it is clear that these amounts will not decrease but increase in the future.

The government clearly cannot continue to carry on as it has: government spending will have to be contained, as will black material expectations. Even a *real* growth in social expenditure of as high as 5 per cent a year for the last quarter of the century would still leave *per capita* social expenditure below 60 per cent of 1975 white levels by the end of the 1990s.

The South African government urgently needs to redefine the whole meaning of 'reform', to ask itself whether it can reduce the white standard of living substantially (it is still at a level far exceeding the resources of the country), while persuading the black majority *not* to determine their material expectations by present white standards. Clearly there will be a conflict between relatively slow increases in average black incomes (and a small reduction in racial disparities through market forces in terms of *primary* income distribution), and greater demands for redistribution through political processes (through the budget or *secondary* income distribution). It is no easy task, to say the least, to predict ways in which this conflict will be resolved.

Faced with a chronic shortage of capital the government is being forced to reassess its position. There is now talk of instituting a 'user charge' for white parents, guaranteeing a minimum standard of education beyond which children would have to be privately funded – a measure which would imply a levy rather than a tax on education. The Ministry of Finance is also resisting the idea of housing South Africa's black population. Controlled urbanisation seems to require a minimum of housing for a minimum number of employees, with the implicit acceptance that the rest of the population will have to be housed almost indefinitely in shanty communities reminiscent of those in Latin America.

Faced with a 60 per cent under-utilisation of capacity in manufacturing industry, local business is calling for sound finance and sound economic management, and an end to the 'social engineering' programmes not only of the 1940s and 1950s (the high-water mark of classical apartheid), but of the reform programme as well. The reforms of the past ten years tend to be dismissed by many as crude attempts to transfer wealth through redistributionist policies which have begun to lose their appeal even in the Soviet Union. If this view is sustained, if businessmen continue to believe the government is playing for limited objectives with hidden agendas, engaging in images and appearances with no clear understanding that it cannot buy itself out of the portending crisis, then there seems little basis for any kind of partnership between the two.

In any event, it is unlikely that the South African business community is really willing to share the responsibility of such a partnership with government. True, there are black schools that need to be built, home loans that need to be advanced, and myriad infrastructural improvements that are urgently required. True, there is talk of using South Africa's liquidity to capitalise the formation of black-owned and black-run companies to build the infrastructure and create the new wealth of which there has been precious little in the past. True, there has even been talk of broadening black equity participation; a move which is resisted by union federations such as COSATU which still prefer to talk of transferring existing resources as if national economies were static, predefined 'pies' that can be rendered 'just' by the simple act of re-slicing. Unfortunately, however, the white business community has not been noted in the past for its confidence in black potential. Such investments do not offer immediate returns; they are not gilt-edged. The concept of broadening black equity participation in companies such as Anglo American is being studied in detail, but exactly how the idea will be implemented will depend on the type of company, the business cycle and the pattern of existing shareholding. As it is, the companies seem to be opposed to providing the kind of funds the Regional Service Councils (RSCs) will need if they are to redistribute income in the way the government intends. South Africa's major businessmen are beginning to argue that the RSCs are another form of indirect taxation which will increase the cost of employment by obliging the community to pass on the cost of the new taxes to the consumer. It is clear that rather than spending more by increasing corporate tax, they would prefer to spend less by reducing taxation – following the US example of deficit financing – even by reducing the upper rate of tax from 47.5 per cent to just under 30 per cent.

As for the second trend – the tentative dismantling of the public sector – many companies are far from happy with schemes for economic decentralisation. Even if they were to work, which is doubtful, the experiment would be prohibitively expensive. The decentralisation of *political* power, which might accompany the redistribution of economic resources, would require elected subordinate levels of government which would probably increase the level of direct demands made on financial resources and might require special fiscal arrangements aimed at resource redistribution at a lower level.

At a time of zero economic growth this could be perceived as a form of double taxation, unaffordable and therefore costly for the citizen, particularly in the type of non-industrialised provincial authorities into which South Africa may yet be divided. Decentralisation as opposed to deregulation is unlikely to attract much support. For some years now, Cabinet Ministers have been talking of carving up South Africa into separate development regions, a symmetrical federation on the regional level, an assymetrical one on the local level. New concepts such as 'consociation', 'concurrent majority' and 'segmental autonomy' have been introduced into the political debate. A form of 'partition' is now regarded by many white politicians as essential for the maintenance of the *capitalist* system. As Professor Lombard pointed out in a report in 1980, the 'political arithmetic of numbers' has been carefully worked out, ruling out the chance of a strategy of co-option that might threaten the power base of the white community.

By comparison, one of the main attractions of the African National Congress (ANC) for the businessmen who met its representatives in Lusaka in 1985 is that, despite the movement's talk of nationalisation, it is strongly committed to preserving the state system which was forged at the turn of the century: a unified state, largely the creation of Cape and British capital, a country that can claim such entrepreneurs as Beit and Rhodes as its founding fathers.

A primary and long-term concern expressed by many businessmen is that in a desperate attempt to retain power, the South African government has begun to think in terms of a decentralised state; either a federation along 'corporate lines', where ethnic classification would form the basis for membership, or a geographically determined confederation, where membership would be defined by territorial location. It would be ironic, indeed, if foreign companies were persuaded to disinvest not by a government which was unwilling to reform the political system, or turn its back on the past, but one which was prepared to destroy that part of South Africa's historical legacy which it still values most highly: the unity of the state.

REFERENCES

H. Adam and K. Moodley, *South Africa without Apartheid* (Cape Town: Maskew Miller, 1986).

M. Forsyth, *Federalism and the Future of South Africa*, (Johannesburg: South Africa Institute of International Affairs, 1984, Bradlow Series No. 2).

M.L. Lipton, *Capitalism and Apartheid* (Aldershot: Gower, 1985). President's

Council, *Report of the Science Committee of the President's Council on Demographic Trends in South Arica*, (Pretoria).
S. Van den Berg, *Long-Term Economic Trends and Development to Prospects in South Africa*, Paper presented at the Institute for African and International Studies, Munich, 16 May 1987.

ACKNOWLEDGEMENT

The author is grateful to the Nuffield Foundation which provided grants for two separate visits to South Africa in August 1986 and July 1987. This chapter is based on interviews conducted during both visits.

10 The South African Crisis: The Major External Actors

James Mayall

INTRODUCTION

Hopes that the defeat of the Third Reich would usher in a new, 'liberal' international order lasted just long enough to secure the establishment of the United Nations Organisation (UNO). Its Charter envisaged a world in which not only would peace-loving countries be secured from aggression by the timely intervention of the Grand Alliance (reconstituted in the Security Council), but it would also be one made safe for constitutional development by the end of empire. Even before the Cold War substituted 'realism' for hope as the basis for relations between the great powers, however, South Africa had sounded a discordant note in the proceedings of the new organisation.

The South African government, then still under the leadership of Jan Smuts, refused to transfer the mandate for South West Africa to the newly created UN Trusteeship Council. South Africa was – as the Western powers insisted and the World Court subsequently ruled – within its rights in adopting this position. The decision none the less dramatised the philosophical divide which already separated South Africa and the European colonial powers. Indeed, from 1946, when India first raised the question of racial discrimination against the Asian population in Natal in the General Assembly, the West has found South Africa to be an embarrassing ally.

Their early embarrassment was deepened after the South African general election of 1948. The successful National Party was led by men who had been openly sympathetic to the Nazis and whose programme of institutionalised apartheid seemed to many to bear an uncomfortable family resemblance to the system against which the Western democracies had taken up arms. Since Western, and particularly British, interests were heavily involved in the South African economy, and since the British government itself was intensely suspicious of the rising tide of anti-colonial sentiment at the United Nations, they were not disposed to make this comparison in public; but the fact that it could be made at all exposed Western governments to pressure from an alliance between liberal opinion at home and anti-colonial nationalism abroad. The United Nations created the stage upon which this alliance was forged.

Pressure on Western governments to 'do something' to bring about the political transformation of South Africa has never been entirely absent since these early post-war episodes, although, as we shall see in a later section of this chapter, its intensity has varied in relation to events within South Africa itself. There have been three such periods of intense pressure and diplomatic activity: following the Sharpeville massacre in 1960, the Soweto uprising in 1976 and the township revolt of 1984. It was Sharpeville that set the pattern for the subsequent international debate. After the shootings, South Africa became the 'moral outcast' of the international order – in much the same way that Turkey had finally become the pariah of the European states system after the Armenian massacres of 1896.

During the meeting of the Security Council convened following the Sharpeville massacre, the Western governments finally accepted the argument that apartheid was a 'special case', and that South Africa could not legitimately shelter from international criticism of its domestic affairs behind Article 2(7) of the Charter. Their concession on this point did not then imply any willingness to support demands for mandatory economic sanctions against South Africa. The resulting ambiguity in Western policy – a willingness to criticise but not to sanction – was understandable: it arose from the contradiction between Western material and strategic interests and Western political values. Having admitted, however, that the South African political system was peculiarly noxious and that, unlike other tyrannies in the post-colonial world, it posed a problem for international order, the West had surrendered a major defence against demands for effective action. Western ambiguity, moreover, created an issue around which the anti-South African (government) alliance could mobilise, Western policy itself becoming the major target of international pressure.

This came from three directions. Western governments were exposed to charges of hypocrisy from Third World countries whose own governments tended to see South Africa as an extension of the 'colonial question' – in other words, a Western responsibility which could only be discharged through the transfer of power. Western policy also provided the Soviet Union and its allies, which have few material interests in the region, with a great deal of scope for propaganda. Finally, Western governments were exposed to pressure from domestic public opinion (persistently from anti-apartheid and human rights activists), but fanning out since 1984, particularly in the United States, to cover a much wider range of interests.[1]

Embattled on three fronts, the official Western response remains, as always, to make the best of a bad job, in the Micawber-like hope that something will eventually happen in South Africa to head off 'violent revolution' while leaving Western interests undisturbed. Politicians are professional optimists and no Western government would be likely to accept this description of their policies in quite such bleak terms. No doubt they would qualify it by pointing to the long and continuing history of Western efforts to engage the South African government in dialogue and to support all those working in South Africa for the peaceful transformation of the society into a 'genuinely multiracial democracy'. Their more pessimistic (or realistic) advisors might put it differently, viewing Western policy as a holding operation, a way of being seen to do something, in the hope that when the balance between repression and revolt in South Africa finally and irrevocably tilts in favour of the latter, Western interests will have been reduced to politically manageable proportions by a 'natural' process of wastage and reorientation.

The West is, of course, an ideological not an empirical or geographical category. Within the Alliance there are significant variations depending on the perceived interests of the different countries, the history of their relations with South Africa, the ways in which they make foreign policy and, more particularly, their different sensitivities to public opinion. These differences confuse the picture, and also probably dilute the impact of Western official pressure on the South African government. None the less, at the strategic level, there is a broad identity of interest – South Africa must change in order to stay the same, i.e. open to the West and part of the Western international economy. But while this objective has remained fairly constant, the international context in which it has been pursued has changed radically. Before attempting to assess the external impact on the South African crisis, therefore, it may be helpful to focus more closely on the nature of Western involvement and the way in which external events have shaped its response to South African developments.

WESTERN INTERESTS

National interests are seldom as self-evident as their advocates may believe. It may be possible, however, as William Foltz suggests in a recent survey of US interests,[2] to identify those 'prudent concerns' to which Western governments habitually refer when defending their policies toward the Republic. These can be conveniently grouped under three headings: economic, strategic and political interests, although there are obvious areas of overlap. I will consider each briefly in turn.

Economic interests

The most obvious way in which the major Western powers have helped to shape the South African situation is through their participation in the economy. Indeed, it is because South Africa is perceived by its enemies to depend so heavily on Western economic support that Western governments are seen as holding the key to the overthrow of the apartheid system. Yet how important the West is to the South African economy, and vice versa, remains difficult to quantify. This is partly because the relevant national statistics are not available in a readily comparable form; partly because the extent of South Africa's exposure in the area of greatest interdependence, namely world capital markets, is difficult to monitor let alone police; and partly because, under the prolonged threat of sanctions, import substitution has greatly reduced the country's overall dependence.

It is certainly true that a great many Western businesses have wholly- or partially-owned subsidiaries in South Africa, although the current wave of divestment and disinvestment is leading to a contraction of their involvement. Nevertheless, it has been a consistent aim of Western policy to support and work with, rather than against, Western business in its relations with the South African government. For some countries, South Africa is also a valuable market for manufacturing industry and an important source of raw materials and foodstuffs.

Beyond these general observations, two more specific features of Western economic involvement are worth noting since they have a direct bearing on the policy debate. The first is the asymmetry between political influence and economic stake. Bluntly put, while the United States and the United Kingdom are the two most important external actors in South Africa, the constraints under which their governments formulate policy are not the same. Although no longer South Africa's principal trading partner, British governments have always been reluctant to take any action which would damage the UK's economic ties with South Africa. Apart from a philosophical objection to the use of economic pressure as an instrument of peacetime foreign policy in any context, this reluctance reflects the fact that for most of the post-war period Britain has enjoyed a healthy surplus in visible bilateral trade.[3] Britain is also the principal source of foreign investment. This has been estimated by the British Industry Committee on South Africa (BICSA – formerly the United Kingdom–South Africa Trade Association, UKSATA), at around £6 billion, representing 45 per cent of all foreign investment in South Africa. For governments which have always had to nurse the balance of payments and which have increasingly faced major unemployment problems, these considerations have always seemed compelling.

As economic hegemon, the United States has not been similarly constrained. It has been observed that

> In aggregate terms, American interests are small and have remained remarkably stable. Since the end of World War II South Africa has accounted annually for about 1 per cent of US foreign trade and between 1–2 per cent of US direct investment overseas. These investments have yielded substantial rates of profit for some US corporations, though smaller than profits elsewhere in Africa. In almost every case South African holdings represent a small part of a US corporation's activity.[4]

The relative economic insignificance of South Africa to the United States has not, however, made the US noticeably more willing than Britain to engage in economic warfare with Pretoria, perhaps because US administrations are afraid (or say they are afraid) of forfeiting South African supplies of strategic minerals to the Soviet Union. The ability to discount the economic costs of a break with South Africa has none the less influenced US reactions to the South African crisis in two ways. First, it has fuelled the tendency, never far below the surface in US political life, to seek economic solutions to political problems, and it has played into the hands of domestic pressure groups.

The current 'epidemic' of corporate disinvestment has now spread to other countries, the decision of Barclays Bank to pull out in December 1986 being a most notable example. The process started and has spread furthest in the United States, as business leaders found that they were spending a disproportionate amount of boardroom time (disproportionate, that is, to the stakes involved) in fighting off pressure from anti-apartheid activists. Even when business has been prepared to face up to this pressure, moreover, the banks have not. It was the decision of Chase Manhattan in 1985 to 'call in' its South

African loans that led other banks to follow suit, precipitating a flight of capital and a heavy fall in the rand. With the banking sector sounding the retreat, primarily for commercial reasons, the way was cleared politically for US 'conversion' to the cause of economic sanctions.[5]

The second feature of Western involvement which bears on the policy debate derives from the first. Bluntly put, the high visibility of British and US involvement (economic in the one case, political in the other), opens up a 'free-rider' option for the other Western powers. The French were the first to exploit this option when, in the mid-1960s, they refused to follow the US and British lead in imposing a unilateral arms embargo, and quickly captured their share of the market. Ten years later, following the mandatory arms embargo imposed by the Security Council in 1977, the French retreated from this position, reduced their economic ties with the Republic, and have generally failed to give public support to British positions taken within the EEC.[6]

It is perhaps not overly cynical to suggest that this change of heart reflected not only the swing to the left in French politics that brought President Mitterrand to power, but the fact that France has less to lose than the other major powers. There is relatively little direct French investment in South Africa. Where the French led, the West Germans and Japanese followed. These countries have overtaken Britain in the South African market but are for the most part able to shelter from public criticism behind British and US policies. Their governments are as deeply opposed to the imposition of economic sanctions as the British and United States governments; indeed, on some issues – for example their refusal to contemplate a ban on South African coal imports – they have been even more intransigent.[7]

Strategic interests

In describing the strategic significance of South Africa to the West, three kinds of arguments are customarily deployed. First, it is pointed out that the West depends on South Africa for a number of industrial and strategic minerals, including metals in the platinum group and chromium and manganese ores, for which the principal alternative supplier is the Soviet Union. The contested significance of this dependence emerges clearly from the clotted prose of a report by the US Secretary of State's Advisory Committee on South Africa, published in January 1987:

> Having viewed the strategic minerals issue through the prisms of several competing schools of thought in the policy community, we are agreed that a minerals cut-off (either by counter-sanctions or by a breakdown of the South African economy and infrastructure) would have an undeniable impact on the United States. In some cases, we could be forced to increase imports from the Soviet Union. But we have concluded that the potential impact of such a denial is not sufficient cause to determine US policy towards South Africa.[8]

It is not clear whether the Committee adopted a unilateral or multilateral approach in reaching this conclusion. Dependence on imports of most raw materials varies significantly among the industrial countries, ranging from Japan's almost total dependence at one end of the spectrum to the near self-sufficiency of the United States at the other. The EEC falls somewhere in between, although for most commodities the position is closer to that of Japan than to the United States.[9] Although the ability of individual countries to survive a major interruption of supplies varies, their interdependence would ensure that the shock from any disruption of supplies would be felt throughout the system. Michael Shafer has plausibly suggested that

> a major or even a potentially major supply interruption could trigger a rash of panic buying that would bid up prices and strain inter-allied relations. Moreover, as the threat of damage to their economies mounted, Western Europe and Japan would pressure the United States to share its mineral stocks. In a crisis, moreover, the United States would find its allies unwilling to take tough unified action because of their high vulnerability.[10]

Second, South Africa is of strategic importance to the West because it commands the sea route between the Atlantic and Indian oceans. The most sensitive commodity involved is undoubtedly oil: the seaways around the Cape currently handle up to 65 per cent of Western Europe's and 28 per cent of the US' oil imports. Although the threat of Soviet interdiction of Western shipping has long been discounted by all except the most ardent cold warriors[11] – apart from the likelihood that it would provoke Western reprisals it would require the deployment of massive naval and air resources – no Western government believes it can afford to be entirely indifferent to the strategic implications of South African geography. In the words of the House of Commons Foreign Affairs Committee Report,

> it remains, and must remain, a priority for British and Alliance policy, that whatever future system of government South Africa chooses for itself, South Africa should remain firmly outside the Soviet sphere of influence and should continue to be allied, if possible more closely, to the defence interests of North America and Western Europe.[12]

The US Secretary of State's Advisory Committee reached an almost identical conclusion.[13]

Geography cannot be divorced from politics. From the point of view of all the Western powers, and above all for the United States, there is finally, therefore, the more vague but ultimately more important interest of denying South Africa to the 'Soviet sphere of interest', and of containing Soviet influence elsewhere in the region. Being indeterminate, this overriding interest is in tension with the other two: in each case it is possible to argue that the West would be better advised to support the status quo in South Africa or the nationalist opposition. Moreover, to the extent that maintaining South Africa in the Western international economy is regarded as a major objective of the containment policy, the strategic dilemma becomes more acute: the longer fundamental change is delayed, it is argued, the more likely that it will involve a radical attack upon capitalist institutions and the market.

Political interests

In the conflict between Western 'values' and material interests, it may seem that the latter always win. There is a sense, however, in which all Western governments regard the defence of these 'values' in South Africa an interest in itself. The fact that these values have been simultaneously endorsed and abused by the South African government creates problems for the West. The abuse weakens faith in the rule of law, and in countries with sizeable black minorities, South Africa's public reliance on democratic forms and institutions (for the white population) arguably undermines confidence in Western democracy and the Western commitment to human rights. Thus, Secretary of State Cyrus Vance explained President Carter's Human Rights policy to the Senate Committee on Foreign Relations in 1980: 'The advancement of human rights is more than an ideal. It, too, is an interest.

Peaceful gains for freedom are also steps towards stability abroad and greater security for America.'[14]

President Reagan's administration has placed much less emphasis on human rights (except as a sub-plot in the policy of confrontation with the Soviet Union), and the governments of the other Western powers are not similarly constrained by political tradition to occupy the 'high moral ground' in foreign policy. However, their willingness to condemn apartheid when they often remain silent about tyrannical forms of government elsewhere none the less suggests their sensitivity on this issue.

The United Kingdom is, in this respect, in a different position from the other Western powers, for two reasons. First, there is what the Foreign Affairs Select Committee refers to as the country's 'colonial legacy'. Whether, as its 1986 report suggests, Britain has a particular moral responsibility for the well-being of the entire South African population (as the result of the British Parliament's surrender of its responsibilities for the 'non-white' population in 1909), is debatable.[15] The government does accept, however, that some 800 000 people in South Africa probably have a right of abode in the United Kingdom.[16] If a genuinely revolutionary confrontation develops in South Africa, Britain could face a problem similar to that faced by France with the return of the *pieds-noirs* from Algeria in the 1960s. No doubt a proportion of the more affluent and skilled would attempt to resettle in Australasia and the Americas – indeed they are already doing so – but the majority would have to be reabsorbed into British society facing economic circumstances which are much less propitious than they were in France at that time.

Second, there is the impact of the South African crisis on the Commonwealth. The consequences of the Commonwealth campaign for sanctions against South Africa will be discussed in the next section of this chapter. Here it is sufficient to note that while, in opposing sanctions, the present British government has split with the majority of other members, there is no clear indication that they dissent from the Foreign Affairs Committee view that 'membership and leadership of the Commonwealth is undoubedly a major diplomatic asset'.[17] They deny that the failure to agree a Commonwealth approach to the problem of South Africa poses a threat to the Commonwealth itself, and argue that 'the Commonwealth is sufficiently mature to accommodate the legitimate differences of view that inevitably arise from time to time amongst its members'.[18] So far, at any rate, there has been no general British retreat from Commonwealth activities as a result of the row over South Africa.

THE INTERNATIONAL CONTEXT

With important exceptions, the South African 'interests' which Western governments have articulated since the National Party came to power in 1947 have remained remarkably stable. By contrast, the international environment has changed dramatically over the same period. Indeed, the exceptional cases where Western interests have been redefined (for example in the British decision not to resist South Africa's withdrawal from the Commonwealth and the termination of the Simonstown naval base agreement), were the result of a perceived need to adjust to external change in order to secure them. They did not arise from an autonomous review of Western interests. Ultimately, no doubt, it is events within South Africa rather than beyond its borders which have forced Western governments to modify their policies. The African National Congress (ANC), for example, has assumed a new prominence and an unprecedented legitimacy in Western capitals in the wake of the urban rebellion (see Chapter 2). Given Western reluctance actively to involve itself, however, it seems unlikely that any departure from established positions would be contemplated without powerful international reinforcement. This has come from four directions: from international institutions, from shifts in the geopolitical balance of power within the southern African region, most recently as a result of South Africa's own regional policies, and from Western fears about Soviet objectives and intentions. Let us consider each in turn.

Institutional pressure

As has been seen, the South African problem was on the international agenda almost from the start of the United Nations, and was acknowledged as an international 'problem' by the Western powers after Sharpeville in 1960. It was kept on the agenda, moreover, as the result of sustained Afro-Asian diplomatic efforts. The demand for the immediate end to apartheid merited a paragraph in the first declaration of the Non-Aligned Movement (NAM) following its inaugural summit in Belgrade in September 1961, and it has been repeated in all subsequent NAM pronouncements. Indeed, since the Bandung Conference in 1955 most international meetings at which the Afro-Asian and Non-Aligned states were represented have included a condemnation of apartheid in their final documents. This form of institutional pressure, which led to South Africa's withdrawal from most international organisations in the UN system in the 1960s, reached a climax in December 1974. Article 16 of the Charter on the Economic Rights and Duties of States sought to establish

> the right and duty of all states individually and collectively to eliminate colonialism, apartheid, racial discrimination, neo-colonialism and all forms of foreign aggression, occupation and domination, and the economic and social consequences thereof, as a prerequisite for development.[19]

It is difficult to know what, if any, impact such ritualised demands have had on Western governments. Probably not much. What is habitual is readily discounted in politics, as in life. On three occasions, however, the ritual was transformed under the pressure of events into a genuinely political statement to which the major powers felt bound to respond. The first followed the establishment of the Organisation of African Unity (OAU) in 1963. The creation of the OAU allowed the African states to concert their policies towards South Africa at the United Nations and elsewhere. Indeed, it required them to do so. The OAU Charter binds its members to pursue the liberation of the Continent, specifically including the end of minority rule in South Africa, by all means at their disposal. From 1963 onwards African members regularly attempted to persuade the Security Council to invoke Chapter VII of the Charter against South Africa, not only in respect of its illegal occupation of Namibia but also because of the South African government's refusal to abandon racial discrimination within the country itself.[20]

Until the 1980s, the OAU was a force to be reckoned with within the southern African diplomacy of the Western powers. First the Americans and then the British introduced unilateral arms embargoes in a scarcely veiled response to African demands during the Security Council meetings of July 1963. At the end of the 1960s the South African attempt to blunt the 'liberation struggle' by engaging in dialogue with 'moderate' African governments was finally frustrated within the OAU – primarily by the diplomatic efforts of Tanzania and Zambia. Although a purely South African policy, the success of dialogue would have had beneficial consequences for Western interests, if only because what financial and arms support the liberation movements received, came predominantly from the Soviet Union and China.

Despite the OAU's operational weakness – it was never able to fulfil its original intention of monopolising all external assistance to the liberation movments – it was able to confer or deny legitimacy on or to any southern African settlement. In 1976 the Front Line States (FLS) were mandated to act for the African states collectively in Rhodesia and Namibia. When Ian Smith made an eleventh-hour political deal with Bishop Abel Muzorewa, it was the OAU which refused to recognise the 'Zimbabwe–Rhodesia' regime, and so frustrated Western efforts to bypass the Patriotic Front. In recent years the OAU has been crippled by internal dissension and it is uncertain whether the organisation can continue to perform the 'legitimating' role – with respect to South Africa – which it played elsewhere in the region during its first twenty years. The principles which it established as a framework for African diplomacy, however, continue to prevent Pretoria from selling to the West its own preferred solution to its internal problems. The fact that no country other than South Africa itself has recognisd any of the 'independent homelands' probably has much to do with the OAU ruling that African states should achieve independence within (and only within) the frontiers established under colonial rule. (It might be noted that if purely empirical criteria were decisive in securing international recognition, there would be little to choose between the claims of the Transkei and Lesotho to sovereign statehood.)

Institutional pressure on the Western powers 'to do something' about South Africa was ratcheted up a second time after the Soweto riots in 1976, and particularly following the death of Steve Biko, the Black Consciousness leader, in police custody. These events led to a new round of Security Council meetings, a mandatory arms embargo – the first time that action had been taken against South Africa under Chapter VII of the Charter – and the introduction of codes of conduct for Western businesses operating in South Africa. The latter were introduced to avoid government embarrassment after it had been revealed, in a successful newspaper campaign in Britain, that many Western businesses were profiting from apartheid by paying their workers below subsistence wages.

Pressure was further intensified following the township revolt of 1984 to mid-1986. The focus now moved to the Commonwealth. At the Commonwealth Summit held in Nassau, Bahamas, in October 1985, a crisis was averted only by the appointment of a Group of Eminent Persons (EPG) to intercede with the South African government. The failure of the Group's mission led to the agreement of a Commonwealth 'package of measures'[21] (most of which the British government continued to resist), and increased pressure for action against apartheid within the EEC. The publication of the Group's report in June 1986 also provided ammunition for those within the United States who were pressing for an end to President Reagan's policy of 'constructive engagement'. In September both Houses of Congress agreed a list of sanctions which went considerably beyond the measures agreed by the Commonwealth and the EEC.[22] The President vetoed the Bill and his veto was, in turn, overruled by the Senate.

Geopolitics

The US policy of constructive engagement was merely the latest in a series of attempts to fashion a credible diplomatic response to what the administration saw as a major geopolitical challenge to Western interests in the region. Whether or not this perception is accurate, it is true that the emergence of the FLS as a regional co-ordinating group for African pressure on the West has complicated the task of 'defending Western interests'.

The geopolitical transformation of southern Africa was the result of two linked events. The first, the Portuguese *coup d'etat* of 1974, led rapidly to the independence of Angola and Mozambique – whose successor governments were linked by treaty with, and in the former case effectively helped to power by, the Soviet Union. For a short period at the beginning of his administration, President Carter attempted to keep the two issues apart, but he was unable to isolate the South African problem wholly from Cold War rivalries and calculations. President Reagan has made no such attempt.

The second event, the independence of Zimbabwe in February 1980, followed from the first. Once independent, Mozambique opened its eastern borders to ZANU guerrillas, to whom it offered a sanctuary where they could assemble, organise and train and from where they could emerge to launch attacks in the Rhodesian countryside. It was eventually Britain which successfully negotiated the transfer of power to Zimbabwe. However, it was the US fear of 'losing' Zimbabwe to Soviet influence in the same way that Angola had been 'lost', which led to a more active United States policy aimed at breaking the long deadlock in the Rhodesian crisis and securing an orderly transfer of power. The crucial breakthrough occurred at a meeting in Pretoria in September 1976 during which Henry Kissinger persuaded Ian Smith to commit himself to majority rule within two years.[23]

The 'liberation' of the entire southern African region, with the exception of Namibia and South Africa itself, created a dilemma for the FLS: how to reconcile the commitment to confronting South Africa, with their economic dependence on the Republic. Their immediate response in 1980 was to create the Southern African

Development Co-ordination Conference (SADCC). SADCC's primary long-term political aim was to reduce dependence on South Africa. Zimbabwe's independence created a parallel dilemma for the West, particularly for Britain whose armed forces had been given the task of integrating the guerrilla forces with the old Rhodesian army. How, in the event of conflict, were British interests in South Africa and Zimbabwe to be reconciled?

At first sight, SADCC created opportunities for the West, since Western governments could now support development projects which made economic sense, regardless of what happened in South Africa. The new organisation was accordingly greeted with enthusiasm by the EEC, the United States and indeed by most donor countries and agencies. But SADCC also sharpened the Western policy dilemma: how to support the independence of its member states without intensifying their confrontation with South Africa and increasing the chances that the South African crisis would escalate into a much wider and unpredictable regional conflict. This danger is most acute in the transport sector, where Western assistance to develop a more effective and independent regional transport network – as in the current project to upgrade the Beira line and modernise Beira port – has created obvious targets for South Africa or South African-backed saboteurs.

Over the past five years Zimbabwe has become dependent for over 85 per cent of its export and import trade on South Africa and its railways and ports, largely because the line that links the country with Maputo, the Mozambique capital, has been kept permanently closed by Mozambique National Resistance (MNR) guerrillas (see Chapter 11). Under an agreement with Mozambique, the Zimbabweans themselves have policed the Beira corridor, the alternative outlet to the sea, and have kept the line open; but they have failed to stop bridges being destroyed and, more recently, direct attacks on trains. It is likely that if the project develops to a point where the line can carry a significantly higher proportion of Zimbabwean traffic than at present (around 10 per cent), sabotage activity will increase.

One possible solution to the security problems that will accompany the successful creation of a SADCC transport network would be for the donor countries to offer military support for the defence of the roads, railways and port facilities involved. Transport security has emerged as an issue of Non-Aligned diplomacy. At the Non-Aligned summit in Harare in September 1986, a 'solidarity fund' was established, with India and Nigeria on the organising committee. During the conference there was also some speculation about an alleged Indian offer of military aid for the defence of the Maputo line – they were apparently considering providing the Mozambique government with MIG fighter jets – and the Nigerians allegedly also expressed interest in deploying troops along the Beira Corridor.

No firm commitments appear to have resulted from these explorations. In any event, a Western force would have greater credibility as a deterrent, both because of its weaponry and because of South Africa's need to retain some Western support. Politically, however, a Western presence would be more problematic for the host countries. There has been some modest British and US military support for Mozambique, largely in the form of training, designed to symbolise Western political support for the FLS in their efforts to reduce dependence on South Africa, and to encourage an alternative strategy to that of punitive economic sanctions. If there has been any serious discussion between the Western powers and the FLS about more visible military support, it has evidently not borne fruit.[24] The basic obstacle is presumably the West's reluctance to accept SADCC as anything more than an economic arrangement, let alone to endorse its role in any strategy of confrontation with Pretoria.

South African destabilisation

It is an open question whether the third major change to which the Western powers have had to adjust – South Africa's deliberate policy of regional destabilisation – is partly of their own, or at least US manufacture. This view is certainly widely held in Zambia and Zimbabwe. There is no doubt that the United States was heavily involved in the diplomacy which led to the Nkomati Accord, the ineffective non-aggression pact between Mozambique and South Africa which was signed in February 1984. With or without Western connivance, however, Pretoria has successfully demonstrated that it can contain any threat to the Republic which emanates from outside. The South African objective does not seem to have been to overthrow existing governments (except in Lesotho, where in January 1986 they imposed a blockade to force a change in a government they themselves had originally brought to power). Rather, they have sought to ensure that their potentially hostile neighbours are kept busy at home and are constantly reminded of the costs of actively supporting the military activities of the ANC, or in any other way posing a threat to South Africa.

The instruments of destabilisation employed by the South African government range from overt and covert support for the MNR in

Mozambique and UNITA in Angola, through economic pressure on the land-locked neighbouring states (such as delays in the handling of essential imports through South African customs or the requirement that all imports be covered by a foreign exchange deposit before transshipment) to direct (although so far largely symbolic) military intervention against alleged ANC targets in neighbouring countries. It was a series of such attacks against targets in Zambia, Zimbabwe and Botswana in May 1986 (none of which had any obvious military rationale) which finally sabotaged the mission of the EPG.

The details of South Africa's sustained harassment of its neighbours are provided in Chapter 11. They are relevant here only in so far as they bear directly on the problems of Western policy. Suffice it to say, therefore, that South Africa's policy has already imposed very heavy costs on the region. According to a document prepared for the Non-Aligned Summit 'it is conservatively estimated that these sanctions have cost South Africa's independent black-ruled neighbours well in excess of US$20 million'.[25] The effects, it is argued, have been devastating for the region as a whole and particularly for Mozambique where in many areas government and administration have been virtually destroyed.

The consequences of this devastation for Western interests and influence are hard to determine. Much depends on the assumptions on which analysis is based. The authors of the document quoted above argue the 'liberal' case for economic sanctions, but draw the implicit – and very questionable – conclusion that because they are suffering already, the FLS would be able and willing to take any amount of punishment in the future out of 'solidarity with their brothers and sisters in their struggle to overthrow apartheid'. An altogether gloomier picture can justifiably be painted. It could be suggested that, given Western determination to counter 'Soviet influence', it was inevitable that South Africa would be allowed a free ride in respect of its own regional policies. Any attempt by Zimbabwe and Zambia to implement economic sanctions could trigger an irrational but still ferocious counter-attack by South Africa, in effect a decision in Pretoria to go for the 'Lesotho option', rather than to continue co-existing with dependent but hostile regimes. This would obviously be contrary to Western interests, if only because it could create a situation which the Soviet Union could exploit if it so chose.

But would it choose to do so? Post-independence developments in Mozambique have not seriously harmed Western interests; indeed, on 'realist' assumptions, it may even have helped since the government, despairing of effective assistance from its Soviet ally, has increasingly turned to the West for help. All that can be said confidently is that South Africa's regional policies have severely sharpened the Western policy dilemma that arises from a desire to protect interests on both sides of the regional divide.

The 'Soviet factor'

The Soviet Union's interests in southern Africa are ideological and historical rather than material. Judging from recent pronouncements, moreover, the Soviet dilemma in the region is how to maintain its political commitments to the MPLA in Angola, Frelimo in Mozambique and to South Africa's ANC, while reassuring the United States that it does not propose any dramatic intervention to force the pace of change in South Africa. Soviet spokesmen have indicated that South Africa is as low a strategic priority for the USSR as it is for the USA, a point which academic writers have often observed but which has been persistently overlooked in political debate.

This absence of material stakes in South Africa, whose defence or expansion might result in observable and public shifts in Soviet policy, means that Moscow's role in the crisis is almost invariably viewed through the prism of rival Western perceptions. On the one side, there are those who maintain that South Africa is the African country in which the Soviet Union has always been most interested; the one African country with an industrial proletariat and a developed form of capitalism whose contradictory class relations have some genuinely revolutionary potential. From this perspective, the fact that the South African Communist Party (SACP) has a long-standing united front with the ANC – the latter has also recently joined the PLO in enjoying embassy status in Moscow[26] – speaks perhaps more eloquently to the Soviet Union's long-term intentions than the evidence of tactical restraint and caution which, on every level except that of propaganda, has always been the hallmark of Soviet policy towards the Republic. On the other side there are those who see the Soviet Union as pre-occupied with its superpower status, and hence unlikely to surrender its regional commitments and allies lightly, but in other respects not disposed to challenge Western policies and interests directly. It is, of course, this tendency in Western political opinion to which the current Soviet leadership addresses itself, for example in publicising its advice to the ANC to leave the 'socialist revolution' for the future and its insistence that the region is not an area of superpower rivalry.[27] But those who view Soviet policy from this perspective do not have to rely solely on official pronouncements – the record of Soviet activity in the region also provides supporting evidence.

The crucial point to note is that since the 1970s (when the collapse of Portugal's African empire provided Moscow with historic opportunities), the most that can be claimed for the Soviet Union's southern African policy is that the relationship with Angola has been consolidated.[28] Despite a record of economic and political failure, the MPLA government has survived; the armed forces have been substantially re-armed with Soviet equipment for the continuing civil war with UNITA; and there have been repeated claims by UNITA leader Jonas Savimbi that Soviet officers have helped to direct the MPLA's military campaign against his own forces, and that Soviet pilots have flown some of the Angolan MIG 23s and MIG 25s in combat.

Whatever the actual scale of their involvement, it is known that the Soviets have impressed on the Americans (in a series of bilateral talks on regional affairs) the strength of their commitment, and have also supported the Angolan government in their refusal to talk to UNITA so long as it is supplied by the United States and South Africa. The message to Washington is unambiguous: the Russians do not intend to be excluded from any peace process in Angola.

Elsewhere in the region, Soviet policy appears to have been much more tentative. Although they have continued to supply Mozambique with some weaponry and with cheap oil, the Frelimo government's request for membership of the COMECON (CMEA) was turned down, and the level of economic and military support was insufficient to save the late President Machel from having to sign the Nkomati Accord in 1984; indeed, to the extent that it signalled a degree of 'realism' in Mozambique's policy, the Soviet Union probably welcomed it, since they had criticised what they viewed as an 'ultra-left' line followed by Frelimo after independence.

In Zimbabwe, the Soviet Union backed Joshua Nkomo's ZAPU throughout the war of independence and continued to do so right up to the pre-independence elections. The result was a predictable cooling in diplomatic relations when Robert Mugabe's ZANU won the elections and formed a government in 1980. Relations have since improved; Mugabe has made a state visit to Moscow and Zimbabwe has officially requested military supplies from the Soviet Union, including MIG 29s. By July 1987, however, nothing had been settled and there was certainly no evidence to suggest that Moscow had encouraged Zimbabwe to carry its flirtation with sanctions against South Africa to the point of implementation.[29]

There is even less that can sensibly be said about the Soviet Union's relations with South Africa itself. Soviet support for the ANC (and its ally the SACP) is not in question – a fact which has undoubtedly gained Moscow diplomatic credit in Africa over the years, since it is in line with official OAU policy. Even at this level of inter-party relations, however, the picture that emerges is less than clearcut.[30]

At the level of state-to-state relations, there seems little doubt that there is regular, if clandestine, consultation between South Africa and the Soviet Union over the marketing of diamond and other commodities where the two states share common interests. The alliance is, however, considered so unholy by both sides that they do not have – nor are they likely to have in the future – any official relations. Despite this antagonism – Moscow's unequivocal support for the ANC/SACP mirrors Pretoria's representation of the Soviet Union as the 'real' enemy in the total onslaught which it faces – nothing in the record of Soviet involvement in southern Africa over the past decade suggests that the Russians are prepared to contemplate a direct confrontation with the West over South Africa, or even with South Africa's own military forces.[31]

In the circumstances, the Soviet impact on the South African crisis seems likely to continue to be indirect, a function of South African and Western perceptions of the Soviet Union's long-run objectives, rather than the result of any determined Soviet policy to play an historical role in shaping the future. In this respect, the major Western fear has always been that the Soviet Union does not have to do anything to 'win' in the long-run. If South Africa cannot reform itself then, at some point, however distant, there is likely to be a revolution. The Soviet Union may not gain directly from the new dispensation, but to the extent that Western interests will be damaged, at least in the short-run, they will gain none the less. It is this spectre which has haunted the Western policy debate on South Africa for more than a generation.

WESTERN POLICIES

If, as noted earlier, Western interests in South Africa have remained relatively constant in a world of flux, Western policies have moved sedately in response to public opinion without ever attempting to lead it. In the background to the debate, two rival views of international society, the 'liberal' and 'realist', confront one another. The official perception is that there is very little Western governments can do to influence the course of events in South Africa (and therefore very little that they should do other than point out to the South African authorities that they are playing into the hands of the Soviet Union). The contrary view is held by a wide and articulate section of international public opinion.

Originally, governments fell back on international law to fend off their critics. The United Kingdom, at any rate, was prepared to defend South Africa against all outside attempts to interfere in its domestic affairs – the Americans were somewhat more equivocal. As noted earlier, after Sharpeville, Western governments conceded that apartheid represented a special case: it was contrary to the UN Charter and should be condemned by the international community whenever possible. Since it did not constitute a threat to international security, the justification under chapter VII for the imposition of sanctions, that was as far as they were prepared to go.

Once the US and UK governments had introduced their own unilateral arms embargoes in 1963 and 1964 they might have been expected to abandon this essentially legal objection to economic sanctions. They have continued to draw a sharp distinction, however, between military and economic sanctions, and to oppose the latter on the grounds that they would be counter-productive, more likely to drive the South African government into the *laager* than to persuade them to introduce significant political reforms, let alone to transfer power to the black majority.

At a meeting of the British Cabinet in 1947, the Commonwealth Secretary Patrick Gordon Walker stated:

> Those who argue that because we dislike the Union's native policy we should ostracise her and have nothing to do with her completely fail to understand the realities of the situation. Such a policy would not only gravely harm us in the defence and economic fields, it would also weaken our power to deter South Africa from foolhardy acts for fear of breaking with us.[32]

This is the core defence which, despite occasional differences among themselves, all Western governments have employed. The argument is often buttressed with another, that to influence the South African government in the direction of 'reform' requires contact and persuasion rather than ostracism and pressure. To this end, official contact has been maintained not merely through the normal networks of bilateral diplomacy and economic co-operation – for example the extension of the Export Credit Guarantee Department (ECGD) or the Export–Import Bank (EXIM) bank cover to British and US exporters respectively – but until very recently through co-operation between the South African and Western intelligence services, and by the practice of officially sponsored visits by South African politicians to Western countries.

The events of 1976–77 and 1984–86 led to modifications in Western policies. The strategy of using the private sector to bring pressure to bear on the South African government began in the United Kingdom in 1974, with the elaboration of a statutory 'code of conduct' for South African subsidiaries of British-owned firms. A 'reporting system' was set up to oversee the operation of the code under which firms were required, among other things, to pay equal pay for equal work and to permit the formation of black trade unions. The European Community (EEC) instituted a code of conduct in 1977, and in the United States, the 'Sullivan principles' were agreed on a voluntary basis by the majority of US firms operating in South Africa – although originally omitting any commitment to recognise trade unions. The British system was later generalised within the EEC. Simultaneously, the Commonwealth produced the 'Gleneagles Agreement' which effectively isolated South Africa from world sport, and the Western powers finally agreed on a mandatory arms embargo.

Over the past ten years, the debate on Western policy has moved backwards and forwards across the Atlantic, with the United States sometimes attempting to provide a lead, and sometimes to blend in with the United Kingdom and the EEC. In the first two years of his presidency (1976–80), Jimmy Carter attempted to differentiate his Southern African policy from that of his predecessor. Richard Nixon had accepted the 'tar baby' option[33] on the advice of his National Security Advisor, Henry Kissinger, and Kissinger's advice was again heeded when Nixon turned his attention to the Rhodesian problem. Here, Kissinger suggested that it would be impossible to secure an orderly transfer of power in Rhodesia without South African co-operation, and that this in turn required the West to show at least tacit 'understanding' of South Africa's domestic problems.

Carter, by contrast, refused to make any concessions to the South African position, insisting that it was necessary and possible to make progress on all three regional problems – Rhodesian independence, Namibia and the dismantling of apartheid in South Africa – simultaneously. A barrage of diplomatic pressure was mounted against

Pretoria: the US military attaché was withdrawn, export bans introduced on any items which might conceivably be put to military use (such as spare tyres for police vehicles) and the Administration put no obstacles in the way of a Congressionally inspired ban on EXIM bank cover for US exports. (This last measure was largely a symbolic gesture as, at the time, private business was able to meet its own financial requirements through the banking system without recourse to government support.) In any event, Carter's South African policy, like his foreign policy in general, fell foul of an increasingly hostile Congress. Well before the end of his term of office, US–South Africa relations had quietly slipped back to the basis of 'business as usual'.

The contrast between President Carter's and President Reagan's policies of constructive engagement is one of style rather than substance.[34] For both administrations, the sticking point was their refusal to impose serious economic sanctions which would both harm their own interests and significantly weaken the South African economy; while the positive inducements which they offered in support of change were equally inadequate. The domestic consequences of the contrast in style, however, were paradoxical; for while Carter courted liberal opinion within the United States but alienated a more conservative Congress, Reagan exploited the drift to the right in US politics and ignored the anti-apartheid and human rights activists, only to find that the revolt in South Africa's townships had engendered a broad bipartisan alliance against his policy of tacit support for the South African government. The Senate's overturning of the President's veto on its proposed package of sanctions represents the single most significant shift in Western policy towards South Africa since 1948.

Although the US administration remains opposed to a sanctions policy, and there must, therefore, be some doubt as to how vigorously they will implement it, the US government is now committed to a more extensive package of restrictive measures than any of the other Western powers. It remains true, of course, that no major United States interest will suffer as a result of these sanctions – no doubt an important reason why it was possible to secure Congressional agreement. However, the Secretary of State's Advisory Committee concluded that the 'sanctions issue' was now closed and that the President should 'begin urgent consultations with our allies (especially Britain, Canada, West Germany, Japan and Israel) to enlist their support for a multilateral programme of sanctions drawn from the list of measures in the Anti-Apartheid Act of 1986'.[35]

As the South African crisis faded from the world's headlines in 1987, the President did not seem to be pursuing this recommendation with any great vigour, to put it mildly. Nevertheless, independently of US policy, the tide of opinion in Western Europe and the Commonwealth was flowing strongly in the same direction, bringing steady pressure to bear on the United Kingdom, which does have important interests at stake, to bring its policies into line. The pressure was applied in earnest at meetings of the EEC in September 1985. It was intensified at the Commonwealth Heads of Government meeting at Nassau in the Bahamas in October of the same year, continued at the meeting of the European Council at the Hague in June 1986 and reached a climax at the mini Commonwealth Summit which met in London in August 1986 to consider the Report of the EPG. At all these meetings the British found themselves isolated in resisting demands for the imposition of further restrictive measures.

While continuing to insist on their basic opposition to punitive sanctions and preference for dialogue, on each occasion the government gave ground. At Luxembourg they extended the existing ban on military trade, which included a ban on nuclear co-operation, and the ban on the sale of oil; they also agreed to discourage scientific and cultural events 'except where these contribute to the ending of apartheid or have no possible role in supporting it', to freeze existing agreements in sporting and security spheres and to recall the British military attaché and refuse to accredit a South African attaché in London. At Nassau they added to this list a ban on all government loans to the South African government, an end to government financing for trade missions and fairs and a ban on the direct import of Krugerrands. At the Hague, following the failure of the EPG mission, they managed to persuade their European partners that Foreign Secretary Sir Geoffrey Howe, in his capacity as President of the Council, should make one final attempt to persuade the South African government to end the State of Emergency, legalise the ANC and other opposition parties and release Nelson Mandela and his colleagues from detention. At the Commonwealth meeting in August, when all the other members agreed to implement the full list of further measures envisaged in the Nassau Accord, the British confined themselves to a voluntary ban on investment in South Africa, a voluntary ban on the promotion of tourism into South Africa and 'to accept and implement any EEC decision to ban the import of coal, iron and steel and of gold coins from South Africa'.

The auguries for Howe's mission could scarcely have been worse, and although President Botha finally agreed to meet him, it ended in predictable failure. If its primary purpose was tactical, however, that is to buy time for the UK government during which the clamour for action against South Africa might fade, it was not altogether unsuccessful. Given the commitment they had already made in June and their widely publicised opposition to further measures, the Presidency of the Foreign Ministers' meeting may have provided the United Kingdom with opportunities for exercising diplomatic influence behind the scenes but it also put them in a somewhat delicate position. At the meeting of the EEC Foreign Ministers held in Brussels on 15 and 16 September 1986 they finally accepted the ban on new investment and on imports of iron, steel and gold coins, all of which had been envisaged in the Hague communiqué. They were, however, saved from having to accept a ban on the import of coal, the sanction most likely to have major adverse effects on the South African economy and on black employment, by West Germany and Portugal who insisted that it should be deleted from the list.[36]

What conclusions can be drawn from this brief survey of British policy? It seems clear from the government's handling of the South African question that their primary objective at all these meetings was to limit the damage to their own interests (and to maintain the support for their policy in the Conservative Party) rather than to make any particular impact within South Africa. The question inevitably arises, therefore, as to whether in giving way to international pressure only at the margin and even then with such obvious reluctance, the message sent to the South African government has not been exactly the opposite to that intended; in other words, a message of comfort and ultimate support. The British government would no doubt deny this interpretation, pointing out that they have made no secret of their belief that the key assumption on which the sanctions campaign is based – that by raising the cost of its policies, the South African government can be persuaded to act reasonably – is false, and that their own preferred policy of encouraging 'peaceful reform' is, by its nature, both long term and incremental in its achievements. The final question to be considered, therefore, is the impact of Western policies on the major internal actors in the South African drama.

THE IMPACT

Whether Western policies have had a serious impact on the South African government's own reform programme – their avowed intention –

is debatable. The South African government, it is said, welcomed some aspects of Western pressure, for example the codes of conduct, even tacitly encouraging South African businesses to test public opinion in advance of changes in the law. It is equally possible, however, to argue that it was the internal contradictions in South African society and the demands of the South African economy, rather than Western pressure, that forced the government to recognise black trade unions and to begin, however tortuously, the process of dismantling the outer ramparts of the apartheid system. Whichever view is taken, it is certain that the West has failed to persuade the National Party to embrace the notion of fundamental political change, that is, a transfer of power from the white minority to the black majority.

The impact of Western policies on South Africa's external relations is equally ambiguous. Over the past two years a key assumption of the US policy of constructive engagement has proved to be false. This was that the South African government would behave reasonably (that is, from a Western point of view) in Namibia and elsewhere in Southern Africa if Western governments showed 'understanding' of South Africa's 'domestic problems' and the fact that the South African government could only move forward at a snail's pace for fear of promoting a 'right-wing backlash'.

At present, however, it is increasingly doubtful whether the Western powers and the South African government have in view the same ultimate destination either at home or abroad. In South Africa, the State of Emergency has effectively ended all talk of an early release for Nelson Mandela and a deal with the ANC. Indeed, all the evidence suggests that the government has set its face against any further concessions to international opinion. Meanwhile, Western governments which once refused to meet the ANC, on the grounds that it advocated the violent overthrow of the South African government, now do so, suggesting at least a shift in their long-term perceptions.

Without a credible policy to offer to their own publics, as well as to the African Commonwealth and non-aligned governments, the Western powers have fallen back on damage limitation, offering marginal and largely symbolic economic sanctions and worthy but equally marginal positive measures to 'buy time' – for example, the British government's aid training programme for blacks. In this respect Western policies towards their own critics have much in common with those of South Africa in responding to official Western demands for evidence of political and economic change. Like South African policy, the Western approach seems increasingly ineffective and US policy has, as we have seen, been overturned by the US Congress, with what results it is too early yet to say.

The reception of Western policies within South Africa varies according to the audience. In a sense, Western governments have a natural constituency in the private sector, particularly the predominantly English-speaking mining, financial and large business interests and their political arm, the Progressive Federal Party (PFP). Chief Buthelezi's Inkatha Movement is the only politically significant black party loosely allied to the white political and economic 'opposition'. Representatives from this constituency are well known and well received in Western capitals and they generally claim similar objectives – 'killing apartheid by economic growth', and making South Africa 'safe for capitalism and democracy', by timely political reform.

This grouping also shares the Western antipathy to economic sanctions, which they see as likely not only to undermine their own interests but to destroy what little room there still exists for manoeuvring the society towards 'less violent' forms of change. It is noticeable, for example, that as the West edged towards sanctions in 1986 in response to international and domestic pressure, the business community found itself a direct target of 'patriotic appeals' from the South African government. There has been some backsliding since a group of business leaders (led by Gavin Relly, chief executive of the Anglo American Corporation) met the ANC in Lusaka in the summer of 1985. The decision of the US Senate to overturn the President's veto on the Congressional package of sanctions was viewed by the United Democratic Front (UDF) and other resistance groups as a major victory. By contrast, even the much milder European package agreed in September 1986 was seen in the business community as well as by the South African government as an ominous portent of things to come. Contingency planning, sanctions-busting preparations, and the purchase of the assets of 'disinvesting' companies by local managements (at rock-bottom prices), flourish; with the result that the business community increasingly looks inwards rather than to its traditional basis of support in the West.

Unfortunately for the West, those who are in sympathy with Western policies seem the least likely to exercise influence in the resolution of the political crisis. It is difficult to measure the impact of Western policies on Pretoria. Clearly, for a long time the South African government was anxious to do what it could in terms of policy presentation to minimise the chances that Western governments would lose patience and acquiesce in Afro-Asian demands for punitive sanctions. Rehabilitation among the Western democracies had, in any case, long been a central objective of South African foreign policy.

No doubt there are still elements within the South African government – particularly in the Department of Foreign Affairs (DFA) – which are anxious not to alienate the West further. But there is also evidence that they are losing ground to those who believe either that the West's bluff has been called and that there are no circumstances under which damaging sanctions will be imposed, or that there is no package of politically acceptable reforms that can prevent their eventual imposition. The role of the international campaign in fuelling the Afrikaner right wing, which in the shape of the Conservative Party (CP) has now replaced the PFP as the official opposition, has almost certainly reinforced the hard-line anti-Westerners within the government. The immediate internal result of the US and EEC decisions on sanctions in September 1986 was to strengthen the government's position, and there was speculation that had President Botha gone for a snap election he would have won at the expense of both the left and the right. In the event, he opted for a Spring election in 1987. Although the government fought it on the sanctions and 'security' issues, and the determination to resist outside interference, the right-wing parties made substantial gains – the 'left' was the only real loser. The result was not auspicious for an early resumption of the government's 'reform' programme.

CONCLUSION

If, from the South African government's point of view, the West has demonstrated its insensitivity to South African problems by entertaining even the minimal sanctions that have so far been introduced, for the black opposition these same measures are widely interpreted as tokenism; final proof that whatever they say to the contrary, the governments of the major powers – and particularly the British – are in fact supporting white supremacy. This interpretation in turn reinforces those in opposition whose interests lie in the further polarisation of the conflict and for whom the ultimate enemy is not so much white power, as South African capitalism.

Others in the resistance fold – particularly elements within the ANC and the UDF – suggest that the West is running a long-term risk of alienating a future government in South Africa, and that those who ultimately gain power are unlikely to forget or to forgive those who frustrated their efforts. Though possible, given the complexity of interests and views in South Africa, this may also prove to be an empty threat. In any event, there is little evidence that this consideration presses very heavily on the Western powers, or, indeed, the Soviet Union.

NOTES

1. Pressure on Western governments for disengagement from South Africa has predictably engendered counter pressures from organised business interests. For the UK, see UKSATA, *British Tråde with South Africa: A Question of National Interest* (London, 1982), and for the USA, C. Young, 'United States Policy Towards Africa: Silver Anniversary Reflections', *African Studies Review*, vol. 27, no. 3, pp. 1–17.
2. W.J. Foltz, 'United States Policy Towards South Africa: Is One Possible?' in G.J. Bender, J.S. Coleman, and R.L. Sklar (eds), *African Crisis Areas and US Foreign Policy* (Berkeley: University of California Press, 1985) pp. 32–48.
3. The trade surplus was estimated at £479 million in 1984 but declined substantially in 1985. It became negative in the early months of 1986 although the government notes that 'a high proportion of imports from South Africa have been diamonds and other goods which are re-exported'. Sixth Report from the Foreign Affairs Committee, Session 1985–86, *South Africa, Observations by the Government* (London: HMSO Cmnd 9925, October 1986), p. 3.
4. Foltz, op. cit. note 2 above, pp. 32–3.
5. c.f. D. Austin, 'A South African Policy: Six Precepts in Search of a Diplomacy?', *International Affairs*, vol. 62, no. 3, Summer 1986, pp. 400–1.
6. See *Financial Times*, 6, 11, and 27 August 1986.
7. The Japanese have generally been reluctant to take any action which will put the country out of step with the US and the rest of the OECD. In September 1986 they announced a series of anodyne measures that simultaneously informed the Americans that any ban on coal would have to be extended to Japanese imports of coal from the east coast of the USA. At present, Japanese ships loading at Philadelphia 'top up' with higher grade coal at Port Elizabeth on the return journey.
8. Report of the Secretary of State's Advisory Committee on South Africa, submitted 29 January 1987, p. 4.
9. The relatively favourable US position is a product not merely of its rich natural endowment but of the huge stockpiles of strategic materials which the government established during the Korean war and have maintained ever since. For a recent analysis of Western vulnerability to

supply disruption see H.W. Maull, 'South Africa's Minerals: the Achilles Heel of Western Economic Security?', *International Affairs*, vol. 62, no. 4, Autumn 1986, pp. 619–26.

10. M. Shafer, 'Mineral Myths', *Foreign Policy*, no. 47, Summer 1982, pp. 154–71. For an African view, see O. Ogunbadejo, *The International Politics of Africa's Strategic Minerals* (London: Croom Helm, 1985).
11. For an account of the Western strategic re-assessment of this possibility see J. Spence, 'Does Pretoria have a Cape card to Play?', *The Times*, 1 September 1986.
12. House of Commons, Sixth Report from the Foreign Affairs Committee, *South Africa*, vol. I (London: HMSO Cmnd 9925, July 1986) p. viii.
13. 'It is important in our long-term strategic interests that South Africa not fall under the control of a government hostile to the United States or one allied with the USSR that might allow the establishment of a Soviet military presence.' Op. cit. note 8 above.
14. *US Foreign Policy Objectives*, Hearings before the Committee on Foreign Relations, US Senate, 96th Congress, Second Session (27 March 1980). See also J. Mayall, 'The United States', in J. Vincent, (ed.), *Foreign Policy and Human Rights: Issues and Responses* (Cambridge: Cambridge University Press, 1986).
15. London: HMSO, Cmnd 9925, para. 6.
16. According to a written answer in the House of Commons, the government estimates 'that there are approximately 300 000 holders of British passports resident in South Africa with a right of abode in the United Kingdom. It is estimated that a further 500 000 could be eligible to a British passport and right of abode.' House of Commons Debates, 26 June 1986, Col. 252.
17. London: HMSO, Cmnd 9925, op. cit., note 3 above, para. 31.
18. Ibid., para. 7.
19. United Nations, General Assembly Official Records, 29th Session, GA/SUP. 31,A/3281.
20. For an assessment of this policy see, *South Africa: Time Running Out, The Report of the Study Commission on US Policy Towards Southern Africa* (Berkeley: University of California Press, 1981), pp. 295–300.
21. These measures had been anticipated at the Nassau meeting and included bans on air-links, new investment and the re-investment of profits, the import of agricultural products, government procurement in South Africa and government contracts with majority-owned South African companies, the promotion of tourism and termination of double taxation agreements and government assistance to investment in and trade with South Africa. For the text of the Commonwealth Accord see *Mission to South Africa, The Commonwealth Report: the Findings of the Commonwealth Eminent Persons Group on Southern Africa* (Harmondsworth: Penguin, 1986) Appendix 1.
22. The US Congressional Bill bans US investment and bank loans, terminates landing rights in the USA, prohibits the import of South African uranium, coal, steel, textiles, military vehicles and agricultural products. The Bill was vetoed by President Reagan who objected, among other things, to a feature of the legislation which sought to restrict US military

assistance to third countries which do not join US sanctions. The Senate overrode his veto by a vote of 78 to 21 on 2 October 1986.

23. L.H. Gann and T.H. Henrikson, *The Struggle for Zimbabwe* (New York: Praeger, 1981), p. 54.
24. When Zimbabwean Prime Minister, Robert Mugabe, visited Moscow in the Autumn of 1986 there were suggestions, not yet confirmed, that the Soviet Union was considering supplying Zimbabwe with an air defence system. There may have been discussions with the UK as well but it is not current British policy to provide such systems on an aid basis.
25. *South Africa Imposes Sanctions Against Neighbours* (Harare: Southern African Research and Documentation Centre), published for the Eighth Summit of the Non-Aligned Movement, Zimbabwe, September 1986, p. 5.
26. This was confirmed in an interview with the BBC programme 'African Perspective' by the Soviet Deputy Foreign Minister, Anatoly Adamishin, following a meeting on 2 July 1987 with US Assistant Secretary of State for African Affairs, Dr Chester Crocker, at the US Embassy in London. See *Front File: Southern Africa Brief* 3, July 1987.
27. Ibid. See also the unsigned article by 'A West European Correspondent' in *Africa Analysis*, 12 December 1986, for an account of the speech delivered by Professor Starushenko to the Second Soviet-African Conference 'on peace, cooperation and social progress' in June 1986. In this speech, Starushenko (one of the Deputy Directors of the Africa Institute in Moscow) encouraged the ANC to 'work out comprehensive guarantees for the white population which could be implemented after the elimination of the regime of apartheid'. Although Starushenko's views do not represent official Soviet policy, he would undoubtedly have received political clearance before delivering the speech.
28. For an account of Gorbachev's apparent re-assessment of the Soviet Union's southern African policy, and of his reinforcement of the Angolan military, see C. Coker, 'The Soviet Union's Year in Africa', in Colin Legam (ed.), *Africa Contemporary Record* 1985–1986 (New York: Africana Publishing Co.) vol. 18, pp. A267–840.
29. See J. Mayall, 'To Sanction or not to Sanction? Rationality and Realism in Southern African Politics', *LSE Quarterly*, vol. 1, no. 4, Winter 1987 pp. 371–94.
30. See note 27 above. See also *Front File*, op. cit. note 26 above.
31. Even if the claims of direct Soviet involvement with the Angolan forces are correct, it has not been on a scale sufficient to deter the South Africans from operating relatively freely in Southern Angola, against SWAPO and in support of UNITA, and apparently maintaining an estimated force of 7000 in the country, *The Times*, 28 July 1987.
32. R. Ovendale, 'The South African Policy of the British Labour Government, 1947–51, *International Affairs*, vol. 59, no. 1, Winter 1982–83, p. 57. See also J. Mayall, 'Africa in Anglo-American Relations' in W.R. Louis and H. Bull (eds), *The Special Relationship: Anglo-American Relations since 1945* (Oxford: Oxford University Press, 1986), pp. 322–40.

33. 'Tar Baby' was the name given to the second of five options in the 1969 National Security Study Memorandum, No. 39, which Henry Kissinger commissioned. It emphasised 'communication' with the white minority regimes in southern Africa including a relaxation of sanctions against Rhodesia which, for chrome imports, was actually realised via the Byrd Amendment. See A. Lake, *The 'Tar Baby' Option: American Policy Towards Southern Rhodesia* (New York: Columbia University Press, 1976).
34. C. Coker, *The United States and South Africa, 1968–1985: Constructive Engagement and its Critics* (New York: Duke University Press, 1986).
35. Advisory Committee Report, op. cit. note 8 above.
36. Portugal, like the United Kingdom, has a colonial legacy – 650 000 Portuguese are resident in South Africa. The government is unwilling to do anything which would make their return to Portugal more likely.

11 Strategy and Power: South Africa and Its Neighbours

Sam C. Nolutshungu

INTRODUCTION

Conflict between South Africa and its neighbours[1] is endemic, pervasive, and costly. On the face of it, the 'contest' is hopelessly uneven, with Pretoria having all the advantages. The neighbouring states are, in a sense, unavoidably 'victims' of the conflagration on the southernmost tip of the continent. However, the ramifications of the southern African conflict extend far beyond the region itself, implicating powerful third parties, and creating strategic problems – and opportunities – for the weaker states.

It is self-evident that conflict *within* South Africa conditions Pretoria's options and behaviour, as well as those of its neighbouring states and beyond. Through discussion of major recent developments in the subcontinent, the present analysis explores the broad outlines of a 'dependent' strategic interaction; an objective of which is to influence the behaviour of third parties who, in turn, will influence its outcome. Both the power and the strategies of the opposed states are contingent upon what ordinary people in South Africa do, and on the role played by states outside the region.

THE CONTEXT OF STRATEGIC INTERACTION

Civil strife within South Africa has adverse consequences for its neighbours, whatever the degree of international action taken against the Pretoria government, and irrespective of their own policies toward South Africa. In the years since the collapse of Portuguese rule in Angola and Mozambique, and particularly since the end of white settler rule in Rhodesia, the ways in which South Africa's difficulties might be exported to its neighbours have become dramatically evident.

Anticipating an escalating guerrilla war launched by the African National Congress (ANC) from bases in the neighbouring countries, Pretoria has used its military and economic might to dissuade its neighbours from harbouring ANC sympathisers and guerrillas. In the 1960s and early 1970s South Africa claimed the 'right of hot pursuit' to cross international boundaries to follow guerrillas who had infiltrated the Republic itself or Namibia. From the late 1970s the policy became more assertive, increasingly involving retaliatory raids deep inside the neighbouring states.

With a view toward the eventual application of trade boycotts by its African neighbours, South Africa began – after Zimbabwean independence – to use armed force to disrupt attempts by the black states to establish alternative trading routes to those it provided, and on which they had become dependent. Pretoria had for some time used economic means to discourage autonomous economic development in the countries within its Customs Union (Botswana, Lesotho and Swaziland) but now extended the policy to the other previously white ruled states.[2] At first it seemed to rely on enticement but soon turned to economic subversion and military coercion to ensure continued dependence.[3]

In its efforts to attract Western support, Pretoria had always made a case for its 'importance in the defence of Western interests' in southern Africa – whether in terms of lucrative business involvement or in countering the supposed 'Soviet threat' in the sub-continent. (The collapse of Portugal's empire and the fact that it was under pressure from avowedly Marxist guerrillas lent some credibility to the latter assertion in Western circles, and led to the unsuccessful South African intervention in the Angolan Civil War.)[4]

The intervention in Angola marked a departure in South African policy: a commitment to direct, coercive interference in neighbouring states which would, in time, allow for the recruitment, training and supply of subversive organisations directed against those states. South Africa's conflicts in Namibia and internally would then be treated as part of a larger military and economic project encompassing the entire region. This would lead to Pretoria supporting, and in varying degrees directing, rebel groups in Angola, Mozambique, Lesotho and Zimbabwe.[5]

For the neighbouring countries, compliance with South African wishes – that they abandon their project of economic de-linkage and join Pretoria's proposed 'constellation of states'; formally refuse succour to South African liberation movements; and generally cease campaigning for the isolation of South Africa – carried dangers as obvious as those flowing from South African economic and military pressure.

Economically, dependence on South Africa was costly and, moreover, made the neighbouring countries vulnerable to the vagaries of South Africa's own internal economic policies. This had been borne out by the experience of the members of the Customs Union. Furthermore, as long as these countries were closely tied to South Africa the chances of autonomous industrial development were slim. They would remain the backward periphery of a relatively highly developed centre; the latter always more attractive to investors, and wielding powerful weapons to thwart effective competition with its own producers.

Politically and ideologically, each of these states knew that too close an association with South Africa would threaten its own legitimacy and provide ammunition for internal opponents. The history of each country's own colonial past and the concomitant popular identification with unenfranchised blacks in South Africa ensured the potency of the issue in domestic politics. Such collaboration could also result in international isolation. In so far as South Africa demanded from these states diplomatic recognition for itself and for its bantustans, it sought humiliating submission and derogated their sovereign status. Moreover, their relations with major external powers would thus always be fraught.

Finally, the possibility that as the conflict intensified, armed South African movements could be compelled to impose their armed struggle upon these states (rather as the Palestinians have had to do in the Middle East), has not been lost on either the liberation movements or the black states.[6]

The South African crisis therefore implicates its neighbours deeply and dangerously at two quite distinct levels: that of the generalised diffusion of conflict – the social conflict in South Africa finding an echo in, integrating with, and augmenting latent social conflict in the neighbouring states; and that of strategic interaction among states.

The focal issue of strategic interaction in southern Africa is heightened international pressure to secure a change of regime in South Africa – specifically through international 'sanctions'. South Africa, of course, wants neither sanctions nor a change of regime. Some of its neighbours want both – though, in many cases, there are qualifications as to the form and extent of the sanctions. The two 'sides' can impose sanctions on each other, but the crucial measures will be those imposed by key trading states outside the region. The measures contemplated by the antagonists in southern Africa, therefore, will be subordinate to their respective attempts to influence the behaviour of third parties. Those who do favour sanctions and may assist international punitive measures, nevertheless do not wish South Africa to impose counter-sanctions on them, nor do they look to their own strength to extract concessions from South Africa.

Pretoria, for its part, would not generally wish to impose sanctions on its neighbours except to dissuade the international economic community from imposing punitive measures on its own economy. (There are exceptions to this, where South Africa has utilised economic sanctions to further its own local aims – the most prominent case being that of Lesotho in 1986.) However, it may wish to retaliate against neighbours supporting sanctions, and reward those helping to frustrate their imposition. Since the behaviour of the neighbouring states is crucial to South Africa's attempts to circumvent sanctions, the policy of coercion and enticement has an importance far exceeding the economic significance of trade within the sub-continent itself.

In the *de facto* context of armed conflict within the region, strategies of economic warfare will always be conditioned by, and linked to, strategies for winning – or helping allies or proxies to win – the wider armed contest. The intensification of armed conflict in and around South Africa could be used by either side to influence both the conduct and the outcome of the international sanctions campaign. For obvious reasons, and on past form, South Africa would favour a strong linkage between the military and economic contests, while its neighbours generally view sanctions as an *alternative* to a military resolution, hoping to avoid such direct involvement. An escalation of military pressure by South Africa may, however, prefigure greater military involvement of third parties in tandem with economic sanctions. This possibility of 'big power' involvement makes the unequal military contest on which a South African 'linkage' strategy would be predicated, potentially more far-reaching for South Africa. I will return to this point presently.

Thus the conflict between South Africa and its neighbours is a 'dependent' one, centred not on their inter-state disputes alone, but on a larger conflict. It involves South Africa's internal political conflict, and all actors in the sub-continent wish to influence the behaviour of third parties. For this reason, the power balances between states within the region are insufficient to determine the outcome of the local conflict.

SOME COMMENTS ON SOUTH AFRICA'S 'TOTAL STRATEGY'

The period of P.W. Botha's leadership from 1978 to the present provides some clues to South Africa's likely strategies both in terms of Pretoria's objectives, the coherence of its response, and its use of 'linkage' strategies.

South Africa has sought to achieve two aims in southern Africa: first, to make the region inhospitable to active opponents of its regime, particularly the ANC; and second, to secure and enlarge its economic and military predominance in the region, thus entrenching its hegemony. For the most part, co-operation has been assumed likely to occur due to interdependencies inherited from the colonial era, while the issue of the ANC presence in the region has, optimistically, been treated as one that could be settled by a combination of military and economic strategies adopted by Pretoria.

However, it has proved impossible for Pretoria to establish a stable hegemonic order, for two main reasons. There is no common security threat facing the countries in the region against which Pretoria can provide protection. The oft-invoked 'communist' or 'Soviet threat' is purely ideological and speculative (see Chapter 10), and although it garnered some sympathy in certain African quarters during the invasion of Angola in 1975, the greatest fear of the neighbouring states remains South Africa itself. In economic terms, South Africa has always had far less to offer than it claims; the 'collective good' it promises simply being the inherited (and rather unattractive) colonial economic dependencies. In any event, most of the neighbouring states look to countries other than South Africa for the development of profitable economic relations. At the level of ideology, apartheid makes acceptance of South African economic leadership exceedingly unpalatable, even to the weakest of them. With the exception of Malawi, each of the neighbouring states has made strenuous (and continuing) efforts to reduce its reliance on Pretoria.

While concern with security has been paramount in South Africa's 'official' thinking, attention has clearly been divided as to how far economic objectives might be traded off for security gains, or *vice versa*. This is prompted by two sets of considerations: Pretoria's recognition of the need for domestic reform, and the fact that it is possible for 'security concerns' to be broadly defined (even changed), according to conditions. Simply put, South Africa could still pursue economic *détente* publicly while ensuring that the region remained unsafe for the ANC through the use of surreptitious, 'non-public' means.

The extent to which South African policy is informed by blueprints for an 'eventual outcome' rather than *ad hoc* 'crisis management' remains an unanswered question. This is despite the pervasive official rhetoric of 'total strategy' and 'ultimate aims'. Moreover, apparent 'wins' and 'losses' do not necessarily evidence a linear lengthening or shortening of the survival of white rule in South Africa. It is clear, for example, that should South Africa accept 'defeat' in Namibia (allowing free elections which the South West African Peoples Organisation (SWAPO) can be expected to win), this may be based more on a wish to conserve resources than on actual weakness. In contrast, South Africa's apparent success in gaining recognition as an intermediary in the Rhodesia/Zimbabwe transition was offset by the victory of the group it least wanted to take control of its northern neighbour.[7]

In many instances, the practical objectives of the 'total strategy' propounded on various occasions by President Botha and General Magnus Malan, have been obscure.[8] For example, in 1984 Mozambique was required to sign a non-aggression pact and evict ANC cadres. It did both, but pressure from the South African-backed Mozambique National Resistance (MNR) continued, as did South African economic pressure to prevent the effective functioning of Mozambiquan ports. To follow its own logic, South Africa's 'constellation of states' project would have been better served by a massive infusion of aid, enabling South Africa to gain control of the Mozambiquan communications and transport infrastructure.

In so far as South African policy has helped to discourage foreign investment and, therefore, economic growth in neighbouring countries (including the member states of the Customs Union), it has reduced the long-term economic attractiveness of South Africa itself. Moreover, policies of economic disruption have been pursued even against countries that are, or have been, South Africa's most important trading partners in Africa, such as Zambia and Zimbabwe.

Finally, while hoping to rely on Western economic and strategic support in the battles that lie ahead. Pretoria has undermined Western confidence – for example, by its military attacks on pro-Western states like Botswana and Lesotho, and through continued destabilisation of Mozambique at a time when Washington believed its own interests to be well served by a stable Machel government.

It might be argued that Pretoria's motive is simply the preservation of the present regime, and not the complicated strategies of 'modernised capitalist domination' which have been attributed to it. If this is so, its 'strategy' demands little more than aggressive defence against all threats to it – the prolongation of the 'endgame', regardless of the costs. Pretoria's actions would then equate with those of the settler *jusqu'au-boutisme* familiar from Algeria to Angola, tragic and irrational.

'Total strategy' achieved a certain credibility at first (now much tarnished) among those who believed that the political aim constituted a purposeful strategy, capable of bringing about an end to the conflict. It was believed that a coalition of 'the military and capital' had ascended to power in South Africa, and that future policies would place a 'class ordering' of the society over the maintenance of apartheid. This would allow South African capital to expand into southern Africa, while paving the way for increased Western business involvement in South Africa itself.[9] In this sense Botha seemed indeed to be a 'reformer'. He was compared by the Mozambiquans, at one stage, to General De Gaulle, who 'understood' the *pieds-noirs* in ways that they themselves evidently did not.[10]

Reforming sex and pass laws, devising a new (though still racist) constitution, initially allowing greater scope for political debate within South Africa; all this, combined with concessions to the 'black middle class', heralded a new direction in the politics of white rule. Then came the chill wind of reaction – the reaction-within-the-reaction – in the face of economic recession and urban revolt.

'Total strategy' came increasingly to rely more on coercion – internally and regionally – than on diplomacy, persuasion or enticement. The West's support for South Africa's use of force in Angola (and by implication in Namibia after President Reagan's accession in 1979), encouraged the Botha regime to pursue its own 'strategic vision' which owed a great deal to the conventional wisdom of western counter-insurgency.

Its 'strategic' element was, in fact, merely an incremental emphasis on the use of force, and was marked by an inability to appreciate the political constraints and possibilities of both its internal opposition and the states over which it sought to exercise hegemony. The result has been a corrosion of the economic base of that hegemony, and an incitement of the opponents it cannot subdue to a greater, one might say reciprocal, stress on violence. The paradox of this 'strategic vision' is that it ultimately nullifies strategy itself: by undermining political imagination it leaves it without a directing purpose; by suppressing politics it effaces the matrix of its rationality. For those within its range, there is no more safety in submission than in resistance.

THE FRONT LINE STATES AND THE 'TOTAL STRATEGY'

While eager to see the end of apartheid (not least because of their emotional commitment to South Africa's black population), none of the Front Line States (FLS) has, in practice, expected an 'all or nothing' solution. Neither in terms of the transformation of the capitalist economy, nor in the area of constitution making would they have held out for a complete accession to the demands of the liberation movement. Even on the question of the length of a hypothetical transition period to majority rule, many would have been, in current parlance, 'moderate'.[11] Many would have welcomed any initiative from Pretoria which enabled them to take full advantage of its more developed economy without risk of political repudiation by their own populace. Many would have been happy to defer their struggles with 'Western imperialism' to better times, rather than be propelled by apartheid into precipitate confrontations. This is as true for Angola and Zimbabwe as it was for Mozambique under Machel after 1983.[12]

Necessarily prone to pragmatism – or 'moderation', thus understood, on such issues simply because they are states – South Africa's neighbours had considerable scope for ambiguity in their dealings with Pretoria. The fact that they could coalesce in the Southern African Development Co-ordination Conference (SADCC), an organisation embracing Marxist Angola, pro-South African Malawi, heavily-infiltrated Swaziland, and the ANC's host, Zambia, suggested that even in seeking to reduce dependence on South Africa, they would be committed to continued links. Beyond SADCC, all of the FLS except Angola and Tanzania continued to trade with South Africa. Many gave no significant assistance to the ANC throughout the 1980s, and some that did were quickly constrained. None, with the exception of Angola, considered challenging South African military superiority – even defensively.

Thus, economically and strategically, the FLS did not pursue any goals that precluded the possibility of a 'co-operative' settlement with South Africa. Yet none has reaped significant benefits in terms of its economy or security. All may find it impossible to continue to comply with South Africa's demand that they exclude the ANC and its sympathisers.

Faced with South African aggression, the FLS have relied for support essentially on world opinion and its effect on Western governments. Towards South Africa itself, their responses have comprised varying degrees of resistance and accommodation – in most cases, more the latter than the former. Some, like Zimbabwe, appear to hold out the hope that the prospect of gainful economic co-operation might restrain Pretoria.[13] In so far as their policies might have been intended to change South Africa, or to secure relatively peaceful conditions in their region, these states must be considered to have failed. For all of them, with or without increasing sanctions, the prospect of greater violence and disruption looms large. It is against this background that their likely roles and fate in relation to the 'sanctions issue' should be considered.

SANCTIONS, THE FRONT LINE STATES, AND THE ANC

From the emergence in the early 1960s of debates over possible international sanctions against South Africa, it was apparent that certain states (Botswana, Lesotho and Swaziland) could be taken 'hostage' by Pretoria.[14] With the revival of the sanctions project, catalysed by the eruption of urban revolt in 1984, Pretoria had hinted that it would impose sanctions of its own against its dependent neighbours: expelling migrant workers, withholding vital supplies which could range from grain to petroleum products, and perhaps denying transport facilities to some of these states. This had seemed to reinforce the argument deployed by many who oppose sanctions (often for entirely selfish reasons), that coercive measures of this kind would hurt the 'wrong people'.

The threat of counter-sanctions has been used against the United States and other Western powers too, though with greater ambivalence. Essentially, the threat of 'retaliation' relates to the strategic minerals which South Africa exports. The rest of its merchandise can be easily obtained elsewhere[15] – in fact, some of South Africa's important exports are extremely vulnerable, agricultural products and coal being cases in point. In reality, South Africa needs its trading partners more than they need its products or its constrained market.

South Africa's current economic difficulties, so evident since the mid-1970s, therefore reduce the credibility of its retaliatory threats. In order to emerge from the recession which has contributed directly to internal black militancy, and a loss of business confidence within the country, South Africa badly needs foreign finance in the form of investments and loans, as well as an expansion of its overseas markets. Moreover, the prospect of more extensive trade sanctions makes it imperative for them to *retain* markets: to provide the means to pay for essential (including strategic) imports which they may be forced to buy at increasing premiums. In order to encourage foreign countries to collude in sanctions busting, South Africa will have to convince them of its 'businesslike' approach – a cause not aided if it unnecessarily provokes important trading states. Markets lost through gestures of defiance may be impossible to recover, while the gestures themselves may make it much easier for pro-sanctions lobbyists to gain public sympathy in Western countries. Historically, such defiance has not served South Africa well as far as Western public opinion is concerned, although it often makes a powerful impression on conservative governments.

Quite evidently, the African states are nowhere near as important for South Africa as the West, and Pretoria may feel less constrained in imposing counter-sanctions on them. However, Africa provides essential markets for some important products: for example chemicals (33 per cent of total exports), machinery (41 per cent), transport equipment (24 per cent), and fruit, grain and vegetables (14 per cent).[16] Moreover, Pretoria would not wish to excite further sympathy for the neighbouring states, thus attracting to them the kind of aid that would reduce their vulnerability. Unless retaliatory measures were so effective as to force the neighbouring states to plead for the *lifting* of sanctions against South Africa, they could thus be counter-productive.

Beyond 'hostage taking', however, the neighbouring states have further potential importance for South Africa. Obviously Pretoria wants trade to persist, as well as its neighbours' (heavy) use of South African rail and port facilities. Equally important, some of these states could be (and to an extent already are) vital collaborators in sanctions busting – in much the same way as Malawi and South Africa itself were for Rhodesia. Coercive measures might be adopted to achieve this, including non-economic initiatives aimed at deposing or destabilising recalcitrant governments. In the lower reaches of subversion, the bribing of key officials is no doubt considered an attractive prospect by Pretoria.

In strategic terms, it is worth noting that the economic 'execution' of hostages works most effectively as a *threat*: once the threat is ignored, it becomes largely self-defeating. It hardly needs to be added that once hostages are 'dead', they retain no value for their captor.

The greatest area of dependence of the neighbouring states (other than the Customs Union states which are inextricably tied up with South Africa) is in road and rail communication and ports. Despite the urgent efforts of the FLS to open trade outlets through Malawi and Tanzania, reliance on South African ports continues. (The exception, the Beira Corridor, is continually subjected to sabotage by South African-backed forces.) This is an important, and potentially subtle, lever for South Africa. For example, Pretoria is capable of imposing differential levies on politically troublesome and less economically important users, like Zambia. This could have a 'moderating' effect on such states as sanctions increase – and even in the event of armed inter-state conflict. The level of subtlety which Pretoria might deploy in this regard is – for all the complex considerations I have described – not easily predictable. Similarly, the precise reasoning behind South Africa's repatriation of some 60 000 Mozambiquan migrant workers, remains the subject of much debate. Certainly, one aim was to demonstrate its ability to 'punish' its neighbours.

Relations between South Africa and Mozambique had deteriorated very quickly after the signing of the Nkomati Accord. South Africa continued to support the MNR; the much vaunted South African investment in Mozambique did not materialise; and far from Botha proving himself a 'regional reformer', he immediately reneged on the substantive content of the pact. Similar South African agreements with other neighbouring states were difficult to envisage as Mozambique began to hint at a reversion to its former stance.

When the ANC appeared to have resumed guerrilla infiltration into South Africa – apparently via Mozambique – Pretoria gave up all pretence of upholding the Accord. That it was prepared to sacrifice such a 'diplomatic coup' in favour of security concerns was an indication of the depth of Pretoria's fear of escalating ANC guerrilla activity. Keeping the ANC 'out' was not only its principal concern, but often overrode trade interests; and played havoc with notions of 'reform' and 'elite-accommodation' at home.

Relations between Mozambique and Malawi also deteriorated, due principally to the MNR's decision to operate from bases in Malawi rather than South Africa – a move encouraged by Pretoria, which sought to disguise the extent of its involvement with the Mozambiquan rebels. The threat of retaliatory action by Mozambique against Pretoria's most compliant collaborator loomed large. All these interlocking dynamics underlined the impracticability (from South Africa's point of view) of a policy of 'tolerance' toward the Frelimo government, while continuing to support its destabilisation. Thus if South Africa 'mourned', as it said it did, the death of Machel, it is nevertheless difficult to see what further use it could have had for him.

Pending international sanctions may have set the seal on Pretoria's choice of destabilisation over *rapprochement*. Mozambique's Beira Corridor was the key to the attempt by other southern African states to reduce their dependence on South Africa. Pretoria needed, at all costs, to ensure that it did not succeed, or, alternatively, that it functioned under a compliant Mozambiquan leadership, controllable by South Africa. It is still a matter of some debate as to whether South Africa prefers a Mozambique in a condition of permanent instability, or the installation of an MNR-based regime. The latter option, if it could possibly be implemented, would involve high costs for South Africa. Among other things, a 'Lebanon' situation might ensue in the form of a counter-counter-revolutionary struggle. This could be valuable to the ANC. Pretoria could not rule out the possibility that the Frelimo government, if mortally threatened, might turn to the USSR for aid (including military aid) on a much larger scale than before – a concern which has also influenced both US and UK policy for some time. This could be regarded by some in South Africa as a *desirable* outcome prompting, they might believe, Western military intervention to counter the 'Soviet threat'. That it may have precisely the opposite effect on the West, prompting them vastly to increase pressure on Pretoria is, if anything, a stronger argument.

In one sense, South Africa's actions over Mozambique were an indirect retaliation against Washington, which had welcomed (and, indeed, urged the implementation of) the Nkomati Accord, for various reasons. The retaliation was not without ambiguity, to the extent that Pretoria was attempting to force a reconsideration of the sanctions campaign, using the fact that the US Administration opposed both the ANC's armed struggle, and the renewed radicalism of Maputo. (Like-minded people may quarrel, of course, only to agree more strongly with each other.) The risk entailed in South Africa's even seeming to disagree is that they may make their allies within the United States more vulnerable to attacks from anti-apartheid campaigners.[17]

South Africa's 'strategic' pattern of coercion and more or less 'impatient' enticement is unlikely to alter in the foreseeable future – even in the event of a change in the South African state's top personnel. There are a variety of reasons for this, which are worth recapitulating at this point. First, the impulse towards coercion has been entrenched over many years in the political culture, and never been effectively challenged from within the white polity. Second, the increasingly (politically) important security forces live by doctrines which are informed by the utilities and details of coercion[18] (see Chapter 7). Third, given South Africa's present conventional arms superiority, certain forms of violent aggression against its neighbours carry relatively few risks, unlike economic levers. Fourth, while South Africa can threaten economic reprisals, it has very little to offer by way of enticement.

A STRATEGY OF 'INTENTIONAL AMBIGUITY'?

In a straightforward 'fight' with South Africa none of the states in SADCC could win. Collectively, it is just feasible that they could win in a protracted, devastating struggle. Neither apocalyptic scenario is at all probable, for all the reasons I have enumerated. Having established that, the political and economic objectives of the neighbouring states are simple enough. Their ideal is economic independence of Pretoria. Failing that, they seek to make the terms of their dependence more favourable, or less unfavourable. They also seek to secure, as quickly as possible and with the minimum cost to themselves, majority rule in South Africa.

With varying degrees of commitment (and still more so, of success) these states have already pursued their economic aims through SADCC. Politically they have moved, falteringly, toward intensive mutual consultation in an attempt to co-ordinate their responses to Pretoria and their demands to the international community – the latter essentially being the call for sanctions. (For historical and geographical reasons Angola has gone furthest in both resisting South African aggression and in supporting the ANC and SWAPO.)

There has been some considerable progress in SADCC's long-term economic initiatives. However, massive external assistance is needed – even more so if sanctions are ratcheted up. This aid would need to be both economic and military. In its efforts to ensure financial support, SADCC has looked primarily to the West. The Soviet Union is, it can be reasonably asserted, wary both of long-term financial commitments and of SADCC itself, which is made up largely of 'pro-Western' (including 'anti-communist') states.[19] Yet, little progress has been made in securing Western military support, and the FLS cannot renounce the option of relying more heavily on Soviet military assistance in the future.

Incremental economic 'de-linking' from South Africa, if financial aid were forthcoming, would be possible for all but the Customs Union states. Military problems are more intractable. There would be little point in expending vast sums of money on oil pipelines, roads, railways and air-freight services if these were constantly subject to South African-inspired sabotage – as is the case in Mozambique and the Benguela railway running through Zaire and Angola. An end to, or at least the establishment of control over, the wars in Angola and Mozambique would be essential.

While condemning both UNITA (National Union for the Total Independence of Angola) and the MNR, African states have until recently given little material help to the respective beleaguered governments. (Zimbabwe's limited engagement in Mozambique is an exception.) With the increased infiltration of the MNR from Malawi into Mozambique – part of a generally higher level of destabilisation in concert with South Africa – Mozambique, Zambia, Zimbabwe and Tanzania have engaged in vigorous diplomacy to warn Blantyre against giving succour to the rebels. While denying its complicity, Malawi has sensed its own vulnerability to counter-destabilisation, but still essentially responds to Pretoria's *diktats*. President Banda's controversial attitudes to a range of issues have provoked considerable ill-feeling in Mozambique and, notably, in the military.[20]

Efforts have also been made to persuade Zaire's President Mobuto to stop supporting UNITA,[21] and Angola has been at pains to play down differences with its neighbour. Some of Savimbi's allies could be persuaded to scale down, if not totally withdraw, their support for him. Savimbi appears to have been attempting to sue for peace, while at the same time making exaggerated claims of success on the battlefield and issuing threats against Zambia.[22] Signs of internal dissension within UNITA have also emerged, extending to hints of disquiet about his leadership. An indication of the worsening of UNITA's fortunes internationally was the decision of the European Assembly to brand it a 'terrorist organisation'.[23]

The reduction of economic dependence, and active encouragement of and participation in sanctions against South Africa necessarily imply grave risks to the security of the neighbouring states. South Africa's 'linkage' of the two areas of activity assures this. However, even if the military decisions evidently entailed in a full-blown strategy of economic de-linking were not taken, there would still be scope for African states to pursue effective strategies against Pretoria which could minimise their own losses.

The approach of the African states to sanctions is likely to be graduated – trade can be expected to be diverted first in 'non-essentials', next in goods that could be obtained elsewhere – even if at a premium – and, eventually, even in essential producer goods. A policy of co-operation in the procurement and distribution of 'substitute goods' from elsewhere, as well as some import-substitution through local industrialisation (even of the cottage-industry type), could relieve some of the inevitable hardship. In this regard, joint approaches to other countries for supplies and investment would be more effective than separate initiatives by different states. Another important factor would be the effective, accelerated political mobilisation of the populations of the African states against apartheid, thus making the inevitable privations more bearable.

The likely variations and ambiguity in the response of the neighbouring states to increasing sanctions could, therefore, be turned to the advantage of the weaker states *if they were consciously acting in concert*. Not only would this high degree of common purpose and co-operation be essential, but they would also have to demonstrate their ability – beyond rhetoric – to absorb the punishment, and convince their own people of the need to do so.

The 'strategy' of intentional ambiguity can be pursued at different levels with broadly similar effects. It is essentially a strategy of discrimination and graduated response – an understanding of *realpolitik*. It can entail confrontation with the South African regime while offering incentives for co-operation to other elements in the South African power bloc; it might imply an increased reliance on traditional aid-donors outside the region while at the same time exploiting every opportunity of increasing the range of external supporters. Bluntly put, what is required is a far higher degree of unity and subtlety both within and among the neighbouring states (and the broader FLS) than has thus far been achieved. It remains to be seen whether such close co-ordination is possible given the particularities of each country and the constraints imposed by South African strategy and power.

CONCLUSION

In any contest with its neighbours, South Africa quite evidently enjoys many advantages, yet these are neither unqualified nor unchallengeable. The neighbouring states can only benefit, in this context, from a variety of factors bearing on South Africa itself. That country's internal conflicts – prompted primarily by the black majority, but also emerging in the white community – appear unresolvable under the present system, thus limiting the state's ability to conceive and implement coherent, long-term strategic goals. This is exacerbated by increasing external pressure, resulting in a heavy reliance on direct coercion at the expense of more sophisticated economic and diplomatic tactics. This, in itself, contributes to tensions within the white power bloc as the influence of the military increases. Further, while in the short run clearly better able to absorb the costs of economic warfare within the region, South Africa's highly urbanised population would accept the privations of international sanctions less peaceably than their neighbours. In a powerful sense, the neighbouring states are inevitably the 'victims' of the social conflict which wracks South Africa, but the factors presented above offer them some encouragement in their refusal simply to capitulate. Perhaps more than any other factor, however, their hope for massive international aid in various forms remains paramount.

Strategy is the business of statecraft; but beyond 'policies' lie much larger processes of historical change. The examination of the origins and parameters of such strategy and policy is useful. And yet, can it be doubted that however slow and painful their unfolding may be for black and white alike, those larger forces do not conspire to preserve white domination in Africa?

NOTES

1. South Africa's 'neighbours', in this chapter, are to be broadly understood as including all those African states which border on South Africa, as well as others in the southern African sub-continent. The 'Front Line

States', when thus specifically referred to, comprise Mozambique, Zambia, Zimbabwe, Tanzania, Angola and Botswana.

2. See J. Hanlon, *Beggar Your Neighbours: Apartheid Power in Southern Africa* (Bloomington: Indiana University Press, 1986), chs. 11 and 12.
3. The balance shifted decisively in favour of coercion at the end of the 1970s after the failure of several diplomatic initiatives. See S. C. Nolutshungu, *South Africa in Africa: a study in ideology and foreign policy* (Manchester: Manchester University Press, 1975); D. Geldenhuys, *The Diplomacy of Isolation: South African Foreign Policy Making* (New York: St Martin's Press, 1984); R. Davies and D. O'Meara, 'Total Strategy in Southern Africa', *Journal of Southern African Studies*, vol. 11, issue 2, pp. 183–211, 1985; and Hanlon, op. cit. note 2 above, ch. 4.
4. J. Marcum, *The Angolan Revolution, Vol. II* (New York: Hoover Institution, 1978); G. Bender, J. Coleman and R. Sklar, *African Crisis Areas and United States Foreign Policy* (Berkeley: University of California Press, 1986).
5. Hanlon, op. cit. note 2 above.
6. This danger appeared very real after the Nkomati Accord was signed, and Swaziland put severe pressure on ANC cadres and sympathisers to leave its territory. (See *Africa Research Bulletin (Pol Ser)*, May 1984, p. 7239; August 1984, p. 7334.) As repression mounts against young militants in the townships at the same time that South Africa seeks to compel its neighbours to deny them refuge, the problem may reassert itself in a more dramatic way. Note also Zambian President Kaunda's warning to Zaire that it would be unsafe to continue to rely on trade routes through South Africa 'as these might be closed by either the South African forces or the freedom fighters'. (*Agence France Presse*, 23 November 1986) [US Dept. of Commerce Foreign Broadcasts Information Service (FBIS): MEA–86–226].
7. South Africa's role is discussed, albeit somewhat sketchily, in J. Davidow, *A Peace in Southern Africa: the Lancaster House Conference on Rhodesia, 1979* (Boulder, Col.: Westview, 1984).
8. See P. Frankel, *Pretoria's Praetorians: civil-military relations in South Africa* (Cambridge: Cambridge University Press, 1984); and Davies and O'Meara, op. cit. note 3 above.
9. In the early days of Botha's reform policy it did seem that business interests would have greater weight. However, later events – including the business leaders' initiative to meet ANC officials in Lusaka (disapproved of by Botha) – indicated that they did not have their finger on the pulse of state policy. Note, in this context, an interview with Botha in *Le Figaro*, Paris, 5 December 1986; also, J. Saul and S. Gelb, *The Crisis in South Africa: Class Defence, Class Revolution* (New York: Monthly Review Press, 1986); Hanlon, op. cit. note 2 above, p. 148. While escalating sanctions might lead to their economic requirements being more readily heeded, it does not follow that their advice on political policy would be decisive.
10. Personal Communication. Harare, January 1985.
11. The demands by the FLS (and of the Commonwealth and Non-Aligned Conferences) for the release of political prisoners, the unbanning of the

ANC and the PAC and 'meaningful negotiations' does not include any specific prescription for the terms of an agreement to end confrontation.

12. Angola's desire for accommodation was reflected in the economic policies it adopted after the Civil War, especially towards US multinationals, and in its willingness on several occasions to enter into negotiation with the US. Zimbabwe's bitterest quarrels with the US have been about South Africa.
13. South African Foreign Minister Pik Botha's threats to retaliate were reported in the *New York Times*, 6 August, 1986. Prime Minister Mugabe has hinted that Zimbabwe would respond by nationalising South African assets in Zimbabwe. (See BBC report of Mugabe's statements in New York on 3 October 1986 [FBIS MEA–86–193].)
14. J. Halpern, *South Africa's Hostages: Basutoland, Bechuanaland and Swaziland* (Harmondsworth: Penguin, 1965).
15. See A. Seidmann, *The Roots of Crisis in Southern Africa* (New Jersey: Africa World Press, 1986), p. 8, and *New York Times*, 6, 9 and 12, 1986.
16. Hanlon, op. cit. note 2 above, p. 281.
17. The isolation of President Reagan due to the Iran arms scandal (*New York Times*, 23 December 1986), which left him facing a Democrat-dominated Congress and substantial bipartisan support for measures against Pretoria, can only make things more difficult. Further, US Secretary of State George Schultz has held an official meeting with ANC President Tambo.
18. As the South African government's authority and ability to maintain stability in its black townships has declined, 'vigilante' activity has increased (see Chapter 5). So, too, has South African unwillingness to contemplate any diplomatic accommodation with its neighbours.
19. Much of the Western aid to SADCC is still in the form of unfulfilled 'pledges'. In some cases donors such as the United Kingdom and the Federal Republic of Germany have tried to use aid to tie the recipient closer to South Africa rather than to further SADCC's aim of increasing independence from Pretoria. A dramatic example of insensitivity to the political difficulties of black states in the region was provided by the IMF which, in giving Zambia a standby credit of £300 million, insisted on its now famous 'conditionality'; the effect of which was to push up the price of maize – the staple food – by 120 per cent, thus provoking riots in the volatile Copperbelt area of Zambia in December 1986.
20. Mozambique Radio commentary, 23 November 1986 [FBIS 24.11.86]. Signs of conciliation include the handing back of Mozambiquan soldiers who had fled into Malawi during fighting with the MNR; the reported departure of some MNR agents from Malawi; and the signing of a co-operation Accord between the two countries including a protocol on security and public order.
21. The *Star*, Johannesburg, 9, 23 September 1986.
22. Ibid.
23. *Agence France Presse*, 23 October 1986 [FBIS MEA–86–206].

12 From Ancient Rome to KwaZulu: Inkatha in South African Politics

John Brewer

INTRODUCTION

Macaulay, in *Lays of Ancient Rome*, wrote of Romans praying to the Tiber for life and arms, but it was the god Janus who was normally guardian of the state's ventures into war. Janus was depicted with two faces, looking in opposite directions, with one signifying opening and beginning, the other closure and ending; he presided over the beginning of all enterprises, being especially invoked in times of conflict and as the protector of trade, when he became the pre-eminent god. Down the centuries the two-faced Janus has been given conflicting attributes. The first is as the bearer and protector of new ventures and beginnings, with one face looking forward from the past, especially toward peace following war. The second connotation is that of deceit and double dealing, with one face pulling in a way opposite to the other, much as in Dryden's lines on Shakespeare: 'He was the very Janus of poets; he wears almost everywhere two faces; and you have scarce begun to admire the one, ere you despise the other.'

A feature of ancient Rome has been recreated in the unlikely wastes of KwaZulu: for Chief Buthelezi and his Inkatha movement are a modern Janus. This is a useful allegory with which to understand their paradoxical position in South African politics. On the one hand, it is possible to see Inkatha's role as forward looking, directed toward the dismantling of apartheid, bearing new beginnings for when this period of South Africa's history closes. Hence Buthelezi's attempt to protect international trade with the West and take black South Africans away from violence toward a negotiated peace on the lines of the KwaZulu-Natal Indaba. The Indaba, for example, provides for a two-chamber legislature, the first consisting of 100 seats which would be elected by universal franchise from constituencies based on economic development regions in KwaZulu and Natal. The second chamber would comprise representatives of ethnic groups, although allowing for a general

'South African' group to accommodate those who refuse to define themselves in terms of the groupings the state currently deploys. The Indaba further proposes an independent judiciary and a Bill of Rights – things which are laudable in sentiment and, as far as they go, beneficial in their effects. Conversely, others suspect deception, either wondering where the opposite face will lead, or noting the difference in the features of the two images; with the second, long-concealed face being a sharp contrast.

The paradox, however, goes deeper. This Janus-like character sustains widely dissimilar interpretations and opinions of the movement, depending upon which face is perceived, with both supporters and opponents being able to draw on evidence to verify their strongly held but opposing beliefs. Supporters point to policies which, with some justification, they see as relatively progressive in intent, while critics claim to identify an uglier side, for which there is also some truth.[1] Anyone assessing these different interpretations in order to try to understand the role played by Buthelezi and Inkatha in South African politics is therefore forced to conclude, as most do, that it is ambiguous. Ancient Rome gives some purchase in unravelling this ambiguity, for it can only be understood as the product of a systematic contradiction which amounts to a Janus face. First, it is useful to have some background information on the movement.

INKATHA AND ITS LEADER

Inkatha was formed in 1975 by Chief Mangosuthu Buthelezi, an hereditary prince of the Zulu royal house and the Chief Minister of KwaZulu, in the context of a long period of quiescence in black politics following the banning of the leading resistance movements in 1960. Its name is replete with cultural and political symbolism. Zulu women carrying water pails and other burdens on their heads use a soft pad or grass coil to ease the discomfort. The pad is called an *inkatha* and it symbolised the purpose of *Inkatha yakwa Zulu* when King Solomon founded the movement in 1928. The title translates literally as 'the grass coil of the Zulu nation' but Solomon's nephew, Chief Buthelezi, renamed it *Inkatha yeNkululeko yeSiswe* – no longer 'of the Zulu', but 'for the freedom of the nation'.[2] The movement deliberately employs this symbolism for political effect. An information booklet on Inkatha, published in Ulundi, the capital of KwaZulu, contains the following description:

> An 'inkatha' is so powerfully woven together that it does not crumble and break, it does not slip and dislodge its burden. An 'inkatha' carries the weight of the nation, the treasures of the nation, and the burden of the people.

The people whom Buthelezi first had in mind were Zulu, as the 1975 Constitution and Aims and Objectives makes clear, so that the movement represented an attempt to marshall a cultural nationalism within the confines of KwaZulu. But with the rapidly changing nature of black politics after the 1976 Soweto uprising, Buthelezi broadened his aspirations and set Inkatha to be a political movement seeking the 'liberation of the poor and under-privileged thoughout the whole of South Africa', as the 1979 Statement of Inkatha Principles puts it.[3] Some critics still describe it as an expression of regional cultural nationalism, but this tends to obscure the role Inkatha plays in the wider political struggle within South Africa. It is a tempting portrayal, however, because the movement has been unable to extend its social and political base much beyond rural KwaZulu.

In the first years after its formation, the movement gained considerable prominence due to a variety of factors. It was the only organisation *in situ* which was able to exploit the new political circumstances following the 1976 uprising, partly because of the banning of the leading Black Consciousness organisations in 1977 and the failure of other nationally-based organisations to emerge until 1979. It was this which also allowed other locally-based organisations like the Soweto Committee of Ten or the Port Elizabeth Black Civic Organisation (PEBCO) to excite national interest. Inkatha's early success in mobilising amongst Zulu people was impressive, especially in its capacity to straddle the urban-rural divide and to incorporate black women. Membership figures rose rapidly; the rise seemed more meteoric than it was because of the absence of other organisations and the fact that other forms of political mobilisation were illegal. Opinion polls among black South Africans in this period attested to the national popularity of Buthelezi, leading some analysts to invest the movement with considerable importance and their analyses gave Buthelezi further legitimacy.[4] Buthelezi's strident comments against the apartheid system were also given considerable coverage in the 'liberal' media which, after the 1976 disturbances, were suddenly discovering the importance of representing black feelings. Buthelezi was also particularly astute in this period in cultivating an image of Inkatha as a movement of compromise to a white audience; to radical black opinion he presented it as the internal wing of the liberation movement, pointing to his international contacts and awards on the one hand, and on the other to continuities with the African National Congress (ANC), and to links with Black Consciousness groups and ex-ANC figures such as Dr Nthato Motlana. The success of this image was reinforced in the short term by endorsement by ANC leaders, who were prepared to meet Buthelezi. A much publicised private meeting took place in London in 1979. A letter, circulated widely during 1979 in the underground inside South Africa, reported ANC President Oliver Tambo's view that participation in the apartheid system was legitimate as long as it was for the right reasons; Buthelezi's supporters initially presented this as ANC acceptance of his position as Chief Minister of KwaZulu. In evidence to the UK Foreign Affairs Committee in the House of Commons in October 1985, Tambo claimed that it was the ANC who suggested to Buthelezi that he form Inkatha, although Buthelezi admits only to keeping the External Mission informed of his intention to found the movement. Either way, very cordial relations existed between Buthelezi and the ANC in the early days.

Academic treatment of the movement lagged well behind these developments and Inkatha's prominence was already receding by the time the first analyses appeared.[5] Most of this work focused on the political role the movement was playing, or could play in the future, and did not provide much of an anatomy of the make-up of the organisation, but interesting features of the movement nonetheless emerged. With regard to the organisational structure of the movement, McCaul reported in 1983 that members were organised into branches of a minimum of 30 which met fortnightly, being in turn grouped into constituencies (which in rural areas coincided with a chief's area of authority), and constituencies into regions, co-ordinated by a Central Committee. There were overlapping structures, such as the Women's Brigade and the Youth Brigade, attempting to harness two powerful sectors in black politics, and various structures within KwaZulu. Increasingly there has been a conflation of the bureaucratic structures of Inkatha and the KwaZulu government. For example, the KwaZulu Cabinet sits *en bloc* on the Central Committee of Inkatha, and the Chief Minister of KwaZulu, Buthelezi, is Inkatha's President. The General Secretary is the movement's leading administrative officer, responsible to the Central Committee, on which he sits, and the incumbent is Minister of Education in KwaZulu. This makes it difficult for people to distinguish between Inkatha's roles in governing KwaZulu and in wider black politics.

The movement's membership has provoked greater academic interest, primarily because it tests Inkatha's claims to be the most popular single political movement and to have members who cut across class and ethnic boundaries – factors which are essential to substantiate the legitimacy of Buthelezi's claims about Inkatha's position in the liberation struggle. Southall has pointed out how difficult it is to take Inkatha's enumeration of its membership at face value because of the high proportion of those who fail to renew subscriptions and the movement's failure to specify the number who are affiliate members only.[6] There is also a suspicion, which seems to be confirmed by empirical evidence,[7] that a number are pressured to join in order to qualify for employment, services and facilities in KwaZulu. For example, the Durban *Daily News* has claimed that Inkatha members have been given preferential treatment in the allocation of housing in KwaMashu township and in the receipt of pensions. Among Buthelezi's critics, tales are common of students having to join the Youth Brigade before they can enrol in school, and of teachers and public servants having to become members in order to obtain employment in the KwaZulu bureaucracy. Students, doctors, teachers and nurses in KwaZulu are required to take oaths of allegiance to the KwaZulu government (and hence to Inkatha as the ruling party) before pursuing their careers.

Buthelezi does, however, attract a sizeable and devoted following, but this is drawn from a very narrow social base, primarily located in rural KwaZulu. Some of Buthelezi's close friends and supporters within the white English-speaking community gave the first outlines of Inkatha's support, but their accounts hardly gave Inkatha credibility as a national movement. One of these, Schlemmer, estimated that in mid-1978, probably at the height of Inkatha's broad appeal, 95 per cent of members were Zulu and of its near one thousand branches, only 36 were outside Natal, with 203 in urban areas.[8] In 1982 Kane-Berman updated Schlemmer's figures only to confirm the general tendency.[9] While Buthelezi made an attempt to widen the ethnic base of Inkatha through the South African Black Alliance (SABA), an amalgam of groups working within apartheid structures, the fact remains that membership is structurally located in rural KwaZulu. Schlemmer uses this social base to explain further features of Inkatha membership. It accounts, for example, for the disproportionate number of females who are members, as a very large number of the economically active males are absent from the rural areas because they are migrant workers. It was also used to explain the large number of members drawn from particular economic and occupational groups, for support was thought to be particularly evident among the non-economically active sectors of KwaZulu, especially schoolchildren; those in the economically active sectors which administer or work within the KwaZulu bureaucracy, such as teachers or civil servants; and members of the professions and business community who service their own people in KwaZulu. However, it is necessary to recall that these are precisely the groups over which Buthelezi has the power to compel membership.

In 1982, in the context of Inkatha's relative decline, Kane-Berman revised his view to argue that the movement was very broadly based in class terms, including a large number of members from the urban proletariat.[10] In fact, my survey of a sample of Inkatha members in KwaMashu confirmed that Inkatha has a stronger connection with the urban proletariat than the tenuous links given it by migrant workers, but the survey allowed no assessment of Inkatha's appeal in other urban townships.[11] Southall claims, however, that this broad class appeal reflects the essentially populist character of the membership, arguing that the petty bourgeoisie in KwaZulu are manipulating this populist base in order to advance their sectional class interest in the political centre.[12] This view of Inkatha's role may well be correct but it is not reflected in the socio-demographic structure and attitudinal characteristics of members; what empirical evidence there is on the membership in KwaMashu shows that it is the members from the urban proletariat who have the highest sense of 'political efficacy', while members drawn from the professional and middle classes have a poor commitment to political activity and lower feelings of personal competence in politics.[13] This confirms the general impression that the politically aware and committed middle classes support the more radical stance taken by the National Forum and the United Democratic Front (UDF), thus giving a class dimension to Inkatha's political conflicts with these organisations.

The social base of the movement gives some clue as to why its political fortunes in black politics ebbed from the late 1970s onwards. It became increasingly difficult for Inkatha to transcend its narrow social base and rid itself of the taint of exclusivist Zulu ethnicity. Buthelezi also came to the view that political and economic conservatism best served the material interests of his economically insecure and under-privileged members. Schlemmer and Moller have shown that most of Inkatha's adult male members came from that section of the black working-class whose political militancy is tempered by severe material insecurity; who depend on chiefs for land allocation and old-age security and who therefore cannot afford to show their frustration in the homeland, resorting to political escapism in religious cults, drugs and alcohol.[14] Beginning in 1978, Buthelezi came by inclination to place Inkatha in the conservative political centre. This was partly as a result of his perception of his members' best interests, but also because of the example given him of the co-option of Muzorewa in Zimbabwe, his increasing association with the white English-speaking business community and their political representatives in the Progressive Federal Party (PFP),[15] and his growing ostracism from radical blacks.

This last feature requires elaboration. The escalating levels of political consciousness among black South Africans in the early 1980s, coupled with the re-emergence of the ANC in internal black politics and the formation of the United Democratic Front, presented Inkatha with competitors in the struggle for national internal leadership. This not only diminished Inkatha's prominence as a political organisation, but also prevented it from claiming legitimacy by styling itself the internal wing of the liberation movement. Inkatha's lurch to the right, as it has been described, led to a deterioration in its relations with radical political movements, and caused Buthelezi to break any alleged 'continuity', distancing himself and Inkatha not only from their tactics but also from their aims and aspirations. This would not in itself be a political problem for Inkatha had not political attitudes hardened among a vast majority of black South Africans, to an extent where the movement is increasingly marginalised and isolated within black politics, and restricted to a diminishing constituency of those who are prepared to accept something considerably less than universal franchise in a unitary state. Inkatha's dilemma was clear even in 1980, when I argued that the longer it was trapped between the pressures of its KwaZulu platform and ostracism from the 'left', the more conservative it was likely to become.[16]

Public opinion polls among black South Africans over the last decade are one measure of Inkatha's decline. In 1977 the report of the Arnold Bergstraesser Institute gained considerable publicity because it revealed Buthelezi to be the most popular leader of those from whom respondents were asked to choose (including Nelson Mandela), with Buthelezi obtaining the support of 53 per cent and Mandela 17.5 per cent. Even outside his power base of Natal, Buthelezi scored higher than Mandela.[17] These figures were heavily influenced by the context of black politics at that time, and by 1981 Schlemmer's research showed that Buthelezi's support had declined to 32.5 per cent, while Mandela's had risen to 34 per cent. Moreover, while Mandela's support was evenly spread across the country, Buthelezi's was restricted to Natal. In the Witwatersrand area, Buthelezi's support had dropped to 17 per cent.[18] Research undertaken in 1985 jointly by the Community Agency for Social Enquiry and the Institute for Black Research (admittedly directed by people opposed to Buthelezi) revealed that Inkatha was supported by only 8 per cent of the sample, while various individuals and groups associated with the 'Congress tradition', such as the ANC and the UDF, were supported by 41 per cent. Buthelezi's long-time opponent Bishop Desmond Tutu received exactly double the support of Buthelezi.[19] Southall cites public opinion surveys in a variety of newspapers during 1985 which asked respondents who they thought was the best leader; the percentage by which Mandela led Buthelezi ranged from between 23 to 48 per cent.[20]

The erosion of Buthelezi's power base is only slightly less pronounced in Natal. As Orkin shows, in the Natal metropolitan region, Buthelezi's support dropped from 75 per cent in 1977 to just under 50 per cent in 1981 and to 33 per cent in 1985.[21] Orkin's 1985 survey suggests that both ethnicity and urbanisation have contributed to the erosion of Inkatha's support. Among Zulu people in Natal, Buthelezi mustered 34 per cent support, while receiving only 11 per cent among Zulus in the urban areas of the Witwatersrand. The figures illustrate a weakening of his support among Zulus as they become urbanised. This is clearly shown by a comparison of levels of support for Buthelezi in the rural and urban areas of Natal, where it is consistently lower in the latter.[22] Clearly, Buthelezi is unable to say he speaks for the majority of Zulus, even in Natal. Among non-Zulus in urban areas outside Natal, Buthelezi garnered only 1.5 per cent support, compared with Mandela's 44.5 per cent. As one moves out of the Natal region and away from Zulu-speakers, Buthelezi's support among urban blacks diminishes, while that of the ANC increases. That is to say, Inkatha's attraction is weakest in the more populous regions, and its association with a Zulu cultural nationalism keeps non-Zulus out. Perhaps most important of all, Inkatha was shown to attract only a minority of Zulus to its laager. In short, Inkatha is losing the battle for popular support, and its social base is slowly narrowing towards the poor and under-privileged in rural KwaZulu.[23]

As political attitudes among the majority of black South Africans have become more militant, Buthelezi can no longer claim that he is simply a cipher for the feelings, frustrations and aspirations of the people – a view he expounded frequently in earlier years, claiming that his 'non-radicalism' on issues such as disinvestment, majority rule and negotiation reflected public opinion. The notions of 'the grassroots' and 'constituency politics' featured prominently in Inkatha propaganda. Other legitimations for his stance have to be sought in the current circumstances, and this is increasingly found in the idea of 'moderation'. He avows the label of 'responsible conservative' and moderate,[24] which removes him further from the centre stage of black politics and creates a certain dissonance with some of his earlier speeches. Many of Buthelezi's recent speeches employ the rhetoric of 'moderation', outlining its virtues at length, suggesting that such moderation is a set of social, political and economic principles and values which govern his position on violence, negotiation, the free enterprise system, disinvestment and a range of other issues. He adheres to these values out of choice and feels obliged to encourage others to pursue them, even if it makes him unpopular. In the period of Buthelezi's earlier prominence and support he adopted the self appellation of 'charismatic leader',[25] but it now seems to be that of martyr. However, critics claim that Buthelezi has merely appropriated the idea of moderation for ideological reasons, and, as we shall see, some aspects of Inkatha's conduct are anything but an example of moderation.

If Inkatha is off the centre stage of black politics, it is, however, certainly not peripheral to South African politics as a whole. In transforming 'moderation' into an ideology, Buthelezi enmeshes Inkatha more firmly into the political and economic interests of English-speaking whites, the PFP, big business and even 'reformers' within the government, placing Inkatha in an alliance with powerful groups at the centre of South African society. Adam and Moodley report an interview with a senior civil servant in 1983 which expresses the government's recognition of this, although Buthelezi would much prefer such remarks to be left unreported.

> We need Buthelezi. Areas under his control have generally been quiet. As long as he uses Inkatha in a responsible way, Buthelezi is no danger. My father would have said, why do you give the bloody Kaffir a platform at all? Why don't you lock them all up? But we can't do this anymore. . . . The government needs Black leaders to talk to.[26]

This raises the issue of just what role Inkatha is playing in South African politics and whom it thinks it is benefiting.

INKATHA'S ROLE IN SOUTH AFRICAN POLITICS

While at the level of popular opinion there are probably many views of Inkatha's role in South African politics, among analysts three broad assessments have emerged. The first is associated with Buthelezi's supporters within the PFP and white 'liberalism' generally. Here, Inkatha is portrayed as using the limited space available under apartheid to expand the middle ground in order to push for a peaceful, non-racial liberal democracy under the free enterprise system. Inkatha is said to be able to achieve this by organising a mass constituency which cannot be by-passed in any future negotiations, giving it the power of veto, and by adhering strictly in its practice and principles to the values of peaceful democratic change, thus educating a constituency which is capable of and sizeable enough to push for change. In this view, what distinguishes Inkatha from most other tendencies within the liberation struggle is simply the tactics employed to achieve commonly agreed goals, with Inkatha preferring peaceful negotiation over violence, disinvestment and boycott. Inkatha becomes a black nationalist movement which has merely chosen different strategies to make reform viable, strategies which Buthelezi's supporters endorse as those more likely to achieve liberation. As Kane-Berman wrote, 'a black political movement set up in a "homeland" under Pretoria's fragmentation policy is now the only organisation able to prevent the final and possibly irreversible break-up of South Africa'.[27] Herein lies its paradox, as Kane-Berman saw it: it was deploying the structures of apartheid to establish a non-racial, liberal-democratic and free enterprise society which was an antithesis of apartheid.

Another interpretation is associated with Southall, and endorsed by others,[28] and argues that the rather limited social base of Inkatha cuts it off from powerful constituencies in the black working-class and that it has compromised itself with the ruling bloc and undergone a move to the right in order to advance both the sectional interests of the African petty bourgeoisie who lead the movement and the interests of capital generally.[29] In this view, Inkatha is not a national liberation movement. It is portrayed as compromising the liberation struggle by putting narrow interests first, and likely to accept participation in some future 'confederal' or 'consociational' political system which merely disguises continued segregation. According to Southall, the paradoxical and ambiguous nature of this role derives from two sources: the fact that it compromises liberation because of the incongruity between Inkatha's rhetoric about ending apartheid and its real intentions; and that its lurch to the right distances it from the masses thus making it incapable of mediating between the state and the popular classes, as it wishes to.[30]

The differences between these two interpretations of Inkatha's role condition how the movement's policies are interpreted by analysts. For example, Buthelezi's opposition to disinvestment and boycotts can be seen as an unwillingness to destroy the foundations of the economy, which must provide sufficient employment in the post-apartheid period to ensure that people's expectations are realisable in what Max Weber calls their life-chances,[31] or, conversely, as naked support for the interests of capital, offering to employers continued profit and a compliant, conciliatory and strike-free workforce. The KwaZulu-Natal Indaba has been variously portrayed. It is seen by supporters as the beginning of non-racial democracy offering, in a microcosm, an example to the government of how to dismantle apartheid peacefully by negotiation, thus proving, as John Bhengu of the Inkatha Youth Brigade claimed in the Johannesburg *Star*, that Buthelezi was using the system only in order to destroy it. It is presented by opponents as separatism writ small, once more avoiding the issue of universal franchise in a unitary state in favour of a compromise between the political and economic interests of the African petty bourgeoisie, white farmers and business in Natal.

A third interpretation of Inkatha offers something of a compromise between the other two. It refrains from making a judgment about either, arguing that in asking whose real interests Inkatha is supposed to serve, one is posing a conceptual rather than an empirical question. Exponents of this view prefer to focus on the more mundane matter of identifying the extent of Inkatha's contradictions, ambiguities and paradoxes.[32] On the one hand it is possible to argue that such an approach asks less fundamental questions, but it also avoids having to give selective answers. However, such an approach is inevitable because I contend that Inkatha is by nature Janus-faced and in order to capture its contradictory character successfuly, it is necessary to focus on both faces simultaneously and to identify the contrast between them, rather than directing attention to one image only, as the preceding interpretations do.

INKATHA: THE MODERN JANUS

The organisation uses two apartheid-sponsored platforms, not one as usually seen. It has the platform of KwaZulu, but in leaving it to operate by conventional means, free of harassment, the state is providing Inkatha with an exclusive channel of opposition; and the state controls both. These two platforms give Inkatha a dual role – as a political party in the sponsored platform of KwaZulu, and as a political movement in wider South African politics, where it uses the second platform. This gives the organisation two contradictory aims. On one hand Inkatha functions as a political party to govern an ethnic base, while as a political movement it calls for solidarity across ethnic divisions among those who are the victims of ethnic fragmentation. Its role as a political party in KwaZulu integrates it into the established social and political order. It may desire the overthrow of that system, but it plays by the existing rules to do it. However, the problem for Inkatha is that its political movement role does not require of its members passive participation through the ballot box, followed by subservience to elected representatives who will agitate for goals via parliamentary means. Its imperative for change is a heightening of experience and consciousness through participation in the struggle, with the collectivity as a whole being the vehicle for change. The role of political party in KwaZulu requires compromise and barter politicking with the state, and an alliance with traditional forces in KwaZulu, such as chiefs. By contrast, in order to win widespread support among black South Africans, Inkatha needs, in its political movement role, to reject the very government with which it negotiates; to transcend the ethnic base it governs; and to decry the traditionalism with which it is in alliance. This results in two sets of constraints on the organisation which are a direct result of its dual role: the tension between being a political movement and a political party, and the problem of using an ethnic base to destroy ethnic fragmentation.

Inkatha can reconcile the conflicting demands of this dual role and deal with the constraints it imposes only by deliberate contradiction and systematic ambiguity. This is where the Janus allegory is useful, for while Inkatha's policies do promise something of a new beginning, the ambiguity contained in its contradictions also embodies a face which is ugly in its contrast with the other. Thus, a movement advocating national liberation and the attenuation of oppression offers its own kind of autocracy within the organisation and the homeland it governs, whether in seeking to outlaw opposition parties in KwaZulu, or requiring students to take oaths of loyalty in order to obtain university bursaries. An organisation committed to pacifism is quite prepared to use violence against its detractors. A rational commitment to black unity is linked to an emotional manipulation of Zulu ethnicity. A movement once strongly against participation in central government initiatives has now become thoroughly immersed in white politics, and is willing to make a number of compromises in its former, more radical policies. Inkatha's ambiguity in these matters reflects its inability to resolve the contradictory demands of its dual role and constitutes its Janus face.

I have discussed these contradictions elsewhere,[33] and will here merely highlight and expand upon one – the issue of violence. This is important because intra-black violence has become a new feature of black politics and Inkatha's stance on this issue serves well to demonstrate its Janus face quality, in both connotations of the term.

In public statements Inkatha is pacifist. In part this reflects Buthelezi's personal commitment to non-violence, as well as to the powerful interest groups with which he is associated who themselves seek a peaceful solution to conflict, but it is also an attempt to define for Inkatha a position different to that of the external liberation movements and their internal supporters. It is not a simple question of Inkatha reserving these pacifist sentiments for Western audiences, where the theme does recur continually, for it is also an important item in internal propaganda. There is only semantic difference between the following two passages, the first delivered in the West, the other aimed at domestic consumption. To the Royal Commonwealth Society in London in April 1987 Buthelezi said:

> I am deeply aware of the potential for violence which exists. I could in fact go on a violent rampage which could leave previous violent episodes as pale reflections of what violence can be like in South Africa. I lead a very angry people . . . It is this very potential for violence which fires our determination now to get the negotiation process under way . . . If violence wins the day, there will be no rule of law and there will be no multi-party democracy, because there will be a South Africa laid waste by it . . . There is a need to develop local and regional power bases in which there are disciplined forces subject to political leadership.[34]

In his King Shaka Day speech in September 1985 Buthelezi said, when referring to the ANC's external mission:

> My brothers and sisters . . . I say to you that I am not prepared to lead black South Africans into one shameful defeat by violence into

> another shameful defeat by violence. I say clearly to the world that black South Africans do not want to conduct their struggle for liberation in this way . . . Black South Africans will not turn to supporting violence *en masse* while there is yet one non-violent action which can succeed.[35]

A number of important themes are inter-woven here. Buthelezi presents Inkatha as a disciplined force led by a leader who eschews violence, which, although it could well become violent, refuses on principle to do so while there is yet one alternative. Some of the principles which are invoked to motivate this pacifism include a belief in negotiation and compromise for their own sake; respect for the law; a belief in a public mandate and a duty toward representing public opinion; and concern about the prospects of peace in the post-apartheid society. Inkatha is offered as the only alternative for all those in South Africa and the West who abhor violence. Reminding the government that Buthelezi leads an angry people is merely a part of his overriding commitment to negotiation, for it places pressure on them to get the process underway. Small wonder then that Buthelezi should be feted for his commitment to non-violence and negotiation, winning fulsome praise abroad as a 'reasonable' man. His international awards include being made an 'Apostle of Peace' and his commitment to the principle of the rule of law is enshrined in four honorary doctorates of law.[36]

In this view Inkatha is a Janus which portends peace, and from the above speeches it is easy to see how this interpretation can be sustained. Yet Janus had two faces looking in opposite directions, and violence has been threatened and used against Inkatha's detractors, opponents and internal dissidents. Violence, of course, is of many types. Symbolic threats are evident in Inkatha's references to the power that lies in Zulu numbers and by allusions to Zulu military traditions. It is an ethnic symbolism which calls upon the Zulu as a proud fighting nation, and such threats thus involve an appeal to Zulu ethnicity. Responding to those who are allegedly engaging in a 'calculated campaign of vilification against the Zulu people', Buthelezi warned that the 'Zulu will respond in kind . . . the campaign will not go unanswered'.[37] The symbolism of the Zulu spear in its folklore is frequently used by Inkatha. At a seminar on the Anglo-Zulu Wars, Buthelezi admitted that the Zulu spear was a precious symbol: 'It remains the powerful symbol which inspires us towards the liberation of our land.'[38]

Much less symbolic are the threats and use of actual physical violence. Many such threats have been made against those who are labelled as extremists, and, significantly, attacks on Inkatha's opponents pre-date the general escalation in state violence from 1985 onwards into which the actions of the 'comrades' and others have to be fitted. Although it may have been a coincidence, it is a matter of historical record that a few days after Buthelezi appeared in Soweto during the 1976 uprising to investigate, among other things, alleged intimidation against Zulu migrant workers, the hostel-dwellers erupted in violence against students. The physical attacks on supporters of the Committee of Ten in the late 1970s appear even less coincidental. To Motlana's criticism of Inkatha, Buthelezi responded by saying 'it may cost him lives'.[39] Inkatha's General Secretary warned that Motlana would be 'dealt with harshly indeed'. Following these threats a mob attacked one Alex Mbatha in Durban in October 1979, believing him to be Motlana coming to speak at an Indian political rally.[40] It was hardly justification to excuse this as impromptu action by peripheral elements when Buthelezi spent the best part of a five-hour speech personally attacking his opponent prior to the assault. No disciplinary measures were taken against the assailants at the time.

Considerable force was used by Inkatha members and officials against KwaMashu pupils during the schools boycott in 1980. Soon after the formation of Inkatha, Buthelezi identified the youth as a crucial group from which to draw energy and support (initially in KwaZulu but then hopefully elsewhere), and it was therefore necessary to counter the more radicalised and politicised tendencies that appeared in the urban townships of KwaZulu. In part this was attempted by reforms of the school curriculum introduced in 1978, which placed the study of Inkatha's ideology, symbols and practices on the syllabus. At a conference of 1500 Zulu educationalists in 1978 the KwaZulu Minister of Education, who became Inkatha General Secretary, informed teachers that they were to acquaint pupils with the role and significance of Inkatha, and were themselves urged to become members. In the KwaZulu Legislative Assembly a year earlier he put this more strongly. Those teachers who remained outside the ambit of Inkatha would not be 'entrusted with the future of our children . . . those teachers who refuse to join Inkatha will not be entrusted to continue teaching'.[41] Time was to be set aside for Inkatha Youth Brigade meetings. A circular issued by the KwaZulu government instructed teachers to give schools the opportunity to form youth brigades and to take part in Inkatha activities. It added that this was a departmental instruction and failure to comply constituted insubordination.[42] Clearly Inkatha was trying to enforce a vacuum – keeping argument and information which challenged the movement out of KwaZulu schools. Violence aided this process, for when the syllabus failed to depoliticise more radical students, Zulu impis tried. Buthelezi warned KwaMashu students who participated in the 1980 Coloured students boycott that they were 'political riff raff' who were throwing down a gauntlet to the movement and would end by having their skulls cracked.[43] The KwaZulu Minister of Education subsequently described the boycotters as the 'real enemy' in South Africa. In a careful analysis of the 1980 boycott in KwaZulu, based partly on interview material, Teague documents how some Inkatha supporters put Buthelezi's warning into practice.[44] For example, a Reverend Mbambo was severely injured on the day of Buthelezi's speech when a mob of two hundred attacked him for allegedly being one of those behind the boycott. For the same reason, police were called in to protect a female councillor from the wrath of a crowd of women who were thought to be from the Inkatha Women's Brigade, and to protect schoolchildren holding a meeting when they were confronted by impis armed with spears, knives and knobkerries. Eleven boycotters were rounded up by Inkatha officials and taken to see Buthelezi. In the court case that followed, it was revealed that one of the pupils had been woken by armed men, handcuffed and taken to a hall where Inkatha officials kept order, from which he was taken in the middle of the night to see Buthelezi, who eventually handed him over to the police. Nor was the violence restricted to those involved in the boycott. Teague claims that there was open conflict between Inkatha members and residents in KwaMashu who opposed the movement.

These incidents occurred at least five years before the wave of intra-black violence which accompanied Inkatha's ideological disputes with resistance movements, and many more have occurred since the general escalation in political violence. Early in 1983, youths alleged to be from the Inkatha Youth Brigade attacked Indian students at the University of Durban-Westville who objected to Buthelezi speaking on the campus. Four students died and one hundred were injured at the University of Zululand when members of Inkatha attacked students who had tried to stop Buthelezi speaking. Some of the students reported hearing the attackers shout, as they ran down the halls of residence, 'We want the Xhosas and Sothos out', and urging Zulu students to join them.[45] One of the students killed was Fumane Marivate who was specifically singled out by the Youth Brigade because of the prominent role he had played in disrupting an earlier speech by the

Inkatha General Secretary. According to one eye witness, the Inkatha youth killed Marivate by hanging him upside down from a tree and beating him until he died. A member of the Inkatha Youth Brigade died the following day in a revenge attack. The UDF, AZASO and AZAPO called for a day of mourning, while Buthelezi blamed the students for allegedly 'saying things which offended' his supporters.[46] In a speech after the violence, Buthelezi expressed regret at the deaths but warned: 'If the kind of provocation continues which we experienced on Saturday, Inkatha youth will demonstrate their strength and their prowess . . . those forces of disunity will be taught a lesson or two if the denigration of Inkatha continues . . . Continuing to label me a sell-out is going to have ugly repercussions.'[47] When the university reopened in 1984 students who received bursaries from the KwaZulu government were told that their grants would be withdrawn unless they signed a declaration undertaking not to criticise Buthelezi, Inkatha or the KwaZulu government.

In November 1983 youths shouting Inkatha slogans invaded a prayer meeting which had been called by an affiliate of the UDF. The police were called to protect UDF supporters, whereupon the youths burnt a bus, slashed tyres and smashed car windows. Chief Mapumulo was assaulted outside the KwaZulu legislative assembly for refusing to join Inkatha. In a violent clash at Lamontville, four youths were killed by Inkatha supporters. Buthelezi condemned both attacks but said that whoever challenged him challenged 'the people' and would be dealt with by the people. In all there were 12 deaths in Durban in clashes between UDF affiliates and Inkatha during 1984. Within weeks of the formation of the Congress of South African Trade Unions (COSATU) in December 1985, its meetings were attacked. During 1985 some of the worst incidents of violence occurred when vigilante groups, who were said to be acting in the name of Inkatha, attacked Indian communities and sacked the historic Gandhi settlement at Phoenix in Inanda.[48] An estimated 70 people died in the fighting. Wellings and Sutcliffe document the violence that accompanied the moves to incorporate urban townships round Durban into KwaZulu,[49] with Inkatha supporters using considerable force to discourage opposition to the consolidation of KwaZulu, and the violence around Pietermaritzburg during 1987 in conflicts between Inkatha and the UDF has become extreme.

A number of points need to be emphasised. Buthelezi's personal commitment to non-violence has not prevented some Inkatha members from using force against political opponents, detractors or dissidents, which contradicts the movement's appellation as moderate. Nor, for a number of reasons, can Inkatha be described as a disciplined movement. Firstly, there is evidence that minor Inkatha officials with arms have been seen leading some of the attacks and encouraging members to violence. Secondly, it is not always in self-defence. Inkatha supporters have indeed been provoked, but many incidents illustrate that Inkatha can get its retaliation in first, and sometimes their attacks are responses to verbal not physical abuse. Thirdly, while Buthelezi has personally disclaimed violence, and he never encourages his members to violence, as critics claim, some of his supporters are over zealous and have got out of control. As speeches quoted here show, Buthelezi dislikes criticism and responds to it with such emotion that it is easy for some supporters to lose sight of the fact that he was only subjected to verbal attack, even though he is not himself averse to vilifying opponents verbally, which supporters may mishear as justification for attacking them. Moreover, some of Buthelezi's remarks are so opaque that supporters can wrongly interpret them as an endorsement of violence. This is encapsulated well in the following remarks: 'We will not tolerate those who make a mockery of . . . Inkatha. These are fighting words and I need a mandate from this conference to back these words up with action if necessary.'[50] Speaking to Inkatha Youth Brigade members, who are responsible for much of the movement's violence, Buthelezi said: 'There was a time when Inkatha was turning the other cheek . . . [and we were regarded as] the cissies of the struggle. [Now] you gird your loins with Inkatha's power and strength to pursue noble objectives. I am very proud of you. You are the joy of my life.'[51]

The intention of physical violence is to inflict injury. There are other forms of violence which create fear without the infliction of injury, and can be called psychological violence. Its intention is to intimidate. Thus, to students on the Indian campus at Durban-Westville who taunted Buthelezi, he made threats of a repeat of the bloody Indian-Zulu riots in 1949. Similar threats were made against Indians in 1976. To the coloured and Indian political groups who opposed contact with Inkatha in the South African Black Alliance, Buthelezi gave a warning of a civil war of black against black. To the editor of the *Sunday Tribune*, who documented Inkatha's violence against boycotting students in May 1980, Buthelezi retorted that he was laying the foundation for anti-white violence. This fear is not only created by the clever use in propaganda of the potential power that lies in Zulu numbers or in past incidents of violence, it comes also from the realisation that Inkatha has the resources and the capacity to carry out its threats. These resources are not just located in the zealousness of the Inkatha Youth Brigade, for Buthelezi has access to the KwaZulu police, with its own paramilitary section. They have controlled political and industrial unrest in KwaZulu, moved against Buthelezi's opponents and imposed Inkatha discipline, and Haysom has documented the connection between Inkatha and right-wing vigilantes.[52]

CONCLUSION

All this happens while Inkatha is praised in the South African and Western media for its willingness to participate in the search for a democratic non-violent future, revealing a failure to understand the significance of its negative image. However, because this Janus quality is inherent to the organisation, deriving from the dual role it is forced to play, Inkatha's position in the liberation struggle ought not to be judged on the positive image alone. Some of Inkatha's policies could well have been conceived in Lusaka, and the Bill of Rights that emerged from the KwaZulu-Natal Indaba is a mirror reflection of the Freedom Charter. But Inkatha will inevitably look in opposite directions simultaneously, and while the movement possesses this dual role these promises will always be compromised by the more negative side of its Janus face. It will not be otherwise until Inkatha rids itself of KwaZulu and Zulu ethnicity and bridges the ostracism from other resistance movements. The proposed statelet of KwaNatal, which has emerged from the Indaba, attempts to achieve the first two objectives, but will not realise the third because of the suspicion amongst many black South Africans, whom Inkatha must attract if it is to extend its support base, that it will deceive and double-deal them; this is the paradox of Janus.

Inkatha's Janus face is, however, both its strength and its weakness. It weakens Inkatha because it creates mistrust of the organisation and its leader amongst the majority of black South Africans, and many besides; but it is its strength because it makes Inkatha a co-optable ally to the powerful political and business interests who want an end to uncertainty in South Africa. Therefore, as Massing notes, Buthelezi will never be strong enough to govern the post-apartheid South Africa by himself, but he is currently too strong for it to be ruled without him.[53] The road to liberation is certainly not easy, as Mandela warned, and Inkatha will accompany this journey for a long time yet.

NOTES

1. As a personal illustration of how this creates an analytical minefield, my own work on Inkatha has been attacked by Buthelezi's critics as pro-Inkatha and an attempt to delegitimise the ANC, while being dismissed out of hand by his supporters as too critical.
2. For a discussion of this see S. Marks, 'Natal, the Zulu Royal Family and the Ideology of Segregation', *Journal of Southern African Studies*, 4, 1978, p. 188.
3. On this change, see J.D. Brewer, *After Soweto: An Unfinished Journey* (Oxford: Clarendon Press, 1987), pp. 355–6.
4. Most notably T. Hanf *et al.*, *Sudafrika: Friedlicher Wandel*, (Munich: Munchen und Mainz 1978). An English edition was published under the title *South Africa: The Prospects of Peaceful Change*, (Rex Collings, 1981).
5. For some early analyses see: J.D. Brewer, 'The Modern Janus: Inkatha's Role in Black Liberation', Institute of Commonwealth Studies, *Societies of Southern Africa in the 19th and 20th Centuries*, vol. 12, 1981; John Kane-Berman, 'Inkatha: The Paradox of South African Politics', *Optima*, vol. 30, no. 2, 1982, pp. 143–77; C. McCaul, *Towards an Understanding of Inkatha*, (Johannesburg: South African Research Services, 1983); L. Schlemmer, 'The Stirring Giant: Observations on the Inkatha and Other Black Political Movements', in Price and Rosberg, *The Apartheid Regime*, (Berkeley: Institute for International Studies, 1980); R. Southall, 'Buthelezi, Inkatha and the Politics of Compromise', *African Affairs*, vol. 80, 1981, pp. 453–81; R. Southall, 'Consociationalism in South Africa: The Buthelezi Commission and Beyond', *Journal of Modern African Studies*, 21, no. 1, 1983, pp. 77–112.
6. R. Southall, 'A Note of Inkatha Membership', *African Affairs*, 85, 1986, p. 579.
7. J.D. Brewer, 'Political Efficacy and Inkatha Membership in Kwa Mashu: A Research Note', *Journal of Commonwealth and Comparative Politics*, vol. 25, no. 2, 1987, pp. 205–6.
8. 'The Stirring Giant', op. cit. n. 5 above, p. 115.
9. 'Inkatha: The Paradox of South African Politics', op. cit. n. 5 above, p. 155.
10. Ibid.
11. J.D. Brewer, 'Inkatha Membership in Kwa Mashu', *African Affairs*, 84, 1985.
12. 'Buthelezi, Inkatha and the Politics of Compromise', op. cit. n. 5 above, pp. 466–7; also 'Consociationalism in South Africa', op. cit. n. 5 above, pp. 110–12.
13. Brewer, 'Political Efficacy and Inkatha Membership in Kwa Mashu', op. cit. n. 7 above.

14. L. Schlemmer and V. Moller, *Migrant Labour in South Africa*, (Durban: University of Natal, Centre for Applied Social Sciences, 1982).
15. For an early statement of this see G. Mare, 'Class Conflict and Ideology Among the Petty Bourgeoisie in the Homelands – Inkatha: A case study', *Conference on the History of Opposition in South Africa*, (Johannesburg, Student Development Studies Group, 1978).
16. Brewer, 'The Modern Janus', op. cit. n. 5 above, p. 100.
17. See T. Hanf *et al*, op. cit. n. 4 above. The following analysis is based on figures provided in M. Orkin, *Disinvestment: The Struggle for the Future*, (Johannesburg: Ravan Press, 1986) pp. 34–49.
18. Orkin, op. cit. n. 17 above, p. 37.
19. Ibid. p. 35.
20. 'A Note on Inkatha Membership', op. cit. n. 6 above, p. 582.
21. Op. cit. n. 17 above, pp. 40–1.
22. See the research discussed in Southall, 'A note on Inkatha Membership', op. cit. n. 6 above, p. 582.
23. Orkin, op. cit. n. 17 above, p. 42.
24. Quoted in H. Adam and K. Moodley, *South Africa Without Apartheid*, (Berkeley: University of California Press, 1986), p. 89.
25. This was a self-assessment reinforced by Buthelezi's biographer B. Temkin, *Gatsha Buthelezi: Zulu Statesman*, (Cape Town: Purnell, 1976).
26. South Africa Without Apartheid, op. cit. n. 24 above, p. 90.
27. 'Inkatha: The Paradox of South African Politics', op. cit. n. 5 above, p. 146.
28. See B. Hirson, *Year of Fire, Year of Ash*, (London: Zed Press, 1979); J. Saul and S. Gelb, *The Crisis in South Africa*, (New York: Monthly Review Press, 1981).
29. Southall, 'Buthelezi, Inkatha and the Politics of Compromise', op. cit. n. 5 above, pp. 466–77; Southall, 'Consociationalism in South Africa', op. cit. n. 5 above, pp. 110–12.
30. Ibid.
31. For a discussion of the economic constraints upon the KwaNatal statelet in meeting these expectations see N. Nattrass, 'The KwaNatal Indaba and the Politics of Promising Too Much', in J.D. Brewer (ed.), *Five Minutes to Midnight: Can South Africa Survive?*, (London: Macmillan, forthcoming).
32. Brewer, 'The Modern Janus', op. cit, n. 5 above; Brewer, *After Soweto*, op. cit. n. 3 above, pp. 338–406.
33. Brewer, *After Soweto*, op. cit. n. 3 above, pp. 352–89.
34. An address to the Royal Commonwealth Society, London, 24 April 1987.
35. King Shaka Day speech, Umlazi, 28 September 1985.
36. He was made an Apostle of Peace (Rastriya Pita) by the Pandit Satyapal Sharma of India in 1983, and his doctorates of law are from the

University of Zululand (1976), University of Cape Town (1979), Tampa University Florida (1985) and Boston University (1986).

37. *Daily News*, 28 April 1978.
38. Ibid., 8 February 1979.
39. *Post Transvaal*, 22 October 1979.
40. Ibid., 17 October 1979.
41. *Rand Daily Mail*, 12 May 1977.
42. *Daily News*, 10 May 1979.
43. *Daily News*, 12 May 1980 and 19 May 1980; also *Natal Mercury*, 19 May 1980.
44. P.-A. Teague, 'A Study of Inkatha yeSizwe's Approach to Youth, With Specific Reference to the Movement's Youth Brigade', BA Hons. Dissertation, University of Cape Town, 1983. The *Daily News*, 9 June 1980, discusses the incident where the student was paraded before Buthelezi.
45. Eye witness account given to Peta-Ann Teague, op. cit. n. 44 above, p. 61.
46. *Guardian*, 3 November 1983.
47. Statement to members of the KwaZulu Legislative Assembly, 31 October 1983, quoted in Teague, op. cit. n. 44 above, p. 63.
48. See H. Hughes, 'Violence in Inanda, August 1985', *Journal of Southern African Studies*, 13, 1987; F. Meer, *Unrest in Natal, August 1985*, (Durban: Institute of Black Research, 1985); A. Sitas, 'Inanda, August 1985', *South African Labour Bulletin*, 11, 1986.
49. 'Inkatha Versus the Rest: Black Opposition to Inkatha and the Incorporation Issue in Durban's African Townships', Development Studies Unit, University of Natal, mimeo, 1986.
50. Presidential Address, Sixth Ordinary General Conference, June 1980, quoted in Teague, op. cit. n. 44 above, p. 53.
51. *Weekly Mail*, 5–11 September 1986.
52. N. Haysom, *Apartheid's Private Army: The Rise of Right-Wing Vigilantes in South Africa*, (London: CIIR, 1986), pp. 80–99.
53. M. Massing, 'The Chief', *New York Review of Books*, 34, 1987.

Chairman's Note

I have listened carefully to the many different points of fact, fantasy, predilection and prediction which were made during the sittings of our Study Group on South Africa.

We were all agreed on the uniqueness of the South African imbroglio. It differs from other post-war liberation struggles at most levels, but chiefly because in most other colonial territories there were few white settlers established over generations. Moreover, most settlers retained links with their countries of origin – which the Afrikaners have not done. Although analogies can be drawn, they are without exception limited.

We were also agreed, by the time of our last meeting, that the auguries for a 'negotiated settlement' – which we understood to mean a substantive reallocation of political power in favour of the representative leaders of the black majority – are poor. This assessment stands in sharp contrast to the cautious optimism expressed by a number of people of varying backgrounds and political persuasions at the time of the visit of the Commonwealth Eminent Persons' Group to South Africa in 1986.

From our discussions, it became clear that the debate within the state power bloc, i.e. those elements discussed in Chapters 6, 7 and 8, is now about the optimum levels of repressive activity. Those voices once urging the necessity of 'reform' – however ill-defined – have been quietened. This situation, predictably, serves to harden prevailing attitudes within the resistance and polarises the political situation yet further.

Beneath the apparently deadlocked surface in South Africa in 1988 there lies a variety of fluid or potentially fluid factors, but the chances of these breaking through the surface and creating opportunities for change are, at present, very slight. The South African government gives no indication of seriously considering any initiative which would loosen its own stranglehold on power – an essential component of any negotiations worth the name. In direct relation to this, the resistance movements become increasingly unwilling to entertain notions of tactical compromise.

For those who abhor the discriminatory and vicious political system in South Africa, this scenario prompts a simple answer to the question

'What is to be done?'. It is to encourage pressure, by whatever means, which will force the rulers of that country to recognise the need for real negotiation if South Africa is not to tear itself apart in the coming years.

John F. Kennedy's much-quoted maxim has seldom been more apposite: 'Those who make peaceful revolution impossible will make violent revolution inevitable.' It is in the nature of politics that deals can be struck in spite of protagonists' vows never to compromise; the simple truth of South Africa today is that the longer the impasse is allowed to continue, the more remote the possibility of a solution becomes.

The nature of that solution is something which cannot yet be guessed, but the best hope of encouraging it is by sustained and unflinching pressure to make South Africa's minority see that their self-interest lies in allowing the rest of the population to share fully in the benefits of living in what should be one of the most favoured and prosperous countries on the African continent. Until they accept that, they should recognise that they will never be able to live at peace again.

To drive this point home is the first step towards ending the continuing cycle of temporary gains and losses which have so debilitating an effect on both state and resistance in South Africa.

ALAN BULLOCK
Chairman

Index

Abbreviations: SA refers to South Africa; see also List of Abbreviations on p.xviii. **Bold** type denotes major references.